QUALITATIVE
DATA ANALYSIS

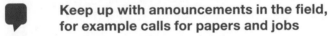
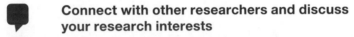

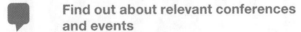

QUALITATIVE
DATA ANALYSIS

PRACTICAL STRATEGIES

PAT BAZELEY

Los Angeles | London | New Delhi
Singapore | Washington DC

Los Angeles | London | New Delhi
Singapore | Washington DC

SAGE Publications Ltd
1 Oliver's Yard
55 City Road
London EC1Y 1SP

SAGE Publications Inc.
2455 Teller Road
Thousand Oaks, California 91320

SAGE Publications India Pvt Ltd
B 1/I 1 Mohan Cooperative Industrial Area
Mathura Road
New Delhi 110 044

SAGE Publications Asia-Pacific Pte Ltd
3 Church Street
#10-04 Samsung Hub
Singapore 049483

Editor: Jai Seaman
Assistant editor: Anna Horvai
Production editor: Ian Antcliff
Copyeditor: Brian Goodale
Proofreader: Jennifer Hinchliffe
Marketing manager: Ben Griffin-Sherwood
Cover design: Lisa Harper
Typeset by: C&M Digitals (P) Ltd, Chennai, India
Printed by: CPI Group (UK) Ltd, Coydon, CR0 4YY

Library of Congress Control Number: 2012944105

British Library Cataloguing in Publication data

A catalogue record for this book is available from the British Library

ISBN 978-1-84920-302-9
ISBN 978-1-84920-303-6 (pbk)

Table of contents

List of figures

List of tables

List of boxes

About the author

Pat Bazeley (PhD, Macquarie University) provides research training and consulting through her company, Research Support P/L, to academics, graduate students and practitioners from a wide range of disciplines in universities and government agencies both within Australia and internationally. Additionally, she has a part-time appointment as Associate Professor in the Centre for Primary Health Care and Equity at the University of New South Wales. Since graduating in psychology she has worked in community development, project consulting and in academic research development. In consequence, she has had experience with research design and methodology broadly across the social sciences. Her particular expertise is in helping researchers to make sense of qualitative and quantitative data and the use of computer programs for management and analysis of data. Her research and publications focus on qualitative and mixed methods data analysis, and on the development and performance of researchers.

Preface

In 1979, Matthew Miles, writing about the 'attractive nuisance' of 'rich, full, earthy, holistic, "real"' qualitative data (p. 590), lamented the lack of available guidance on how to manage the labour intensive task of working through the large bank of raw field notes he and his team had rapidly amassed in a four-year, case-study-based evaluation project. With colleague Michael Huberman, he set out to share the practical strategies they had developed over their years of evaluative field research in education. The result was a landmark book, first published in 1984 and updated in 1994, entitled *Qualitative Data Analysis: A Sourcebook of New Methods.* I discovered this book in March 1989, when I was privileged to participate in a weekend workshop on qualitative data analysis conducted by Matthew Miles at Macquarie University, Sydney – my first formal instruction on methods I had been attempting to employ, as a community psychologist, since my student days in the 1960s and 1970s.

This book builds on the tradition, so well laid out by Miles and Huberman, of providing to researchers working with qualitative data a series of practical strategies that they can draw on to steer their path toward enlightening and well-founded conclusions. With limited technology available at the time, Miles and Huberman built much of their analysis strategy around the use of visual displays and hand-drawn, matrix-based comparative pattern analyses. As I worked over many years with qualitative researchers struggling with coded data, I began to teach them to *Describe*, *Compare*, and *Relate* as a simple 'formula' to take them beyond simply 'identifying themes' when they wrote about what they had learned. In this book I have extended this approach to cover a three-stage analysis journey, with steps identified by some simple mnemonics: *Read* and *Reflect*, *Explore* and *Play*, *Code* and *Connect*, *Review* and *Refine* to start the analytic process; *Describe*, *Compare*, and *Relate* to deepen it; then *Extract* and *Explain*, so that you can *Contend*, *Defend*, and *Extend* to bring it to a conclusion. Throughout the process, you will benefit also from taking time out to *Wander* and *Ponder*, allowing your brain to make connections and ideas to gel. This book is unashamedly about the 'doing tools' for analysis, although it both draws on and places these tools within the context of the 'thinking tools' provided by different methodological approaches.[1]

While the need to apply sharp observation, clear thinking, and a strong dash of creativity to the task of data analysis has not changed, developments in technology over the past two decades have created new opportunities for data gathering and new tools to assist and refine analysis. In seeking to meet the needs of researchers struggling with banks of complex data, I endeavour to marry the wisdom of the past with the possibilities of the present, to arrive at ways to think about data and ways to work with data so as to release their riches, to advance understanding, and perhaps to contribute to a more fair and just society.

Software, symbols, and sample data

To illustrate the strategies I describe, I have drawn on my own and others' research. In particular, I draw on examples from an ongoing project about researchers and researching that was built largely on secondary data and created primarily for teaching purposes. In the Researchers project, I am asking how people become researchers, what their experience is of being a researcher, and how that impacts on their continuing involvement in research. Data for the project were extracted from interviews conducted for earlier, related projects. These were supplemented by focus group data and by other interviews drawn from the public domain.

Students in the twenty-first century expect to use computers for any kind of task, and their professors are gradually catching on to the advantages of doing so as well. Strategies for analysis are illustrated using 'pencil and paper' methods, standard MS Office software, and two specialised qualitative data analysis programs, NVivo (www.qsrinternational.com) and MAXQDA (www.maxqda. com). Other qualitative data analysis software (QDAS) you might encounter at your institution includes Atlas.ti, HyperResearch, and QDA Miner. Many of the processes I illustrate with NVivo or MAXQDA have direct parallels in those alternative programs. Further information on software options is available through the CAQDAS website: caqdas.soc.surrey.ac.uk. Developers' websites typically provide access to demonstration copies and tutorials, as well as

---

[1]This helpful distinction between methodology as providing the thinking tools for research and methods as providing the doing tools was proposed by Giddings and Grant (2009).

the usual information on purchasing, system requirements, and training opportunities. If you are not using software for analysis, I strongly encourage you to investigate those options, and to do so as early as possible in your project planning.

You will find the following symbols used throughout this book:

▶   represents a task or activity you can do to put a strategy into action;

✅   suggests a tip that will help you 'get it right';

❗   issues a warning about something that can go wrong or do damage to your analysis.

Acknowledgements

Miles and Huberman's text was a critical early influence on my development as a qualitative researcher. Lyn Richards and Barbara Bowers, through their mentoring, broadened and deepened my interpretive skills. Authors too numerous to mention have extended my knowledge and understanding – and have enthused me with a desire to experiment with different ways of doing and thinking methods. Lynn Kemp has, over many years, shared my enthusiasm for exploring and experimenting with new and different ways of working with data.

That this book exists at all is due to Patrick Brindle, former research methods commissioning editor for Sage Publications. His trust that a relatively unknown writer in qualitative methods could write a practical guidebook to qualitative analysis saw it initiated, and his early guidance was critical in ensuring that it retained its practical focus. Jai Seaman, his successor, has applied gentle pressure and strong encouragement in the final stages.

Reviewers and students also provided encouragement. Joe Maxwell has been especially helpful in providing critical review that both challenged and supported my writing; I appreciate the time and the care he gave to the task.

My family and friends have put up with being more or less ignored, and with hearing about not much else from me other than about 'the book'. Thanks for sticking with me! Special thanks go to Jane Mears who kept visiting anyway, made sure I had plenty of greens, and provided a sounding board: an extraordinary friend!

I am indebted to my students, clients, and colleagues for what I have learned from them, and for their readiness to allow me to share from their experience and projects.

And finally, I must acknowledge the heritage of many qualitative researchers from times past whose work continues to provide foundations for and influence analysis strategies – also their publishers who have generously given permission for use of figures and tables from their work.

PART 1

PREPARING THE WAY: LAYING THE FOUNDATIONS FOR ANALYSIS

Preparation for analysis begins when your research project begins. From the time of its conception you will take steps that will facilitate or hinder your interpretation and explanation of the phenomena you observe. In Part 1 of this book, therefore, I lay out those things that you need to consider in planning your project, and in managing and preparing data for analysis.

Analysis is laid on the foundation of our understanding about how the world works, what makes it what it is (ontology); and of how we, as human beings, can understand and learn about that world and especially about the world of people (epistemology). For example, our understanding of the nature of reality and truth and whether we discover, interpret, or construct realities and truths influence our choices of topic, methods, and conclusions. Although these foundations may remain implicit rather than explicit, thinking about them sharpens and enriches our analysis, and our understanding of these things impacts on how we assess the trustworthiness of our conclusions.

A variety of traditions about how to learn about the social world has grown up over the past century of scholarship and research as people have developed a method that works, considered its foundations, and gradually codified it to the point where it has become known as a particular 'methodology'. Each of these traditions started out as a solution to a problem of how to observe and understand some particular aspect of the social world. As you face your own research problem, you can learn from others' experiences and the methodologies they have developed, but ultimately, you will make your own decisions about how best to solve your research problem. Essentially, this is a book about strategies, informed by but not tied to those who have gone before, to help you to do that. We begin the analytic journey from the beginning, building on foundations, thinking about purposes, framing questions, and determining methods for answering them – all from the perspective of how these activities will influence our capacity to analyse and interpret the data we gather.

1

Foundations for thinking and working qualitatively

Qualitative analysis is like the qualitative data with which one works: intense, engaging, challenging, non-linear, contextualised, and highly variable. It is potentially productive of fresh insights and deep understanding. Yet when people think about reports from qualitative analysis, (too often) they visualise description heavily laden with participant quotes. All of us carry ideas (right or wrong) about what it means to do qualitative research and analysis. Some will be aware of the many different approaches that come under that rubric, and some will have considered the more complex issues of how philosophical and methodological perspectives intersect with qualitative data and analysis. This chapter is designed to lay a foundation for the analysis strategies that follow. Read it now to catch a vision of the analysis path laid out in this book, but return to it again later when, especially for those new to qualitative methods, the foundational material in it will have acquired more meaning.

In this introductory chapter:

- catch a glimpse of my hands-on, down-to-earth approach to qualitative analysis;
- understand the central role of 'the case' in qualitative analysis;
- examine your purpose in undertaking a qualitative project;
- learn to appreciate methodological traditions, but also to recognise there will be variations from those in the methods people use;
- consider the contribution and impact on analysis of explicit and implicit world views;
- think about using software for analysis.

Thinking qualitatively

Qualitative research[1] is a covering term for a variety of approaches to research that tend to focus on the *qualities* of things more than their *quantity*.

---

[1] I use this term because it is an accepted convention for parsimoniously describing a large class of data and approaches used in research. Your research might deal with quantities or qualities of phenomena. Qualitative research focuses on the latter.

Describing qualitative data as 'sexy', Matthew Miles and Michael Huberman suggested:

> They are a source of well-grounded, rich descriptions and explanation of processes in identifiable local contexts. With qualitative data one can preserve chronological flow, see precisely which events led to which consequences, and derive fruitful explanations. Then, too, good qualitative data are more likely to lead to serendipitous findings and to new integrations; they help researchers to get beyond initial conceptions and to generate or revise conceptual frameworks. (1994: 1)

Researchers engaging in a qualitative study focus on observing, describing, interpreting, and analysing the way that people experience, act on, or think about themselves and the world around them. *Analysis* has been described as involving 'a close engagement with one's [data], and the illumination of their meaning and significance through insightful and technically sophisticated work' (Antaki, Billig, Edwards, & Potter, 2003: 30). In this book, you will find both simple and sophisticated strategies for analysis that will deepen your understanding and enrich interpretation.

The activity of analysing qualitative data is an extension of the kind of analysis we do in everyday life (Schatzman, 1991; Stake, 2010). We bring to data our inherent skills of critical thinking. Our interpretation is coloured by our previous and current personal, social, and cultural experience. The sharpening of our interpretive skills in everyday life is important because, as human beings, we act, and influence others, on the basis of our interpretations of who they are and what they say. Similarly, as researchers, we act, and influence others, on the basis of our interpretations of what we observe, hear, and read. Development of our analytic skills prepares us for a struggle with meanings as we attempt to understand the complexities of human experience.

Understanding the complexities of the human condition will take the qualitative researcher through and beyond description to concept development and theory building (Harper, 1992). Juliet Corbin (in conversation with Cisneros-Puebla, 2004) lamented the shifting emphasis in qualitative methods to more rapid analyses, dramatisation of findings, and consequent superficiality and lack of theory development – just as Anselm Strauss (1995), her mentor, had lamented a decade earlier the lack of discussion about the development and testing of theory from data in his discipline of sociology. Theory building, involving conceptualisation, linking, and explanation based on careful analysis and interpretation of data, was something he saw as central to the discipline.

While analysis is locally focused initially, the capacity to generalise in some form or another is usually wanted from a qualitative study, so that it has significance beyond the novel value of simply telling a story or representing points of view. Such generalisation can take multiple forms, but derives more often from understanding and application of the *processes* analysed, rather than from descriptive reports of various experiences or characteristics from across a limited sample.

Focus on cases

Qualitative analysis is fundamentally case oriented. Data are contributed by and analysis is centred around cases – the single entity or multiple instances of a phenomenon that become the focus of study. This case-oriented approach of qualitative analysis emphasises the situated interrelatedness of different features and causes within each example of that phenomenon. It gives agency to cases, rather than to variables (Abbott, 1992). Note the difference, for example, between the statements: 'With their lack of education, Bill and Stephen struggled to find meaningful work'; and 'Low education predicts poor employment options.' The case focus of qualitative research enables you to explore Bill's and Stephen's struggles, the difficulties they face in an increasingly technological society, and the impact on their sense of personhood. We begin to see them as 'real people' – people who become lost in a variable-based 'statement of fact' about the relationship between education and employment options.[2]

Your study might be based on one case, a few cases, or many cases. Cases of the same type will be similar enough to be seen as examples of the same phenomenon, yet with distinctions that enable comparison across them, such as pupils in a class, or a series of letters from a soldier at war. Cases have a degree of fluidity in qualitative research: 'What is a case?' and 'What is this a case of?' might be redefined through the course of your project, as your analysis and interpretation of those data impact, refine, or change your understanding of what it is you are studying.

Cases can take multiple forms. You might interview a series of unconnected individuals, each one being a case, say, of someone who has experienced divorce, or who has been to Machu Picchu. A primary case might be studied through illustrative subunits embedded within it; thus a corporation could be the case, with one or more specific departments or products studied as illustrative cases within that corporation (Yin, 2003). Cases might be layered, for example where schools, classes, and the pupils in them are each treated as cases at different levels. Robert Yin emphasised the bounded nature of the case, and warned to 'beware' of cases which are not easily defined in terms of their boundaries – their beginning and end points. David Byrne (2009a: 2), in contrast, described cases as complex systems interacting and intersecting with other surrounding complex systems. Hence the difficulty of defining 'What is a case?'

While Yin equates *cases* with *units of analysis*, Ragin (1992) distinguishes between *theoretical* cases and *empirical* cases, where (a) theoretical cases are the entities or phenomena about which you want to draw conclusions and potentially make generalisations, and (b) empirical cases equate to the units of analysis for which you gather data and by which you manipulate those data. In most studies

---

[2]It is for these reasons that I introduce the notion of cases here, rather than waiting to introduce cases as an aspect of sampling.

your theoretical and empirical cases will be the same, but there are situations in which the qualitative researcher might study a number of units of analysis that together comprise or inform a single case. An example would be where a carer and the doctor are interviewed as well as the person who is ill (with the latter being the focus of the case).

To the extent that 'a case ... is one among others' (Stake, 2000: 436), it can inform our understanding of the wider group. 'Cases are generally characterized on the one hand by their concreteness and circumstantial specificity and on the other by their theoretical interest or generalizability' (Schwandt, 2007: 27). 'The "point of view" of the individual informant is the basis for understanding the shared points of view of the group ... to which the subject belongs' (Harper, 1992: 141). The point of view of individuals is also the basis for comprehending and understanding diversity of views (Maxwell, 2012). Multiple case studies based on systematic comparison (structured qualitative interpretation) extend the value of the single case study through developing explanatory theory in the context of complex, multiple causality (Byrne, 2009a).

- Because a case is embedded in a broader context, investigation of the case will inevitably lead you into that broader context. Douglas Harper (1992), for example, learned about the culture and relationships of a whole community through his case study of Willie, the rural mechanic.
- The basic structural dimensions of social order will be reflected in any case drawn from that society (Silverman, 2010). Norman Denzin, drawing on Jean-Paul Sartre and focusing on people as cases for study, described every person as being a universal singular – 'a singular instance of the universal themes that structure his or her moment in history' (2001: 162):

  No person is ever just an individual. He or she must be studied as a single instance of more universal social experiences and social processes. The person, Sartre (1981) states, is 'summed up and for this reason universalized by his epoch, he in turn resumes it by reproducing himself in it as a singularity' (p. ix). Every person is like every other person but like no other person. Interpretive studies ... attempt to uncover this complex interrelationship between the universal and the singular, between private troubles and public issues in a person's life. In this way, all interpretive studies are biographical and historical. They are always fitted to the historical moment that surrounds the subject's life experiences. (2001: 39)

- Understanding local causality qualitatively, through identifying the complex network of mechanisms linking events and processes in a single case, is an essential basis for understanding regularity and divergence in a pattern of causation (Maxwell, 2012; Miles & Huberman, 1994).

Seeing social research as being focused around cases has significance with respect to the issue of generalisation. In particular, understanding what can be learned from a single case has important implications for the ability of qualitative researchers to generalise from their data – an issue that is taken up in Chapter 13.

More immediately, clarifying what (you think) are the cases that will provide the basis for your empirical data gathering will:

- intersect with clarifying what your study is about;
- provide a basis for sampling strategies;
- be useful in thinking about how to organise your data; and
- focus your analysis, reminding you of the contextual embeddedness, narrative sequencing, and complexity of each case.

Research purposes: what do you want to achieve?

Think through the personal, practical, and/or intellectual elements of your purpose in engaging in qualitative research (Maxwell, 2013).[3]

Personal goals usually motivate you to embark on a particular study. Research topics often come out of personal experience. We seek through the research to better understand our own experience; we wish to authenticate and share something new we have learned; or we want to instigate change so that others can benefit from our experience. Sometimes we are driven by personal curiosity. Personally, I'm fascinated with solving puzzles: how can I make this work, how can I find this out?[4] Too often, in the increasingly competitive and commercial world of universities, we are pushed into engaging in a study or selecting a particular topic for research because of the dictates of career advancement, funding imperatives, or restricted opportunities for choice. Individual curiosity and personal experience are not *sufficient* reasons for choosing a topic to investigate (Thorne, 2008), but they are needed for you to stay motivated enough to work through the often overwhelmingly messy, complex, and voluminous data generated through a qualitative investigation. Your personal goals and preferences in doing research can become a source of bias, however, as they influence not only your choices of topic and method, but the very way in which you interact with your participants (or data) and conduct your analysis.

Practical goals 'are focused on *accomplishing* something – meeting some need, changing some situation, or achieving some objective' (Maxwell, 2013: 28). These are often value driven. They provide a justification for your research; they are outcome focused.

Intellectual goals 'are focused on *understanding* something – gaining insight into what is going on and why this is happening, or answering some question that previous research has not adequately addressed' (2013: 28). These contribute

---

[3]These purposes would apply equally well to other kinds of research.

[4]Hence my later career choices of working in developmental roles where I primarily work with others on solving these issues, but leave them to complete the 'hard yards' of working through to reach an answer to their questions!

to the stock of academic knowledge. Maxwell suggested five intellectual goals particularly suited to qualitative research (your project will not necessarily be guided by all of these):

1   Understanding the *meaning*, for participants in the study, of the events, situations, experiences, and actions they are involved with or engage in. ...

2   Understanding the particular *contexts* within which the participants act, and the influence that this context has on their actions. ...

3   Understanding the *process* by which events and actions take place. ...

4   Identifying *unanticipated* phenomena and influences, and generating new, 'grounded' theories about the latter. ...

5   Developing *causal explanations*. (2013: 30–1, emphasis added)

Establishing a clear purpose is a first step to shaping a project, and is critical to all further steps continuing through to the eventual presentation of your analysis. Throughout this book, therefore, you will find references to the need to have established the focus and goals of your research, if not the exact questions you wish to answer with your research. Exercise 1, at the end of this chapter, provides some questions to help you clarify why you are undertaking this study. Even if it changes, it is important for you to attempt to complete the sentence:

The purpose of this study is ...

▶   Do it now; check it often; revise if necessary!

Thinking methods (and methodology)

When you have decided upon your goal, the question becomes: how are you going to get there? And once you have data, what are you going to do with them? There is no one way, nor a right way, to approach data. No formula exists to transform data into findings (Patton, 2002: 432). In this context, qualitative research has become 'a complex, changing and contested field – a site of multiple methodologies and research practices' (Punch, 1998: 139).

Methodology is 'a theory of how inquiry should proceed' (Schwandt, 2007: 193), embracing philosophy, assumptions about validity, and sometimes preferred methods. Methodologies that most researchers have heard of (but might have trouble defining) include ethnography, grounded theory, phenomenology, case study, narrative analysis, and discourse analysis. *Methods* are the tools employed by a researcher to investigate a problem, to find out what is going on there. Whereas methodologies are often (but not exclusively) associated with particular philosophical traditions, methods are guided but not prescribed by a particular philosophical or methodological perspective. There are multiple strategies for making and analysing data. Some methodological traditions, such as ethnography, have a long history, while others burgeoned in the latter half of the twentieth century.[5] Within these established methodological approaches there has been constant evolution of ideas and variety in schools of thought,[6] while new approaches continue to emerge from within and across disciplines to become codified as new methodologies.[7]

There is a great deal of 'posturing' about methodology. 'When such everyday behaviors as watching and asking become the basis for a role definition as "qualitative researchers", small wonder that we look for impressive-sounding labels that help to validate us as the self-appointed observers of our fellow humans' (Wolcott, 1992: 23–4). Students are expected to name the methodology they have used for their dissertation research, and in so doing risk condemnation by an examiner for lack of purity in the way they have practised it. Valerie Janesick coined the term *methodolatry* to describe 'a preoccupation with selecting and finding methods to the exclusion of the actual substance of the story being told. Methodolatry is the idolatry of method, or a slavish attachment and devotion to method, that so often overtakes the discourse in the education and human services fields' (2000: 390).

Each of the different qualitatively oriented methodological traditions has developed in response to a need for a way of tackling a particular type of research problem. Each is designed to guide researchers regarding how best to satisfy particular interpretive goals and the associated questions they then ask.

---

[5]Phenomenology first emerged as a methodology for research in the early part of the twentieth century. Grounded theory 'went public' in the 1960s with the publication of Glaser and Strauss' now classic text (where, incidentally, the *methodology* was referred to as constant comparative analysis rather than grounded theory). Discourse analysis and its offshoots developed with the rise of poststructural (deconstructivist) challenges to traditional approaches.

[6]For example: Glaser and Strauss' (1967) original approach to developing grounded theory moved in different directions as each of these authors reasserted (Glaser, 1978; 1992) or developed (Strauss, 1987) their approach from different paradigmatic bases, contributing to a (rather acrimonious, partly personality based) rift between them. Grounded theory methods were taken by their students in new directions, such as dimensional analysis, situational analysis, constructivism, that emphasised one or other particular element while still retaining an essential core of practices around the use of constant comparative techniques, openness to evolving data, and theoretical sampling (Morse, Stern, Corbin, Bowers, Charmaz, & Clarke, 2009). Husserlian phenomenology sought to ascertain the nature of one's own immediate pre-conceptual experience, with the researcher's past history and ideas put aside during the descriptive process, but newer understandings of phenomenology, influenced by pragmatism and constructivism, give more recognition to the subjectivity of reported experiences (e.g., Smith, Flowers, & Larkin, 2009). Performance ethnography (Alexander, 2005; Denzin, 2003) and autoethnography (Ellis, 2004), connected only loosely to their ethnography namesake, are promoted as the new, significant methods for the twenty-first century.

[7]For example, Thorne has proposed interpretive description as a methodology for the practice-oriented disciplines, seeing it as 'a more appropriate and viable option than watering down or modifying phenomenology, ethnography or grounded theory and hoping no one notices the methodological violations' (2008: 35).

Each has contributed richly to our heritage as qualitative researchers, between them providing rationale and approaches for a variety of data gathering methods and analysis procedures. In the context of extensively reviewing a wide range of different approaches to qualitative research, however, Michael Quinn Patton recommended adopting 'a stance of methodological enlightenment and tolerance, namely, that methodological orthodoxy, superiority, and purity should yield to methodological appropriateness, pragmatism, and mutual respect' (2002: 68). Methodological writing largely arises out of 'moments of scholarly reflection in a research career that, for the writer, encapsulate some research skills that the writer has learned' so that, as you apply your judgement to assess the usefulness of these ideas and skills, 'the reading of methodology (and going on methods courses) becomes a "time-out" in a brain gymnasium for social researchers' (Seale, 2004: 413). Approach classical or established methodologies, therefore, as a guide to inform rather than a set of rules to follow (Dey, 2004). Over the years, my personal mantra has become: *Be informed by methodology, but not a slave to it.*[8] Reading methodological literature always sends me diving for a notebook and pen (or keyboard); it prompts so many trains of thought. In this book I draw on the 'scholarly reflections' of writers across a broad methodological spectrum, combing them for practical strategies and wise counsel to inform the task of analysing qualitative data. References to specific methodologies are intended not to make you expert in those approaches, but rather to encourage you to use the ideas contained within them to prompt fresh ideas and questions about your own project.

'Methods in use'

Several authors, in describing approaches taken to mixed methods research, have observed that there is little correspondence between methods as described in texts, and 'methods in use' (Bryman, 2006; Harden & Thomas, 2005; Maxwell & Loomis, 2003). In qualitative projects, too, there are marked discrepancies between theory and practice when it comes to methods, and even more when researchers claim to be following a particular methodological tradition:

> If you want to understand what a science is, you should look in the first instance not at its theories or its findings, and certainly not what its apologists say about it; you should look at what the practitioners of it do. (Geertz, 1973: 9)

> I begin to see that the whole idea of a method for discovering things is *ex post facto*. You succeed in doing something, or you do something so well that you yourself want to know how you did it. So you go back, trying to re-create the steps that led you, not quite by accident, not quite by design, to where you wanted to be. You call that re-creation your 'method'. (Koller, 1983: 88, quoted by Sandelowski, 2008: 11)

---

[8] By 'methodology' here I mean defined and recognised methodological traditions, such as grounded theory, phenomenology, case study, ethnography.

To us it seems clear that research is actually more a craft than a slavish adherence to methodological rules. No study conforms exactly to a standard methodology; each one calls for the researcher to bend the methodology to the peculiarities of the setting. (Miles & Huberman, 1994: 5)

I wonder if Margarete Sandelowski (2000) wrote her article on qualitative description out of frustration – the kind I have experienced when students come to me with a good question, useful data, and some meaningful insights, but are struggling because someone has told them that they have to name the methodology that they are working in and then they are trapped into trying to show how what they have done fits that methodology. Sandelowski (2000) and Thorne (2008) differ with respect to the relevance of a disciplinary base to methodology, but nevertheless agree on the need for intellectual honesty and methodological integrity in research products. Rather than 'forcing on an ill-fitting shoe', it is better to ensure (and show) that the conclusions being drawn have coherence and validity in terms of purpose, questions, sampling, data gathered, and methods of analysis (Maxwell, 2013). 'For me, the importance of method is not whose approach one chooses but the "quality" of the research findings produced by any approach' (Corbin, 2009: 52; see also Box 1.1).

Box 1.1

The processes of research – in practice

In their book *Doing Exemplary Research*, Peter Frost and Ralph Stablein (1992) asked the authors of seven award-winning or otherwise exemplary articles in organisation studies to describe the process of developing their research, carrying it out, and producing the publication. Each account is illustrated with excerpts from the original articles, and each is followed by commentaries from experienced researcher-editors. These authors talk about the mishaps, dead ends, chance events, frustrations, and pleasures occurring along their research journeys – journeys that sometimes involved radical shifts in direction, scrapping detailed analyses, disputes among team members, and long pathways to publication with multiple rejections on the way. In producing their exemplary papers, these authors demonstrated the benefits of persistence, immersion, emotional involvement, collaboration with a team and/or with colleagues and journal editors, participation in conferences, and working toward getting published. These various authors write with great candour and, in particular, show that the research process does not necessarily follow a classical linear pathway.

A significant concern with modifying, mixing, or being pragmatically pluralistic or eclectic in designing a methodological approach is that firm disciplinary foundations will be lost, with a consequent loss of standards for research practice also (Thorne, 2008). The term 'blitzkrieg ethnography', for example, has been applied to 'hit and run' work conducted in a number of evaluation studies claiming an ethnographic component, where there has not been lengthy immersion in the site (Rist, 1980: 9).

Valid application of a methodology assumes you have adopted *all* its core values and its techniques, but 'no abstract processes of analysis, no matter how eloquently named and finely described, can substitute for the skill, knowledge, experience, creativity, diligence, and work of the qualitative analyst' (Patton, 2002: 432). If you are guided by but do not fully adopt a traditional methodology, then recognise and declare the ways in which the elements which make it both coherent and distinctive have been modified, and the implications of doing so, particularly for the quality and generalisability of the results. A pragmatic approach to methods choices does *not* mean being careless, disrespectful of tradition, or sloppy! Different approaches emphasise different aspects, but across these, 'it is possible to develop practical standards – workable across different perspectives – for judging the goodness of conclusions' (Miles & Huberman, 1994: 5). What readers most need to know is what actual steps you took in obtaining the results you present, so they can make their own judgements about the 'goodness' of your conclusions. A label will not tell them that.

Working qualitatively

Miles and Huberman (1994: 10) observed that qualitative analysis comprises 'three concurrent flows of activity: data reduction, data display, and conclusion drawing/verification'. Their 'interactive' model showing the cyclical nature of qualitative work is reproduced in Figure 1.1. Critically, they emphasised that:

- each of these three components continues during and after data collection;
- data reduction involves analytic choices and therefore is part of data analysis;

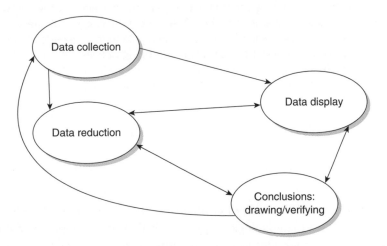

Figure 1.1   Components of data analysis: Miles and Huberman's interactive model
Source: Miles & Huberman, 1994: 12, Figure 1.4

- data display serves to organise and compress information, making it amenable to further analysis and interpretation;
- meanings drawn from the data have to be tested against the data, with more being sought as necessary.

Like Miles and Huberman, I see analysis as a recursive process, one that progresses eventually through a number of interactive stages. It involves a two-steps-forward, one-step-backward path traversing three main sectors, reaching always toward the goal of insightful understanding of your cases and topic of investigation. To help you find your way, I offer the simple mnemonics outlined in the Preface and illustrated in Figure 1.2 as an aid to recalling the steps that will take you forward. They don't fit all situations and they are not fail-safe, but perhaps they will remind you of steps to take and help you make progress when you're stuck.

Planning the route: setting up for analysis

Philosophical and methodological foundations for research are considered as a contextualising perspective for my approach to qualitative analysis. The focus then shifts to practical issues to consider when you are setting up a project because they impact on analysis – designing for analysis, and managing the data that you are going to be working with. Like swimmers who dive into the dazzling Australian surf without first checking for rocks, rips, and dumpers, being beguiled by the excitement of data gathering and launching in without any plan for design or management is courting danger – and is sometimes fatal.[9]

- *Foundations* for analysis are ultimately laid in the philosophical, methodological, and theoretical perspectives that you adopt. These will be gradually articulated as you continue to reflect on your research experience.
- *Design* for analysis before you start to gather data. In a sense, you begin to analyse from the moment you begin to break your problem down into researchable questions. Consider how others have approached this topic and the questions arising from their work. Also consider how theory might inform what you want to do: building a framework that will help to refine your questions and approach. Then, as you plan your methods for generating data, develop a strategy for analysing them, and for checking the trustworthiness of the ideas and conclusions you might come up with, all the while keeping your goals and questions in focus.
- *Manage* data generated through fieldwork or deskwork effectively and efficiently, so that data and emerging ideas are not lost, so that you will be able to build an analysis and track the progress of your analysis, and so that you will be able to locate the evidence required to test and support the results you are putting forward.

---

[9]Like others who have worked as project consultants, there have been many occasions on which I have been called in *after* data have been collected. 'Resuscitation' can be effective, but you are always left wishing you had been called in at design stage.

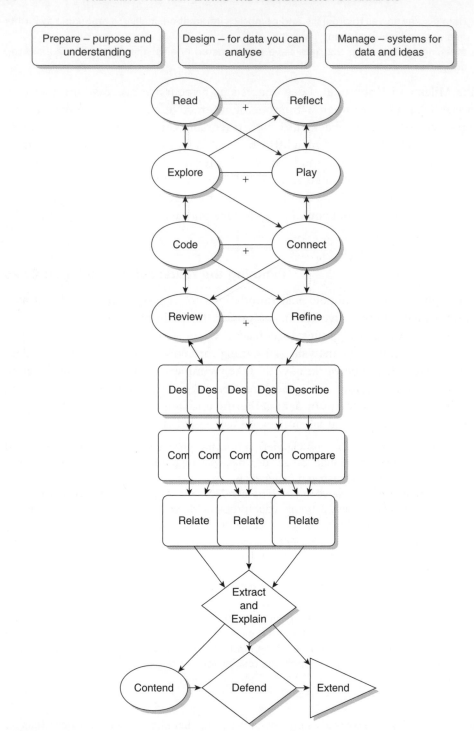

Figure 1.2   Stepping through analysis

Working with data: a pathway into analysis

Analysis takes another step forward when you start gathering data and begin to reflect on them. Develop a sense of the whole and see connections across parts before breaking it into components – and reflect again on the whole as you review your work. Coding data is the steady work component of the analytic process, necessary to gain meaningful results supported by data. It involves seeing and interpreting what has been said, written, or done; reflecting on evolving categories; deciding what is important to follow up. You will take quite a few steps to complete this section of the pathway, and this often requires moving back to go forward. Sequence, therefore, is not a strong feature of this second part of the journey; feel free to dip in and out as you *Read* and *Reflect*, *Explore* and *Play*, *Code* and *Connect*, *Review* and *Refine* your way through your data (Figure 1.2).

- *Read* and *Reflect* to gain holistic perspective on each individual data source and on the project as a whole. Record initial impressions, identify and note key points raised within each data source, and consider how each reinforces, extends, or challenges previous sources.
- *Explore*: investigate the terrain, not just what is covered by your data, but also what surrounds them. Take on the constant adventure of looking with fresh eyes and finding something new.
- … and *Play* games with your data. Explore and play with possibilities. Doing so will spur your imagination and help you to see and test connections.
- *Code*: careful, thoughtful coding ensures familiarity with the detail of data, prompts reflective questioning around developing categories, and builds a comprehensive picture of what the data are dealing with. A well-structured coding system provides a solid base of concepts and categories to work with, and serves as an effective management tool to facilitate further analysis. It enables interrogation of the data and expedites retrieval of evidence to support emerging ideas and conclusions.
- … and *Connect*: coding on its own is insufficient to build understanding. That requires making connections across and through the narratives, accounts, and other data that you have, to build a storyline, or to more deeply understand how your participants have made meaning of their experience.
- *Review* and *Refine* throughout the process of coding, connecting, and visualising your data. Stop to review and reflect on what it is you are extracting and seeing. Maybe split, merge, or rearrange concepts, group them or link them to reflect growing understanding. Record the process of your research, the decisions you make, in journals or memos to prompt deeper reflection. This will provide an audit trail to aid transparency when you later seek to show how you arrived at your conclusions.

Work back and forth through the various data sources, giving each the benefit of its individual perspective, but also placing each in the context of the growing whole. Later work in this stage may necessitate your reviewing and perhaps recoding previous work with a different set of eyes. The constant challenge is to keep a sense of both case and project narratives while also working with detail in segments of text. After a period of being immersed in the data, take time out for a 'scholarly walk'; even a brief stroll can be a productive distraction.

Beyond codes and themes: analytic writing

Let's assume you have observed closely and thought critically as you coded, connected, and refined your data, but you are still experiencing a block in moving forward from observations, codes, concepts, and rough notes to analysis and writing. To facilitate this exciting but often overwhelming task of working through analysis that goes beyond simple descriptive reporting of 'themes' to building an interpretive model, I suggest taking three steps at a time, moving through a *Describe, Compare, Relate* sequence for each of your categories or themes (Figure 1.2).[10] Repeat these three sequential steps for each concept or theme, recording preliminary results as you go. The writing process itself is an added stimulus to deeper analysis, hence my description of this stage as analytic writing.

- *Describe* as a starting point. Review the context for the study to provide a background against which further analyses will be read. Then, move to the first major category or theme. Describe and record its characteristics and boundaries. *How* did people talk about this aspect, and *how many* talked about it? What's *not* included? As an extension of this process, build metacodes or pattern codes, or perhaps detour to develop a significant theoretical concept.
- *Compare* differences across contrasting cases, demographic groups, or variations in context for the category or theme you have just described. Ask questions of your data about who, why, what, when? Is this theme more or less frequently occurring in different cases or for different groups? Is it expressed differently by different groups? How does it differ in different contexts? Record meaningful associations: doing so will prompt further questions in your mind. Record, also, non-meaningful associations: not only is it important to know if certain groups or contexts are similar, but recording these means you won't have to waste time later rechecking.
- *Relate* this category or theme to others already written about. Ask more questions to prompt and guide this process. What was it that made one group different from another with respect to this category or theme; was it because …? Does it make a difference if …? Look for patterns of association in codes or themes across cases, and between sets of codes in your data. Under what conditions does this category or theme arise? Does it have the same form of expression in all circumstances? What else is involved in relation to it? What precedes or follows? Record the questions you ask, and the results you find (or don't find). As you relate categories and identify patterns of interaction you will be helped to structure your writing because relating is best done to categories already discussed; you will be forced to think about what the reader already needs to know before they can understand what you are now writing about.

---

[10]I first presented these three steps as a means of moving beyond identification of themes in qualitative analysis at the 4th International Qualitative Research Convention, organised by the Qualitative Research Association of Malaysia, at Selangor, Malaysia, 3–5 September 2007. That keynote paper has since been published in the *Malaysian Qualitative Research Journal* (Bazeley, 2009); its contents provided the germ of many of the ideas found in this book.

Refining analysis: making sense of it all

By now, you will have become very familiar with your data, and you will be developing clear ideas about how they might all fit together. It's time to *Extract* relevant data and *Explain* how phenomena have come about (Figure 1.2), to place your work in a broader context, and to present new information and a point of view on your subject matter that is supported by your data, in a way that will convince your various audiences. In doing so, you will find yourself repeatedly stepping back to step forward. You're well into the writing process, but in that process, each time you describe an experience or a phenomenon, write about a connection, argue a theory, or test a conclusion, you will find yourself returning to the evidence you have been working with and refining your analyses to check how things work and to make sure you've got it right. Here's where the audit trail you've been keeping becomes critical. How did you arrive at that idea or conclusion? What evidence do you have with which to *Contend*, *Defend*, and *Extend* what you have learned, so that you can present a convincing argument for a reader, and knowledge to build on for others?

- *Extract* and *Explain* through description, theory development, and visual modelling in a way that builds focus and demonstrates coherence, firm evidence, and sound argument. How do all the patterns and associations and explanations you have developed along the way come together? Then use that to:
- *Contend*: what is it that you want to convey to your audience? Out of all the data and ideas you have, can you focus them to arrive at conclusions that answer the questions and meet the purposes you set for your work (in their original or modified versions)? Create rich, interpretive description, develop and argue a thesis, build a model that encapsulates it all, and support it from your data and analyses.
- *Defend* by attending to the basis for your arguments, showing how your conclusions follow from your data, dealing with rival explanations and negative cases along the way. The ease with which you can defend your work will depend on the thoroughness of your analyses on the way through, along with your reflexive records of how you proceeded.
- *Extend* the value of what you have done beyond the immediate setting. Have you provided sufficient contextualisation to allow appropriation to parallel settings? Are your concepts sufficiently developed through abstraction and elaboration to render them useful in a broader context? Will your theoretical propositions 'stand up' so as to allow prediction? Will your work contribute to a wider body of literature to allow for synthesis and extension of knowledge and practice in and beyond your discipline?

Working qualitatively – using software

The availability of software and advances in technology have impacted on how research is done. The internet has become a major vehicle for generating data; the availability of and changes in recording equipment have changed the level and kind of detail available for analysis; advances in computing have led to the development and use of data mining procedures for both numbers and texts.

Software designed for analysis of qualitative data has increased our capacity to retrieve, sort, and interrogate unstructured data in ways that were unimaginable with pencil and paper. As its use has become more widespread, so also has its functionality extended well beyond the original tools for coding and retrieving text that characterised its early development. The ability to support multiple data types, multimedia and web-based sources, complex data arrangements and querying requirements, multi-site teamwork, and extensive memoing, linking, and visualisation of data are all now standard features of qualitative analysis software.

Historically, the use of software facilitated some activities, such as coding, and limited others, such as seeing a document as a whole or scribbling memos along-side text. Residual concerns relate to four issues:

- that computers distance researchers from their data;
- that computers foster the dominance of code and retrieve as a strategy for analysis;
- that computers lead to the mechanisation of analysis; and
- a misperception that computers provide a method of analysis or dictate use of a particular approach (Bazeley, 2007).

It is important that software is seen as providing tools to support rather than drive analysis. Most programs have sufficient flexibility in design that they can be adapted to a researcher's chosen methodological approach. Software *will not* do an analysis for you, nor can it think for you. Rather, its data management and querying capacity supports you to carry out *your* analysis by removing the limitations imposed by paper processing and human memory.

The process of coding using software encourages an attention to detail and constant review, to create an unusual degree of 'closeness' to data. At the same time, coded segments can always be viewed within a larger context; thinking and reviewing are supported by memo writing and visualisation as well as coding; links between and across data segments, sources, codes and coded passages, and even external files are readily established and mapped; and analysis tools to track and assess associations between codes are more flexible, are more easily accessed, and provide more visually accessible reporting than do manual methods.

Electronic tools, such as those provided by the internet and software, extend and change what researchers can achieve using data in ways that depend on both the design of the tool and the ability of the user to apply it to their own purposes. On the negative side, novices, in particular, can 'mess up' without realising they have done so (Gilbert, 2002), affecting the reliability or trustworthiness of results. There is a learning curve involved for those using new software for the first time, so it is a good idea to start using it with a small project, or at a very early stage with a few notes or articles. Most of the strategies I suggest in the pages that follow can be done with or without computer software, but those who use software will be well rewarded by having greater flexibility and power in working with their data, and in saving time in the longer term.

Foundations for working qualitatively

There have been long-standing debates about the nature of reality and knowledge, and how that impacts on choices made in a research programme. When a research participant describes an event or tells a story about their life, do we read that as a description of what really happened, or as an account that reveals how that person made sense of that event or experience – their situated reality? How can we discover why people act the way they do? Indeed, is it possible to know this at all; what does it mean to *know* anything? Such considerations have impacted on research as arguments over what are best, or right, or simply appropriate ways of understanding the world we live in. In the 1970s, arguments about approaches to social research stemmed from what was seen as an overreliance on measurement of observable aspects of social phenomena, to the neglect of understanding the meaning of events and experiences for people. This shift in emphasis laid the foundation for the acceptance and development of qualitative approaches to social research within the broader academic setting. This simple dichotomy in perspectives has since broadened to include a whole array of enquiry paradigms and methodological approaches.

The word 'paradigm' is most commonly used in a metaphysical sense to describe a coherent worldview. It provides a basis for understanding the nature of reality (the world we live in), and provides guidance on how that reality can be known and understood (*ontology* and *epistemology*, respectively). These mental models (Greene, 2007) or knowledge claims (Creswell, 2003) guide us as to what is considered important, legitimate, and reasonable in research, and colour our assumptions about whether we can discover reality, or truth. By extension, a paradigm also describes shared beliefs deriving from a common disciplinary tradition and literature among a community of scholars that provide a basis for determining what are seen as appropriate questions and strategies within that community (Morgan, 2007).

When I first started academic study in the 1960s, the unquestioned goal of social science and behavioural research, especially in my primary discipline of psychology, was to emulate scientific research by engaging in objective empiricism. Deductive logic, hypothesis testing, experimental method, and direct observation of outcomes were givens on the path to knowledge. During my graduate studies and then as a community-based research practitioner I necessarily developed a far more pragmatic and eclectic approach, drawing on whatever data and whatever methods would assist in answering the questions I needed to address. Paradigmatic debates, as such, were never raised, but this had changed by the time I returned to academia in the 1990s, at the latter end of the period known as the paradigm wars. In a sense, my experience is an endorsement of Clive Seale's view:

> I do not think social researchers wanting to produce good-quality work need to be
> over-concerned with the problem of philosophical foundations, or the lack of them,

since the practical task of doing a research project does not require these things to be resolved at the philosophical level. Neither should they be too worried about political correctness, since this can get in the way of creativity just as much as the blind methodological rule-following of the (mythical) positivist. (2004: 411)

At some stage, however, probably not too far down the research track, you *will* find yourself engaging with issues of ontology and epistemology and the debates surrounding these in order to inform your own research. As you do, you will begin to realise that your view of the world has been implicitly impacting on how you approach the tasks of research, even if you were not especially aware of it (Mertens, 2010). Reflectively struggling with these various debates *does* sharpen thinking, to prompt a more challenging analysis.

Some of the issues to think through include:

- Do social phenomena have an existence or a meaning apart from our conception of them? To what extent are concepts (including the concepts of various stakeholders) shared?
- Whose reality is being considered in research? Especially with reference to issues of power, whose reality will be privileged in an investigation?
- Should one observe from a distance or closely? Does distance provide objectivity with neutrality or does closeness provide objectivity through detailed understanding?
- Is objectivity even possible? Or desirable?
- What might be considered as evidence? What might validity, or 'truth', mean in the context of different understandings of reality?
- How do these issues impact on your choices about what might be worthy of investigation, the focus of your research, and the role of mental and emotional phenomena in research?
- Whose interest is being served by your research? Is it benefiting the 'common (wo)man', the marginalised, or the already rich and powerful?
- What defines ethical practice in research?

Paradigmatic issues such as these often take on more meaning and can be better recognised and understood once one has had some research experience (Patton, 2002), so you may want to return for refreshment to these questions, or other philosophical reading, at a later time.

Ontological and epistemological perspectives

It is not the purpose of this book to delve into the full range of enquiry paradigms and perspectives in detail. Rather, I will give a few brief pointers to just some of those that have influenced several qualitative research traditions, including strategies described in chapters to follow.[11]

---

[11]If forced to identify my paradigmatic position, I would describe myself as a pragmatic, critical realist with a transformative perspective.

Critical realism

Critical realism[12] accords broadly with a 'common-sense', natural way to view the world: 'The defining feature of realism is the belief that there is a world existing independently of our knowledge of it' (Sayer, 2000: 2). Realists distinguish between empirical (experienced) reality and actual reality (what is there or what happens whether we experience it or not). Theories about a real phenomenon might change, but that does not change actual reality.[13] Mental properties and processes (including our own and others' emotions, goals, attitudes, and intentions) are equally part of the real world, acting in interaction with physical properties and processes, with consequences for both (Maxwell, 2012).

Reality can be known only through our senses. Epistemologically, we construct reality (Sayer preferred the term 'construe') as we interact with both the physical and mental aspects of it. Our perspective on reality, therefore, is partial, fallible, and subject to revision. Our construction of reality influences our actions, and thereby, recursively, has consequences for reality in both its physical and mental aspects (Box 1.2).

Realist philosophy has much to say about social processes, and takes a strong position in its approach to understanding and investigating causation. Realists argue that it is necessary to explain events, not just to document regularities in them – to identify the physical or mental mechanisms, processes, structures, and other contextual forces that account for events or observed regularities (House, 1991; Maxwell, 2012; Sayer, 2000). (Critical realist contributions to understanding causation are discussed further in Chapter 11.)

Box 1.2

Research from a critical realist perspective

John Eastwood (2011) worked within a critical realist framework to construct an explanatory theory of maternal depression and neighbourhood context using statistical, geospatial, and qualitative data and analyses. Having identified the contextual conditions associated with incidence of maternal depression, he then explored the mechanisms through which these conditions might

(Continued)

---

[12]Realism is written about with a range of adjectives attached to it including, for example, scientific (or empirical) realism, naive realism, experiential realism, natural realism. The terms 'realism' and 'critical realism' are often used synonymously in social science writing (e.g., by Maxwell, 2012).

[13]Sayer (2000) and others use the example of man's belief that the world was flat to illustrate this point.

(Continued)

contribute to depression in new mothers. He found that economic and social marginalisation could create difficulty in accessing support in areas with otherwise strong bonding networks, creating a sense of isolation and loss of control. When these latter conditions were further combined with a culturally generated incongruity between expectations and the reality of motherhood, manifested as a sense of pervasive loss and loneliness, stress resulted and the mother-to-be became depressed during the antenatal stage. Antenatal stress and depression contributed to difficult infant temperament which, when the baby was born, added to the already existing stressful mix, with the consequence of a high risk of maternal depression, and poorer health and social outcomes for the baby.

Pragmatism and symbolic interactionism

Pragmatists also believe all knowledge is tentative, and needs to be tested against experience. Reality for any person is derived directly from their experience. Knowledge results from discovering the conditions and consequences of experience, and we learn through reflection on our experience (Box 1.3). Seeing knowledge as a human construction does not mean that anything is possible; rather, it is a reconstruction of something that exists, and the 'truth' of that knowledge is tested through action, by whether it is matched by experience (Biesta, 2010).

Objects we perceive (including both physical and social objects) acquire meaning through our transactions with those objects over time. To me, a length of board suspended across two short posts is a seat where I can rest when my feet are tired; to my grandson, it is something to walk along (a balance beam). Meaning is thus culturally (contextually and temporally) determined. Once an experience becomes defined and labelled, we tend to interpret it in the terms ascribed to that label and to neglect features from a wider perspective that don't fit. Our consciousness and self-consciousness are similarly dependent on our interaction with society (intersubjectivity), as we view ourselves (and other things) from the standpoint of others (Mead, 1934).

Pragmatism and its derivative, symbolic interactionism, have influenced the development of many approaches to qualitative analysis, and grounded theory in particular, by emphasising:

- a focus on the transactional – action-based – nature of experience as this is affected by different conditions, and the consequences of action under those different conditions;
- a notion that one's ideas about self are built through interaction with others and hence are a reflection of the society of which one is part;
- a need to observe and interpret data from the point of view of the person providing them, as that is the basis for that person's thinking and consequent action.

Box 1.3

Symbolic interactionism at work in research

The classic study 'How to become a marihuana user' was undertaken by Howard Becker ([1953] 2006) as a consequence of observations during his graduate-student experiences of playing jazz piano in a Chicago nightclub.

Becker interviewed 50 people from a variety of social positions with different levels of experience in using marihuana. He found that the novice user of marihuana has to learn how to use the drug in order to gain any effect; has to overcome negative, often frightening, physiological reactions; has to learn from others to recognise the symptoms of being high on the drug; and then has to learn through association with more experienced users to interpret the effects as pleasurable. He concluded that persisting and feeling pleasure, for a person who uses the drug, is behaviour that is learned through others' naming of the experience as pleasurable and the new user's consequent renaming of ambiguous experiences as enjoyable. Continued use depends on the user continuing to conceive of marihuana as something that gives pleasure; it may cease for a time, therefore, after an incident in which particularly negative effects are experienced (with restarting again being through the influence of friends), or if alcohol use dulls the effects of marihuana use. Use was not associated with particular personality types or physiological characteristics, as was held by conventional wisdom at the time.

Constructivism

Constructivists acknowledge multiple realities, working from the premise that knowledge is constructed through discourse in the context of individual histories and social interaction (Schwandt, 2000). Some constructivists accept that there is a pre-existing real world that provides a basis for our perceptions, although it has no meaning until conscious minds engage with it. Others argue that reality is purely created or constructed by minds, through discourse – that even 'self-evident' things like man and woman are produced through complicated discursive practices. For all constructivists, knowledge is constructed rather than received or discovered, and our concepts, beliefs, and theories about the objects and experiences with which we engage will be continually modified in the light of new experience (Schwandt, 2007). Epistemologically, constructivists' ideas reflect those also found in critical realist and pragmatist epistemologies, but they differ ontologically (Box 1.4).

Box 1.4

A constructivist's view of chronic illness

'Constructivists study *how* – and sometimes *why* – participants construct meanings and actions in specific situations' (Charmaz, 2006: 130); thus any analysis will be contextually situated. In researching how chronically ill people constructed time, Kathy Charmaz found they dealt with

(Continued)

(Continued)

their illness by living each day, one day at a time, not planning for future days. This construction of time allowed them to focus on their illness and its treatment in the present moment, and thus to control their days and manage their emotions. She quotes one of her participants:

> I try to live one day at a time because it is just less frightening … I could just get really tied up in what might happen [death or further deterioration] since so much has happened in the last six months [multiple complications and iatrogenic diseases]. But what good does it do? I can only handle today? (2006: 147)

In constructing her analysis, Charmaz interpreted the range of tacit meanings in people's statements of experience that she has gathered together under each category, rather than simply describing those experiences. Others coming from a similar perspective and with similar experience of the data might arrive at the same interpretation, but without that similar perspective, they might see and emphasise different aspects of their participants' experiences.

Theoretical and ideological perspectives

Emerging theoretical and ideological perspectives – sometimes also referred to as paradigms – are becoming increasingly influential in the fields of qualitative and mixed methods research. Typically these are designed to alert you to important biases which implicitly or explicitly influence the way you approach your questions, your participants, and your methods. Essentially, however, they reflect value orientations rather than epistemologies.

Transformative perspective

Qualitative researchers became concerned that the research agenda has been too much under the direction of powerful researchers or the interests of funders they represent, to the neglect of those who are marginalised in society and less articulate. In response, some have adopted a 'transformative' or 'emancipatory' perspective as a basis for the work they do. A transformative approach is broadly compatible with critical realism (House, 1991; Maxwell & Mittapalli, 2010).

Coming from a background of work with people with a low-incidence disability, Donna Mertens (2007; 2009) articulated a widely applicable 'transformative paradigm' for qualitative and mixed methods research as 'a framework for examining assumptions that explicitly address power issues, social justice, and cultural complexity throughout the research process' (2007: 212–13; see Box 1.5). Researchers and community members may have different understandings of reality as a consequence of unearned privilege; thus to promote social transformation with increased social justice, 'it is necessary to be explicit about the social, political, cultural, economic, ethic, racial, gender, age and disability values that define realities' (2007: 216). In a transformative approach, community members are involved in determining the research focus, with involvement continuing throughout the project.

Results from the research must be meaningful and accessible to community members, as a further demonstration of respect for those who contributed and as a prompt, where appropriate, to local action.

Box 1.5

A transformative study

Donna Mertens was asked by a consulting firm, on contract to a US state department of education, to gather evaluation data relating to problems being experienced at a residential school for deaf pupils. She reported:

> The consulting firm did not mention sexual abuse in our initial communications, but I asked for copies of the request for proposal and the proposal. The first line in the request for proposal stated, 'Because of serious allegations of sexual abuse at the residential school for the deaf, an external evaluator should be brought into the school to systematically study the context of the school.' When I mentioned this to the contact person at the consulting firm, it was acknowledged as a problem, but it was suggested that we could address it by using a survey to ask if the curriculum included sex education and if the students could lock their doors at night. I indicated that I thought the problem was more complex than that, but I was willing to go to the school and discuss the evaluation project with the school officials.

> On my arrival, I met with the four men who constituted the upper management of the school. For about 30 minutes, they talked about the need to look at the curriculum and the administrative structure. They did not mention the topic of sexual abuse. So I raised the topic by saying, 'I am a bit confused. I have been here for about a half hour, and no one has yet mentioned the issue of sexual abuse which is the basis for the State Department of Education requirement of an external evaluation.'

> After some chair scraping and coughing, one school administrator said, 'That happened last year and I am sure if you ask people they will say that they just want to move on.' The administrators were correct that the incidents that resulted in the termination of the superintendent's contract and the jailing of two staff members had happened in the spring of the year, and I was there in the fall. I assured them that it was indeed quite possible that some people would say that they would prefer to move on, but it was important for me to ask a wide range of people two questions: What were the factors that allowed the sexual abuse to happen? And what would need to be changed in order to reduce the probability that it would recur? I found that there were many answers to these questions, one of which was a desire to not talk about it and move on. However, *allowing those with power to frame the questions and methods would have resulted in a continuation of an overall context that had permitted many young deaf people to be seriously psychologically and physically hurt.* (Mertens, 2007: 214–15, emphasis added; see also Mertens, 1999)

Feminism and other standpoint theories

Other theorists have observed that knowledge is situated by the experiences and orientation of the person. As Ezzy has stated, 'all knowledge is knowledge from where a person stands' (2002: 20). Standpoint theories, which include feminist theory, queer theory, and race theory, typically focus on the identity and concerns of particular sectors of society, but with broader implications for the way in which research is done. Feminist researchers have, for example, responded to the implicit treatment of women as 'other' (i.e., defined only with reference to men), the stereotyping of women and women's roles (Box 1.6), and the unequal treatment of women in research by asking questions such as: 'Are there "women's ways of knowing" and is there a body of "women's knowledge"?' These lead to the further question: 'How does the knowledge women produce about themselves differ from that produced by men?'

In approaching any research topic, standpoint theorists attend to ensuring that the voices of marginalised, misrepresented, or subjugated groups are heard through the ways in which research is designed, conducted, and reported. 'Subjugated knowledges can be key to social change, not because they are the whole truth, but because they include information and ways of thinking which dominant groups have a vested interest in suppressing' (New, 1998: 360). Postmodern writing, particularly the work of Michel Foucault on gender and power, has had a significant influence on the development of these theories, with the analysis (and deconstruction) of historical discourses being an influential research strategy. As with the transformative perspective, power is a central issue to be understood, demystified, and addressed throughout the research process.

Box 1.6

Competing discourses in Indian media representations of female entrepreneurs

The media play an important role in shaping representations of masculinity and femininity and, in doing so, exercise subtle control over women's bodies and behaviour. In a critical discourse analysis of 46 'human interest' feature articles from Indian newspapers and magazines over a period of change in the Indian economy, Radha Iyer (2009) identified contradictory discourses of femininity, patriarchy, and becoming.

In these articles, the discourse of femininity focused on women's physical attributes as women, or, through metaphor, to their roles as homemakers (e.g., 'making kitchen soup for the skin') and as mothers. These 'girls' are described as powerless followers, rather than creative, risk-taking, owners of their ventures. Similarly, the discourse of patriarchy foregrounds the traditional roles of the women, and their dependence on their families for support in their business.

Discourses that illustrated resistance and difference focused on women's being and becoming entrepreneurs in ways that transgressed their socially provided roles, and showed female entrepreneurs as subject rather than as 'other'. They recorded these women as speaking of having adjusted their identities, of making deliberate and sometimes arduous choices, of taking control, and of doing so with confidence. At the same time these women continued to recognise their traditional societal roles, reflecting the complexity of competing subjectivities.

Working qualitatively: implications for analysis

Any attempt to definitively set criteria for what qualifies exclusively as qualitative research is doomed to failure. Qualitative research and analysis are expected to demonstrate features that include, for example, seeking an insider view of the social world, using an inductive (emergent) approach, and working intensively with small samples. These features are, nevertheless, neither essential for, nor exclusive to, thinking and working qualitatively, but rather are just some of a broad class of strategies that may be part of working qualitatively. Within this context of indefinite and infinite variability, and without being exclusive or prescriptive, Table 1.1 points ahead by outlining characteristics seen as common to many qualitative approaches to research, with their implications for undertaking analysis.

Table 1.1 Common features of qualitative research and implications for analysis

Characteristic	Implications for analysis
Intense or prolonged contact with an everyday life situation	Data management system is essential Analysis starts as data are gathered Openness to new directions as new information comes to hand Seek new or further data on the basis of emerging ideas
Looking for 'insider' viewpoint; seeing things from the participant's perspective	Deep attentiveness to participants' viewpoints 'Bracketing' and/or recognising one's own preconceptions
Data usually in the form of words rather than numbers	Use of hermeneutic rather than statistical techniques Less clearly defined strategies for analysis Emphasis on interpretation rather than manipulation of data
Labour-intensive	Allow a period at least two to five times as long for analysis as for generating data The bulk of the work for the project as a whole (and time needed) comes *after* data are gathered, rather than before
Emphasis on context – 'holistic' and 'naturalistic'	Always consider the impact of the setting for the data Analysis is a messy process involving consideration of multiple elements and factors at the same time
Methods are non-reductive	All methods have to be reductive to some degree in order to organise and make sense of data, but with qualitative analysis access to data in its original form is usually retained

(Continued)

Table 1.1 (Continued)

Characteristic	Implications for analysis
Theory emergent; inductive or abductive	More often starts with an idea or a general question than with the goal of testing details of an existing theory Immersion in data as a primary source of understanding
Enormous variety in forms of data used and approaches to using them	Multiple options available for analysing an issue Choices made in the context of research purpose Benefit of flexibility and breadth of researcher skill
Openness and flexibility	Adapt methods in response to unanticipated findings Avoid drawing conclusions early, and hold them lightly
Focus on process rather than variance	Linkages between elements in data are as much or more of a focus than the elements themselves Seeking explanation rather than correlation
Focus on interpretation	Meanings are constructed within subjective and inter-subjective experience
Possibility of multiple interpretations	Focus on those that: • serve the research purpose • are internally consistent • are theoretically sound
Researcher as instrument	The instrument is non-standardised! Need for skills training Need for a sharp, analytic, but empathic mind
Lacking clear criteria for rigour and quality	Importance of 'audit trail' to track generation of and document the basis for interpretive ideas and conclusions Maintain a strong evidentiary database to support results
Limited capacity to generalise	Focus on local rather than universal meanings Be specific about the context of these results Focus on understanding process rather than describing range or coverage

Writing about foundations

Each chapter will conclude with some brief suggestions for researchers for writing about the issues covered as they prepare their work for presentation (especially for those writing a dissertation).

In the introduction

▶ Describe the purpose for your study:
  o what 'problem' prompted it;
  o what your study is intended to achieve; and
  o why it matters.

▶ Explain how or why a qualitative approach will help you achieve your purpose.

▶ If you have a particular agenda or bias in your approach to this topic, indicate that here – and justify it.

At the start of the methodology chapter (usually)

▶ Outline your understanding of the nature of reality and of how people gain knowledge of the world around them. Include also any value perspectives you have that will influence your approach to gaining knowledge through research.

▶ If you are adopting an established methodology, review the essential characteristics of this methodology, and your rationale for choosing it (this has to accord with your purpose).

Given you are not writing a textbook on the subject, you do *not* need to review every available approach to either the philosophical or the methodological foundations for a study. Rather, simply identify and explain your chosen approach, and provide your rationale for making that choice.

Exercises

Exercise 1: Thinking qualitatively

▶ Take an article from a newspaper or a magazine, and with a group of friends identify the author's purpose and how they achieve that. Note the language used, the way in which the article has been constructed, the selection of 'evidence', and the degree of confidence you might have in the conclusions.

▶ Take an article that is based on a statistically analysed survey, and consider how you might look at the same issues utilising a qualitative perspective.

Exercise 2: Research purposes

▶ Identify your *personal* goal(s) in doing this research:
  ○ How might these impact on your motivation?
  ○ And on the validity of your conclusions?

▶ Whose interest does this research serve (who are the *stakeholders*)?
  ○ Who has or needs the knowledge?
  ○ Who has the power?

▶ What *practical* (problem, policy) goals does your project serve? What will it accomplish? (These *do not* lead directly to research questions; they are too open ended or value laden.)

▶ What *intellectual* goals does your project serve? What will it help you *understand*? (These generally *do* lead directly to research questions.)

Exercise 3: Paradigmatic foundations

▶ Have members of your small group each read a research article or two that rely on analysis of qualitative data, and attempt to discern the underlying ontological and epistemological assumptions the author(s) of the study have made (these are rarely spelt out). Then have the group meet and discuss what they each have found. The purpose is not to name the approach so much as to identify the assumptions that feature in it.

▶ In a group, identify a research problem, and then design how the questions might look if that problem is viewed from different philosophical, methodological, or stakeholder perspectives.

Further reading

Stake (2010) is a recent, readable introduction to and overview of qualitative approaches to research.

Brinkmann (2012) draws on a solid foundation of philosophy, theory, and literary writing to show how you can build an achievable qualitative project from the experiences and materials available to you in your everyday life.

Patton (2002: Chapter 3) provides an extensive overview of qualitative approaches and methodologies.

Becker (1998): when I first read this book, I thought it was chaotic, as Becker has a tendency to wander all around his point in the process of making it. I came back to it later and loved it. I keep on coming back to it for ideas and stimulation.

Ragin and Becker (1992): *What is a case?* contains the contributions of eight social scientists to a conference designed to explore this question. This is not introductory material, but interesting reading for those who want to think more deeply.

Frost and Stablein (1992) review the ups and downs of seven research journeys in their field of organisation studies, in their quest to identify what makes for exemplary research. Learn from their experiences, especially things that will encourage you when your research doesn't go according to plan.

Mertens (2009) presents research methods within a strong social justice (transformative) framework.

Morse (1999) describes a pluralistic approach to methodology in the context of exploring the complex concept and process of providing comfort in a trauma (emergency) room.

Greene (2007: Chapter 3), having lived through it and been part of it, offers a very balanced and readable historical account of the whole period of ferment in paradigms and methods from the 1970s through to the turn of the century.

Crotty (1998) is a widely read text that gives a detailed review of major ontological and epistemological positions.

Denzin and Lincoln (1994; 2000; 2005; 2011): each edition of the *Handbook of qualitative research* has offered a section on paradigms and perspectives, with multiple contributions covering a range of perspectives, and with a trend over the various editions toward including more that might loosely be categorised as 'postmodernist'.

Maxwell (2012) argues cogently for the value of a critical realist perspective for qualitative research, which he then illustrates with examples from his own research.

O'Brien (2006) provides an extensive selection of classic and more recent readings from a pragmatist, constructivist, or symbolic interactionist perspective, with a commentary. This is a book to relax with and enjoy.

Shin, Kim, and Chung (2009) tabulate a brief summary of the steps taken in analysis for several major approaches to each of phenomenology, grounded theory, ethnography, and general qualitative analysis, as used by authors of 464 articles in *Qualitative Health Research* and 89 in the Korean journal *Qualitative Research*.

Schwandt's (2007) *Dictionary of qualitative inquiry* is a useful resource to keep handy for a digest of information on all those terms you're meeting that you don't understand.

Davidson and di Gregorio (2011) review where software has come from in relation to qualitative analysis and where it is going to with increasing use of Web 2.0 tools for research. It provides a positive change from most reviews of software in qualitative methods texts that are clearly written by non-users who draw on out-of-date texts for their commentary.

2
Designing for analysis

As a dancer embracing styles from classical through to modern who also researches, Valerie Janesick (2000) found many parallels between the processes of choreography and research design. Choreography – and design – progresses through three stages:

- a warm-up and preparation stage – thinking through questions and appropriate strategies;
- exploration, tryout, workout – conducting pilot work to test strategies;
- illumination and formulation – completion of the plan.

This chapter will take you through these stages as you plan for gathering and working with qualitative data – ensuring that strategies are designed *with analysis in mind*. Design that facilitates analysis will allow you to generate data that will:

- stimulate thinking about the phenomenon being investigated;
- provide new understanding of inherent concepts, processes, and/or issues;
- lead to the development of fresh ideas and insights; and
- provide an evidentiary database to draw from in building and verifying conclusions.

Design: giving form to ideas

Dance is a mixture of set routines and improvised moments. Like the choreographer, a researcher captures complexity while being rigorous but also flexible about approach (Janesick, 2000). Design keeps the study centred around its purposes, while accommodating the inevitable twists and turns occasioned by real-world contingencies as they are met in 'naturalistic inquiry'.

Good design embodies both artistic merit and practical utility (fitness for purpose). In social research, creative and sensitive planning is required to balance the goals of the researcher with the needs, goals, and wishes of others participating in or otherwise impacted by the research.

Designing qualitative research: 'planned flexibility'

Despite the need to 'plan for engaging in systematic inquiry' and its 'pristine and logical presentation in journal articles ... real research is often confusing, messy, intensely frustrating, and fundamentally nonlinear' (Marshall & Rossman,

2006: 24, 23). Qualitative research calls, therefore, for considerable flexibility in design.

Research designs can vary from those in which every last detail pertaining to data collection and analysis is pre-specified, to those in which only the research problem and the broad approach to that problem are outlined prior to the commencement of data collection. Each of these extremes can be problematic. The danger of a tightly specified approach means that you might miss the critical new information or understanding your data might give you. A broadly specified approach, unless it is embedded within a history of engagement with the topic and researcher experience in data gathering and analysis, risks ineffective research strategies and analysis with no conclusions. That leaves you with a middle road of *planned flexibility* – veering more to the planned side for multi-site, multi-investigator, or theory-testing projects, and more to flexibility for exploratory, single-investigator, descriptive, or theory-generating projects.

Planning helps to ensure the research remains purposeful, and that practical considerations impacting on achieving those purposes have been thought through. Having *flexibility* in design means that it will be possible to adjust specific questions and methods as required on the basis of field experience, and that the possibility of changes has been considered, with these being allowed for as contingencies in the planning phase. Contingencies include finding new opportunities through unexpected events or connections, as well as potential limitations, such as finding that you can no longer access a particular site for fieldwork as originally planned or that a gatekeeper is limiting access to participants. Your preliminary analyses might reveal a surprise factor, requiring changes to check out its possibilities: perhaps your method of data collection isn't giving you the information you most need, or the funding agency offers you a reduced budget. No design is perfect, 'there are always trade-offs' (Patton, 2002: 223).[1]

Frameworks for design

Marshall and Rossman identified three challenges in designing a qualitative study that is to be presented in the form of a proposal:

a developing a conceptual framework for the study that is thorough, concise, and elegant;

b planning a design that is systematic and manageable, yet flexible; and

c integrating these into a coherent document that convinces the proposal readers (a funding agency or dissertation committee) that the study should be done, can be done, and will be done. (2006: 10–11)

---

[1]These are often discussed as 'limitations' of the study, referred to in either the methodology or the final discussion, depending on whether they were anticipated or unanticipated.

This led them to specify three interactive components in developing a project proposal:

- The conceptual framework, providing the rationale for the study.
- The design and methods, developed out of the conceptual framework, questions, and methodological literature. This involves consideration of the assumptions of qualitative approaches; site and sample selection; overall design and data collection methods; field-work practice; ethical issues; resource needs; and the trustworthiness of the overall design.
- Researcher competence – demonstrating that the researcher has the competence to carry out the study.

Coherent interactivity between major components of design is the key feature of Maxwell's (2013) research design framework (Figure 2.1). Maxwell explicitly rejected the idea of a cyclic or linear sequencing of the different components. Rather, 'the different parts of a design form an integrated and interacting whole, with each component closely tied to several others' (2013: 4). Research questions are the heart or hub of design, rather than the starting point; they both inform and are responsive to other components. The upper and lower triangles in his model each form closely integrated clusters that 'resonate'. While the connections shown have a certain amount of elasticity (to reflect necessary flexibility in design), should any connection be stretched to breaking point, the whole design will become ineffective. Environmental factors such as paradigmatic framework, available resources, and the research setting also impact on the design process, but they are not a core component of the design process itself; ethical considerations are an issue for *every* part of design.

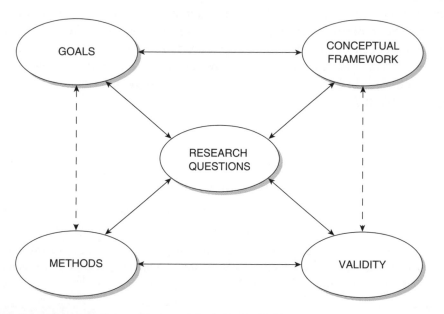

Figure 2.1   Maxwell's interactive model of research design
Source: Maxwell, 2013: 5, Figure 1.1

Designing for analysis

Analysis strategies are intimately linked with questions of research design. A well-designed study facilitates analysis.

- The conceptual framework (literature, theory, paradigmatic foundations) provides a foundation, focus, and starting point for the analysis. It may hold clues to analysis puzzles along the way, and eventually it can provide a reference point against which to check (and report) your analysis.
- Questions focus the analysis around the purpose.
- Data gathering and sampling strategies ensure that appropriate data are obtained for analysis.
- Data management and storage strategies ensure that data are accessible for review and analysis.
- Initial exploratory work allows for testing the analytic value of proposed strategies.

Focusing the study

Having thought about the critical issue that you want to explore or investigate, why you want to do that, and who will be interested in the results of your investigation (cf. Chapter 1), you've decided that the best approach to take is to employ some kind of qualitative approach – but as you begin to think through what it might involve and you test out a few ideas in practice, the enormity of the task becomes apparent. To ensure it is doable, be prepared to let go of some aspects, the associated questions that just *might* prove interesting, to fine-tune and focus the study.

Good design breaks down a complex issue and broad interest to something that can be managed in limited time, with limited resources, and still produce useful results (Flick, 2007a). Think about this task as breaking the topic into 'bite-sized chunks' to be tackled one at a time. See this as part of an early strategic planning process, otherwise attention will be scattered and effort will be ineffectively applied.

- ▶ Identify the various facets of your research problem, and explore how each might be investigated; or
- ▶ Identify steps or stages in the development of the phenomenon or process you are researching (i.e., not the research process itself), to help in breaking the study down into chunks based on those steps.

Which of the elements identified will best suit your purpose in doing the study, *at this stage*? Don't be surprised if you find that you don't get much further than investigating the first of these for your current project.

There are resources and strategies available to assist as you begin to focus your study and place boundaries around it. The order in which I discuss them here is approximate; you are likely to move back and forth between them as you refine your plans for the task ahead. *Record all of your ideas and your thoughts about them throughout the focusing process* – preferably electronically. For now, it is wise to store all ideas, however wild. You may come back to one and follow it up; you may find that a fleeting idea you record now provides a clue to a puzzle you encounter later.

Draw on experience – your own and others'

▶ Start by thinking through your own experience of the problem you are studying:
  ○ What is the background to the topic and your interest in it?
  ○ What expectations, beliefs and assumptions do you have relating to it?

▶ Based on your experience, try writing about the topic, or drawing it, then use that writing or drawing to identify key components of the problem, and possible relationships between them. These will be explored during your analysis.

▶ Now, focus in on those components and relationships that seem most central to the problem, or that mark a critical step in the pathway, and shape some ideas around those – but don't dismiss the others just yet, you might still need to go there.

▶ Try your ideas out on your colleagues:
  ○ Does anyone else think the topic is of interest? If not, they, and possibly others, won't be interested in your contribution to it either.
  ○ Do they know anything about it? 'Pick their brains' for ideas.
  ○ To whom or to what resources can they refer you?
  ○ Can they help you identify the most critical issues in the area?

Discussions with colleagues are a rich source of knowledge, ideas, and critique; this is a primary benefit of being part of a research centre or collegial network.[2] After these discussions you will have the confidence to go ahead, and/or a refined set of ideas – or you will have realised that you need to start again.

If you can create an appropriate opportunity while you are developing and refining your thoughts about your study, test your idea early in a kind of 'pre-pilot' exploration. Possibilities include:

▶ Visit a site like those you are interested in studying and observe what is happening there. You might also check out whether you are likely to encounter access problems if you locate your study in that or a similar site.

▶ Use some existing or publicly available data to explore background factors and potential foci, or to trial techniques (and software) for analysis. Use stories from newspapers, magazines, and film. Explore public documents or websites. Draw on the social science data archives now available in many countries; these make existing data available at low cost to researchers for secondary analysis or teaching purposes.

---

[2]In 1976, Pelz and Andrews reported that the most productive of the 1300 researchers they studied were those who had *more* frequent contact with a *wider* circle of professional colleagues. For those who don't have such a network close at hand, the internet now offers opportunities to link with others with similar interests internationally through interest-based forums. Conferences also provide an opportunity to present and discuss your ideas with others.

► Explore the topic by discussing it with willing friends or relatives, especially if they share any similarities with those who will be your eventual participants.[3]

By now you will have one or two ideas that are taking shape and possibly a raft of associated questions that are interesting but not central to the main idea. As you start to draw boundaries around the idea, sit other ideas in a folder somewhere for possible retrieval on another day – a day that might come sooner or later, depending on how your ideas progress through other phases of refinement.

Extract data and ideas from the literature

Engaging with the literature has been likened to engaging in a conversation (Marshall & Rossman, 2006: 43). Conversations are two-way: as you learn from the literature, critique it also (Box 2.1). Treat literature as data to be analysed like any other data. Have it do double work: test out your data analysis strategies and skills by working analytically with articles or notes you have made, just as you would for interview material or other documents, while you also use these sources to clarify and refine your topic and design.[4] Well used, it will contextualise and provide a starting framework for your data collection *and analysis*. Knowledge of the technical literature once a study is under way increases 'theoretical sensitivity' (Strauss, 1987: 12); it 'gets researchers away from too literal an immersion in the materials ... and quickly gets them to thinking in terms of explicit concepts and their relationships' (1987: 29).

Box 2.1

Breadth versus focus in a dissertation literature review

In 2005, the *Educational Researcher* published an article by David Boote and Penny Beile advocating scholarly thoroughness and breadth in a doctoral candidate's review of the literature. It prompted a sharp response from Joseph Maxwell followed by a rejoinder from the original

(Continued)

---

[3]Be aware that doing so can have unintended consequences. Maxwell observed: 'Several of my students have had very uncomfortable and unproductive interviews with people whom they knew well, and with whom (despite my expressed concerns) they didn't anticipate any problems. They had failed to realize that these participants perceived the interview very differently from how the student saw it. These perceptions involved, among other issues, fear of the possible consequences of what they said (particularly if the interview is recorded), power differences between the student and the interviewee, a lack of understanding of the purpose of the study and what the student would do with the interview data, and even the setting of the interview itself' (2013: 93).

[4]The recently developed capacity of qualitative software to import pdf documents or a whole bibliographic database with attached pdf sources means that you can also experiment with using software for analysis when reviewing your literature.

(Continued)

authors. Essentially, Boote and Beile argued that good and useful (education) research is based on sound scholarship – a sophisticated knowledge of and capacity to analyse and synthesise the research literature in one's field of specialisation. 'A substantive, thorough, sophisticated literature review is a pre-condition for doing substantive, thorough, sophisticated research' (2005: 3).

In his response, Maxwell (2006: 28) argued that Boote and Beile had missed the central criterion of *relevance* of the literature for informing a planned study. He suggested: (a) it is more important for a student to learn *how* to locate and evaluate literature for any field in which they might develop an interest than to become familiar with a broad range of literature in one field; and (b) a student should learn to draw on relevant literature from a range of disciplines, lest they fail to see alternative ways of viewing their problem.

I see three essential foci to be aware of (and make notes about) when reading literature as you plan your study:

▶ From research studies already done, gain and evaluate information and ideas about *the substantive focus* (the topic) of your research project.

▶ From both research studies and the broader, theoretical literature, identify *theoretical contributions* to understanding your research problem.

▶ From research studies in your topic area, note and review the type and adequacy of the *research methods* others have used in studying this question.

The substantive focus: what is known, where are the debates?

There is always literature that can inform your topic. If you really think you have found an area that has not been written about at all, first ask yourself why that might be and whether it really warrants a research study. If it passes that test, then think through the broader context in which it sits and about related areas from which you can learn. The person using an email forum some years ago who lamented a lack of literature about the settlement of Vietnamese refugees in a small rural town could have found literature about settlement of refugees more generally, research on settlement patterns for Vietnamese refugees in cities around the world, and stories or studies of the experiences of anyone moving to live in a small rural town in that country. All these sources existed, and all could provide guidance for the design of the study and inform later analysis.

Regardless of your methodological approach, reading will alert you to ways of thinking about the topic that you'd never imagined, and is *always* stimulating. Play with the ideas, contemplate the challenges, find the contradictions and the gaps, and direct your research and analysis to those.

Theoretical contributions from the literature

This is where you can really come up with some unexpected ideas. Be stimulated by the perspectives of major social theorists. How would your plans for analysis be impacted, for example, if you applied ideas from Foucault's writing about gender and power, or Bourdieu's concepts of cultural, social, economic, and symbolic capital, or Bandura's social learning theory, or Festinger's model of cognitive dissonance, or Jung's theory of personality archetypes? Box 2.2 provides a small example of just how different the perspectives and emphases of different major theorists can be. Consider older as well as more recent theoretical writing, and perhaps build some comparisons of different perspectives into your analysis plan.

Box 2.2

Doors into theoretical perspectives

Cooper (2008) very effectively illustrated the impact of social theory on how the world might be perceived by describing the potential interests that three eminent social theorists and others might have in studying something as prosaic as the doors in public or institutional buildings. Thus, he suggested, Latour might consider how the technology of the door controls the behaviour of those going through it; Goffman might note how facial expressions change as someone passes through a door that serves as a boundary between public and private spaces; Foucault might look at how the architecture of the door concretises disciplinary power, for example, by facilitating surveillance and control in a prison or a school; historical sociologists could consider that, increasingly, doors in public spaces are being designed and used in ways that reduce risk – risk of intrusion in some settings, and risk of litigation in others; while the feminist observes customs and conventions of gendered behaviour in relation to doors.

Consider general, substantive, and local theories that have been developed around your topic, the relationships that others have identified, and the explanations they have developed, and also the 'naive' theories that are found in popular literature. Anticipate patterns you might find in your data, work through alternative possible explanations, and then think about what the implications of these explanations would be, as pointers to things you would need to observe or assess (Maxwell, 2013). The theoretical reading you do will inform your planning, and then as you work on, it will increase your sensitivity to things in your data that do or don't fit.

Although more often designed with the intention of developing theory, a qualitative project can be designed to test or elaborate theory (Box 2.3). In that case, the theory or theories being tested will explicitly inform the design and provide a template for analysis. My experience in such cases, however, is that the theory needs still to be held 'lightly', as the data that come in do not always fit *a priori* codes and assumed relationships; indeed, it might be that something else altogether is found to be responsible for an observed pattern.

Box 2.3

A theory-based model of immunisation compliance

The model of factors potentially impacting on on-time immunisation compliance in Figure 2.2 was developed out of decision making theory, social support theory, self-efficacy theory, research literature on immunisation compliance, and previous research experience. The study that was subsequently designed involved a combination of survey and interview data that included structured questions, open-ended narrative, decision mapping, and mapping of egonets at intervals over a period from pre-birth to six months post-birth for a sample of parents from three socioeconomically different areas, to capture and test the relevance of all the specified social, emotional, and cognitive elements included in the model.

The Scene +	The Actors →	The Decision +	The Event →	Consequences
Societal expectations	**The parent/carer**	Influence from information sources	Ease of obtaining immunisation service	Immunisation occurs:
School entry requirements	Carer coping and self-efficacy	Consistency of information	Integration with well-baby service	• On time
Prevalence of disease	Carer health beliefs (locus of control)	Reminders	Familiarity of environment	• Late or Incomplete
Recent publicity re immunisation	Carer disposition (anxiety, depression, caution)	Risk – considering probabilities	Personalised vs. 'cattle line'	• Not at all
Publicity re adverse effects (of disease, of vaccine)	Carer's personal experience of diseases, vaccines	Ambiguity of outcomes	Preparation for event	
Efficiency in vaccine distribution	Needle phobia	Fear of brain damage	Daily hassles, e.g., work, other children	
	Carer's social integration	Fear of baby suffering	Access to social support	
	The child	Avoidance of regret	Routine ↔ Stressful	
	General health status	Influence by experts		
	Irritability	Customary behaviour		
	'Vulnerability' with specific health problems, e.g., asthma			
	Health professionals			
	(doctor, EC nurses)			
	Attitudes conveyed and advice given			
	Level of agreement between professionals			
	Cautiousness re 'contraindications' (e.g., colds)			
	Knowledge re contraindications			
	Practice management, affecting opportunistic immunisation			

Figure 2.2   Theoretical framework for a proposed study of immunisation compliance

Does prior reading (substantive or theoretical) bias analysis?

The short answer to this question is: probably no more (and potentially less) than your prior assumptions would have done, without further reading. If your reading is thorough, then it will alert you to *alternative* views on the topic (and associated theory and methods), and open up debates in the area for you to explore. Seek out different perspectives, read on the topic from disciplines other than your own, consider more than one theoretical basis (Box 2.4). Analyse assumptions and premises to identify and question what has contributed to their being accepted as 'given'. Challenge each component in your framework. Keep a journal to record this process. When you come to collecting and analysing data, consider them first of all at face value to see what they are saying, and then you might deliberately introduce some ideas from existing research and theory, to assess the data against those.

Box 2.4

When initial assumptions don't fit: the social shaping of money

After the banking system was deregulated in Australia, Supriya Singh (1997) sought to investigate the impact on families, but rather than talking about changes in the way they managed money and banking, couples talked about how money intersected with their marriage relationship. This shift in direction was accompanied by a further surprise, for their money-in-marriage concerns were not related to the classic issues of gender, power, or equality as might be predicted from the economic management literature. Singh found, instead, that aspects of jointness and sharing in relation to the joint bank account were emphasised. Reading now in the sociological and anthropological literature, her reanalysis led her to theorise about the social shaping of money and to a concept of 'ritual information' to describe this cultural pattern.

Using the literature to learn from others' methods

Review *methods* used by others who have investigated your topic, as part of your review of the literature. Consider the kinds of data that those different methods generated and how these were, or might be, analysed. This will provide ideas to emulate or to critique (Box 2.5). It is unfortunate that the size restrictions of journal articles often mean that authors do not expand on the methods they have used, with details of what worked well and particularly of methods they tried that didn't work well. For those of interest but with insufficient detail, use the email address usually provided to contact the author with specific questions seeking further detail. Most authors are happy to answer a specific enquiry that demonstrates you have read and thought about the issue, but very general 'How should I study this topic?' email requests implying a lack of effort on your part are likely to go unanswered (as they do also on listservs).

Box 2.5

Reviewing the literature for methodological insights

To explore and learn

To conceptualise the situated meaning of wellbeing at a systemic level in one workplace, Joanne Abbey, an organisational psychologist and doctoral student, needed to find approaches and methods that revealed how the workplace related to employees' subjective, interior awareness of personal needs, feelings, disappointments, successes, losses, and achievements. Phenomenography was decided upon as being appropriate to the idea of viewing and research-ing wellbeing as a systemic construct. Attracted by Sykes, Friedman, Rosenfeld, and Weiss' (2006) approach to learning from personal experience about success in schools, Joanne tested questions from their interview protocol in pilot interviews. These questions were modified to suit the focus on wellbeing. Because wellbeing is not clearly defined, she decided to use visual methods. Her search led her to ZMET (Zaltman, 1996). ZMET utilises the projective value of visual images as metaphors to communicate social meaning, thought, embodied experience, and emotions. She asked her study participants to select (and bring to their interviews) images that directly represented aspects of what wellbeing meant to them in their workplace. She com-bined a modified ZMET interview protocol (to discuss these images) with questions from Sykes et al.'s 'Learning from success' (to elicit emblematic wellbeing experiences). This approach was modified once more during data gathering and initial coding, to ensure maximum value was gained from interviews. The advantage of customising both approach and method was that interview data unambiguously related to the question of interest: what did wellbeing at work mean to these employees?

To critique

When Rod Gutierrez (2006) reviewed the literature on psychological injury in the workplace, he noted the methodology used in each of the studies he reviewed. He found research in the area was characterised by small-sample case studies; the condition itself was ill-defined, with very few studies confirming the clinical status of the claimant; the target population was identified only after their claim had been accepted, and so almost no studies included comparison cases whose claim had been rejected; the claimant's reports were relied upon for assessment of workplace precipitating conditions; and, importantly, almost all research had begun with the assumption that psychological injury at work was a direct consequence of occupational stress. Having established the methodological inadequacy and theoretical limitations of previous stud-ies, Gutierrez reconceptualised psychological injury as a biopsychosocial event occurring in the context of work and in interaction with an ever-evolving political-legal system (the workers' compensation system). He then set about examining possible causal factors for psychological injury by applying both statistical and textual analyses to qualitative reports from claimants, their employers, and an independent psychologist for a moderately large ($N = 156$) sample of cases from a variety of occupations and with varied outcomes (injury claim accepted, claim denied, not eligible to claim).

Develop a conceptual framework for the study

By helping to refine and clarify research questions, and in providing substantive and theoretical bases for them, your conceptual framework provides both a boundary and a focus for data collection and analysis. This will give you, as the researcher, a sense of direction and also some sense of control over the study, both of which are important for allowing you to move on. As you plan your study, and as you start to develop analysis categories, it is helpful to keep challenging what you are doing to maintain focus. This is not to stop you from picking up on new leads as you begin to analyse your data, but to help ensure that whatever you do will contribute to wherever the final analysis takes you.

Map the framework

Visualising or mapping a conceptual or theoretical framework at the beginning of your project can help in identifying the assumptions you hold about what your topic involves and how things relate to each other. More than anything else, however, working through the development of a conceptual framework will sharpen the focus of your study, helping you to formulate your questions and to determine what is needed to answer them.

Begin to visualise this framework by drawing on your own experience and assumptions very early in the planning process, and then progressively refine this as you proceed to read and to build your knowledge and understanding. As you progressively identify elements or concepts being studied, use links to show connections between them. Conceptual frameworks are best done graphically, rather than in text. Having to get the entire framework on a single page obliges you to specify the bins that hold discrete phenomena, to map likely relationships, to divide variables that are conceptually or functionally distinct, and to work with all of the information at once (Miles & Huberman, 1994: 22). Archive progressive copies of these maps as part of your audit trail for the project, or because you might need to revert to an earlier idea.

To map a conceptual framework (Maxwell, 2013; Miles & Huberman, 1994; Strauss, 1987; Box 2.6):

▶ Identify a list of relevant concepts (also people).
▶ Place each of these on cards or create objects in a computer diagram.
▶ Push the cards around a table, or the icons around a screen (using modelling software), to get a sense of grouping and order.
▶ As you identify each item to be placed in the model, ask what else might be associated with it. Add any additional items to those you already have.
▶ Connect each concept to show relationships with other items. If you are working with cards on a table, you might have to move to a paper or whiteboard version at this stage.

▶ Adjust the locations of concepts and links and add feedback loops, to improve the model.

▶ Add colour, thickness and labels to lines, to add clarity or emphasis to the model.

If you're struggling for what to put into your concept map, try these ideas:

▶ Think about keywords you use when talking about the topic. Make these into concepts in your theory and map.

▶ Take something you've already written and map the implicit theory embedded within it.

▶ Identify a key concept and brainstorm around this.

▶ Ask someone to interview you about your topic, probing for what is going on and why. Have them make notes as they do, and use these as the basis for a map.

▶ If you are exploring theoretical contributions to the topic, try mapping the relevant components of each theory.

▶ Look for the conflicts and gaps in your model – the bits you struggle to place. Ask whether you need to explore these in your project. What would be needed to fill in gaps or connect isolates?

▶ If you are working with a team, have each team member attempt a concept map, compare versions, discuss, and revise. This has the secondary benefit of ensuring that all team members are agreed regarding the direction of the study.

Finally, after you have a map that satisfies you (for the present!):

▶ Identify:
  o the actors in the situation;
  o the contextual factors;
  o the activities or processes to be studied;
  o the initial relationships to be examined.

▶ Write a narrative of what the map says about what you are studying, emphasising the meaning of the arrows.

Box 2.6

Mapping a conceptual framework

When I started to look at the development of researchers, I already had an understanding of at least two very different pathways into research. There were those who had always been inclined to want to ask questions and discover new information, or who enjoyed puzzles; and there were those who responded to the pressure of workplace demands to undertake research, some of whom then became highly committed to a research pathway. Sampling, therefore, needed to cover both of these routes. Additionally, drawing a simple map (Figure 2.3) made clear to me that establishing the major source of motivation did not explain eventual engagement with research, that other elements (environmental and personal) were also necessary for research to happen.

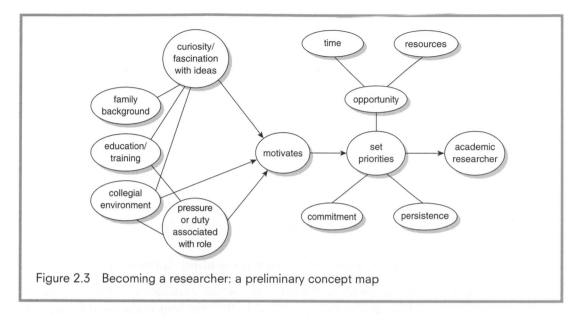

Figure 2.3   Becoming a researcher: a preliminary concept map

Develop a logic model

Logic modelling is a particular form of concept mapping that provides a sound basis for exploring process, particularly causal pathways in evaluation studies and in studies of change (AusAID, 2005; Knowlton & Phillips, 2009; Patton, 2002; Yin, 2003). Logic models 'are a graphic way to organize information and display thinking ... [They] describe planned action and its expected results. A model is a snapshot of an individual's or group's current thinking about how their idea or program might work' (Knowlton & Phillips, 2009: 4). The steps work as a series of 'if–then' sequences (Figure 2.4) based on a theoretical model of change, in which assumptions – informed by beliefs and knowledge about how strategies will lead to change – are named. The development of a model is best approached as a team task, involving colleagues and key stakeholders (AusAID, 2005).

To develop a logic model:

▶ Clarify the scope of the investigation or analysis. Gather preliminary information on the main issues.

▶ Identify the problem or goal or end point of a process, and ask what has to be in place for that to come about.

▶ Work back through each step and ask what would be necessary for that condition to be present.

▶ Keep going until you reach some potential root causes.

▶ Consider, also, potential additional (unintended) impacts of intermediate processes.

For an action project, the logic model will point to specific places to intervene so as to change the process. For a research evaluation of an intervention, it will

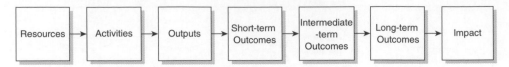

Figure 2.4   A basic program logic model
Source: Knowlton & Phillips, 2009: 37, Figure 3.2

point to intermediate programme elements that had to be in place for an outcome to occur, thus clarifying what has to be assessed to understand the process by which an intervention did or did not achieve its goals.[5] These principles for setting up intermediate observation points are not limited to evaluation studies; they can be applied to a range of process-oriented studies.

Develop (analysable and answerable) research questions

Research questions are derived from your purpose, mediated by your conceptual framework. They clarify what you need to find out and understand in order to achieve your practical and/or intellectual purposes; they will be expressed differently from the way you wrote your purpose, especially if that purpose was expressed in practical terms. (Similarly, the questions you ask of participants will be derived from your research questions but also different from them.) Once you have worked out your purpose, think of developing questions as a funnelling process in which you narrow down from a broad goal or topic area through a conceptual framework to particular questions.

Questions cannot be adequately formulated without your having already completed some theoretical or practical work, and preferably both. They are often modified as you proceed in your study and gain more understanding of the issues relating to your topic – during the design phase and again during the data gathering and analysis phases. There is no standard formula for designing research questions, and no agreement between major authors about how focused or open they should be. The primary issues are that your research questions provide direction for, and set boundaries around, your research plans (Green, 2008).

The questions that are developed out of the purpose and conceptual framework for the study are key to focusing data collection and for developing an approach to analysis, guiding what is relevant and not relevant throughout the data gathering and analysis periods (Box 2.7). Clarify the terms that you use in them, and specify the assumptions underlying them. As you begin to formulate your questions, imagine possible answers to those questions and the kind of evidence you require to support those answers, checking that they are capable of

---

[5]The AusAID framework recommends applying 'SMART indicators' (Specific, Measurable, Attainable, Relevant, and Timely) to each point along the way for evaluation purposes.

being answered. Again, working through these issues in discussion with a small group can be very helpful.

Box 2.7

The tortuous path to developing a practice-relevant research question

Anne Bunde-Birouste's project developed from a passion that she believes makes the impossible possible. She wanted to address the refugee settlement situation in a way that was sensitive to what young people were going through in the transition from refugee camp to Australia, and so she established Football United®, a programme using football (soccer) as a vehicle to support refugee youth settlement. But she was also a university lecturer (in health promotion), and was needing to embark on a doctoral project. By focusing her research on Football United®, she was better able to reconcile these three areas of demand on her time. Having dismissed the idea of using a phenomenological approach to look at her experience (and the adviser who suggested it), she set out with an exploratory initial question about identifying the political and organisational challenges and barriers to a programme such as Football United®, and a new adviser.

Meanwhile, the programme was gaining momentum, and data for evaluation of it were coming in. Anne was now reading literature on diffusion of innovation, participatory action research, and related topics, but none seemed to immediately connect with what was happening in the field, or to clarify the question she needed to ask for her dissertation. It was through being immersed in the programme and the evaluation, and having to clarify it for others, that the primary question to frame her research became clear. From a starting point of 'How do you turn a vision into a programme?', the question has evolved to become, more specifically: 'How does one turn a good idea into a viable programme that contributes to building social inclusion in multi-ethnic communities consisting largely of refugees from fragile and conflict-impacted areas?' Literature on the complexities of responsive programme design that results in an innovative project has been difficult to locate, although the literature on diffusion has become relevant as the programme model is adopted elsewhere. Now, through a process of community reflexive practice, she is engaged in answering her question, writing in an autoethnographic style that reflects her intimate involvement with both the organisation and the research.

Designing for data that can be analysed

The primary criterion in deciding on a design for data gathering, whether you are working within an established methodology or one that is purpose built for this study, will be to consider the implications of your research questions, within the context of your conceptual framework: what kind of data will be required to answer them? How will you analyse that kind of data, in order to find your answers? In a sense, you are building a logic model of how you plan to get from data to conclusions – the steps that will be needed on the way, and what you need to do to realise each of those steps and move forward. What sources of evidence, treated in what ways, will provide what you need? Will you have adequate resources to support data gathering? The time, money, and skills you have available each impact on your options. In a qualitative study, *data analysis will take much longer to complete than the time taken to gather the data*. In a three-year dissertation study using qualitative data, for example, you would be well advised to plan for primary data collection to occur *early* in the second year, if not before.

What did you learn from the methodological aspects of the literature that you surveyed about how others had approached analysis of their data, in your field of enquiry? Observe hints, limitations, and benefits that authors have mentioned about the analysis aspects of their various methods and learn from their experiences.

This is a time, also, where you might look to established methodological tradi- tions for guidance, as it is in their ways of thinking about and working with data that they have most to offer, despite their tendency to present (or imply) analysis principles rather than spell out clear strategies. Learn from these established approaches; become aware of all the necessary and sufficient elements in those you are considering using. Those who follow through carefully on the principles of a particular methodology will find benefit in doing so as each forms a coherent approach, but alternatively you may choose to use their frameworks for stimulation and ideas without becoming a card-carrying follower of a particular approach – providing the package that you put together is focused and coherent.

The most important lesson you can learn at this stage is to *plan for data analy- sis at the same time as you design your methods for gathering data*, that is, *before* you go into 'the field'. Patton (2002) identified the top 10 pieces of advice offered on a qualitative listserv to someone thinking about using qualitative methods. An example of number six in frequency was:

> Figure out analysis before you gather data. I've talked with lots of advanced grad stu- dents who rushed to collect data before they knew anything about analyzing it – and lived to regret it, big time. This is true for statistical data and quantitative data, but somehow people seem to think that qualitative data are easy to analyze. No way. That's a big-time NO WAY. And don't think that the new software will solve the problem. Another big-time NO WAY. You, that's YOU, still have to analyze the data. (2002: 34)

Identifying and selecting cases

Are you studying people, situations, documents, sites, time periods, organisa- tions, events or concepts? One, several, or many? Deciding what the case or cases are for your study and what to use as a unit of analysis are early actions that will have a profound effect on later analysis. Cases, and/or the units of analysis embedded in them, become the basis for making comparisons and exploring relationships between various aspects of experience (cf. Chapter 1).

Let's say you are studying a community association (or perhaps two or three associations). The study of the community association is likely to include data from multiple sources, including multiple people. If the focus of the study (and the basis for comparison and generalisation from the study) is the community association, then the association is the case, and if you are studying only one or a small number, then this would generally be described as a case study or multiple case studies. The theoretical interest is focused on the association (even if the empirical cases, or units of analysis, are the people in it). A study of *people* involved in one or more community associations is different; then the people involved are the cases, but you would be unlikely to call this a case study unless, for example, your study is about volunteering and the people are simply embedded examples of that behaviour (so that volunteering is the 'case' being studied). The complication, as you can see from this example, is that there is a fluidity about how you define your cases: 'As a general guide, your tentative definition of the unit of analysis (and therefore of the case) is related to the way you have defined your initial research questions', and 'selection of the appropriate unit of analysis will occur when you accurately specify your primary research questions' (Yin, 2003: 23, 24). If your questions and conceptual framework are clear, it takes only minutes to define the case type (what kinds of units you are using) and thence the cases for the study (Miles & Huberman, 1994).

Most research texts list a variety of strategies available to the qualitative researcher for selecting (sampling) cases. Patton (2002: 243–4) provides a particularly comprehensive list of 18 mostly purposeful sampling strategies, supported by a discussion of each. Essentially, sampling strategies vary with regard to whether one is looking to learn from variation, including extreme cases, or from typical or homogeneous cases; whether sampling is theoretically based or opportunistic; whether it relies on foreknowledge of potential cases or not; and so on. There are several ways in which sampling strategies particularly impact on or are impacted by proposed analysis strategies, which are relevant to consider here, however.

- The extent of homogeneity or diversity in the sample may impact on the extent to which you focus on within-case or cross-case analyses. Limited variation allows for intensive study of a particular phenomenon within a particular context; variation or stratification on a criterion relevant to the question allows for comparative analyses.
- The terms 'purposive sampling' and 'theoretical sampling' are often used in the context of emergent qualitative research. Often samples are initially purposive in that they are selected especially to meet particular research goals or to provide variation; they are then supplemented by a theoretical sample which is designed to allow exploration of questions that arise from initial analyses. Becker's 'trick' in relation to sampling was 'to insist that nothing that can be imagined is impossible, so we should look for the most unlikely things that we can think of and incorporate their existence, or the possibility of their existence, into our thinking' (1998: 85–6). Particularly with theoretical sampling, your strategy for choosing cases is intimately linked with ongoing analysis, and criteria for choices will shift in response to new information, as it arises. Thus, data collection methods may be altered or new cases or new data added during a study to better ground the theory being developed.
- The issue of when to stop sampling new cases (or within a case for a case study) also is likely to be dictated more by the purpose of the study and the progress of the

analysis than it is by probability-based criteria for generalisation of findings. The term that is often applied as an analysis-based criterion for ceasing the addition of new cases is *saturation*. Saturation generally means that no new information is being added to coding categories (data saturation), or to the emerging theory (theoretical saturation), through adding further cases to the analysis (Corbin & Strauss, 2008; Strauss, 1987). The difficulties of predicting how many cases will provide saturation were observed by Janice Morse:

> Estimating the number of participants in a study required to reach saturation depends on a number of factors, including the quality of data, the scope of the study, the nature of the topic, the amount of useful information obtained from each participant, the number of interviews per participant, the use of shadowed data [reporting on others' experiences], and the qualitative method and study design used. Once all of these factors are considered, you may not be much further ahead in predicting the exact number, but you will be able to defend the estimated range presented in your proposal. Because the actual number of participants is still an unknown, should data collection not proceed smoothly when writing the proposal, it is wise to overestimate the sample size rather than to underestimate so that funds are available to collect all the necessary data. (2000: 3)

When Baker and Edwards (2012) sought the views of a range of 14 established writers in the field of qualitative methods on the issue of sample size, the most common response was 'It depends', although what it depended upon was different for each. When a team of researchers set out to test the notion of saturation, 12 cases were found to be sufficient for the development of *descriptive* categories in a homogeneous group (Box 2.8) – but note (a) the conditional nature of their conclusion that you could well need more for your purpose, and (b) no new categories is a far shallower criterion than having fully developed categories to which no new information is being added.

Box 2.8

When is saturation reached? An experiment in sample size

Based on a thematic analysis of structured interviews regarding accuracy and social desirability in reporting sexual behaviour, conducted with 60 women in two West African countries at high risk for acquisition of HIV, Guest, Bunce, and Johnson (2006) experimented to determine the point at which data saturation (i.e., no further development of their codebook) was reached. They documented the extent of thematic development – new codes and changes to existing codes – after coding each set of six interviews, through 10 sets in total.

Starting with interviews from Ghana, they found that 80 per cent of their 109 codes were created from the first set of six interviews, and that 92 per cent were identified after a further six interviews. The remaining nine codes identified were used infrequently. They then worked on the data from Nigeria and found they had to add just five new codes, only one of which was substantively new.

They made a total of 36 revisions to codes, the majority of these occurring within the second set of six interviews to be coded (i.e., numbers 7–12). Most changes were about when to use the code, rather than the substantive content of the code. The reliability of the relative frequency with which different codes were applied also stabilised very early; codes that were important early in the analysis remained important throughout.

Noting that 'it really depends on how you want to use your data and what you want to achieve from your analysis', the authors concluded that '*if* the goal is to describe a shared perception, belief, or behavior among a relatively homogeneous group, then a sample of twelve will likely be sufficient, as it was in our study' (2006: 76, emphasis added).

Relationships and responsibility to participants

Not all qualitative research involves direct interaction with people, but most does. Qualitative analysts honour the role their participants play in the research they do, for it is the participants' perspectives on the topic of the research and their interpretation of what is going on that the researcher is (usually) seeking to understand and present. Seek agreements with stakeholders and clear ground rules with participants about what they expect from the analysis and their part (if any) in producing or vetting reports and academic papers. Relationships with participants are complicated when you are engaged in research where anonymity can be difficult to guarantee, for example, within an organisation or a small community.

Obtaining data of any sort is not a neutral activity. When researchers observe, they change the dynamics of a situation, with implications for the people involved and for the data they have to analyse. An interview, for example, might bring particular issues to the fore for the interviewee, or the process might lead the interviewee to new insights about their situation. Northcutt and McCoy (2004) observed that even at the level of the physical, particles with quantum relationships to each other vary in their state and behaviour depending on the method by which they are observed. This research-action thesis (Sanford, 1970) was evidenced in my own doctoral work in public housing apartments where resident-prompted community action was the practical consequence of data gathering about mental health needs and resources, both before data were analysed and after results were made available to residents (Bazeley, 1977).

Because you impact on people participating in your research, your roles and responsibilities as a researcher are brought into focus. Questions about these have arisen more commonly in recent decades as qualitative approaches to research and alternative paradigms for the development of new knowledge have gained more currency, but the questions apply equally to all research methods that involve or otherwise impact on people. Participants might become more directly involved in a project through designing questions, gathering data, or contributing to analysis of the data.

Cultural sensitivity, appropriateness, and power issues impact also on gaining access to data, on the quality of data, and on the potential for you to misinterpret the data you do get – even within one's home country and broad cultural group (Box 2.9).

| Box 2.9 |

Cultural issues in data gathering

When Bugi Sumirat, from the Ministry of Forestry of Indonesia, attempted to ask members of forest-dependent communities in Indonesia their opinions on various matters using scaled items as part of his doctoral studies for Charles Sturt University, the respondents wanted to know from him how they should answer, even when he insisted it was their opinion that he wanted. Because he was an educated person, he was respected as being more knowledgeable and authoritative, and so his opinion would be more important. He therefore had to switch to a more open-ended style of interviewing, to gather the data that he wanted.

Fry, Chantavanich, and Chantavanich (1981) reviewed studies in which concepts and measures had to be redefined to suit Thai understanding. They found, for example, that school status was determined not on being private or public, but on being 'a school with a name', as determined by reputational interviewing, as well as by having a lot of students score well in the final board exams. Ethnic status was not about being Chinese – Chinese in Thailand are Thai – but about the degree to which one is Thai of Chinese descent, evidenced in a range of language and cultural practices. Economic status could not be measured by asking about income, but rather had to be assessed by possession of important consumer goods. Emic (interview) data and analyses were needed, therefore, to determine how to measure relevant variables.

The issue of the *power of the researcher* in relation to participants was addressed more specifically by Degenhardt (2006; Degenhardt & Duignan, 2010) with respect to the problems associated with being an insider researcher who also is in a position of power in the organisation being studied. As principal of an elite private school, she was responsible, for example, for employment of staff and for arbitration of issues arising in the running of the school. From her experience she developed the Powerful Insider Research Method to model the strategies she developed to manage her potentially conflicting roles (Box 2.10). Similar issues of power and trustworthiness of research arise wherever 'insider' evaluation research is conducted in an organisation involved in a change process.

| Box 2.10 |

Participant-researcher-leader? Instigating change, protecting participants *and* developing trustworthy research

In her evaluative case study of the 'reinvention' of the secondary girls' school of which she was principal, Leoni Degenhardt had to balance the roles of researcher, principal, change agent, and 'human being' while also protecting staff, students, and other people connected with the school (Degenhardt, 2006). She developed elaborate systems to protect the anonymity of staff, students, and parents who were interviewed or who participated in focus groups as part of the research, at some cost to the quality of her data. Additionally, she established two committees at the beginning of the research process:

- A verity committee, comprising a chair with a reputation for integrity amongst all staff and three others selected by the chair from staff members who applied. This committee acted as point of reference for any member of the school community who had a concern with any aspect of the research.
- A critical panel, comprising three external experts in education from varied working environments. The panel was charged with safeguarding the research against possible claims of bias coming from the researcher's position in the school.

Each was set up, after careful consideration and consultation, with transparent terms of reference and with a backup procedure for dealing with disagreement. Nevertheless, tension between being directly involved in a process of change and needing detachment from that process to allow observation and analysis proved to be a challenge. She found that a combination of autoethnography and transpersonal research methods 'was useful to this researcher/principal in making sense of the personal struggles and soul-searching that were part of this study and of the reinventing of the school' (Degenhardt and Duignan, 2010: 73).

With the steps that Degenhardt took to protect the school community, no one refused permission for the research to proceed, and the methods and model she developed 'for the most part, successfully overcame these problems' (2010: 72). She presented her method, the Powerful Insider Research Method (PIRM), as a model that combined the research traditions of autoethnography and transpersonal research methods with the methodological innovation of the two committees (Figure 2.5).

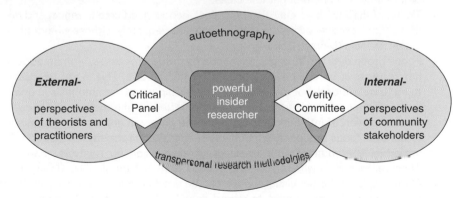

Figure 2.5 PIRM – Powerful Insider Research Method: a research model for use by insider researchers in positions of power in their own organisation

Source: Degenhardt, 2006: 293, Figure 9.6

Designing data collection tools and strategies

Methods of making or gathering data have changed remarkably over the past decade, with increasing use of the web and other electronic and multimedia sources. Regardless of how they came to you, however, you will be dealing with text sources and observations of behaviour recorded in field notes or using images, audio, or video. These kinds of technological changes impact more on strategies for obtaining and managing data than on strategies for analysing them.

'Everything has the potential to be data, but nothing becomes data without the intervention of a researcher who takes note – and often makes note – of some things to the exclusion of others' (Wolcott, 1994: 3–4). The data gathering methods you choose and the way you manage and work with your data directly impact on the direction and effectiveness of your analysis and reporting. When you are choosing methods, consider:

- the kind of data each method could generate;
- whether you will be able to manage and make use of (analyse) those data;
- how you will record additional or incidental contextual information; and
- *how each item of data you plan to obtain will assist you to answer your questions.*

For example:

- Quality of data is impacted by your style and skill in interviewing. Be very aware of your focus but keep prepared questions to a minimum, otherwise you will be so concerned about asking the next question that you will miss and/or cut short something interesting that the interviewee is saying. Instead, learn to ask the interviewee, in a non-directive way, to elaborate on their answers, to contribute to depth of analysis: 'Can you tell me more about that?', 'How does that work?' Some of the best data I've seen was obtained by Lynn Kemp (1999) when she went to people with spinal injury with a single question: 'You came home from hospital and ...?' Most interviews continued for two to three hours before they could be brought to a close.
- Timing of the interviews may also be critical. People need time to reflect and make sense of a difficult experience before they are able to adequately express what that experience meant to them (Morse, 1999).
- Focus group data are strongly influenced by group processes, with homogeneous and heterogeneous groups having quite different dynamics. This is not necessarily something to be avoided, but rather can be capitalised on as the emphasis in analysis shifts from information obtained to the interaction effect within the group. Unless you need the stimulation of interaction to generate the data you are looking for, use interviews rather than focus groups as a much easier and often more effective option. To identify individual contributions to a focus group discussion for analysis, plan to have an observer recording who is speaking at each turn, and the first word they say.
- Photographs and other visual images can be used both to elicit data and, by either the researcher or the researched, to record data. Visual records, such as photographs and videos, allow for 'second-chance' observation and analysis with the possibility of catching details of events that happened too quickly to take in at the time (Flick, 2009). While they have the appearance of objectivity, much depends on the angle of vision, the extent to which the subject of the image was aware of being photographed, and the relationship between the photographer and the people being photographed or filmed.

- Decide what demographic and contextual information will be relevant and design a means of obtaining it. You will benefit from being able to use this information to make comparisons between subgroups in your sample.
- Plan to keep field notes throughout your study. Wherever possible, carry a notebook or recorder. Use them to record the physical and social context as well as events, actions, or whatever is the focus of your study, even if you are relying primarily on interviews or focus groups. Note the ease or difficulty of access; note discussions when appointments are being made. Context is critical to interpreting data, and it is critical to being able to generalise from data.
- Employ multiple investigators (e.g., on field visits) to gain the benefit of the different perspectives of multiple observers. Similarly, seeking data of more than one type can help to overcome the limitations of any one type (e.g., Fleisher, 2000: 242).
- Be aware that data build up very quickly in a qualitative project. You need therefore to be checking their quality and usefulness from the start. Too often I have had students come to a workshop to learn how to use analysis software, having collected 'all' their data, only to find that the data they have are either inadequate or inappropriate for their research purpose and question. You can also generate very large quantities of data; the question then is whether you have the management systems, time, and analysis strategies needed to deal with those large quantities.

Pilot research and initial exploration

Put all your proposed research procedures, including strategies for analysis, through a 'dry run' with the kind of settings or people who will eventually become your research focus. This will allow you to determine whether your design will generate analysable data that are relevant to your purpose, and will help you to assess how long analysis is likely to take. Marshall and Rossman (2006) have suggested that pilot work also helps you understand yourself as a researcher.

There is a tradition of treating data generated through pilot research as material to be discarded, but in qualitative work they retain value, even if you change direction somewhat and the initial data gathered do not cover everything you eventually want. Keep those data, but mark them so that you know at which stage in the project's history they were created. As well as the data contained within, those records provide an archive of the steps you took in designing your approach to your study.

Planning for quality and credibility of conclusions

Why would anyone believe your results and conclusions? The quality and credibility of conclusions drawn from a project depend on:

- clarity of purpose and questions, and soundness of the underlying conceptual basis;
- the usefulness of the design in fulfilling the purpose;
- the sensitivity, openness, and commitment of the researcher in conducting the study;
- the level of critical thinking, depth, and thoroughness of the analysis; and
- your thoroughness and skill in pulling together an argument for your conclusions.

At the *design* stage, plan to:

▶ Have a research partner or a critical friend who can question your approach, and then later your analyses, checking for bias from preconceptions.

▶ Show how you'll use but not be limited by previous literature, and check your data against it, particularly where your design does not allow for internal comparisons.

▶ Record your preconceptions, and check the openness of your questions and responses during your interactions with people, so you can then assess whether you have influenced the data you collected through reactivity with participants.

▶ Build in time and additional data sources for cross-checking conclusions and explanations, then look for evidence that conflicts with your conclusions.

▶ Generate and assess alternative explanations for what you have found.

▶ Build in systems for moderating the influence of 'stand-out' data (e.g., so you won't be tempted to rely on or present single quotes as evidence for a 'theme' or conclusion).

▶ Assess the potential limitations of your study, and develop ways to counter as many of these as possible.

▶ Set up a note-taking system that clearly identifies data sources, and your reflections on data.

▶ Keep an audit trail of data collection and analytic strategies.

▶ Predetermine what kind of information and conclusions you want to be able to share with others from your study. Plan the write-up. What reports will you generate? Who are they for? Who else might be interested? This will all help to further define what sort of data you need, and your approach to analysis.[6]

No matter what steps you take, you cannot guarantee your conclusions. Careful, coordinated design and attention to these elements will, however, improve the likelihood of a trustworthy outcome. More guidelines for ensuring the trustworthiness of your conclusions are provided in Chapter 13.

Designing for an audience

Some years ago now, in response to a brief survey, 127 academic researchers in the creative arts, social sciences, education, and humanities disciplines in a regional university indicated the audiences to whom their research was directed (Bazeley, 2006b). The answers given were able to be categorised in ways that largely reflected different types of research (as defined by the Australian Research Council). Disciplinary differences were evident in the results obtained from that investigation (Table 2.1), but what was most surprising across all those disciplines was the proportion of researchers who targeted non-academic audiences for some or all of their research, including in disciplines such as psychology and history.

Who are the stakeholders for your research? To whom will the results be directed? An academic audience (including national research funding bodies) will be looking for rigour in the approach you have taken to your design and

---

[6]Marshall and Rossman (2006), Maxwell (2013), Miles and Huberman (1994), and Yin (2003) all write about validity issues.

Table 2.1 Audiences for research across three discipline groups

Target audience*	Typical type of research	Creative arts and design (N = 26)	Humanities (N = 44)	Social sciences (N = 57)
Academic	Pure/basic	8	30	39
Government	Strategic	0	4	7
Practitioners	Applied	16	5	50
General public	Any of the above	18	21	15

*More than one response was recorded for a number of respondents.
Source: Bazeley, 2006b: 222

analysis and for what your project has added to knowledge and understanding of issues in the discipline. Strategic research for government (or business or industry) maintains high standards of rigour, but also includes consideration of where and how the results might or will be used, and their potential impact on policy and people. For a practitioner audience, clarity and credibility are important, but the critical issue is how applicable your results are going to be to their working needs; thus an analysis of this factor becomes an important design input. Research that leads to products for direct consumption by the general public (which might be anything from multimedia public installations to magazine or newspaper articles or books) might be derived from an academically oriented design, but the packaging of it will, of course, be very different. Indeed, if academics producing research for government, professional, practitioner, or general public audiences wish to climb up the academic ladder at all, they will need to separately produce additional academic outputs from their work (Bazeley et al., 1996; Box 2.11).

Box 2.11

Writing for an academic audience?

Antjie Krog (2010) recounts how, soon after her appointment as a lecturer in literature at a university in South Africa, a conversation with the dean of research about her publications (a non-fiction book, poetry, and newspaper articles) for the current year went as follows:

'Why do my publications not count?'

'It's not peer reviewed.'

'It was reviewed in all the newspapers!'

(Continued)

(Continued)

'But not by peers.'

Wondering why the professors teaching literature would not be regarded as my peers I asked, 'So who are my peers?'

'Of course you are peerless,' this was said somewhat snottily, 'but I mean the people in your field.'

'So what is my field?'

'The people working ...' and his hands fluttered 'in the areas about which you write.'

'Well,' I said, 'when I look at their work I see that they all quote me.'

His face suddenly beamed: 'So you see! You are raw material!' (2010: 129)

She then reported: 'After being downgraded to raw material, I duly applied to attend a workshop on how to write unraw material so as to meet one's peers through unread but accredited journals' (2010: 130).

Putting it all together

For something to work, all parts have to be in place, well fitting, and 'tightened' (Wolcott, 2009). However, given my earlier emphasis on flexibility in design, and regular comments about being open to new directions either as you deal with contingencies or as you respond to data already obtained and considered, what does it mean to have a well-developed, tight design, and why is it so important? In his interactive model for design, Maxwell (2013) emphasised that all five components (purpose, conceptual framework, research questions, methods, and approach to validity) must be addressed at the design stage, and that there must be compatibility between them. A well-developed, tight design is one where such compatibility is evident.

One helpful strategy to use as part of your design process, as a way of ensuring that all parts come together, is to create a table (or tables) listing the questions you are asking with additional columns to record the purpose that each is meeting; the theory behind the question; the sources of data that will provide the answers (or specific items within each data source); from whom or where those data will be obtained; at what stage of the project; and how they will be processed (e.g., Table 2.2 in Box 2.12). You might then create a second version that identifies each source of data and shows what questions will be answered by each, and in the case of the example shown it would be helpful to arrange a version of it based on timing of data collection. These tables will help also when you come to presenting to others what you are doing or have done.

Box 2.12

Planning for a study of on-time immunisation

Overall purpose: to refine a model predicting on-time immunisation of children, and to apply this model in improving the design of immunisation services (cf. Figure 2.2).

Sample: recruit 60 mothers from three areas, to 'guarantee' data from 30 on three occasions, and data (including scale and survey questions) from an additional 18 on the third occasion only (to not predispose behaviour).

Final outcome: compliance with two, four, and six months schedule assessed by telephone at seven months.

Table 2.2   Questions and methods for a study of 'on-time' immunisation compliance (partial table only)

Specific research questions re impact of:	Theoretical basis	Data sources and timing	Data analysis
Disposition and coping style of the parent	Self-efficacy theory; parental efficacy	Interview re expectations and priorities for child generally: pre-birth, 2 weeks post-birth Survey questions and scaled items: 2 and 10 weeks post-birth	Statistical analyses of scales and survey items; content coding of interviews; comparative analyses and interrelationships between variables and between qualitative concepts and quantitative variables
Experience and beliefs about diseases, vaccines, and control over health of child	Personal history Health locus of control	Narrative re experience + health locus of control scale: 2 and 10 weeks post birth	
Social integration of the parent • information and social influence • availability of social support	Social influence – normalising Social support theory	Social network analysis (egonets) and associated immunisation-related accounts re members of the egonet: 10 weeks post-birth	Extent, centrality, density, considered in relation to description given of belief and support from each network member; interrelationship with other data, e.g., with self-efficacy, locus of control, needle phobia, support to attend clinic, compliance
Assessing probabilities and decision making under conditions of ambiguity and risk	Decision making theory	Narrative re process of going (or not going) for immunisation; mapping of decision-making – 10 weeks post-birth	Narrative analysis re story of the day; mapping and coding of decision steps and influences using modelling software; comparative analyses and relationships with other data, e.g., self-efficacy, locus of control, social support, household circumstances, compliance

Writing about design

Sometimes it is easier to name the overall design after you have worked through the methods used to answer your questions. If you cannot give your design a name then focus instead, for now at least, on describing its component parts and how they fit together to meet your purposes.

In the introduction

▶ As part of the road map for your project and dissertation, provide a brief descriptive paragraph that sums up your overall research approach and design for your project.

In the review of the literature

▶ Conclude your review with the conceptual framework you developed for your study, showing how it was informed by the substantive and theoretical literature. Clearly articulate the aims and questions for the study, either here or at the beginning of the next chapter, showing how the questions identified for the study are derived from the conceptual framework.

In the methodology chapter

After a statement regarding your general philosophical and methodological approach to the questions of the study (as outlined in Chapter 1), provide:

- An overview of your proposed research strategy.
- Reasons for the choices you have made, showing how they will answer the questions you have identified.
- Details of how you actually went about the study, including:
  - sequencing or phasing of substudies (if relevant);
  - selection of sites and/or participants and/or other sources of data, and a rationale for these choices;
  - choice of data collection tools and strategies;
  - management of the data;
  - strategies for analysis of data;
  - strategies for verification of data; and
  - limitations of the design, including a description of the contingencies you faced and how you modified the design to allow for these.
- This chapter should also contain a statement regarding procedures taken to ensure ethical conduct of the research.

It is often useful to include a table such as Table 2.2 to provide an overview or final summary for your methods.

Exercises

Exercise 1: Thinking through possibilities

As part of the planning phase, anticipate a pattern you might expect to observe in relation to your topic, and ask:

▶ What are the elements that make up this pattern? What might produce it? What other things might you expect to see associated with it?

▶ What other explanation could there be? What would I have to see, to determine which explanation best fits? Where or how would each become evident?

▶ What would I need to do to locate and investigate this evidence?

Exercise 2: Conceptual framework

▶ Is there an established theoretical approach to your topic? What happens if you abandon the assumptions of that approach? What do alternative approaches suggest?

▶ Map the elements and relationships suggested by (a) your own experience and (b) one or two alternative approaches to the topic. What implications do these have for the topic?

Exercise 3: A researchable problem?

▶ What do you already know? (Can you guess the answer to your research questions?)

▶ What would you need to find out to meet your goals and answer your questions?

▶ Is the information likely to be available and how can you obtain it?

▶ What skills are required to deal with the information? Do you have these or do you know where you can obtain them?

▶ How will you know when you've got the answer?

Exercise 4: Checking the integration of your research design

Consider each of Maxwell's (2013) five components (Figure 2.1), and demonstrate the compatibility of the following relationships in your study:

▶ purpose (or goals) with your research questions

▶ purpose and questions with your conceptual framework

▶ purpose and questions with methods

▶ conceptual framework with strategies for ensuring validity

▶ methods with strategies for ensuring validity.

Further reading

Maxwell (2013) comprehensively and helpfully suggests tried and tested strategies that will assist you to *develop* ideas and design your qualitative study.

Marshall and Rossman (2010) provide ideas to help you with your study design, in the context of writing a proposal.

Flick (2007a) similarly covers design issues you need to consider in writing a research proposal, while Flick (2009) puts design issues into the larger context of conducting different types of qualitative research more generally.

Patton (2002) comprehensively covers all major aspects of methods in conducting qualitative research. Draw on this for ideas and understanding when you are at the design stage.

Hammersley and Atkinson (2007: Chapter 2) describe design issues specific to planning an ethnographic (field research) project. In Chapter 10 they review ethical issues in field research, including gaining informed consent (e.g., as a participant observer), privacy, harm, and exploitation.

There are, additionally, many other general texts available which cover topics in designing postgraduate research, writing research proposals, or conducting qualitative research studies that will provide you with design ideas. Other more specific references include:

Knowlton and Phillips (2009) and AusAID (2005) for logic modelling and logframe analysis.

Baker and Edwards (2012) for a comprehensive discussion of sample sizes by a panel of experts, supplemented by student experiences.

Kvale (1996) or Kvale (2007) for designing interviews.

Landier et al. (2011) and Yorgason et al. (2010) each provide an example of writing up their study design and methods within the context of a journal article.

Bruce (2007) described in detail some of the methods dilemmas she faced in translating a grounded theory study from planning to practice.

3

Managing and preparing data for analysis

Data have to be documented to become useful as a source and then as evidence for analysis. Any work you do with data, even so apparently mundane as management, has (at least) two analytic consequences:

- whenever you work with data, you are prompted to think about them; and
- the way you manage data impacts on the efficiency and effectiveness of your analysis.

In this chapter:

- learn to develop systems for recording and storing information you will use as data or with data.

There is a difference between having data, and having data that can be analysed! View this chapter as a resource. It is quite procedural, and some parts will seem very basic to those who have grown up on a keyboard, but if you get it right it will stand you in good stead, and if you get it wrong it really matters. Familiarise yourself with its content, then dip back into it as needed.

Before data collection

'Qualitative studies, especially those done by the lone researcher or the novice graduate student, are notorious for their vulnerability to poor study management' (Miles & Huberman, 1994: 43). The advent of a computer on everyone's desk does not seem to have changed this situation, nor has it solved the infamous 'I have a thousand pages of transcript; what do I do now?' question that Kvale (1996) addressed, and which now (with use of digital technology) seems to arise with even greater regularity. The time to figure these things out, of course, is *before* you gather data, not afterwards – not even during. Preparation for your qualitative (or mixed methods) data, beyond framework, questions, and design issues, includes:

- Being aware of the different forms the data might come in, and determining what you plan to do with each of these once you have them, in order to keep track of them all.
- Planning the steps you will take to understand and interpret the data.
- Setting up any necessary databases or other storage facilities for data.

- Becoming familiar with any computer software you plan to use, including analysis software:
  - learn how to manipulate text and to format it appropriately in your word processor, for example, using tools like Replace and Styles (with keyboard shortcuts assigned) for any repetitive tasks;
  - learn how to create a basic spreadsheet, as a means for keeping a record of sampling and data sources, as well as for recording background information about each source of data for your study;
  - learn to use analysis software early, using your research journals and notes; you will benefit from indexing (coding) them as well as your data.
- Identifying 'deliverables': what is expected to come from these data, and for whom; and where they will take you.

Keeping organised, available, and usable data records

The bottom line here is systems, systems, systems! From the alternatives suggested, choose and apply those strategies that are relevant to your situation.[1]

▶ Ensure that every item, whether physical artefact, paper copy, or electronic record, is labelled with a meaningful name or pseudonym and the date of acquisition, and that critical source information is identified on or within it.

▶ If you are working with paper-based data, create a summary record or cover sheet with standardised fields for recording contact data and additional information (Figure 3.1). Mark each page of an attached copy with a name or code that links it to the cover sheet.

▶ Whether working electronically or on paper, create a spreadsheet or database that includes:
  - the name or code identifying the associated document or file;
  - where the document or file is stored;
  - what kind of data they are;
  - when they were collected;
  - where they were collected;
  - from whom they were obtained;
  - anything else relevant to your project, for example, demographic information relating to each of your participants.

  Creating this record in a spreadsheet or database will allow you to quickly find any item and its associated details, as well as to check, for example, the status of any source in your project (e.g., for an audio file, whether it has been transcribed, edited, and coded).

▶ As much as possible, make a note of the broad content of each source of data as soon as they become available:
  - If you are working with paper copies of sources and/or handwritten field notes and journals, create and maintain an index for your materials according to the major categories of what they cover (do this as you collect or write each item, so the task doesn't become impossible). Creating a record of keywords with source IDs and section or page numbers will ensure that, regardless of the system you have for storing items, you will be able to locate all your source material for a particular topic.

---

[1]General guidelines for (a) managing files on your computer and (b) using formatting features in Word are available at www.researchsupport.com.au.

- ○ If you record data using a word processor, use or insert keywords into the text, for later searching and coding.
- ○ If you record directly into qualitative software, code and classify your notes as you write them (Box 3.1).

▶ If you are working primarily with paper records, include an additional field in your spreadsheet or database to store the index of keywords *with page numbers* as part of the more general record for that source. Use of Find (Ctrl + F) with the keyword would then quickly identify all sources you have with data on that topic.

In practice, it can be difficult to maintain this level of discipline in record keeping, especially if, for example, you get home late after a torrid community meeting, or large quantities of data are suddenly piling up. Discipline in doing so, however, pays dividends in saved time later and in quality of evidence for your analysis and conclusions.

Project: *Careers Research*   Record ID: *24*

Source: *Helen Jones*   Date of contact: *2/3/09*

Location: *Her staff office*   Conducted by: *Pat B*

Affiliation: *Xyz University*   Discipline: *Health*

Gender: *F*   Age group: *30s*

Position: *Lecturer*   Career stage: *Early*

Location of original recording: *Careers Research\Interview Data\Audio files*

Transcribed?   Yes ✔   No ...   Edited?   Yes ...   No ✔

Reason for contact: *Practitioner rather than researcher orientation*

Context: *Practitioner-researcher, part of large team, does the computer databases. Still doing PhD.*

Main points / impressions: *Very harmonious team. Clearly enjoys her role in working with them. Comfortable with computers and databases. More hesitant about PhD research.*

Points to follow up:

- *Role of teams: e.g., How critical is team experience for new researchers? What does it provide that others don't get (would having a mentor do the same thing)?*
- *When does working with a team make for more or less engagement with research? What if team is conflictual or exploitative – does that impact on desire to do research, or just on working with that group?*
- *Role/time conflicts: e.g. between work for team project and PhD research (also with teaching).*

Keywords: *teams; time issues; practitioner research*

Figure 3.1   Contact summary record (paper version)

Box 3.1

Two contrasting approaches to managing data

Storing handwritten notes

William Foote Whyte spent over three years (in the late 1930s) living in and observing 'street corner society' in an Italian immigrant community in Boston. His record of that experience and what he learned from it about the structure of social groups has become a classic in sociological literature. His book contains, also, an appendix in which he recorded how he went about the study, including his approach to organising data records.

> In the very early stage of exploration, I simply put all the notes, in chronological order, in a single folder. As I was to go on to study a number of different groups and problems, it was obvious that this was no solution at all.

> I had to subdivide the notes. There seemed to be two main possibilities. I could organize the notes topically, with folders for politics, rackets, the church, the family, and so on. Or I could organize the notes in terms of the groups on which they were based, which would mean having folders on the Nortons, the Italian Community Club, and so on. …

> As the material in the folders piled up, I came to realize that the organization of notes by social groups fitted in with the way in which my study was developing. For example, we have a college-boy member of the Italian Community Club saying: 'These racketeers give our district a bad name. They should really be cleaned out of here.' And we have a member of the Nortons saying: 'These racketeers are really all right. When you need help, they'll give it to you. The legitimate businessman – he won't even give you the time of day.' Should these notes be filed under 'Racketeers, attitudes toward'? If so they would only show that there are conflicting attitudes toward racketeers in Cornerville … It seemed to me of much greater scientific interest to be able to relate the attitude to the group in which the individual participated. This shows why two individuals could be expected to have quite different attitudes on a given topic.

> As time went on, even the notes in one folder grew beyond the point where my memory would allow me to locate any given item rapidly. Then I devised a rudimentary indexing system. (Whyte, [1943] 1993: 307–8)

Managing sources using QDA software

Over a period of 18 months I was engaged in an ethnographic study exploring research cultures and performance in the arts, humanities, education, and social sciences disciplines within a regional university, involving 300 staff members across seven schools, to determine strategies for increasing the visibility of their research. Data for the study were derived from observations, interviews, surveys, media materials, and administrative records. All materials were recorded, managed, and analysed using qualitative software, with individual staff members being designated as empirical cases (units of analysis) for the project:

- Field observations, notes from interviews and casual conversations, copy from media, and notes from school-based working documents (e.g., applications for support of various kinds) were recorded progressively in ongoing documents for each of the seven schools. Each entry was identified for source of the information, staff member(s) involved, date, etc. Each was coded as it was entered (or soon after) for staff member (case) and for issues raised related to research performance.

- Survey responses (gathered via email) were coded for staff member and content, including their area of research and other related information.
- School, research centre, and staff members' web pages were reviewed, with relevant information extracted and similarly coded for staff member and content.
- Publication and funding records, derived as two documents from administrative spreadsheets, were coded for research area and auto coded for staff member.
- Policy documents, strategic plans, etc. were imported and coded for any relevant issues.
- Demographic and academic status details were recorded as attributes of cases, i.e., for each staff member.
- Notes from published literature on research development and performance issues were imported and coded for content within the software.

Cases were grouped within schools. Content codes were grouped according to research topic, research approach, program issues, assessment issues, and production issues.
As a result:

- The research interests and related experience of any staff member could be immediately retrieved at any time.
- A record of all current research activity relating to any topic could be retrieved, along with who was involved in research on that topic and in what way. This information was then able to be reported both by school and by potential areas of interest, to guide further development.
- Issues impeding or promoting the visibility of research could be reviewed; analysed in relation to discipline, level of appointment, etc.; then discussed, strategised, and reported.

Recording and preparing data for analysis

How you make data records or prepare information for analysis in your research study depends on:

- the kinds of data you are working with – whether they comprise field notes or other observations; cultural and other objects; records from interviews, focus groups, or other conversations; newspaper reports or other media; electronic data from blogs, forums, or other websites; and so on;
- the methodological approach you will be taking to the analysis of those documents; and
- whether you plan to analyse them as paper/physical records, multimedia files, or electronically, using a word processor, a spreadsheet or database, or qualitative analysis software.

Additionally:

- As a general guideline, record and use pseudonyms for participants (also sites and organisations) from the start of your working with your data. These names become more familiar to you than the real names of those involved, while also being more meaningful than a case number would be. (Keep the master list that links names and pseudonyms in a location separate from the data.)

Ethnographic or case study field notes and observations

Exploratory ethnographic or case study fieldwork involves observations, spontaneous or planned interviews and discussions, site-based and team meetings, visual records, and documentary records. This type of research is therefore one of the most difficult to manage from the point of view of record keeping and data management. To begin with, you will want to record 'everything', generating large volumes of diverse information. Only as the study develops and begins to take shape will you feel safe in focusing and hence limiting what you record or store. Having a clear conceptual framework will assist from the start in providing direction about what might be relevant; undertaking analysis along the way will be vital to clarifying the ongoing direction.

Record concrete detail in field notes, including those things that locals would see as meaningful, rather than just recording labels or making general statements (Emerson, Fretz, & Shaw, 1995; Hammersley & Atkinson, 2007). 'The ethnographer "inscribes" social discourse; *he writes it down*. In so doing, he turns it from a passing event, which exists only in its own moment of occurrence, into an account, which exists in its inscription and can be reconsulted' (Geertz, 1973: 19). As an event or experience is observed and recorded, write 'lushly' and 'loosely' to provide a 'richer matrix to start from' (Goffman, 1989: 131). 'Write down whatever impressions occur ... to react rather than to sift out what may seem important, because it is often difficult to know what will and will not be useful in the future' (Eisenhardt, 2002: 15). Some selection and reduction in the details of what occurred are inevitable, nevertheless, and the focus in what you record might change over the course of the project.

In the process of constructing field notes, the writer also makes sense of his or her observations, but records them without using evaluative forms of expression (Emerson et al., 1995). Record actual words spoken wherever possible, making sure the words of those you are observing are clearly distinguishable from your own. One suggestion is to use double, single, or no quotation marks to distinguish the degree of accuracy with which spoken words have been recorded. Always locate the context of spoken words: who said them, who else was there, where they were, when it was, and what else was going on (Box 3.2).

Poor field notes are as much use for analysis and evidence as a blurred photograph (Hammersley & Atkinson, 2007). If possible, record observations before talking to others or engaging in further observations. Have a quiet corner where you can discreetly escape to make notes, or, if your role allows it, make notes as you observe: Whyte ([1943] 1993) took on the role of secretary in the Italian Community Club he was studying so that he could take notes unobtrusively in their meetings. At the very least, jot some words and phrases to prompt recall when you return later (that day!) to expand the record.

| Box 3.2 |

Observations in a delivery suite

These notes are part of those recorded by Jan Wheeler, a clinical midwifery consultant, during one of several sessions observing what midwives did to minimise perineal trauma for Asian women during the second stage of normal labour and birth.

Key: M = midwife, W = woman, P = partner, DS = delivery suite

0945 The M rang me and said that the W was fully dilated and wanted to push. I had been recruiting women in the ante-natal clinic after talking to the W & P in DS. I ran quickly to DS.

I entered the DS room after knocking.

The woman was in a semi-recumbent position on the bed uncovered by the blanket, genital area exposed, legs apart and using the gas. The Midwife was talking to W and then she removed the gas.

M asked if a contraction had started – W nodded in agreement. M said 'push into your bottom' – a calm, gentle voice. 'Push again into your bottom; use the pain, excellent work. Has the pain gone?' W agreed quietly. M said 'Then just relax.'

W laying quietly, eyes closed. M checked the foetal heart sounds (FHS) with the CTG. P was standing near the window, opposite but well away from W. Went towards the bed to help, unsure, stepping back. M not talking to P, working around him. <<Not encouraging him to interact or showing him how to support the W.>>

Another contraction … M 'Good work, well done, push the baby out.' Checked FHS with CTG … M 'baby is still very happy' (quiet laugh).

P standing near the window, arms folded. M sitting on metal chair (between P and the W) next to the bed near W. Has hand on W's abdomen feeling for a contraction. M 'OK, big breath in … You are doing fantastic. Would you like a drink of water? No? OK.' M checks FHS with CTG, sits down on chair.

W quiet, lays there, doesn't say or do anything – looking at partner. Partner moves around to opposite side of the bed from M. Moves close to bedside near W. Holds his hands together, does not touch W. M sits quietly, with hand intermittently moving/resting on W's abdomen.

Field notes have traditionally been recorded in handwritten journals, but these do not facilitate analytic work. While preliminary notes may have been recorded by hand while on site to insure against loss of detail, a full version should be recorded digitally as soon as possible after the event or experience. Options include typing directly into a word processor document or qualitative analysis software; using voice to text software (e.g., Dragon Dictate); or (especially for a team project) using a blog to record the notes (Box 3.3).

▶ Identify all entries with a date and location (usually in a header of some sort).

▶ Incorporate image data into these records wherever it is available.

▶ To facilitate later analysis, paragraph the text, inserting one or more standardised keywords within each paragraph.

Box 3.3

Using a blog to record field notes

As well as text-based notes, a blog allows you to store images, and hyperlinks to other web-based files (pdfs, MS Office documents, audio, and video). Invited contributors (i.e., other team members) can comment on each post. Entries are date stamped and can be categorised; there is a text search function, and users can click to access an archive of posts.

Documentary, image, and web-based sources

Who produced a document, for whom, and for what purposes are highly relevant to analysis (Flick, 2009). These kinds of sources vary regarding whether:

- they are original (primary) or secondary sources;
- they were solicited (e.g., essays) or unsolicited (e.g., reports, administrative sources);
- they were private or public, official or unofficial;
- you have access to and can record a full copy, part, summary, or notes only;
- for downloaded sources, whether they come as a single file for each item (e.g., report), or with multiple items together in a source (e.g., blog/forum contributions on a thread; newspaper articles on a topic; set of images);
- they comprise text or visual records, and how they can be accessed for reading;
- if images associated with text-based material, whether the images were used to elicit, supplement, or record responses.

Include categories to check for these items in the cover sheets, spreadsheet, or database that records content details about each source, for all documentary sources.

Downloaded sources often come as multiple items together. Given these are already in electronic form, it then makes sense to make use of word processor features (e.g., using Format or Special features accessed by clicking on More in the Replace dialogue) to appropriately format records. Auto coding, content coding, and query features available in QDA software or specialist content analysis software can then take advantage of formatting features to work with the data (Box 3.4).

Paper-based documents pose a different set of data management issues, with options including scanning each page as an image or as readable text; working with it in its original (paper) format; or making notes and working from those. They also create a storage issue, and the necessity to record where, in the storage system, each one is located.

┐ **Box 3.4** ┌

Using software to manage downloaded sources

Jannet Pendleton, at the University of Technology, Sydney, used company media releases and newspaper articles in her doctoral study of a public relations (PR) campaign by a pharmaceutical company to have a new vaccine added to the government prescribing list for children in Australia (allowing parents to access it free of charge). While media releases came as single-item sources, the newspaper articles were downloaded in batches by date for each newspaper. The articles were prepared for coding and analysis using NVivo by turning the article header into a heading style, with the date of the article following. Each newspaper article within a batch, once imported into NVivo, was able to be auto coded as a case identified by its header, with month of publication, source (which newspaper), type (tabloid, broadsheet), and geographic area either stored as attributes of the case or coded. Queries based on this information combined with further coding of content have allowed her to trace the story elements and PR strategies used in the campaign over time, by different news sources, and to explore the link between media releases, newspaper reports, and subsequent government verbal and policy-action responses.

Using a spreadsheet or database to record observations or notes

Where you are recording structured observations or verbal data that do not warrant a detailed analysis of (almost) every word, recording brief quotes and/or text summaries combined with categorical and ratings information in your spreadsheet or database can provide a great deal of information for analysis, including overviews and comparisons, relatively quickly. Set aside a column in the table for each aspect of the data you want to consider; then in the row assigned for each case, enter a summary statement or brief quote that epitomises the information coming from that source for each aspect (Figure 3.2). Text responses to short-answer questions in a questionnaire or survey are typically already in this format. Data of this type in software such as Excel, Access, or similar programs can be easily resorted and 'cut' in different ways, allowing you to explore comparative patterns of these text entries based on category values for demographic and other variables. If finer coding of the content of the cells is required, the spreadsheet or database can be imported into qualitative analysis software to facilitate this.

Interviews and focus groups

Traditionally, interviews and other conversational data were recorded in notes either during or as soon as possible after the conversation occurred. Because technology is now so readily available, it has become more or less

Site	% 0–4 served	wait area	wait – queuing	organisation	imm site & reason	pace	integration with community health
outer metro 1	3	cosy	self-sort, wait 5 min	screen from wait area, not from queue	thigh – recommended site	slow, friendly 4 min	Poor: "I tell my nurses to send them to the doctors"
outer metro 2	7	large room, cold	take a number, wait 8 min	private – away from queue	buttock – less pain (not rec)	no rush, supportive 6 min	Neutral/neg: don't influence – distrustful
metro	70	hall, noisy, crowded	hard with older toddlers, wait 4 min	6 at a time, then come back into hall	thigh – faster	busy, formal, 1.5 min	High: EC nurses guide from EC clinic to adjacent hall for vacc.
metro	30	shared hall	self-sort, 6 min	screen from wait area, not from queue	upper arm – faster	moderate, friendly 3 min	Lukewarm: advise mothers to go

Figure 3.2   Record of observations from immunisation clinics (Bazeley & Kemp, 1995)

expected that interviews and other participant contributions will be recorded digitally, perhaps using a video recorder, and then transcribed. But is this always necessary?

If you are engaging in sociolinguistic, phenomenological, or psychological analysis, you will benefit greatly from having your interviews and other sources fully transcribed. The structure of conversation and turn-taking is important for linguistic research, and details of how people understand and feel and respond, sometimes their barely conscious thoughts, matter for other approaches. *But*, when nuances of expression are not needed for the analytic purpose of the research (e.g., when what is required from the research is to extract 'factual' information about how something was done, or a list of relevant issues or indicators), verbatim transcriptions may not be necessary and notes may be sufficient for the purpose. *Using a computer program to assist analysis does not automatically mean you are required to use full transcripts.*

When I had assistants interviewing researchers about the impact of receiving a small grant on their development as researchers, the conversations were recorded. Much of the recorded conversation was not directly relevant to the topic of my research, however (researchers have an irrepressible urge always to tell what their research is about), and so the interviewers typed notes from the recordings, supplemented by occasional direct quotes. In a different setting, two researchers each took notes from an interview, and their notes were combined to create a final version for analysis. In another setting again, when Australia's corporate watchdog set out to investigate 'boiler room' share-selling scams, the researchers worked entirely from notes they recorded during their telephone conversations with those who had been approached by the scammers. These were sufficient to trace the chain of events and their responses to those as told by the interviewees (Australian Securities and Investments Commission, 2002).

Working from notes can have the added advantage of a much reduced body of data to work through, although the data can be much more dense (as was the case in the boiler room study), making working with that body of data somewhat more difficult in the sense that coding may be attached to smaller and less contextualised units of data. The key disadvantage of working from notes is their incompleteness and therefore the potential for selectivity and bias in the record, given that it is not possible to record absolutely everything that was said. Having a recording as a backup (if appropriate) can be helpful in overcoming this; or alternatively, have a second person involved in the interview or focus group, so that one can focus on recording while the other directs the conversation, with both able to contribute to the record of the conversation.

Transcription[2]

What appears at first sight as a purely mechanical task is, in fact, plagued with interpretive difficulties. First, this is when you discover the real value of using a high-quality recorder for your interviews or, even more so, for group discussions (using two is recommended for the latter). There is also real value in doing your own transcribing, if at all possible – building intimate knowledge of your data. At the very least, if another person typed the transcripts, it is absolutely essential for the person who did the interview to review and edit the transcript while listening carefully to the recording. A typist who unintentionally reorders or omits words or fragments (such as *n't* from the end of a verb) can totally reverse the intended meaning of a sentence. Check also the placement of full stops (periods) and commas.

The flat form of the written words loses the emotional overtones and nuances of the spoken text, and so, as well as corrections, it is beneficial for the interviewer to format or annotate the text to assist in communicating what actually occurred with a view to the purpose and the intended audience for the transcription. The goal in transcribing is to be as true to the conversation as possible, yet pragmatic in dealing with the data. Some issues and suggestions follow:[3]

- A full transcript will include all 'ums', 'mmms', repetitions and the like. Repetitions communicate something about the thinking or emotion of the interviewee. Watch for typists who think they are helping by 'tidying up' the text! Repeated denials may in fact indicate an opposite meaning of what the respondent at first appeared to be saying. 'Ums' may indicate hesitation or some other concern about the topic being discussed or event

---

[2]Most of these guidelines on transcription were originally published in Bazeley (2007).

[3]Kvale (1996) and Mishler (1991) provided useful discussions and examples of these and other issues involved in transcription.

being recalled, although if they are simply a regularly occurring pattern of speech, the decision may be different.

- In the same vein, don't correct incomplete sentences (which tend to represent the way people talk) or poor grammar; it is important to capture the form and style of the participant's expression.
- Note events which create interruptions to the flow of the interview, for example: (tape off), (telephone rings). Note also other things that happen which may influence interpretation of the text (mother enters room).
- Record non-verbal and emotional elements of the conversation, such as (pause), (long pause), (laughter), (very emotional at this point). For some purposes, such as various forms of sociolinguistic analysis, even more detail may be required (e.g., the exact length of the pause, overlaps in talking). Emotional tone and use of rhetoric are important to record. For example, something said sarcastically, if simply recorded verbatim, may convey the opposite of the meaning intended.
- Include and identify the interviewer's questions and comments as they occur within the transcript. These are essential to provide context for the responses.
- If one of the speakers (or the interviewer) provides, say, a non-intrusive affirmation of what another is saying, one option is to record that affirmation simply by placing it in parentheses or square brackets within the flow of text [*Int*.: mmm], rather than taking a new paragraph and unnecessarily breaking up the text flow. This is especially important if you are using a computer program that allows you to retrieve the paragraph-based context of coded segments.
- Digressions from the topic of the interview are a controversial issue. The decision about whether or not to include that text centres on whether there is any meaning in the digression. Unless there clearly is significance (or might be) in what was said, it is usually sufficient to skip the detail of that part of the conversation, and just record that there was a discussion about gardening, or comparing anecdotes about bringing up boys (when the topic of the study was something quite different), and perhaps how long it went for. In practical terms, whether or not these digressions are included in full will often depend on who is doing the transcribing; rarely will a disinterested typist be allowed responsibility for omitting a portion of the text.
- As you are listening to a tape and taking notes or transcribing, you may come to some point in the conversation that is particularly interesting or potent, where emotions are running high, or to an amusing exchange. Make a note in the document as to where that interesting bit is located in the original source, e.g., (10:35). This will facilitate linking directly from your document to an external file with the tape extract, should you wish to be reminded of the tenor of that exchange.
- Some researchers like to comment on (annotate) the text as they are transcribing or editing it. If you do this, then enclose your comment in unique markers to set it apart from the transcribed text: <<comment>>.
- Keep a master copy of the text of transcripts (or notes) in its spoken order and context rather than rearranging its content as points under predetermined topics.
- Provide clear, written decision and formatting guidelines to your typist. You might also ask your typist to record her reflections on what she was hearing in the tapes as she transcribed them.
- An hour of interview takes most typists about four hours to transcribe (assuming a good quality recording) and generates approximately 25 pages of single-spaced typed transcript – something to keep in mind when you are planning how many interviews to

conduct![4] Transcribing a focus group discussion is much slower, taking as much as eight hours per hour of recording. An alternative to typing (sometimes faster, and less stress on wrists) is to use a voice recognition program; currently these require that you repeat what was said while you listen to the original (like translating at a conference), as the software will recognise only the voice for which it has been trained.

 Record whatever procedural decisions are made, first for the typist(s), to ensure consistency in the transcription process, and then for the report, to aid interpretation from the data.

Formatting transcriptions

The approach taken to formatting interview and focus group records depends on the approach being adopted for analysis, and whether or not analysis is computer assisted. For all forms of analysis, it is important to record who is speaking, especially to distinguish the interviewer's words from those of the person responding.[5] Those working with linguistic records or doing conversation analysis employ detailed punctuation conventions to mark the expression used in the text, such as emphasis, extending a word, taking in a breath, raising or dropping volume (Box 3.5). They, and typically also those working in discourse analysis, also number lines in the text. Narrative researchers, in contrast, are more likely to focus on whole paragraphs, seeking to preserve the total integrity of the text and the flow of the story. Phenomenologists often use two or three columns, with the text recorded in one, a first-level interpretation in the next, and possibly a more abstract level of interpretation in the third (cf. Figure 7.4). Grounded theorists (and others) working on paper like to use double-spaced text and wide margins or an additional column, to allow for first-level line-by-line codes and comments.

Box 3.5

Text formatted for conversation analysis

```
1  Joy:    =eh Well surely she's clever ↓mentally isn't s[he
2  Les:                                               [Oh I don't
3          know'bout ↑that, I mean uh I don'think it's all that
4          difficult really
```

(Continued)

---

[4] I generally estimate that, *in addition to* time spent in preliminary reading and writing reflections, it will take a minimum of three to four hours to code an hour of transcribed interview *once the coding system is well established.*

[5] Check how best to do this, for the software you are using.

(Continued)

```
 5        (0.4)
 6 Joy:   What.
 7        (0.5)
 8 Les:   If you've got- if you got the schooling an' the
 9        back↑ground ih-uh (.) (      )-
10        (0.4)
11 Joy:   Oh[no(h)o perhaps that's what it is I don't know
12 Les:     [(      )
13 Les:   ↓No[:::,]
14 Joy:      [(    ) |Oh well I don't ↓know though I d- I should
15        imagine she is clever her children'r clever aren't they,
16        .hhhh yih know I[mean]
17 Les:                   [NO::]↑: no they're not. Only: one is
18        outst↓andingly clever wuh- an:' the other- .hh
19        an:'°Rebecca didn't get t'college,°
```

Source: Drew, 2003: 154

The use of computers changes the need to leave blank columns for comments, because codes and annotations or memos can be recorded and viewed without requiring additional space within the source (Figure 3.3; the text of the memo is

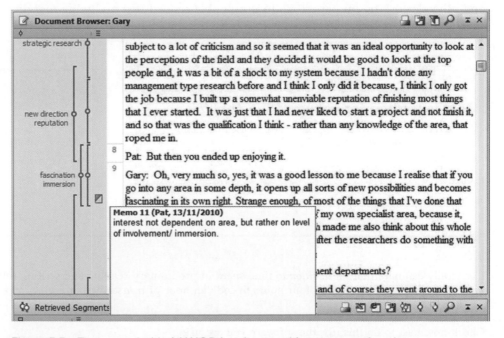

Figure 3.3   Text recorded in MAXQDA software with memos and codes

shown on hovering the mouse pointer over its marginal symbol, or a longer memo can be viewed by double-clicking the symbol). Additionally, speaker identification can be used to automatically code text for who said it, a feature that is especially valuable for multi-person interviews, meetings, and focus groups. Those employing structured interviews might also choose to insert standardised headings (NVivo) or field markers (MAXQDA) for questions, and auto code on that basis as well, although in my experience, even structured interviews rarely follow a guide sufficiently tightly for doing so to be of value. This technique can be of value, however, for formal documents such as structured policy submissions, while mixed forms of data from structured questionnaires can be imported into either of these programs directly from Excel, to allow for auto coding of questions. Those choosing to use computer software for analysis would be well advised to review guidelines for formatting documents in their particular software, with a view to taking advantage of the tools it provides for automation wherever possible (cf. Chapter 6).

Translation of text

Translation is 'a boundary crossing between two cultures' (Halai, 2007: 345). Translation is often necessary in cross-cultural research, especially where the principal researcher(s) do not speak other languages or do not speak them fluently or in a way that is sensitive to local culture. Hazards in cross-cultural research arise from variations in culture, dialect, use of idiom, or other linguistic devices (Esposito, 2001). Having compared two styles of translations for focus groups conducted with Spanish-speaking women – one in which a fluent interpreter translated in real time and was recorded in English, and another in which the Spanish recording was transcribed and translated word-for-word – Esposito found the meaning-based translation better preserved the emic quality of the dialogue. If you are not the translator, involve the translator in the analysis to help ensure retention of the original meaning of the texts and to explain the concepts the participant is using.

Researchers working in a second language (such as students studying in a foreign country) often struggle to transcribe, translate, and interpret personal and often very emotive text from interviews (or focus groups) they have conducted in their own language (Box 3.6). If trying to work in a foreign language means that too much meaning is lost and interpretation is difficult and shallow, transcribe and analyse your interviews in their original language. Interpret what you have found and then work on recording your conclusions in the required language. Use occasional phrases (or brief quotes) from the original language in the final report as needed, accompanied by a parenthesised translation or an explanation where you can't directly translate.

Box 3.6

Strategies for working with bilingual data

Working in Pakistan but studying in Canada, Nelofer Halai (2007) undertook to co-construct a life history with an Urdu- and English-speaking science teacher. As well as observing 30 lessons and gathering other classroom documents, she recorded 13 interviews conducted primarily in Urdu. Parts of the interviews, however, were in English, a language both women spoke fluently. Urdu adopts many technical words for a specialised science vocabulary from English, and also some common words like 'school'. It is also common for some English words to be substituted for Urdu words in everyday language, even where the latter are available.

After some '*ad hoc* decision making' she developed guidelines for the person transcribing the interviews, and, from her further experience, set out the strategies she became comfortable with in developing her 'transmuted' texts. She described four stages:

1 Handwritten transcription using native scripts for each of the different components, as spoken – but did that mean 'school' should be written in English or Urdu script? After (heavily) editing professional transcriptions she decided there was no such thing as 'perfection' and that she should opt for what was manageable, readable, and interpretable.
2 Typed transcription requiring bilingual-capable software. This was complicated by Urdu being a right to left language, and English being left to right, so again, it required lot of proof reading.
3 Translation: after trying to just do those sections needed for her report, she decided to translate the whole of a few selected interviews. In doing so, she sought 'inexact equivalence', using translated quotations in her report.
4 Transliteration: where an exact translation was unavailable, she used an Urdu word or phrase in the text, with a footnote explaining the meaning. Where English words had a local meaning, she provided the contextual meaning in brackets.

Visual records

Because photographs and other visual images are impacted by the intention and understanding of the photographer, as well as by selection of content and form of presentation, recording the context of and purpose for the creation of the image is critical. Many of the issues in storing and managing documentary sources apply also to photographs, including how to select, group, and sequence them; and whether to work with them in their original format (now facilitated by a variety of software tools) or with texts generated from them. Recent developments allow storage and coding of images with associated commentary in most qualitative analysis software products. Any editing required for image data should be completed before import. Similarly, audio or video files and associated transcripts (imported or created in the software) can be stored as parallel records

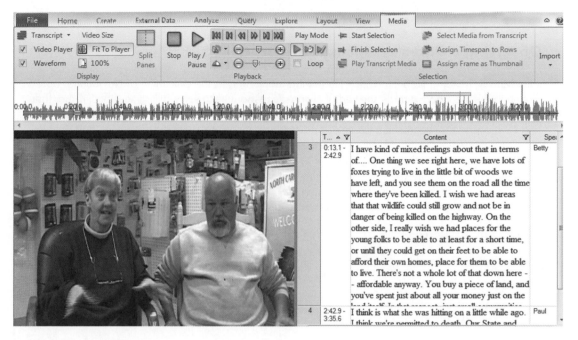

Figure 3.4   Transcribed video record in NVivo

in most qualitative programs,[6] allowing for observation of non-verbal cues along with transcribed text (Figure 3.4).[7]

An alternative way to use software is to work with a standard transcript that has embedded hyperlinks to video clips or sound-bites cut from the original video or audio files, so that a click will take you to see or hear critical expressions or gestures as they occurred.

If material has been recorded using audio or video (especially audio), it can be more efficient in the long run to have a transcript (or notes) instead of or as well as the video to work with (Box 3.7), particularly if the content is a straightforward interview or group discussion:

- it allows for *very* much faster visual scanning, coding, and retrieval of material; and
- it can be easier to take in everything that was said.

---

[6]Transana is an open-source program designed specifically and only for working with audio and video files.

[7]A comprehensive paper on the options and issues in 'Using and preparing multimedia data in CAQDAS packages' is available through the CAQDAS website at caqdas.soc. surrey.ac.uk under Resources > > Working Papers.

Box 3.7

Observing children's responses to story-telling

Julie Mundy-Taylor, a librarian working in teacher education at the University of Newcastle, opted to transcribe the video records she had of children's responses to story-telling sessions, rather than to work directly from the video. She prepared the transcripts by using different styles or colours of text to show a story segment, children's verbalisations associated with that segment, and descriptions of gestures and other physical responses from the children during that segment. Each child's response was identified by their name (as in the sample below). Recording the 'event' and her observations in this way was time consuming, but it has enabled Julie to explore the response of each particular child over the course of several stories and sessions, as well as to compare responses of subgroups and of the children as a whole to different types of story-telling sessions.

Little half-chick 3HE[8]

This next story comes from Spain.

1.38.25 Little half-chick

There was once a Spanish hen,
> *Bridget looks at Arthur*
> *Perry looks down at floor*

and she hatched out a brood of beautiful chicks.
> *Arthur looks at teller*
> *Bruce puts chin in hands*
> *Bridget looks at teller*
> *Leanne plays with fingers*
> *Ruby looks at teller*

Gold and brown and black; all of them lovely; all of them healthy; except for one. And he was a half-chick.
> *Jarrod sits up straight*
> *Celia has mouth open*
> *Grant frowns*
> *Linda pulls face*
> *Arthur looks worried*
> *Georgia has mouth open*
> *Brenda looks worried*

He only had one wing,
> *Matt throws head back*
> *Celia gasps*

and one leg,
> *Bruce gasps*

---

[8]The use of a heading style allowed for auto coding of each story-telling as a separate instance, with it then being able to be associated with attribute data for which story it was, where it came in the sequence of stories for that day, which grade level it was being told to, whether that class had had high or low exposure to story-telling, and whether or not additional props were used as part of the telling. Data for each individual child in each class were identified and coded (as a case) using a text query, allowing each to be linked with relevant attribute data.

half a head
  'Oh poor thing' – Lennon
  Derek frowns
one eye, and half a beak.
  'One beak?' – Perry
  Perry looks at teller
But don't feel sorry for half-chick
  Linda smiles ...

The importance of context

In the qualitative methods literature, attention to context (e.g., through 'naturalistic observation') is one of the most frequently identified defining characteristics of a qualitative approach to research. Regardless of your primary mode of data collection, observations will help to balance the perspectives you gain from your participants. 'The "background details" we include are, in fact, much more important than mere background, not just local color thrown in to give off a little verisimilitude. They are the environing *conditions* under which the things we studied ... exist' (Becker, 1998: 54). The meaning of speech, action, or anything else of interest to a behavioural scientist is always situated, and laws of behaviour cannot be assumed to hold independently of context. Even the meaning of a physical 'fact' is context dependent; for example, a person of 170 cm height would have been seen as tall in nineteenth-century Europe, but is short in the twenty-first century in The Netherlands.[9] Different contexts create varying conditions for action, such that different consequences result. Awareness of context during analysis contributes, therefore, to meaningful and appropriate *interpretation* of what has been observed or told and to understanding relationships between structure and process.

Full description of the context in which a study takes place is necessary not only for understanding the case, but also to allow case-to-case *transfer* of the knowledge gained, the application of theoretical insights to a new setting (Firestone, 1993; Mishler, 1979), or to facilitate further analysis and understanding through replicative or comparative studies (Yin, 2003). You can learn something of a more general phenomenon from a particular example. At the same time, you cannot afford to ignore the influence of place, local situation, or collective practices and understandings on that example, even if you don't yet understand how every aspect might be relevant.

---

[9]Such context dependence raises the issue of how specific one needs to be in describing such elements. In the 'simple' case of heights, is it sufficient to say 'Manfred was short for his years', or would it be better to record both the individual's height and either give a comparative statement or actually provide the prevailing average for heights? As a general rule I would argue for taking the 'middle road' (height plus comparative statement), but the answer depends of course on the reason for one's interest, and the importance of the individual's height in that particular context.

Contextual information is employed at three levels from the general to the particular:

- broader contextual information that situates the whole project;
- background features of particular sources or cases that are constant throughout the study but which vary across sources or cases; and
- situational information relevant to specific recorded events or experiences within the data sources.

Recording contextual information

Contextual or situational factors range in scale from local interactions and discursive practices to statistics relating to national and international settings. Take advantage of the possibilities provided by the development of technology for recording and presenting visual information. Store images, or insert into text; map location details using geographic information systems (GIS) software or Google Earth; draw diagrams and modify them using drawing or modelling software as new information comes to hand. Many of these forms of display, which facilitate understanding of the way in which relationships and other factors influence the people or events, are amenable to showing changes over time (Box 3.8). Recording these assists also in making you alert to these factors when you are coding or otherwise working with text or images.

Field notes accompanying specific sources will be noted in memos attached to the source, as observations noted within the source, or as annotations or marginal notes on the text – wherever they are best placed to ensure they will enter the analyst's awareness as they work with the data. These could include things like references to features or people or experiences in the interviewee's world that need to be explained to a listener or reader (including the interviewer or analyst when they encounter that text at a later time), as well as who was present in the room, interruptions to an interview, what happened immediately before or after an event or exchange, what kind of recorder was used (video, voice, telephone, notes), and whether particular information came before or after the recorder was turned off. Any or all of these have implications for your interpretation of those data, and potentially give meaning to events or comments that would not otherwise make sense.

Box 3.8

Displaying organisational context

James Hunter, in the International School of Business and Technology at the University of New England, studied the consequences for continuing managers and new contractual employees of a decision to outsource the meter reading activities of a publicly listed Australian energy company. Figure 3.5 shows the organisational context for each of the people he interviewed for his case study before and after the outsourcing process.

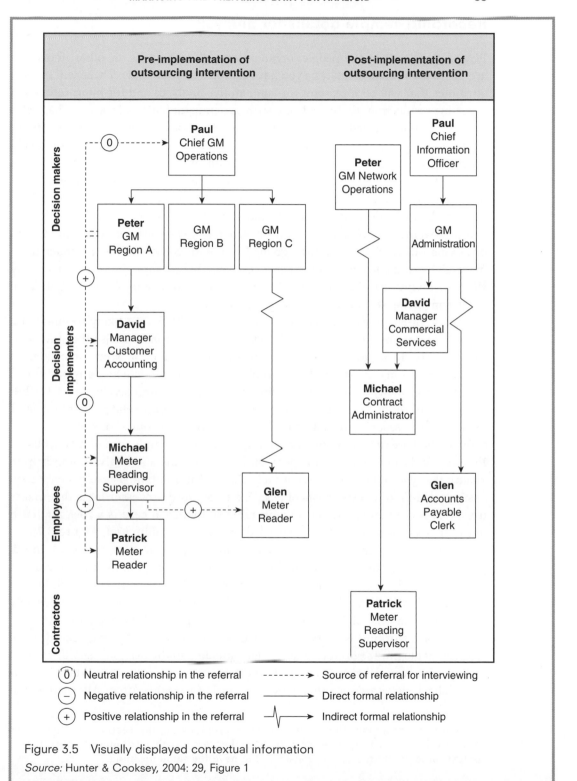

Figure 3.5   Visually displayed contextual information
Source: Hunter & Cooksey, 2004: 29, Figure 1

Recording sample details for analysis

Record details about the people, organisations, places, events, or other items that are the cases or units of analysis you have sampled in your study. These will include attributes that will be important for comparative analyses and for interpreting and reporting results from those analyses, such as demographic details, and perhaps also timing, locations, scaled measures, and other categorical variables.[10] It matters for both analyst and reader, for example, that interviews were eventually conducted primarily within the lower ranks of staff in an organisation (especially if it was intended to interview higher ranks but they were 'too busy' or otherwise unco-operative); gender and discipline of individuals whose data are being reviewed are likely to be relevant in any study of academic life and work; observing childbirth amongst women of South East Asian extraction is a very different experience from observing Middle Eastern women giving birth, with consequences for understand-ing midwives' management practices and caring behaviours; dates matter for any study involving historical analysis of any kind; and likewise timing for longitudinal studies involving several waves of data collection.

Theory, previous experience, and the advice of others are likely to guide you initially in determining which attributes to include to contextualise the study and for analysis. Ideas about additional details that would be worth considering might arise during the study. Try to complete all attribute data and any additional details for as many sources as possible (perhaps also purposively direct further sampling to explore their relevance) and store them with related data, for later exploration in association with the coded data for each source or case.

When you are dealing with data used to describe a sample, use of a checklist at the time of data collection will speed up both recording and analysis, and help to ensure that you remember to record all relevant information. These data are then easily transferred to a spreadsheet (e.g., Excel) or word processor table that makes it easy to review and sort. Set up your table so that each case is a row, and each item for which a value is to be recorded has its own column (cf. Figure 3.7). Be aware that in any kind of table (MS Word table, spreadsheet, or database), multi-ple entries within the same cell prevent effective sorting for comparative analysis or counting. Thus, for example, to record the ages of more than one child, use separate columns for each child, or to record occupations for people who possibly hold more than one job, allow two columns (Occupation 1, Occupation 2).

If you are working with paper records, ensure that you have a record of all relevant demographic or other source data attached to the original records for that source. You would be well advised, additionally, to include these data in your spreadsheet, database, or other tabular records for each source. Alternatively, if

---

[10]In statistical programs the details being referred to in this section are known as variables, but in most qualitative programs they are called attributes. In the current context these two terms can be considered to have the same meaning.

you are using qualitative software, the software will provide ways either of directly recording these details so they attach to the source or case, or of importing them from a spreadsheet; to find out how to do this, likely words to check in the Help files will be *attribute* or *variable*.

Recording data in one or other of these ways helps to make data collection more systematic, enables easy checking and verification of information, encourages comparability, and permits simple counting for analysis and reporting purposes.

Reporting sample details

When it is time to report on who your participants were, include enough detail to satisfy readers that you have considered potentially relevant details, so they can evaluate, interpret, trust, *and apply* the results you report. Summarise those details relevant to your study, for example, the proportions that are male and female, urban or rural, and so on. This information will be critical when you interpret further data, and to the reader for assessing the meaning and significance of what has been found.

If your data are in a Word table, you can sort by the values for a column and then count (e.g., Figure 3.6) – not the best method if you have a lot of cases!

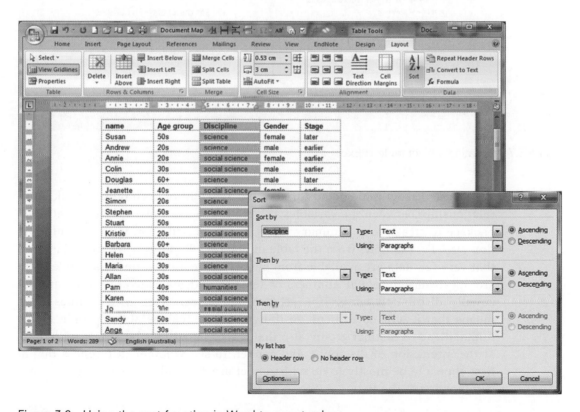

Figure 3.6   Using the sort function in Word to count values

A better (and easier) way of summarising the data is to use a pivot table in Excel (Figures 3.7 and 3.8). Alternatively, export the data to a statistical package and obtain column frequencies and cross-tabulations there; or if your data have been entered or imported into qualitative software, that software will be able to report the total number of sources or cases for each value of an attribute.

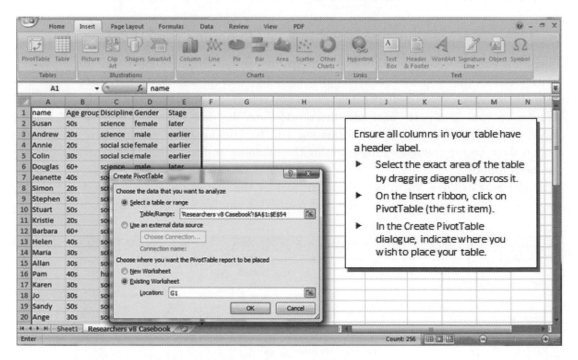

Figure 3.7   Creating a pivot table in Excel

Because demographic details are not independent of each other, check inter-relationships between the variables as well. If you use a pivot table or statistical package to create your summary totals, it will provide you with this information also. For example, from the table in Figure 3.8, you can see from the totals that very few data are available from people in the humanities, and while there are approximately equal numbers of females and males overall, they are not equally distributed across the science and social science disciplines. This means that it will be difficult to draw any conclusions about people in the humanities as a distinct group; also that it will sometimes be necessary to look at the interaction of discipline and gender, to see whether differences that at first appear to be mostly to do with gender are not really about discipline, or a combination of the two.

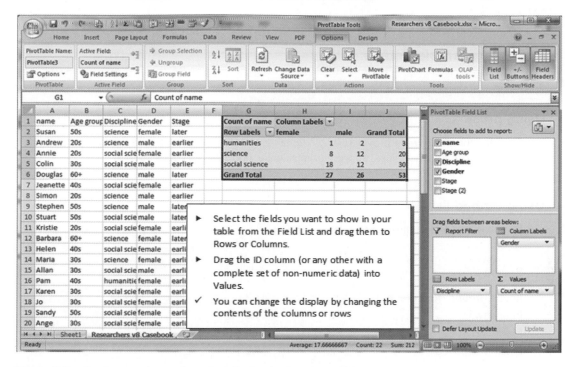

Figure 3.8 Setting up the options for display in the pivot table

For most studies it will be sufficient to report figures for the sample as a whole, rather than to list individual cases with their data, particularly in the body of the report. If individual case data really do need to be reported (say, in an appendix to a dissertation), be careful that individuals are not identifiable from it, particularly if passages from transcripts quoted in the report are also identified in a way that links them to sample details.

Where sample details to be reported involve more than one or two items, or there are a large number of values within any attribute or variable, reporting in regular prose becomes tedious to do as well as being difficult for the reader to absorb. Use lists, tables, and/or charts to provide efficient ways of displaying important demographic information that readily communicate to the reader. Each table or graph must be referred to in the text, but don't repeat all of the details from the table or graph in the text (see examples and alternatives in Box 3.9). At some point in the report, the implications of uneven sampling (as in this example) for interpreting outcomes will have to be addressed. Even if some demographic or similar detail was considered in relation to the qualitative data and found not to be important, it could still be worth including it and reporting its lack of significance, especially if theory had suggested it might be relevant.

Box 3.9

Reporting sample details

(Examples are drawn from the Researchers project.)

Using prose

Data for the study were provided by 27 females and 26 males. Just three had a disciplinary affiliation with the humanities, 20 were from science, and 30 from social science.[11]

Using tabbed lists

Data were gathered through a variety of sources:

Source	N	%[12]
Focus groups (four groups)	25	47.2
Interviews	13	24.5
Media sources	13	24.5
Email responses	2	3.8

Because interviews and media sources were both secondary rather than primary sources, material drawn from them did not necessarily directly address the questions for the study. Additionally, most media reports, the email responses, and one of the focus groups were quite brief and therefore provided limited (although useful) coverage of the issues raised by the study. This potentially uneven coverage of the issues for the study means that case counts must always be treated with caution, with actual sources being checked to establish their significance in drawing conclusions about patterns in the data.

Using tables

A further complication is that different sources tapped into different disciplinary groups (Table 3.1). In particular, the focus groups were primarily with social scientists, and the media interviews were primarily with scientists.

---

[11]Rules for reporting numbers include not starting a sentence with a numeral (write it in words), and using words rather than numerals for numbers less than 10 unless they are part of a string of numerical data, e.g., in a results section.

[12]Percentages should not be reported where the total N is less than 20. Also, percentages should always be reported to the same number of decimal places throughout a single piece of writing, even if that means adding .0 or .00 to a number.

Table 3.1 Disciplines sampled through different sources

Source	Discipline			Total
	Humanities	Science	Social science	
Email	0	0	2	2
Focus group	2	2	21	25
Interview	1	6	6	13
Media	0	12	1	13
Total	3	20	30	53

Using charts

The gender breakdown across disciplines also was uneven, predictably with more males in science and more females in social science (Figure 3.9).

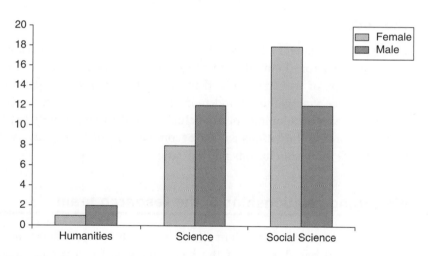

Figure 3.9   Distribution of genders across disciplines

Checks and balances for data

Member checking

Member checking is a strategy for confirmation of findings as they are being developed during or at the conclusion of analysis (cf. Chapter 13). Some, however, insist on returning all data, especially interview transcripts, to their sources for validation, correction, or further approval before analysis. Where there are issues of fact in question, this can indeed be of value. Or, if the interviewee requests that you do so, then you are obliged to comply with that request. Where the interview has broached deep personal issues or emotional experiences, member checking of this type is counter-indicated, however. The interview itself may have been a cathartic experience, and the ethical interviewer will have ensured that a satisfactory conclusion was reached and debriefing occurred before leaving the interviewee. To return the transcript, in such cases, would serve to reawaken the emotions, but this time without the support and wind-down provided by the interviewer.

On a practical level, most interviewees simply hate seeing their spoken words recorded as text, with all their hesitations, 'ums', and incomplete sentences. Others, once the interview is completed, are simply not interested. An alternative strategy is to provide a summary of the findings of the research to those who register interest in receiving it, giving them the opportunity to provide feedback to the researcher (preferably in time to incorporate their ideas into the final analyses and reports of the research).

The audit trail

Throughout all stages of data collection, keep a record of decisions made and your rationale for them. Record these in a project journal, or in a dedicated memo as part of a software-based project. This record is important for tracing how evidence was gathered and managed as the project developed – evidence you will use in developing your conclusions and to help others see the basis for them. Recording limitations as you become aware of them, also, will allow you to moderate your conclusions appropriately.

Managing relationships in the research team

It is a not uncommon experience for a research team to find that the research assistant who has done all of the basic analysis for a project (e.g., coding of interview transcripts) disappears just before final reports are due to be prepared – leaving the chief investigators in an embarrassing situation where they are frantically trying to 'get on top of the data' sufficiently to write reports for industry partners or funders and academic publications. Rarely is justice done in such a situation to the richness of the data that have been gathered, and worse, the reported results are likely to be heavily influenced by the first impressions of the chief investigators.

Miles and Huberman offered very useful advice about status issues. Valuing each team member's contribution to all aspects of the research not only helps to prevent such a situation from occurring, but also contributes to ensuring quality outcomes:

Avoid sharp senior–junior divisions of labor, such as having juniors do the fieldwork and the seniors do the analysis and writing. Senior people need to be directly involved in data collection in order to have a concrete feel for what the field setting is like. Junior people will function poorly as 'hired hands'. Both need to be actively and mutually engaged in thinking about the project and the meaning of emerging findings. You cannot be a 'principal investigator' in a field study without spending time in the field. (1994: 46)

Right from the start it is important to build a shared conceptual framework and understanding of the research questions, and to discuss priorities and strategies as well as insights in coding and analysis. Negotiating who publishes what (and whose names will be on it) *early* in the project is also critical for continuing good relations.[13]

Writing about data management

In the methodology chapter

▶ Outline your storage and data management strategies, e.g., indicate what kinds of data were stored, and the manual and/or computer systems you used to keep records.

▶ Report ways in which your data were recorded, transcribed, translated, or otherwise transformed for analysis.

▶ Note the implications that any of these things had for the way you conducted your analysis.

▶ Record the steps you took to ensure the integrity of your data.

Report sample details

▶ In the methodology chapter, or at the beginning of your results. Provide additional detail in an appendix, if required.

Exercises

Exercise 1: Recording data

▶ Listen to and record a short news broadcast, making notes as you go. A couple of hours later, after you have done something different, make notes again (without consulting the first lot of notes).

▶ Then try making notes from a recording; and finally, transcribe the recording.

▶ Compare the results of the four methods of recording what was said.

---

[13]I have a strong belief that research assistants who make significant contributions to the work should receive recognition as co-authors and not just an acknowledgement at the end of the article.

Exercise 2: Storing data

▶ List the various data sources you are likely to use in a project of your own.

▶ Design a record form to keep track of these data (preferably using table-based software).

▶ Identify any special formatting requirements any sources might have, given the way you want to analyse them.

▶ Identify where and how you plan to store each type of data source (i.e., documents, videos, pictures, etc.) you are likely to encounter.

▶ Make a list of the kind of demographic and other attribute data you might want to use, and design a checklist for recording it.

PART 2

WORKING WITH DATA: A PATHWAY INTO ANALYSIS

In 1620, Francis Bacon wrote:

> The more ancient of the Greeks (whose writings are lost) took up with better judgement a position between these two extremes – between the presumption of pronouncing on everything, and the despair of comprehending anything; and though frequently and bitterly complaining of the difficulty of enquiry and the obscurity of things, and like impatient horses champing at the bit, they did not the less follow up their object and engage with Nature; thinking (it seems) that this very question – viz., whether or not anything can be known – was to be settled not by arguing, but by trying. And yet they too, trusting entirely to the force of their understanding, applied no rule, but made everything turn upon hard thinking and perpetual working and exercise of the mind. (Preface to *Novum Organum II*, from *The Great Instauration*)

Hard thinking and perpetual work (or hard work and perpetual thinking) are indeed the basic ingredients of data analysis. Lace these with some stimulating 'exercising of the mind' as you play with the ideas arising from your working with and through the data sources you've gathered.

As you progress through these chapters, you are moving beyond preparation and onto the analytic pathway. This is where much of the 'hard work' of analysis is done, yet it rarely rates a mention when the work is published. There will be flashes of excitement as you gain fresh insight; there will be times when you feel buried in a morass of data. The strategies outlined in the next four chapters are designed to give you both a broad picture view and a detailed view of the data sources you are gathering, and to keep you moving forward to an ever-deepening understanding of the phenomena that prompted your research questions. You will not use all of these strategies; select just those that are appropriate to your current purpose and questions, and come back another time for another project.

Keep up a diary or journal of your research as you take steps along the way. As you record your reflections on the journey so far, that will prompt further thoughts about your data, and ideas for what to do or look for next. And, it will mean you don't face a blank slate when it comes time to write something for presentation or publication or examination.

Data samples: becoming and being a researcher

These extracts from four of the interviews in the Researchers project will be referred to throughout the text of this part of the book, to illustrate strategies and principles.

Shane – senior lecturer in humanities

Shane: I decided fairly early on, I suppose, in my career as an undergraduate that I wanted to pursue history, I guess because other people told me I was good at it. And so when you get told that sort of thing and it gets reinforced a few times, then you decide you may as well pursue it. So that's how I got into history.

Pat: Can you pinpoint a time when research became a particular interest to you, or was it just something that always seems to have been there?

Shane: Yes I can, with precision. Second year at Greenfield, which was the first time I was encouraged to consider working with primary sources. In that Australian history subject I was doing then, we were told we had to develop essay topics for a major essay, which was not a huge piece of work, 3000 words or so, and we were encouraged to use primary sources if we could and I decided to. I decided to use the [city daily] as the main one and I also used some government papers, and so I started doing that sort of work in second year which I guess a lot of students would never do as undergraduates but would come to in fourth year – in their honours year. And I enjoyed that a lot. I enjoyed the sensuous feel of century-old newsprint. I think, in those days, in the early seventies, we didn't suffer under the huge disabilities we do today, having to use microfilm instead of the real thing. Maybe I wouldn't have been so keen on it today, because there is this sensual quality to using aged papers. It's not nearly as much fun with microfilm. It's a lot harder too, hard on the eyes and also harder to scan. It's much easier to scan the real thing. Microfilm has its limitations. If you're trying to read a paper like the [city daily] for a year, it's quite a big task, even scanning it, let alone if you're trying to do a long period, and on a microfilm you have to go through each page. So it would be at that point I think.

Pat: And so it was something about dealing with primary sources?

Shane: Dealing with primary sources is what I enjoyed, and doing something original; and the feedback I received from my lecturers was very favourable. 'This is marvellous work that you're doing Shane, keep it up' was the response and so –

Pat: You mentioned before that was one of the things that led you into studying history, that positive reinforcement and encouragement –

Shane: And I enjoyed doing it. It was interesting, you're looking at the lives of people and it's pleasant to read this sort of material. So you can have, you can lead the life of peering into the past and understanding people's lives.

Pat: And trying to make sense of what's happening

Shane: Trying to make sense of, you've got the benefit of hindsight. You've got the benefit also of other people writing about it as well. So it exists in some kind of intellectual context. So that's good. And it's always good to look at new areas. My PhD area had hardly been looked at before and certainly not in English to any significant extent at all. So that was exciting even in those dark moments when you think, 'Oh my God, how am I going to manage all that?' when you come home.

Pat: It must be a problem to organise all the material.

Shane: Yes, well it's all in there, I can show you this, I use cards, I can show you what they look like. [Lifts a box of cards down from top shelf in his office.] Once you get past doing all those notes, putting it all together, once you've written it, you see in the visual side of things you can start doing visual research, if you're looking at publication. Nowadays most books are illustrated, so then you start doing the visual research, and look for the visual sources; and I love doing that.

Pat: Scouring old papers and things, for all those photographs.

Shane: Yes, although in those days newspapers didn't publish photographs. You don't have photographs in newspapers really until the thirties, but it's looking at albums and private collections. And that's lovely work, it's intellectually demanding, looking at pictures. ...

Elizabeth – early career researcher in psychology

Elizabeth: ... Research has sort of been, I have grown up in this sort of very academic background, research has been just one of things that people do as long as I remember, and it was always presented as something that was interesting and exciting because you actually found out new things and people passed through our home who had discovered new things, which we talked about over the dinner tables so – And my first job, I did mathematics, not with a view to doing research, it was just my best subject at school, I did a maths degree and I did a little bit of psychology so I could understand my parents <<both professors of psychology>>. Then I found that because I had not done anything useful like statistics or computing along with my maths, there was not really a lot I could do with that so I got a job in the public service as a clerk and went back and did the rest of my psychology part-time and then I got a job in crime research and that gave me a whole new focus on research because here people were doing research that really affected people's lives and legislation and working on things like bail reform and discovered that, whereas white people in Central Australia basically places like Alice and the Northern Territory, $1 was their bail amount for being drunk, Aborigines were charged $10 which of course meant that they could not pay it, they stayed in jail, the white people got out. We did a whole range of things, looked at homosexual offences as they were then, John Smith did a project with us, back in the mid seventies I guess. That was good in what was a sense that research really can change people's lives through legislation. Then I went off and had children and became a depressed housewife, and my friend said why don't you get a part-time job Elizabeth, lots of women feel better with a part-time job. Places like [town] and [regional centre] have the highest unemployment in Australia, don't be silly, there aren't any jobs, and certainly none that would be any less boring than being at home with the kids. But nevertheless to prove the point I had to buy Saturday's paper and sure enough there was a job for a research assistant, with experience in research, preferably an honours degree, not necessarily, make your own hours and the topic was disability and I had a child that was disabled, so there I was experienced with disability as well, I mean talk about made to measure job. That was at [health college], which was doable, especially with your own hours approach. So that was good, I got back into that and my boss was very encouraging and the other women I worked with were encouraging and I was back at uni within a year with a view to doing honours and PhD on account I wanted to be a researcher instead of a research assistant. So I guess for me it has always been there. …

Lynn: When there are so many conflicting priorities, it must be so easy to say well OK I am getting paid to teach, so I have to do that, and I am a mum, so I have to do that, we will just let the research slide because – how do you keep it up there in your priorities?

Elizabeth: Well I have certain days of the week just for research days and it is amazing just how many things that just don't have to be done. So two days a week are teaching days … and those two days tended to drive me a bit crazy but it meant that I usually only needed to come in one other day of the week and sometimes not even that so it gave me really two days free to work on research and writing and you have to be ruthless about it, that is just, as far as I am concerned it is my job description to do that. You have to scribble them out in your diary, make appointments with yourself, it started well because when I got the job I had done the first draft of my PhD but it was not, but I knew that I had to get it in … so it meant that I really had to be quite ruthless and luckily the guy that had left the job left me all the stuff, left me all the lecture notes and things like that. There are times to be innovative and there are time be grateful so I just used the material that he had left for me and then worked the two other days of the week on getting my thesis in, so having started with that pattern it is easier to continue, and I enjoy the research, it is not like it is a chore to do, I find the writing hard, some words don't come easily to me, I guess it is getting a bit easier, although it tends to be that once I have worked on something for a long time, the sixth rewrite, I think, I am getting better at this, then I start on the next thing and seems like I am starting back at the beginning again, but I am not, I am getting better. At least there is something to show for it at the end, with the writing, it was a lot of the other aspects of the research, you can spend a long long time on and there is still nothing to show for it, so.

Frank – professor of economics

Pat: Where have you come from in research terms?

Frank: My PhD was both a theoretical and empirical piece of work, I was using techniques which were novel at the time. (Interruption by secretary.) I was using novel mathematical dynamic techniques and theory and also I was testing these models out econometrically on cross country data. I think it was a strong PhD, I had a strong supervisor, he was regarded as – it is fair to say he would have been in the top five in his area, say, in the world.

Pat: So having that strong supervisor would have been important?

Frank: That strong supervisor was very important, so I then teamed up quite soon with another 'young turk', if you like. He had in fact finished his PhD from a different university, just the way the cookie crumbled, we both ended up new lecturers in a different university in Britain, and we hit it off and both of us were interested in making some sort of an impact, so basically we were young and single and just really went for it. We ended up in a space of – after our first year we would have had about 10 papers on the go, after two to three years.

Pat: On that same area?

Frank: Yes. We enjoyed it, we ended up getting invited – our two names became synonymous with this certain approach, and we went around Britain and into Europe giving research papers and getting ourselves published.

Pat: So you've got a reputation.

Frank: Yes, it wasn't a – you've got to keep that going for basically 10 years before you build up a reputation. Those in the know in the area knew that we were up and coming and we knew that they knew that we were up and coming, because they'd start writing to us and asking us. We basically knew that it was us carving out a niche for ourselves in the research part of the profession and that was our key to success so we kept at it. Eventually we both went apart and our research paths have diverged.

Pat: Was that because you moved geographically or you'd done as much as you could as partners?

Frank: Yes, we got tired in that area and wanted to diversify – so we both ended up, we still wrote papers together but increasingly did research with other people and diversified, etc., now we're totally diverged. Basically good PhD, get stuck in, the lesson is seek out somebody that you can work with I think, and, I'm not saying that just from a personal point of view. You stimulate each other, you keep each other back in the office, when you go out in the pub you are talking research, when you go to bed at night you are thinking it. You motivate each other, you …

Pat: You did say this was when you were single?

Frank: That's right, yes. So it was pretty intensive, but very enjoyable. For people who are married and have families, I fully concur you can't do that. Nowadays, I'm married and I've got a family, so I can't do it, but nevertheless I've got the research culture in me, so I still find myself, maybe early in the morning maybe, if my kids wake me up at six to seven or sometimes I wake up before them or I go and have a read or, late at night I'll go home and I'm not sleepy, I'll go and read something. You get that research culture into you and it's quite exciting now. That's one of the things about it, I find it's exciting when you are abreast of new ideas. It's fulfilling too when people ring you up and ask you to go and speak. That appeals to a rather Neanderthal emotion. There's lots of different aspects of research that can provide the motivation to keep going. There's always the basic one, if you want to be an academic in today's world, you have to do research.

Stuart – professor of psychology

Christine: Going even further back, what made you decide you wanted to do research?

Stuart: I did my degree as an evening student because I didn't have any money so I was working towards the end of it, and when I finished my fourth year I spoke to my then supervisor. And he said to me, 'You know you're good at this and academia needs talented people and you know, you owe it to yourself not to go out into business and make money but to hang around' and I kind of bought that argument. I've always liked the freedom of academia. I like teaching too, you know, it's wonderful to get people, particularly in the area I work in, which is pretty hard, it's getting hard, particularly for someone like me who has no maths and no physics and no you know, no real science background. It's lovely to teach students and watch their eyes light up, you know, that's fun too, but research is I think most rewarding because you're tackling a problem that you yourself have invented. I still draw my own graphs and stuff, like I massage my own data – I like doing all that kind of stuff. I guess it's just thrilling. And also it's, in the years when I've had postgraduate students, there's just nothing nicer than a lab full of eager students you know and you banter and you joke and you send each other up but all the time you're also working towards this research goal. It's terrific.

4

Read, reflect, and connect: initial explorations of data

Look at a light beam in a dark environment, and you will see specks of dust that reflect the light. Look along the beam, and you will see whatever the beam is shining on. When we come to coding data, we will be looking at fractals of information – specks of dust reflecting the light – but we need, before that, to take a different perspective and look along the whole beam to see where the light is focused.

The strategies outlined here are designed for an initial foray into new data sources, in expectation of more concentrated work to come. The 'moral' of this chapter is that time you take to become familiar with and reflect on each source of data as it becomes available is not wasted time. It will shine light onto the focal point for your study.

The *read*, *reflect*, *play*, and *explore* strategies described in this chapter are designed, therefore, to assist you to:

- gain familiarity with the scope and content of each new data source;
- build a contextualised and holistic understanding of the people, events, and ideas being investigated, and the connections within and between them;
- understand the perspective of participants;
- review assumptions to further shape data gathering;
- develop a framework for further analyses; and
- record any ideas and understandings that are generated as you do these things.

Read, and read again

Read through a *whole* transcript, set of notes, or other source document or review an entire recording to remind yourself of the depth and breadth of its content – even if you were the person who produced it. A beginning task in analysing an item of data is to build a sense of the whole, to capture the essential nature of what was being spoken of or observed, before you break down the detail within it. Read rapidly to start, approaching your notes or texts 'as if they had been written by a stranger' (Emerson et al., 1995: 145).[1]

After an initial rapid reading, read more actively by paying attention to, and thinking about, each element that is covered. Celia Orona (1990: 1249) described this process well. After her initial interviews, she 'literally sat for days on end with the transcribed interviews spread out before [her], absorbing them into [her] consciousness and letting them "float" about', writing memos to catch her 'flights of fancy', questions emerging, and ideas prompted by her reading. These memos and scribbled notes themselves became data to be sifted and categorised. She reports reviewing literature on her topic, talking to colleagues and professionals in the field, and continuing with coding and writing memos, 'But most of all, I walked; I sat; I day dreamed.' Only then, having reformulated her thesis question on the basis of her initial interviews (cf. Box 4.8), did she add further interviews.

Write as you read

The 'emergence' of themes and theory depends entirely on the work you do with your data. Record analytic thoughts as they arise. Writing 'often provides sharp, sunlit moments of clarity or insight – little conceptual epiphanies' (Miles & Huberman, 1994: 74).

Reflect in a research journal and/or memos

Having read and saturated your thoughts with the contents of a particular data item, allow yourself an opportunity to process it all. Avoid premature closure by reflecting in a research journal or writing a memo. This kind of writing is like having a discussion with yourself, and the discipline of doing it adds enormously to the depth of your analytic thinking.

For each data item that you gather:

▶ summarise the key points to take forward from this item on an attached page or in a (referenced and time-stamped) project journal; or

▶ update the notes you made about issues raised by it, as recorded on the cover sheet or spreadsheet record; or

---

[1]Our attention as observers becomes drawn by any unexpected or out-of-place features in a scene more than by those features we would expect to see. Similarly our first impressions as readers can be caught by particular words, phrases, or incidents, because they don't fit expectations, the language is colourful. or the story engages, to the neglect of the stronger themes.

▶ write about what you have learned from it and the ideas stimulated by it; and/or

▶ create a diagram that captures processes described or discussed within it.

Project journals (as distinct from field notes) are used throughout a project to make observations or record thinking that is more detailed or more reflective than that usually found in brief annotations or marginal comments. Notes about things that are seen or said become an important component in any project, regardless of methodological approach or type of data. You are likely to develop different types of reflective records, for different purposes, as you progress through your study, but the habit of recording ideas and 'musings' starts before data collection, and continues throughout data collection, analysis, and writing.

> Looking back over my journals and memos from several research projects, there is a pattern in how they developed that is similar to the pattern described by Strauss (1987). My journals begin with questions, suggestions about what I expect to find, and ideas for reading. They move through notes that remind me of people I should talk to about my findings, suggestions for sampling, detailed discussions of particular interviews, and thoughts about how particular books I was reading might relate to the interview material. They also contain attempts to develop categories and concepts, linking these to particular participants or observations. Towards the end of the journal I begin to focus more on the structure of the analysis as a whole and how particular cases might fit into, or suggest modifications to, this structure. (Ezzy, 2002: 72)

Use the project journal to record thoughts arising from or relevant to the project as a whole. Record freely, without worrying too much about style or formal structure. The most important thing is to capture ideas while they are present in your mind, as they have a nasty habit of disappearing all too rapidly. At this stage you will not know what will be useful and what will not; it doesn't matter if later they appear to be not particularly sensible.

▶ Push your thinking in memos and journals by asking yourself questions about what you are learning from this experience, and how this case or this incident differs from previous ones.

▶ Discuss aspects of what you are observing with colleagues, and record points from those discussions.

Include also your day-to-day feelings as you go about your work and your responses to the situations you encounter or the things you hear. Use memos to unblock, to integrate, to crystallise, or to 'blue sky' (Orona, 1990: 1260). Journalling or memo writing are essentially private tasks, but as you work through your personal responses, you gain more insight into the broader significance of what you are seeing and hearing. In that sense, then, this kind of writing assists in the process of turning private thoughts into public knowledge through becoming a vital source of both ideas and justification for your ideas in your later analyses and writing (Hammersley & Atkinson, 2007).

In some projects, the project journal will be the only reflective document you have; in others, it will be one of many. Opinions and experience differ on whether it is better: to work with a single, separate journal; to incorporate your ideas and responses to observations into your field notes; or to create different journals for different elements of the study (e.g., substantive reflections, methodological notes, analytic memos). Experiment to find which best suits your style and project. Additional reflective memos about particular objects, texts, people, or concepts might be associated with whole sources, coding categories, or parts of sources. The project journal and memos related to coding categories often contribute directly to sections of your project reports. Using qualitative software to keep a running journal of ideas as part of your project allows you to maintain linkages with original sources, and facilitates retrieval of ideas about specific topics (Figure 4.1).

Tips for journal writing:

- ✓ Wherever ideas are prompted by a particular data item, make sure to reference the source, and record the date of writing.
- ✓ Clearly distinguish between observations, analytic comments, and interpretive comments in your journals and memos.
- ✓ If you are using a word processor to record your journal, insert keywords into the text, to facilitate retrieval of ideas. If you are using qualitative software, code your journals and memos as you write.[2]

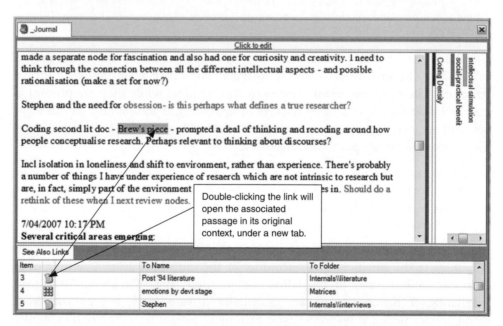

Figure 4.1   Keeping a journal in NVivo, with links to source data or other items

---

[2]MAXQDA allows you to attach a series of codes to each whole memo, and to retrieve any memos thereby linked to any code; NVivo allows you to code the specific content of any memo – memos behave like any other document.

Annotate text

Brief thoughts, observations, or comments occurring during reading might be noted in bracketed insertions, margins, table columns, or attached comments. These record:

- additional information to clarify the text, or noting something that might be of use in a later reading of the material;
- fleeting 'as you go' ideas; and
- cross-references pointing to where related information can be found.

For example, if a participant refers to someone by name, annotate that text to record the position of that person in relation to the participant. If, however, the participant was expressing a negative opinion about that person, note a passing thought, say, about how hearsay evidence can build or break reputations. Later you might develop this thought into an analytic memo. If you have other material on this topic, or someone else has talked about it, then note that link.

There are multiple ways of recording annotations or comments on paper, in a word processor, or using qualitative software:

▶ Insert the comments into the text, making sure your comments are clearly demarcated from observations or transcribed material (e.g., <<swimming coach>>). This is especially useful if the thought occurs as you are transcribing text.

▶ Set your observations and transcriptions out with wide margins to allow for handwritten annotations on the text.

▶ Select relevant text and link a comment, using your word processor (Figure 4.2).[3]

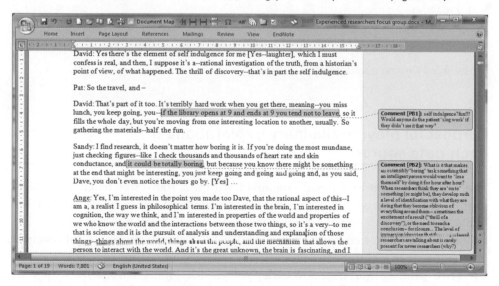

Figure 4.2   Observations recorded using the comments field in Word

---

[3]Comments made using Word are lost if the source is then imported into qualitative software.

- ▶ Record data in a table, placing comments or interpretations on the same row, in the adjacent column.
- ▶ Use the facility for annotations, comments or linked memos in your qualitative analysis program. In both MAXQDA and NVivo, comments (recorded as memos, Figure 3.5 and 4.1, or as annotations, Figure 4.3) can be linked with particular words or text segments. For both programs, recorded comments can be retrieved when viewing either the source or coded text.
- ▶ Use hyperlinks in qualitative software to record (and open) connections with related text within the project, or with other files stored on your computer.

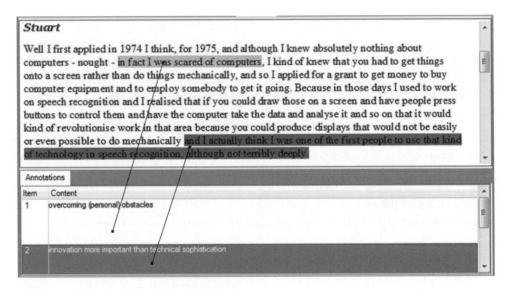

Figure 4.3   Viewing annotations in NVivo

Purposeful play: preliminary explorations of each data source

The amount of text and detail contained within a transcript or an alternative source can be overwhelming when first encountered, so ways to 'lighten up' while still coming to grips with what you have can be both fun and helpful. The strategies I've suggested here are designed to be used selectively; in this era, not even full-time students (or researchers) have the luxury of time to play with them all! Their primary purpose is to assist you in developing familiarity with your data sources, and in seeing them holistically, before you begin to segment and code elements in those sources.

Write a news bulletin

▶ Attempt to sum up the whole source in a few short sentences, much in the style of a news bulletin or press release. How would you title the piece? What is the main message for the reader? What keywords would you put on it for indexing or archiving purposes?

For Shane's story (cf. Shane's interview at the beginning of Part 2), you might focus initially on a descriptive sentence or two about when he first engaged in a serious piece of research and how he was encouraged in doing so – but then the key point about the story is his passion for the type of data he works with, and the careful investigation involved in the kind of research he does, so perhaps your bulletin might start with that. Either would work, and both are relevant to the whole. For an attention-grabbing headline, you might use something dramatic like *A passionate affair* or perhaps *Love those data!*

Writing a bulletin will help you to encapsulate the essential points of the source, to see this case, or incident, or document as a whole, before tackling the detail of it. But don't allow the overview to limit your vision as you move on to consider the detail; Shane's news story could equally well have been about the encouragement he received as a student.

Create a profile

▶ Create a brief word picture to profile the person, event, or situation that is your data source. What features would you focus your profile around?

Short profiles that include key points made during an interview or key observations made during an event help to concentrate your attention on significant features. When I profiled Frank as a researcher, for example, I focused on his strong research ethic, assimilated through supervisory and collegial relationships during his PhD and early academic experiences, and his focused approach to building a research career.

Write the text as a poem

▶ Turn a transcript into a poem; create a ballad from interview text. Use participants' words as much as possible.

Again, this strategy can lead you to identify features on which you might focus further analysis. Here's my brief attempt with Frank's text – no pretence of sophistication here!

> We teamed up, that 'young turk' and I;
> Carved out a niche together.
> Careers progressed, we both moved on.
> I think back to what we did then,
> Long nights of argument – and work;
> Ambition strong, time to achieve.
> That gets much harder now,
> But still fulfilment comes
> When recognition flows.
> Research culture – in your blood,
> Never lets you go.

Similarly, imagine the kind of musical accompaniment that would attend the reading of the poem or the telling of a participant's story. For example, for Shane's text, the music would have a slower, romantic tone, while Frank's could be accompanied by something with a faster, more strident pace.

Think of a 'far-out' comparison

The well-known Chicago sociologist, Everett Hughes, illustrated the use of 'far-out' comparisons by comparing the work of psychiatrists and prostitutes: both see themselves as members of professions with paying clients who reveal intimate problems, and with whom they maintain emotional distance (Corbin, 2009). Patton (2002) reported a study in which the police were thought about as victims, as a means of sensitising the researchers to relevant concepts.

Such comparisons help you to think more abstractly about properties that are shared in common, and those that are different. For example, if Shane's developing interest in research focuses around a *turning point*, one might then think about turning points in the context, say, of religious conversion. Religious conversions can be quite dramatic: they are usually accompanied by strong emotion, they typically occur in a context of influence from others, and they set a direction for the person's life. Think through each of these aspects in relation to Shane. Do any apply? How does Shane's experience differ from that? What memos need to be written, and what keywords would capture that experience or those ideas?

Create a snapshot or vignette

Review photographs and video records for contextual detail that you may have forgotten or missed when you were directly observing places or events or activities. Exploring a snapshot taken in mid-action can reveal previously unnoticed detail while capturing essential actors, actions and responses.

▶ Select or create snapshots from video files, and then study the various elements in these scenes in detail: details of the setting, who is there, where they are in relation to each other, expressions on faces.

▶ If you are working with text, try creating a word picture, or vignette, of a scene that captures some action or interaction described in the text. Add in some visual detail to illuminate the picture from the text or from your recollection of the person you spoke to. If you don't know the person, or the source is printed material rather than a person, you might create an image of what they might have looked like, based on what they said.

▶ Note the details you see or describe, as they will contribute directly to further analysis. If you are having to use your imagination, reflect briefly on what you come up with as that also might lead to some insight about the data. (Don't worry if it doesn't, it was fun to try anyway!)

Scribble and doodle

If you work with paper copies of transcripts or other written (or visual) materials, then, with pencil in hand:

▶ underline important words or phrases;

▶ draw lines to link connected ideas;

▶ scribble in the margins to note ideas flowing from the text;

▶ doodle in the margins to show possible relationships between concepts or ideas (Figure 4.4).

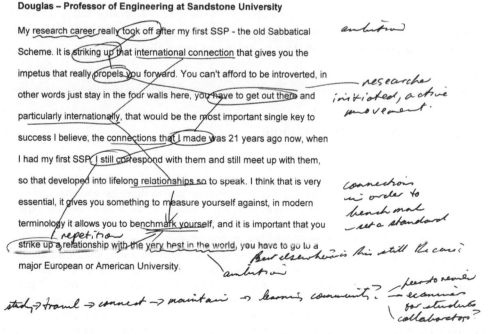

Figure 4.4   Making notes on text

Investigate a puzzle

Does anything stand out as surprising or puzzling, given what you expected from prior reading, general knowledge, or theoretical understanding? Are there inconsistencies in people's accounts, do they use unusual terms?

▶ Identify a puzzle in your data to 'kick-start' your analysis (Silverman, 2000: 135). Then ask, 'What is going on here?' and 'Why?'

▶ Use your journal to write a 'letter' to a colleague about the puzzle, describing it, asking questions about it, and having the colleague 'ask' questions of you, so that the imagined dialogue helps to clarify the puzzle (Orona, 1990).

Silverman (2000) was puzzled when a recipient of advice did not respond to it in any way. He looked for other comparable situations, and found that adolescents given advice without seeking it don't respond, nor do people who might perceive the advice as chastising them if there are other people present. He then puzzled about what keeping silent might achieve when advice is not sought or is designed to chastise.

Use data as a springboard into ideas

▶ Take a small item of data, and 'bounce off' from that to explore the ideas it generates (Box 4.1).

It always amazes me how much potential a sentence or two has for generating ideas. Analysis, itself, is much more systematic, but the ideas from this exploratory process can prove highly productive in guiding further analysis. It is best done in discussion with a peer, a supervisor, or a small group, but with some practice you can do it on your own (maybe use a recorder to catch ideas 'on the fly', rather than interrupt the flow by trying to write them down).

Box 4.1

Generating ideas from a data sample

When Andrea Stern, at the University of Sydney, was investigating the operationalisation of a service-level agreement between a major construction company and an IT support company, she found that technicians in the IT company referred to 'the shoulder tap' to describe what happened when someone needed service quickly. This expression prompted questions about queuing: how long the service queue was, what the protocol for servicing said (it was supposed to be provided strictly in order of request), why people needed to queue in the first place, who was likely to apply the shoulder tap, and how the technicians responded to that in determining who should be given service. These questions evolved into a series of queries to be answered about issues of who had power, the abuse of power and possibly gender, the pressure on technicians to comply and the implications of doing so (both organisationally and personally), and related issues of personal versus professional relationships across the two companies. Exploring the one local (emic) term had prompted and provided a focus for consideration of issues at the heart of the study.

Explore with a team; debrief with a peer

▶ Meet with a team or with peers on a regular basis to discuss issues arising in your research, canvass ideas about the meaning and relevance of data, and refine interpretations. Note new issues to be followed up. Tape team meetings and make notes or transcribe them to create memo files.

Establishing a system for peer debriefing (and for recording notes from the debriefing sessions) is especially important for solo researchers who do not have the benefit of a research team (Box 4.2). My students often (digitally) record supervision sessions, especially when we are reviewing data and looking at potential directions for analysis.

Box 4.2

Debriefing following interviews

Wendy Minato, a doctoral candidate at Charles Sturt University, was engaged in a study of natural resource management in a rural area in south-eastern Australia where 'lifestyle owners' were coming in to live alongside long-established farmers. After a week of interviewing in the area and reviewing her data, she was discussing what she had found so far with her supervisors, one of whom was writing words and phrases she used on a whiteboard as she talked. What they noticed was the number of stories Wendy was telling about how people were feeling obliged to conform to local expectations regarding weed and pest control, and how they shouldn't undermine the efforts of other farmers. The idea of *obligation* and words like *ought* and *should* came up frequently, prompting the idea of normative behaviour. As a consequence, Wendy went back to the library to investigate the concept and process of establishing norms, found a fit, and explored it in further interviews; this then became a core concept in her thesis.

Beyond serving to stimulate or deepen interpretive reflection, regular discussions amongst members of a research team are essential just to ensure that interviewing or other data collection remains 'on the same page', and when coding begins, to ensure a common framework for analysis. Working with an experienced team is especially valuable for novice researchers.

Explore with (computer-based) content analysis

There are many forms of content analysis for text-based data, from simple word lists and searches to the use of specialised coding dictionaries (cf. Chapter 6). The simplest and most appropriate at this exploratory stage is to use software that will display and count the words that are in selected texts, and then provide a facility for retrieving all the passages that use particular words (Figure 4.5). Try

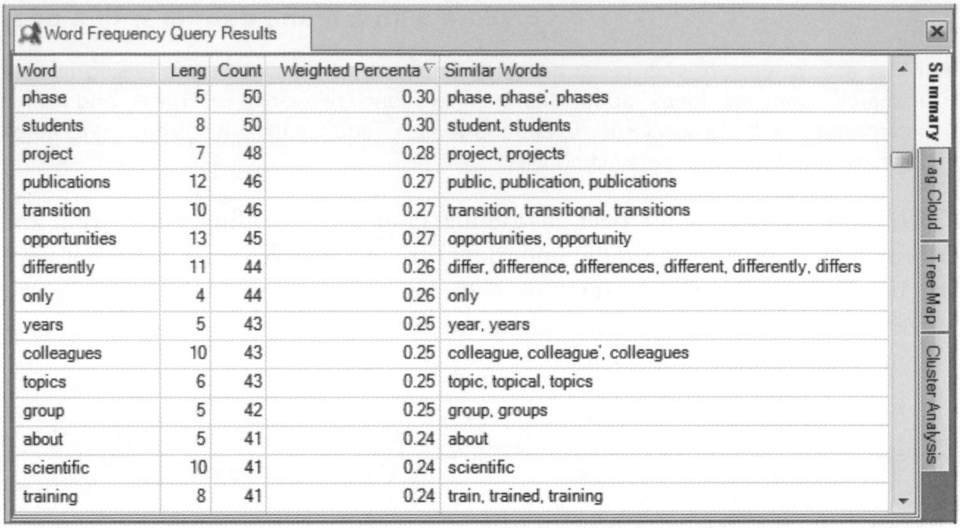

Word	Leng	Count	Weighted Percenta ▽	Similar Words
phase	5	50	0.30	phase, phase', phases
students	8	50	0.30	student, students
project	7	48	0.28	project, projects
publications	12	46	0.27	public, publication, publications
transition	10	46	0.27	transition, transitional, transitions
opportunities	13	45	0.27	opportunities, opportunity
differently	11	44	0.26	differ, difference, differences, different, differently, differs
only	4	44	0.26	only
years	5	43	0.25	year, years
colleagues	10	43	0.25	colleague, colleague', colleagues
topics	6	43	0.25	topic, topical, topics
group	5	42	0.25	group, groups
about	5	41	0.24	about
scientific	10	41	0.24	scientific
training	8	41	0.24	train, trained, training

Word Frequency Query Results

Summary · Tag Cloud · Tree Map · Cluster Analysis

Figure 4.5   Word frequency counts in NVivo, allowing various display options

following up words like 'because', just to see where they lead you.[4] Sometimes you will be surprised by the frequency with which some words appear. Most qualitative software programs provide this kind of tool; alternatively there are free content-listing programs that can be downloaded from the internet.

Express through painting or performance

A Chinese brush artist might prepare by making detailed studies and sketches, but will then work spontaneously and from memory to create a free-flowing painting that captures his emotional response to the blossom, animal, or scene he has studied (Rae, 2003).

▶ After you have read, explored, and absorbed your data, walk away to ponder, and then express your thoughts and feelings through painting or drawing, or perhaps in unscripted performance. What captures the essence of this item of data for you? What are your lingering thoughts? Now, as you write, record, draw, or paint, these become ideas to work with, in the context of these and other data.

Create a display

Supplement your preliminary accounts with diagrams or models where these help to sequence and/or make sense of the information contained within a source. Most

---

[4]In some programs, *because* is listed (by default) as a stop word. This means it won't be found via either word frequency or text search queries. You will need to modify the stop word list via the program's options.

qualitative software programs now have modelling modules to facilitate developing diagrams, allowing for rearrangement of elements during construction and easy modification when additional information becomes available. Alternatively, play at sketching ideas with pencil and paper. Some of these diagrams and models will be developed further, as analysis and theory building proceed.

▶ Use a network diagram to show the relationship of this case to other people. Whyte's ([1943] 1993) observational notes were supported by diagrams mapping team relations in the groups he was observing in Cornerville.

▶ Sketch out a timeline to show the historical development of an organisation or a situation; a series of critical incidents; or a sequence of events you observed or as described by a participant. Add contextual information to these timelines.

▶ Draw a 'map' to show the pathway taken between the start and finish of a process. Each observation or interview will potentially add further information to a section of the line.

▶ Sketch the relative locations of related objects or events or people, as observed, described, or otherwise revealed.

▶ Create a diagram with a person or event in the centre and radial links to significant others, with the length of the link and the size of 'the other' based on importance to and distance from the central person or event.

▶ Map a participant's explanatory pathway to show the assumptions behind, and the logic employed for, the decisions he or she made.

Explore the storylines

Stories, as a form of communication, make up an important part of our everyday lives. Stories have structure, they serve particular functions as part of our communicating, and they reveal ways in which we make meaning of the events and circumstances in our lives. When we, as researchers, observe a scene, a story unfolds before us; when we interview people in an open and flexible way, they provide us with short stories embedded within the larger narrative of their lives. Accounts are given to explain, justify, excuse, or legitimate behaviour (Coffey & Atkinson, 1996). Stories and accounts reveal the embedded ways in which members of a particular cultural or social group comprehend their world. Popular literature, art, and music that are produced, read, observed, and listened to by members of a society, similarly, reveal to us something of the structure and character of that society, and how meaning is attributed to objects and events by its people (Poirier & Ayres, 2002).

Analysis is as much about identifying the larger significance and meaning of objects and events for a participant, about finding the connections – the interdependencies – within and across data, as it is about segmenting and coding data. Connections are evident in accounts people give of aspects of their lives, and various statements that people make might be constructed into a cohesive narrative describing some larger aspect of their experience. We shall return to the task of a more detailed analysis of the structure, meaning, and functional significance of participants' narratives in Chapter 7, but for now your primary concern will be to explore the clues these stories and accounts provide through their telling that will help you to maintain a sense of the connectedness of the data once you begin to focus on their detail.

Locate stories and accounts

Identify, in your field notes, interviews, or other data, the short stories and accounts used by participants to convey experiences or describe events (e.g., Box 4.3). Then ask:

▶ What do you learn from their choices in how they tell the stories? What function does the story have for the teller and the listeners?

▶ How does each participant make meaning of the events or experiences they describe?

▶ Explore and record these purposes and meanings, making sure you keep the link from your notes to the story which prompted your understanding. Is there a pattern to their stories and meaning making?

▶ When do participants feel they need to give an account for their actions? What are the ways in which they do that (what counts as justification for this group)?

Box 4.3

Seeing and interpreting the storyline

When Douglas, a professor of engineering at Sandstone University, explained the key to the development of his career as a researcher – a key he wants to share with others – his didactic account, given originally in the context of a project focusing on early career researchers, benefited from some rearrangement to identify and interpret the storyline. Thus his brief account (cf. Figure 4.4)[5] became:

> When I had my first period of study leave 21 years ago, I linked up with [professors] at [major European university]. It was difficult because I was rather introverted, but I realised I had to 'get out there' to be able to move ahead. The connections I made there have become lifelong relationships, people I still correspond with and meet with. They provide me with a measure of where I'm at, a benchmark on standards of performance. Those international connections were (are) the key to my success. (He now encourages all of his graduate students to travel in the same way.)

As he tells the story here, the critical meaning given to the international connections he actively developed and still maintains was that they allow for (continuing) benchmarking in relation to

---

[5]One would, of course, normally be working with longer texts than this short sample.

professional (academic research) standards: the message to up-and-coming researchers is that they have to measure themselves against (and be inspired by?) the best. One would expect, incidentally, that for 'lifelong relationships' to be maintained over 21 years there would also be a degree of friendship involved, although surprisingly this was not explicitly mentioned. (Is this a puzzle to investigate, or just typical information-focused engineer-speak?)

Create the overarching narrative

A narrative helps to preserve the flow of the story as a whole. Meanings of statements, including those not evident when statements are viewed in isolation, become more apparent in the context of the whole. Together, these statements add up to a larger narrative about some aspect of an interviewee's life. Creating the overarching narrative is especially important in cases where the data in their raw form are somewhat disjointed, or come in multiple forms and packages.

In more complex case studies, where there is danger of 'death by data asphyxiation', pulling together information from your various sources to write up each case as a single, short descriptive profile, perhaps using a proforma, will help you keep perspective while you deal with the variety and volume of those multiple sources and forms of data (Eisenhardt, 2002). The goal here is not to develop a complex interpretive or analytic description, but simply to gain familiarity with and integrate the content of each case as preparation for more detailed study; later you will work with or add to that case description to identify patterns and linkages within it, as further preparation for identifying cross-case patterns.

To create the narrative (these strategies are alternative approaches):

▶ Identify and synthesise the storyline: reduce the text to those elements that are essential, and record in the same order as they were told.

▶ Create a sequenced narrative that captures what is going on for a particular participant or case. Give the narrative a beginning, a middle, and an end (Box 4.3).

▶ Where there are several sources available to inform a single case narrative, construct a single coherent and 'complete' version from all available sources (Box 4.4).

▶ On computer, use the software's in-text linking or hyperlinking system to sequentially link elements of a narrative that unfolds over several, dispersed, sources (Box 4.5).

To review the narrative (see also Chapter 7):

▶ Identify the main characters in the narrative, noting how they respond to each other and to the reported experiences.

▶ Within the narrative, identify key events and experiences, and what it is that marks different 'chapters' in the narrative.

▶ Seek out a core theme to describe the narrative as a whole, and/or a subtheme for each chapter in the narrative.

▶ Note the form of the narrative, e.g., is it orderly or 'all over the place'; is it told with or without emotion?

Box 4.4

Creating a single sequenced narrative from multiple sources

Jim Cumming, in his PhD research on pathways through doctoral research, created an extended narrative for each of his 10 cases from interviews conducted with a doctoral candidate, as well as with two individuals identified by each candidate as having significantly influenced their research and learning. The additional individuals selected by the candidates included supervisors, peers, other academics, and technicians. He then applied narrative analysis to each of his constructed case narratives to portray distinctive elements of doctoral work and its associated outcomes, from which he developed a model of doctoral enterprise (Cumming, 2007).

Box 4.5

Linking parts of a dispersed narrative

A story may develop in 'bits', scattered among other incidents from across several sources, through repeat interviews, or from dispersed sources gathered over different places or times. Such was the story of the governess, hired to assist with schooling for young children on a cattle station in northern Australia, who came – and rapidly went. It was told through a series of seven emails, as different people shared over time through an online list maintained for women living in these isolated situations.[6] Use of 'see also links' in NVivo[7] allowed the story to be told in sequence, whereas coding gathered the pieces in a non-sequential order determined by the source name. See also links can be used to link from a particular text or multimedia passage to whole project items such as another source, a memo, a coding category, or a model, *or* they can be used to link to data segments in the same or another source (cf. Figure 4.1). When retrieved, the linked material is shown in context, and the link can be extended from that point to another passage or item.

Explore similarities and contrasts in stories

When stories vary in their telling, comparison of one incident or telling with another reveals dimensions of experience that vary under different circumstances of experiencing or telling (Box 4.6).

---

[6]These data were recorded in the Bush Schooling tutorial written for an early version of NVivo by Leonie Daws.

[7]In NVivo, see also links are one-way links. These allow for the creation of a new link from already linked text.

▶ If an idea is repeated within an interview, or from one interview to another, compare the tellings to discern the differences. What do these differences signify?

▶ Compare one incident with another similar but not identical incident. Do the differences in context or circumstances make for a difference in outcomes? What does this tell you about the way that the processes or actions involved can vary, and the implications of those variations?

Box 4.6

Cultural contrasts in stories

People from different social or cultural groups will tell the same type of story with variations that reflect their particular culture, thus revealing cultural and social meanings. Bernard and Ryan (2010) provide two examples:

• In a study of responses to rape by Bletzer and Koss (2006), Anglo and Mexican American women expressed thoughts of revenge against those who had raped them, in contrast to Cheyenne women who did not, but all three of these cultural groups spoke of feeling soiled and dirty as a consequence of the rape.

• Matthews (1992) found that different gender groups have different patterns of telling a traditional Mexican folk tale (*La Llorona*, the weeping woman) in which one or other partner to a marriage is unfaithful, leading to the suicide of the woman, based on their understanding of sexual behaviour – that women are sexually uncontrolled versus men are insatiable. Virtually all tellings incorporated the suicide, as within that culture, where exchange of resources is part of the arrangement of a marriage, suicide is the only way a woman can end a marriage.

Explore a metaphor (or two)

A metaphor is a way of grasping abstract ideas by mapping them on to more con-crete ones (Lakoff & Johnson, 1980): for example, we *consume* and *digest* informa-tion and *construct*, *build*, or *grow* theories. The metaphor facilitates understanding, communication, and remembering through using something familiar – such as eating, building, or agriculture – to explain or describe something that may be new or more difficult to comprehend. Thus these simple metaphors effectively convey the idea that information is absorbed into our being, and that theories develop through active intervention, they don't just suddenly appear.

When a participant uses a metaphor, they communicate something about how an experience has been perceived. The different metaphors that people use for pain – a fire or a cage to describe the pain from angina, for example – help to express the nature of the pain that is being experienced. The metaphors they use also reveal something of the culture, conventions, and language of the people or situations they describe.

▶ Study the metaphors that people use when they speak (e.g., Box 4.7). What do these metaphors describe? What image does each portray of the object, event, or experience being described?

▶ What was the speaker's purpose in using the metaphor?

▶ What does the metaphor tell you about the cultural domain of the speaker? 'Metaphors … express specific values, collective identities, shared knowledge, and common vocabularies' (Coffey & Atkinson, 1996: 86).

▶ Change the metaphor in a sentence, to explore how that changes the meaning. For example, consider what an argument would look like if it was referred to as a dance rather than a battle (Lakoff & Johnson, 1980).

| Box 4.7 |

Metaphors used by researchers

Stuart: I *massage* my own data.

David: It's an *immersion* in something utterly different each time.

Ange: … the *indulgence* of the [full-time] PhD process.

Stephen: … the best and most creative work is done when a person is obsessed, when it *sits under their skin* and it's never far from what they are doing.

Barbara: [describing the progress of her research development] I went just *one foot after the other*, straight down the *track*.

Annie: I *drifted* into research.

Explore language; look for emic concepts or 'indigenous terms'

Indigenous or folk terms are culturally encoded local terms or other symbols used by a number of participants to refer to a class of physical or social objects (Patton, 2002; Spradley, 1970). James Spradley studied homeless people who referred to a place to sleep as a *flop*. This could describe a park bench, a doorway, a stairwell, a graveyard. If such a term is recognised during the data gathering process, it can be usefully explored with participants to identify the attributes or characteristics that distinguish its use and that separate it from another term. See how these participants make sense of their world, to develop an emic account. For example, the term *bludger* is used in Australia to depict someone who imposes on others' generosity but doesn't contribute themselves. It may be used in the work setting for someone who doesn't pull their weight in the team; often it is combined pejoratively with *dole* to refer to young adults who persistently rely on welfare rather than working. Identification of this word prompts questions such as why some Australians refer to politicians as a *bunch of bludgers*, and what distinguishes a *dole bludger* from a *welfare cheat*. Indigenous terms and emic typologies provide insight into the perspective of participants; their use in a report also makes feedback more comprehensible to participants (Patton, 2002).

▶ Identify local (indigenous) terms for physical and social objects in the environment. What special meaning do they convey with regard to that object, for this group?

▶ Look to see how the regular way people from particular groups name a concept or express an idea might be influencing the way they then perceive that object and behave toward it.

Exploring context

Situational information relating to specific events or experiences, including the physical settings in which particular events occur, the timing of events, or changes in circumstances, will vary throughout the data sources. Show how they relate to experiences or events being studied through a variety of visual techniques, in memos, and by using additional codes on relevant text (cf. Chapter 6). Details might include aspects such as whether the exchange between the service provider and client took place in the provider's office, the waiting room, the local shops, or the client's home; or a timeline for the introduction of new procedures. They help interpret why an exchange or event, or the response to it, took a particular 'shape', or they will be used to compare experiences in different settings or at different times.

Visual and tabular displays including photographs, maps, timelines, organisational charts, flow charts, graphs, and other diagrams are used for recording, interpreting, and communicating a range of contextual information. For example:

▶ Add relevant contextual details on a network chart or in an organisation chart (cf. Chapter 3). In describing their study of the introduction of a new reading programme into schools, Miles and Huberman (1994) provided examples of the ways in which they used a network chart to show patterns of giving and receiving assistance between (hierarchically ordered) members in an organisation. They used an organisational chart to show positions of authority in the system, job titles, who advocated for the innovation, who used it, people's attitudes to it, and whether relationships between pairs of people were positive, ambivalent, or neutral. This became useful in understanding the behaviour of individuals. They advise the user to 'remember that you are not simply drawing a standard organizational chart, but are mapping salient properties of the context. Remember, too, that your chart will not be exhaustive or complete: It is a collection of organizational fragments or excerpts' (1994: 104–5).

▶ Employ maps or diagrams to assist in exploring the locational relationship of sites or events or people referred to by your participants, perhaps supplemented by photographs of features of interest (Figure 4.6). Innovations in the use of mapping and other visual methods in providing contextual data for exploratory data analysis, made possible by advances in technology, include linking with other forms of digital data, data exploration tools, and three-dimensional fly-bys. These tools 'enhance the visual, iterative exploration of data, allow simultaneous attention to both the particular and the general, the concrete and the abstract, at multiple scales, and accommodate multiple interpretations of the world and diverse views of reality' (Knigge & Cope, 2006: 2027). For example, if you are using MAXQDA, then you can apply an image or a map (e.g., from Google Earth) as a background in MAXMaps, and then add other project detail to it, such as icons for texts or codes to show relative positioning and links to show connections.

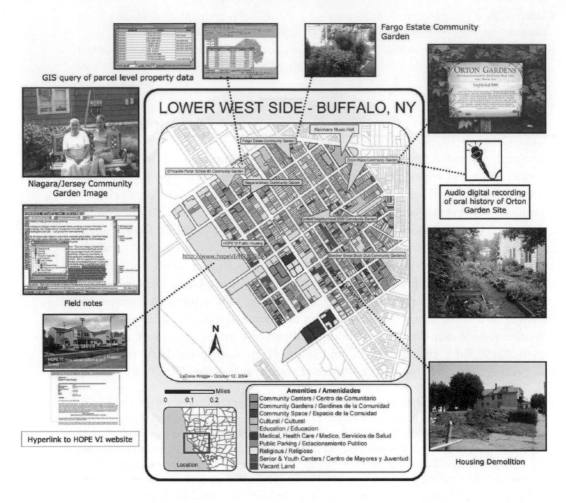

Figure 4.6   Use of mapping combined with qualitative data to explore the role of community gardens in a socially and ethnically diverse neighbourhood

Source: Knigge & Cope, 2006: 2030

Identify relevant categories and concepts

By playing with and exploring your data in the various ways outlined above, you will have identified quite a few categories and concepts that will help to describe or abstract from them. Put these together with critical categories developed from the reading you did when planning your topic,[8] along with nouns and verbs from your research questions, and you will find you have already created a starter set of codes to use when locating and indexing relevant parts of your data.

---

[8]Not all of the latter will attract data; that is of interest in itself.

For example:

▶ Having written the news bulletin about your source, identify keywords of the kind that could be applied to that article for use with online search tools. These are likely to be appropriate codes to include in your analysis.

▶ If you have written a memo about a 'far-out' comparison, code the memo to generate a set of useful categories or concepts based on the dimensions that came out of the comparison.

▶ Review the marginal notes or comments you have written, to identify keywords used in them.

▶ Review the list of words that appeared most frequently in your texts for potential coding categories.

▶ Identify elements of the data relating to narrative focus, plot, and chronology.

In the next two chapters you will focus on the logic and practice of coding to build your understanding of what it is you are doing when you code and what you can achieve by doing it, supported by ideas and strategies to draw on for ways to code your data.

Involving participants in early analysis

Involvement of co-researchers in the construction of data is increasingly common-place, but they are less often involved in analysis. Experience of and strategies for involving participants in analysis of data have been reported by some, for example:

• In research undertaken from a feminist standpoint, examining survival from childhood sexual abuse, Morrow (Morrow & Smith, 1995) interviewed 11 participants. Seven of these then participated in a series of focus group sessions with her in which they explored emerging categories from the data as well as their own research questions. Four women continued on to spend over a year with Morrow as participant co-researchers – working as co-analysts of the data from the focus group. They used their 'natural intuitive analytic skills' as well as skills taught by the researcher to engage in participant verification, analyse videotapes of original group sessions, suggest categories, and revise emerging theory.

• In a comparatively less intensive and very structured process of involvement, Northcutt and McCoy (2004) created a method which they refer to as Interactive Qualitative Analysis (IQA). In an IQA enquiry, they have focus group participants write statements about the topic being discussed. Group members then define 'affinities' to cluster the statements. This is followed by the group's defining, through a comparative process, relationships between pairs of affinities. An interrelationship diagram is created from this information and is further refined to generate a mindmap of influences and outcomes that shows the dynamics of the system. The investigators construct a parallel mindmap based on interview data with the participants, for comparison with the group's map. Reporting from IQA draws, almost entirely, from the words of the participants, with the ideas from different constituent groups being relayed back to participants as a primary mechanism of intervention.

In each of these examples, participants worked *only* with their jointly produced data, and not directly with interviews or other individual data associated with the projects.

Refocus, ready for the next phase

Having ensured your overall familiarity with your first data sources, you are now in a good position for gathering more data, or for launching into more detailed work, coding and connecting elements within those sources. Take stock by evaluating shifts in your thinking as a consequence of early data, and clarify the all-important focus of your project (Box 4.8). These activities have immediate implications for further sampling and data design, as well as for continuing data analysis.

▶ Review key themes – those that seemed important enough for you to have noted immediately after the data source was recorded. How do you see them now?
▶ Check the assumptions you began with. Have they held up with the advent of data?
▶ With the exploratory thinking your initial sources have generated, you may have moved on from, or lost sight of, your original purpose. This is a good time to remind yourself of the purpose you set out with, evaluate what you have learned, and firm up the direction for further data gathering and analysis.
▶ This is also a very good time to return to the literature, especially if your focus is shifting.

The techniques that have been outlined in this chapter should not be forgotten once the first few sources have been examined. Many of the strategies will continue to be relevant for initial analyses of each and every new source that is obtained. If you reach a stage where they can teach you nothing new about new sources, then perhaps you have sufficient data already to answer your questions; or, if you haven't already, you need to move into a deeper analytic mode to determine what you can and can't learn from your data.

⎤ **Box 4.8** ⎡

Refocusing a project following initial interviews

From her experience of working as a student in an adult day health centre for physically and mentally impaired elderly people, Celia Orona (1990) was prompted to ask questions about how families coped with caring for a member with Alzheimer's disease, and in particular (for her thesis topic) how they made the decision to institutionalise the family member. She reports the first response she had to her decision making question:

Decision? Decision? There was no decision. When it came time, I had no choice. It's like falling in love, no one has to tell you. You know.

She continued:

> What I was struck by as I listened to her were my own feelings. I sensed somehow that I had heard another theme. Much as a person working absentmindedly hears an unusual sound in the background and becomes alert, I left her home with that kind of uneasy, perplexed feeling. (1990: 1248)

Her next two interviewees, similarly, had little to say about decision making. By the time of placement, the person they had known intimately was gone, and the person they were placing in care was a stranger. She read and reread these three initial interviews, coded them and wrote marginal comments. Out of this, she began to understand her disquiet, and to identify the underlying issue she had heard as one of identity loss. For further interviews, her focus shifted from decision making to temporal and other aspects of identity loss in a dyadic relationship in the context of Alzheimer's disease, and this remained her focus for the rest of the project.

Writing about preliminary analysis

Two approaches to beginning analytical writing can help with overcoming the mental barriers many face:

1 Start small. Write about one event, one case, one situation. Start descriptively, but then begin to entertain any questions that come to your mind as you write, and explore those. Soon you will be expanding into other areas, and your analysis and writing will be on its way.

2 Simply 'jot' ideas as they come to you – but do it in a word processor, placing each idea under a heading *that is formatted with a heading style.*[9] Then turn on the Document Map in the Navigation pane (View menu): this will allow you to hyperlink to any part of your document so you can jot more ideas under the relevant heading. When you want to sort the ideas you've been gathering, switch to Outline View to rearrange them. Once you have a collection of ideas in any section, turn them into 'proper' text. If you have a problem with paragraphing when you are writing, use a low-level heading for every paragraph (this will help you keep to the point, and also to sort paragraphs), and then delete them in the final presentation.

In the methodology chapter

▶ As part of your description of the analysis steps you took in your project, describe your approach to working with your initial data sources. This is particularly important if, as a result of that early analysis, your project took a new direction.

▶ Note also the techniques you used to ensure you are seeing your data holistically and in context, as a balance to the more detailed and segmented view you will have in some of your later analytic work.

---

[9]Check Styles in Help if you are unsure, or access guidelines on using formatting features of Word from www.researchsupport.com.au.

As part of your presentation of results

▶ Start to draft some ideas about the kinds of things you are finding out from your initial analytic steps (e.g., using the strategies above). These are likely to become modified and perhaps drastically changed before you finish your project, but the process of writing always helps you to think analytically and clearly, and making an early start has significant value in overcoming writers' block, even if you end up changing it all.

▶ Write about an interesting case from or story told in your data, to use as a vignette or example in your results.

Exercises

Exercise 1: Explore and play

▶ Apply some of the strategies outlined in this chapter to your own data. Alternatively, if you do not have your own data yet, try applying some to the extract from Elizabeth's interview, recorded at the beginning of Part 2.

Further reading

Corbin, in Corbin and Strauss (2008: Chapters 8–12), provides an extensive range of examples of memoing as part of her analysis of interviews with three war veterans.

Emerson et al. (1995: Chapter 6) introduce their chapter on analysis with useful questions and strategies to apply once you have data.

Coffey and Atkinson (1996: Chapter 4) discuss a range of approaches relevant for an initial look at the language within your texts, including analysis of metaphors and domain analysis.

Spradley (1979) describes a range of 'classic' approaches to gathering and analysing ethnographic interview data, including taxonomic, domain, and componential analyses. Most of these are reviewed also by Bernard and Ryan (2010).

5

Codes and coding: principles and practice

Coding provides a means of purposefully managing, locating, identifying, sifting, sorting, and querying data. It is not a mechanistic, data reduction process, but rather one designed to stimulate and facilitate analysis. Either explicitly or implicitly, it is a necessary step in most approaches to qualitative analysis, yet forms of coding, approaches taken to coding, and specific purposes for coding vary enormously.

In this chapter, develop an understanding of:

- when and how to make use of coding;
- different kinds of coding;
- strategies for managing the process of coding;
- how coding strategies differ in different situations;
- reliability and validity in coding.

Read this chapter in association with the next. As you begin to apply codes, you will need also to know how to identify and name coding categories.

Using codes to work with data

Coding is a fundamental skill for qualitative analysis. Coding is not an end in itself, but a purposeful step to somewhere. It provides a means of access to evidence; it is a tool for querying data, for testing assumptions and conclusions. But what makes for proficient coding? And how does one become a proficient coder? Four things stand out for me in reply to these two questions: responsiveness to data; focus on purpose; learning through observation of and discussion with experienced others; and practice. You *can* learn to code effectively and well.

When you code for qualitative analysis, you will label a passage of data with a code based on your understanding of what that passage is about. The label (code) is then used both to *represent* and to *access* that passage along with other data that are the same or similar. When you review the code, you have access to and can retrieve all the data represented by that code. Qualitative coding is about data retention, rather than data reduction (Richards, 2009).

Coding typically moves through at least two major stages: an initial stage of identification and labelling, variously referred to as first-level, initial, or open coding (using *a priori* or emergent codes); and a second stage of refining or interpreting to develop more analytical categories or clusters, often referred to as focused coding (Saldaña, 2009). Initially your focus will be on working through your sources; later in the project you will be focusing your thinking more around your codes and coded data.

Different kinds of codes are used to help you focus and develop ideas. Codes range from being purely descriptive of circumstances (sometimes referred to as structural codes) or descriptive of actions or events or experiences, to categorising topics or issues, through to naming more interpretive or analytical concepts (Gibbs, 2007; Richards, 2009). Thus, this event occurred *in the playground*, it describes an act of one child *ridiculing* another, it is about *bullying*, it is a reflection of *cultural stereotyping.* Coding is 'entirely dependent on close reading – they are not mechanical tasks. It is not good enough to skim a transcript or set of field notes and to have a broad sense of "what it's all about", cherrypicking bits of data for quotation' (Hammersley & Atkinson, 2007: 162). When codes involve interpreting data within their context, they give meaning to data. The task of coding assists the researcher to break out of an 'imprisonment in the story' to see new connections and alternative ways of framing and interpreting a text or situation (Maxwell & Miller, 2008: 469).

The evolving understanding that occurs as you move from data to description to analysis means that coding occurs in a cyclical, or recursive, process (Miles & Huberman, 1994). First, new data may add new categories to the analysis. Categories that appear interesting but which are inadequately developed prompt you to seek further data. Inevitably, initial codes will be revised as work proceeds, necessitating review of sources coded earlier. Finally, categories that are developed during coding will be further reviewed and refined before final analysis proceeds. 'Codes are organizing principles that are not set in stone. They are our own creations, in that we identify and select them ourselves; they are tools to think with. They can be expanded, changed, or scrapped altogether as our ideas develop through repeated interactions with the data' (Coffey & Atkinson, 1996: 32).

Tips for coders:

- ✅ Codes can be descriptive, topical, or analytical; codes can be used to serve many purposes.
- ✅ Use coding to stimulate thinking about what is going on in the data.

✅ Coding helps you to attend to the detail of the data. This may be the most valuable contribution of the exercise of coding data, for some researchers.

✅ Your coding will develop, so never be afraid to reconfigure a code or coding system (archive the earlier version for security).

Use coding to:

- manage (keep track of) your data;
- build ideas from your data;
- facilitate asking questions of your data.

Coding to manage (keep track of) data

When you go to use a reference book, two of the most valuable tools in being able to make use of the information in that book are the contents page and an adequate index. Coding data has been likened to indexing a book (Kelle, 2004; Patton, 2002). An entry in an index provides a pointer to where something can be found in the text. Indexing doesn't imply or involve segmenting text (cutting it up); rather, it is a reference to a place in the original source where you can find relevant material. Indexing is an especially useful strategy if you are working on paper, as it allows the records to be maintained in their entirety, while also allowing you to access and review all the material on a particular topic (Hammersley & Atkinson, 2007). Retrieving everything you know about a particular topic or drawing comparisons across groups or contexts for each coding category becomes rather complicated if you rely on indexing, however.

Coding takes you a step further than indexing: as well as helping you locate data, it serves as a way of *sorting* and ordering data – 'the undigested complexity' of field notes, transcripts, documents, pictures, ideas – so that you can keep track of what you have on any topic and easily find what you want, when you want it (Patton, 2002). By placing similar material together into its own place, you can review everything that was said or that is known about a topic or an issue without having to sift through each of the original sources (Box 5.1).

▶ Sort your data according to any or all of what type of data they are, the period they relate to, the setting they came from. Material might be placed in piles, boxes, or files or stored in computerised coding categories: here are the first set of interviews with community leaders and those are the later ones; there are the notes from each series of planning meetings; these blog entries have been sorted according to the web archive from which they came.

▶ Sort your notes and other data also according to particular topics: this is about the level of physical amenity in the area; here are data relating to cooperation (or lack of) between service providers.

Make extra copies (if necessary), so you can put each piece into as many places as are needed. Alternatively, if you use qualitative software, the same part of the data can be coded to as many categories as are needed to fully describe it.

Box 5.1

Coding to manage data

Whenever I have to bring varied sources together and sort out the ideas I am gaining from them, I resort to coding those sources. In such cases, the coding is usually designed just as a way of locating data, rather than as a tool for asking questions of the data (querying), although it has the potential to be developed later for deeper analysis.

Some years ago I was asked to redesign a survey that was a fifth and final data collection point in a 10-year community capacity-building project in an area of economic and social disadvantage. The goal for this final data collection was twofold: to provide a final review to be compared with what had been found before; and to contribute to theoretical development about the association between social capital, community intervention, and health outcomes. In order simply to keep track of the kinds of questions that had been asked, what had been found so far, and old and new theoretical perspectives on each of the issues addressed, I coded questions asked in and reports from earlier surveys, summaries of issues raised in interviews by various stakeholders during the project, and notes from the theoretical literature. This coded material, covering everything currently known for this community on each of the areas being investigated, served to inform the development of the final survey instrument and related theoretical questions.

Coding to build ideas

At a descriptive level, naming a code provides a label that represents what passages of data are about, so they can be located. More importantly, however, naming data *connects* them with other data; data are retained. Coding 'leads you from the data to the idea, and from the idea to all the data pertaining to that idea' (Morse & Richards, 2002: 115).

> If sensing a pattern or 'occurrence' can be called seeing, then the encoding of it can be called seeing as. That is, you first make the observation that something important or notable is occurring, and then you classify or describe it ... the seeing as provides us with a link between a new or emergent pattern and any and all patterns that we have observed and considered previously. It also provides a link to any and all patterns that others have observed and considered previously through reading. (Boyatzis, 1998: 4)

As all the data about one idea are brought together through coding they are recontextualised: 'Coding is also a way of *fracturing* data, breaking data up, and disaggregating records. Once coded, the data look different, as they are seen and heard through the category rather than the research event' (Morse & Richards, 2002: 115). Recontextualisation in this way is not about loss of context, but about seeing data in a *new* context (Box 5.2).

Box 5.2

Building an idea (and analysis) through coding

Shane is an experienced historian. I had asked him about his journey into research and he responded by giving an account of an experience of working with primary sources in his second year as an undergraduate.

For some time I struggled with how to code Shane's references to working with old newspapers:

And I enjoyed that a lot. I enjoyed the sensuous feel of century-old newsprint … Maybe I wouldn't have been so keen on it today, because there is this sensual quality to using aged papers. It's not nearly as much fun with microfilm.

Picking up on his emotional responses was not a problem, but there was greater significance in this: what exactly was it about being involved in working with data that gave rise to the degree of passion that he was expressing? What I was seeing here then 'rang a bell' with something that had caught my attention long ago from Frost and Stablein's (1992) book, *Doing exemplary research*. In their final chapter, these authors summed up what they had learned about the defining characteristics of exemplary research. They called the second of these 'handling your own rat' to express the idea that excellent research comes from being in direct contact with one's data, and doing one's own data analysis. Shane, here, was talking about being in direct, literal, physical and intellectual contact with his data, and about loving that experience. The code I arrived at, then, was *intimate contact with data*. As I reviewed his interview, I could see the same idea expressed again when he was talking about gathering visual material:

You don't have photographs in newspapers really until the thirties, but it's looking at albums and private collections. And that's lovely work, it's intellectually demanding, looking at pictures.

Identifying and naming this code alerted me to other instances where this could be seen. Stuart provided one:

but research is I think most rewarding because you're tackling a problem that you yourself have invented. I still draw my own graphs and stuff, like I massage my own data – I like doing all that kind of stuff. I guess it's just thrilling.

The massage metaphor Stuart uses here in describing how he handles his data reinforces the image of 'skin-to-skin' intimacy. And then, from Paul, participating in a discussion with other experienced researchers:

getting the data and thinking about what it actually means, you know, and being able to get other people's data and think about that too, and then try and shuffle it into some sort of order, so that it makes sense beyond – you know, the bits and pieces, that's what it's about.

From Susan, talking about experimenting with chemical compounds:

and then we had to try and understand why every time you looked at it, it seemed to be adopting some different shape and because of that, more out of interest, because we couldn't understand it and it just got us sucked in, why on earth is this doing this to us.

(Continued)

(Continued)

And from Beverley in a focus group discussion:

> but I can remember when I got results in from that – you sort of get bogged down in all this psychological theory and you, you, you put all these hypotheses together and you make all these predictions – ah hah! – now are you going to get them? … and there were the differences! Wow! They really exist. The *p* is zero zero zero!

But being close to your data is not always a positive experience! Beverley again:

> other people seem to do experiments and write them up and do the next experiment and write it up and – I don't seem to do that. I seem to sort of be having to go back to my initial dataset and because it was a qualitative one and because I'm an amateur at it, you know ((self-deprecating tone)) so I kept going back and saying 'What am I going to do with this stuff?' you know, and sort of finding new stuff there and thinking this isn't supposed to be my whole PhD, this is only supposed to be the beginning, but – ((deep breath))

Intimacy can be threatening to the fumbling novice!

Now thinking primarily in terms of the category, I widened the net a little. For example, Frank talked with strong emotion about being immersed in research and the consequent stimulation of ideas, although for him it was also very much about sharing that immersion with a colleague. As I continued to work, the code for *intimacy with data* morphed into a code for *immersion,* and as I reviewed other related codes, I found many more passages which spoke of immersion that had not originally been coded as such, each of which enriched my understanding. Now I was thinking about and working with a concept rather than cases, although there was constant reference back to the original data for checking on accuracy of interpretation. (I later came to see immersion as a necessary but not sufficient dimension of obsession – a characteristic that was itself widely considered to be necessary for 'good research' and 'really getting somewhere'.)

Coding to facilitate asking questions of the data

When data are coded, it becomes possible to ask questions of them, beyond simply retrieving all the data identified by a particular code. Asking questions of the data – challenging the data – is perhaps one of the most important skills you can develop. Be ruthless in asking 'So what?' or 'What's going on here?' or 'Why is that?' For example, you might start by simply *comparing* reports of a local event by new and longer-term residents of the area, or you could compare the range of different issues experienced in living in the area that are reported by these two groups. Chapter 9 provides many examples of ways of doing this.

Alternatively, you might consider whether residents who raise an issue of 'hoons' creating traffic noise are also the people who complain about the dirty state of the local shopping precinct. And did they say whether one or other or both of these problems have always been there or are they both recent? Or, do those who enjoy the country-like atmosphere of the area in which they live also enjoy entertaining at home? What are the styles of entertaining, or social life more generally, that are enjoyed by residents of different areas, and to what extent is this related to their attitude to the area? These kind of *relational* data questions are addressed in Chapter 10. Coding data is a facilitator for answering all these kinds of questions.

Writing analytic memos and keeping an audit trail

Throughout the process of coding, building memos about concepts is critical. Note why *this* code is important to consider, any regular or especially notable associations it appears to have with other codes, questions that arise in relation to the concept it represents, ideas that come from theoretical or fanciful comparisons, and so on. Memos are especially important for higher-level concepts; these will contribute significantly to the eventual writing up of the project. By recording also the circumstances under which a concept comes up for discussion, and links between this concept and another, you will contribute to later theory building and reporting your analysis.

In addition to memos relating to specific codes, keep notes in a journal or research diary about decisions made in relation to coding (cf. Figure 4.1). These will be important later in helping to explain and justify how you arrived at the conclusions you have reached.

Memos about concepts can be recorded in a notebook, on a sheet in an indexed folder, using a word processor, or using qualitative software (Figure 5.1). Further examples of ways to record memos were illustrated in Chapter 4.

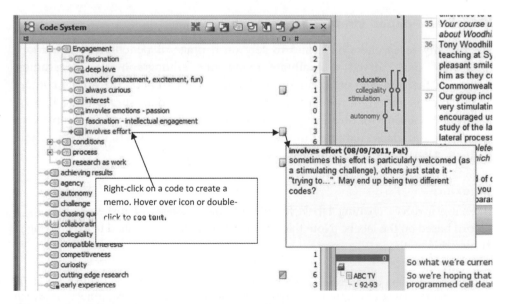

Figure 5.1   Linking a memo to a code in MAXQDA

Tips for coders:

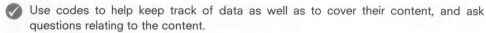 Use codes to help keep track of data as well as to cover their content, and ask questions relating to the content.

Record the decisions you make about coding.

Record ideas you have while you are coding about analysis and questions to ask.

Practical tools for coding

The strategies described in Chapter 4 were designed primarily to help you become familiar with each data source as it became available to you. Now it is time to work systematically through each data source, to build a database of evidence that will provide you with insights into the experiences or processes you want to understand, and serve as a resource for testing and supporting the conclusions you will develop.

There are multiple strategies that researchers have developed for coding data. In this section I review a range of possibilities for both manual and computer systems.[1] If this is your first attempt to systematically code data:

▶ Experiment to start with, until you find a strategy you are comfortable with.

▶ Start small: avoid stepping into a major project with a strategy that you haven't tried before.

▶ Try running some simple analyses based on your first sample of coding, to ensure it will work for your purposes.

▶ Spend some time working through your first few sources with someone who is more experienced; become an apprentice to develop competency in the craft of coding.

'Pencil-and-paper' strategies for coding

Historically researchers have had to rely on a range of pencil-and-paper tools, and these have served to facilitate many fine ethnographies, case studies, grounded theories, and other analyses. For some researchers, the tactile contact with paper is important, as is their ability to sit with data surrounding them – giving them a sense of physically handling and juggling the words or pictures as they tease out ideas contained in them, and a sense of understanding the whole picture. Alternative methods for working 'manually' follow.

Indexing

Indexing involves creating labels for identifiable passages of text, and making a record based on the labels. (Note that multiple labels can be applied to any passage.) To use this method:

---

[1] Novice researchers often (mistakenly) imagine that if they have a small amount of data, it is not worth using a computer for coding and analysis. The smallest project for which I used a computer consisted of nine pages only of data, but using it was invaluable for helping me to organise the concepts contained in those nine pages.

► Sequentially number the lines, paragraphs, pages, or other units in your sources.

► Record your code, accompanied by the appropriate sequential number to identify both the source and the specific location within it. If you find more passages on the same topic, add to your previous record, just as an index for a book is built. If you don't have a predetermined coding system to work from, then you will probably find this easiest to do:

o by creating a card for each code, on which you record reference details for each passage you find for that code, along with a brief reminder of the content of each passage (Turner, 1981);

o as a list into which you can insert new codes, using your word processor or a spreadsheet.

► Record also associations between codes as you go (e.g., the other codes you are using for the same passages).

Marking transcripts or other physical records

Pencil and paper coders format their data so that they have wide margins in which to record codes. Use margins to:

► Write in as many keywords as are necessary to describe the adjacent passage or text or element of the picture; and/or

► Read through sufficient data to be able to decide at least the kinds of codes you might want to use, and develop a shorthand code system from those; then use the margin space to write in the codes you are using (this does not allow for much flexibility).[2]

✓ Always keep a clean copy of the original data, as a backup resource.

► Keep a journal in which you record notes about the content of each code, and of the associations you are noting between it and other codes.

Sorting to create codes

For the first sorting strategy you will need to make multiple copies of each source (ensuring that an intact original is kept on file). Clearly label each copy of each page with essential identifying information:

► Cut out passages from *copies of* the original that are about particular topics or issues or points of relevance with regard to the goals of your project. *Make sure each piece is labelled with its source ID, page, and paragraph number as you copy or cut it from the page.* Make as many copies as you need for the number of categories that apply to that segment.

► Place these in separate piles or hang folders, to represent the various categories.

A second sorting approach uses either short segments of text, or statements drawn from the text that are exemplar quotes regarding ideas present throughout the text. Paste these exemplars onto small cards so that the identifying and

---

[2]Examples of manual coding structures can be found in Miles and Huberman (1994: 59–60) and Patton (2002: 464, 516–17).

descriptive information about the source or the context of the quote can be recorded on the back of the card (Bernard & Ryan, 2010).

▶ Sort the cards into groups, based on similarity of content. This might be done by spreading them across a table and gradually pushing them into piles, then naming the piles.

▶ Alternatively, have pairs of researchers working on the sorting task, with their conversations being recorded as they do so.

The discussions coders have about the piles or the pairs of quotes are as valuable to the researcher as the final sorts are, in providing an understanding of the issues covered by the quotes (Box 5.3).

⌐ Box 5.3 ⌐

Working as a team to create and sort 'chunks of data'

Here is how Scott, Bergeman, Verney, Longenbaker, Markey, and Bisconti described their sorting process:

Working with another member of the research team, we separated the transcribed interviews into units of meaning. Constantly comparing these units with each other, these chunks of data were grouped into emergent categories. A rule for inclusion and exclusion was written for each category, describing the essence of the units in that category. Eventually in this iterative process, the rules were developed into propositional statements that served as tentative findings for a specific theme. The research team then synthesized the propositional statements into an overall understanding of the phenomena. To build rigor into the work, the research team consulted with peer debriefers. (2007: 248–9)

Problems in using paper methods for coding

When you are coding, it is ideal to have both the benefit of being able to see in one place all the data pertaining to a particular code, and also to be able to see the data for which a particular combination of codes applies. A difficulty in deciding about methods of coding, if you are limited to manual (pencil-and-paper or cut-and-paste) approaches, is that while each method has particular benefits, it loses some or all of the benefit that pertains to the other. Thus:

• Indexing or marking techniques, provided an accompanying tally sheet and journal record is maintained, give the best access to patterns of association in the data, but make it more difficult to assemble original data associated with either individual codes or combinations of codes.

• Sorting techniques give the most rapid access to all the evidence gathered relating to a particular code, but are less helpful when it comes to looking at the connection of codes.

Either way, full benefit will depend closely on the care with which you record what you are noticing and thinking as you code. Otherwise, reports will be descriptive (a list of annotated concepts or 'themes') without analyses of associations between themes, or analytical without descriptive depth to provide context and interpretive understanding for the reader.

Using a computer for coding

Software tools to support analysis have now become readily available and are increasingly being adopted by researchers analysing qualitative data. Essentially, using computer software, especially those programs developed specifically for qualitative data analysis, will give you the benefits of *both* the indexing/marking and sorting approaches outlined above, *and more*, with much greater flexibility and speed.

Using standard MS Office software

Everyday MS Office software can assist with sorting and indexing text, albeit *in a limited way*.

Sorting text using Word

At a very simple level, one might *copy* and paste passages of text from an original source into another document where the material is organised by topic (or, less conveniently, into separate documents for each topic). Some text might be pasted multiple times, if multiple codes apply to it.

▶ Use styled headings to identify the topics for the sorted text. Doing so allows you to (a) use the Document Map (Navigation pane) to hyperlink to any heading in the document, for rapid access; and (b) to create a table of contents for the topics in the document (with page numbers).
▶ Record the source ID and paragraph numbers for the original version each time you paste a passage of text.
✔ If you are pasting the text into multiple places, include (with the ID information) a comment with each paste to indicate where else it has been placed.

An alternative approach is to insert keywords into the text, so that relevant passages for any topic can be found using Word's Find function. While these methods can help you to locate all your material on a particular topic, they are not helpful for finding patterns of relationships between categories.

Indexing with Excel

Indexing can be recorded in Excel (or alternative spreadsheet) rather than on paper or cards. This will facilitate pattern searching within and across sources, as well as retrieval (Figure 5.2 shows coding for the passage shown in Figure 5.3).

▶ Ensure your sources have numbered paragraphs.
▶ Each time you identify something in the source to be coded, use a new row in the spreadsheet to record (in column A) the source ID combined with the *single* paragraph number for the material being coded.

✓ You will benefit from always using the same number of digits for numbers; so, for example, if your source has 597 paragraphs, start numbering with 001 (this impacts on sorting). At the same time, don't start an ID with 0, as Excel will drop leading 0s.

▶ In column B for that row, record the code. If you want to code it with three codes, use three rows.

▶ If the code applies to more than one paragraph, repeat the code in a new row for each one.

▶ Use a third column to record a very brief summary of the content for each code for each unit of data, or to paste in a brief quote from the original text. Format the column so the text wraps in the cells if you are using more than a few words.

✓ You can attach a brief memo to a cell in Excel. Cells with a memo are marked with a triangle in the top right corner, and the memo can be seen by hovering over the cell with your mouse pointer.

For retrieval:

▶ Use the software's sort function (cf. Chapter 3) on column B to find all the paragraphs in which material for a particular code appears. Sort on column A to find all the codes that co-occur within each paragraph of data (some of these may be incidental and have no significance).

	A	B	C	D	E	F
1	Source ID	Code	Text			
2	A2	career	In and out of research "I drifted"			
3	A2	educ	hons PhD postdoc			
4	A2	opp	offered postdoc	Pat: reactive rather than proactive		
5	A3	career	not planned			
6	A3	uncertainty	about research			
7	A5	goals	prefers teaching			
8						

Figure 5.2 Recording indexing in Excel, to allow sorting by paragraph or by code

Using qualitative software

When you code using qualitative software, you create within the software a storage area for each topic or concept, in which references to large or small segments of text, image, sound, or video are recorded.

Most software has a similar approach to the coding process:

▶ Import the sources to be coded (this usually *copies* the source into the project file).

▶ Create coding categories either before or during coding. These can be changed and reorganised at any time without loss of data.

▶ Use drag-and-drop to code highlighted text in the imported source at a particular code (Figure 5.3).

✔ Sources can be edited after import, but it is better to set them up appropriately beforehand.

✔ Sources can be of different types, including text, video, audio, and images, and in various formats.[3]

✔ Most software offers ways of automating routine coding (such as for who is speaking in a focus group, or what question is being answered in a questionnaire). These documents usually require special formatting *before* they are imported.

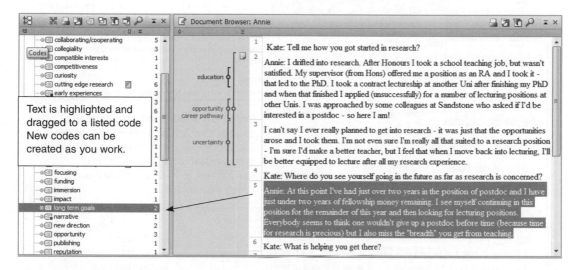

Figure 5.3   Coding using MAXQDA

What is stored, when you code, are not actual segments of data, but *references* to the exact location of the coded data in the source file. Using those references, the software is able to locate and retrieve all the coded passages for a particular code or combination of codes from the source records (Figure 5.4). The passages themselves are never copied, cut, or physically moved as they are coded. Unlike cut-up photocopies on the sitting room floor or in hanging files:

• the source always remains intact;
• information about the source of a quote is always preserved and is displayed whenever a segment is displayed;

---

[3]Exactly what can be imported, in what format, depends on the software being used.

- changes made to the source are (usually) immediately reflected in the coded text segment;[4] and

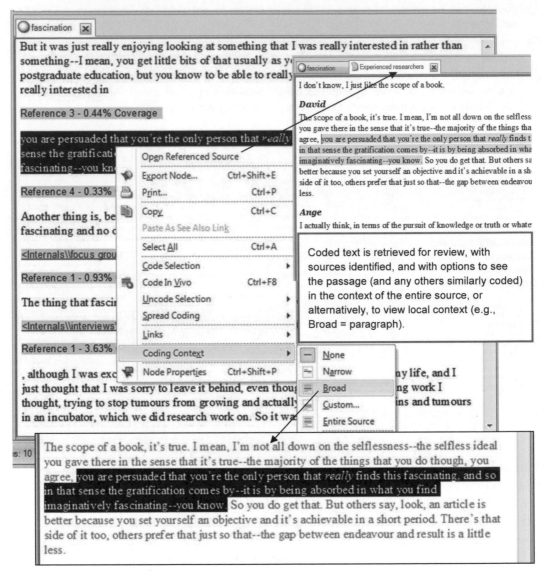

Figure 5.4   Code and context retrieval using NVivo

---

[4]Qualitative software programs vary in the degree of flexibility and integrity they have with regard to editing of texts already imported, particularly once they have been coded. Some are better than others at adjusting the coding that has already been applied to take account of the editing changes. Check this feature carefully before making changes to text that has been coded in the software you are using.

- a coded segment can immediately be seen together with other similarly coded material (Figure 5.4); but also
- it is always possible to view the coded passage in its original context; and
- passages can (and should!) be coded with multiple codes, with queries rapidly able to find passages coded by co-occurring codes.

Computer-based coding of qualitative data is potentially more complex and more detailed than manual thematic sorting. Rather than identifying a passage with one all-inclusive thematic code, when using a computer the coder can separately identify, by using several codes on the same passage, what is going on, contextual factors such as when, where, and who is involved, what attitudes, feelings, or responses are being revealed, what issues are raised, what the outcome is, and so on, with the confidence that the computer can reconnect codes used for the same passage of text. Attending to these different aspects as you work through the data encourages a greater level of attention to nuances in the data and often leads to deeper insights than would otherwise occur. Immediately data are coded in this way, almost limitless possibilities for review, sorting, and sifting of text segments become possible (Bazeley, 2007; Bazeley & Jackson, in press; Lewins & Silver, in press).

Problems in using computer software

There are dangers to watch for when using a computer for coding. There is a tendency for users, especially novice users, to:

- create and record too many data in too much detail, simply because the computer can handle them more efficiently than can be done using paper methods;
- rely on coding and retrieving descriptive codes or simple themes, without taking advantage of the linking, memoing, and analysis tools provided by their software;
- become obsessed with the *task* of coding (often referred to as 'the coding trap'), to the exclusion of imaginative and reflective thinking, linking, and memo writing (Johnston, 2006).

The point, as always with computers, is to make the computer work for you; don't work for it!

As with any new software, there is a learning curve when you first start using qualitative software. Basic tasks like coding and code retrieval are usually quite straightforward to learn, but some form of guidance or training is likely to be needed to really benefit from the more sophisticated management and analysis tools provided by software. Developers offer a range of training tools (video tutorials, extensive online help), workshops, webinars, and web-based Q&A forums to assist the process.

Creating a codebook

A codebook holds a digest of your codes and categories, something that assists the lone coder in being consistent in the application of codes. A codebook is essential for team coding, to ensure all team members are applying codes in a similar way. It will probably be useful to have it in two forms: a full reference version with detailed descriptions of each code and where and how each has been used, and a briefer summary containing the labels you are using for each code and a very brief definition, useful to have nearby as you are coding.

Expect the codebook to be a work in progress, so you will need to reprint it multiple times.[5] This applies even if you start with a predetermined list of relevant codes; it can be surprising how often something that *should* have been relevant turns out to not be so, while other codes need to be elaborated or added.

Codebooks for working manually

Because you don't have rapid access to review material already coded, your codebook will need to contain considerable detail to make it useful as a reference for your coding (MacQueen, McLellan, Kay and Milstein, 1998). Useful information to record includes:

- a short label suitable to apply in a margin;
- both brief and fuller definitions;
- inclusion and exclusion criteria; and
- typical examples (Table 5.1).

Table 5.1   Example of a codebook entry

Code	STIM – Intellectual stimulation
Definition	Any evidence of where thinking processes have been 'turned on' by research or research related activity in a way that serves to motivate them to do more.
When to use	Use specifically where something has the effect of stimulating further creative/research thinking or activity. Often overlaps with other intellectual process codes (use more than one where appropriate).
When not to use	e.g., where simply talking about the challenge of a task associated with research, such as admin.
Example	'You stimulate each other, ... you are talking research, when you go to bed at night you are thinking it.' 'Getting the data...wanting to know.'

Codebooks for computer software

If you are using a word processor or spreadsheet to record coding, then you will benefit from creating a codebook in a similar way to that for manual-based methods.

---

[5]The worst situation I ever encountered, in this regard, was the government employee who, after modifying her codes a couple of times, decided that she could now laminate the list, never to change it again. Unsurprisingly, she rapidly became totally bored with the whole task of coding, and never completed the project.

For those working on specialised qualitative analysis software, there are ways of recording the same type of code information in the software, such that it can be easily retrieved as needed, or printed off for reference, as a list of codes or codes with definitions.

- In MAXQDA, definitions, additional commentary, and reflective thoughts for particular codes can be recorded in memos attached to those codes. The code system can be exported or printed with or without the additional memo information.
- In NVivo, definitions for particular codes can be recorded in the properties dialogue box for those codes. The screen display can be customised to show these definitions whenever codes are listed. Additional commentary and other reflective thoughts about a code are recorded in a memo attached to that code. The list of codes with definitions can be exported or printed, as can the text of individual memos.

Including data about participants or other sources

This is a largely mechanical task (for everyone, not just those using computers) that can be dealt with whenever convenient in your project; perhaps you have already done it as part of preparing your data and storing your data records.

For each of your sources and/or units of analysis (if these don't equate to sources), you will almost always want to code or otherwise record some useful classifying information. This will allow you to identify the context of a particular coded passage, for example, whether it was said by a Londoner or a Parisian, when you are thinking about or reporting that passage. More importantly for analysis, it will allow you to make comparisons by sorting all the data with a particular code according to where they have come from, for example, to compare all the comments on cooperation by females with all those from males. If you are using software, you might also be able to use this kind of classification to compare whole patterns of responses, such as the differences in the range of emotions expressed by beginning researchers compared with those who are more experienced. Such comparisons will contribute significantly to your analysis (cf. Chapter 9).

The two issues for now are: what kind of demographic or variable data will be needed; and how best to record the information so that it can be used for those later comparisons.

Demographic information is the most obvious kind of data to record: things like gender, location, role, age. If you are working in a project where survey data are available for the same participants, you might also want to record responses they made to categorical questions ('Did you experience discrimination often, sometimes, or never?') or perhaps even scaled information ('On a 10-point scale, what was your level of pain today?') to consider along with the qualitative data. What you record will be governed by two factors: what information is relevant to the issues your project is addressing; and your capacity to use the data for analysis – the latter being governed largely by whether you are working manually or using a computer.

Those working with paper records will need to ensure, if they cut them up, that they have a labelling system for the sorted segments that allows them to retrieve relevant demographic data. For those who are recording text data into columns or fields in a spreadsheet or database, then additional columns or fields can be set up within those programs to record associated data. Or, if you are using qualitative software, most current packages provide for recording this kind of classificatory information (typically referred to as 'attributes') so that it is linked to the sources and/or cases, but stored separately from the coding system.[6] This is because such information is relevant to the whole source or case, whereas coding is usually applied to selected segments of data only.

Sometimes you are unaware of just what variables to apply until you are working through the data source, or you might decide during the coding process that you now wish to classify people on another variable or attribute, such as a dominant attitude, or the presence or absence of a particular experience in their lives. This is usually possible, but the thing to remember, if you are doing so, is that the classification you use has to 'fit' *all* of the data for that source or case – otherwise it is better to use coding, applied to the relevant passages only.

Methods decisions in coding

Some of you will have generated some codes already, based on the suggestions in the previous chapter. Maybe you have also explored some techniques for coding. Those experiences provide a good background against which to make some decisions about the way you are going to approach coding for your current project.

Keeping your purpose in focus

The first and most important thing to consider is your purpose in coding. Before you start, remind yourself of the aims and objectives for your project and the questions your research is designed to answer, as these will critically influence what you will look for in coding your data. Then, as your list of codes grows, periodically review them in the light of your questions. Will they give you access to the kind of data that will allow you to answer them?

---

[6]Many of these software programs allow, also, for this kind of data to be imported directly from a spreadsheet.

Tips for coders:

- ✓ Paste a copy of the questions for your project on the wall near your workspace.
- ✓ Challenge each code you create. Ask: why am I interested in that?[7]
- ✓ Have a trial run to see if you can answer your questions from the codes you have created. Are there any gaps that need filling?
- ✓ 'Park' data and ideas that are interesting but not immediately relevant (use a single code). Ignore or remove any that are neither interesting nor relevant.

Breadth versus detail in coding

Will you start generating codes by marking or sorting data into broad categories or by working line-by-line or even phrase-by-phrase? Bernard and Ryan (2010) evocatively characterised different approaches to the task of coding as lumping and splitting, with 'splitters' maximising differences between text passages as they look for fine-grained themes or categories, while 'lumpers' ignore the finer nuances in the text as they look for overarching themes or areas of discussion.

In practice, most people will engage in a combination of both splitting and lumping, if not at the start, then certainly during the course of their project. For example, you might:

▶ Use broad codes indicating areas to revisit if it is too early to comprehend detail in those areas.

▶ Focus on the detail of a few rich paragraphs if you are feeling lost in the whole. Qualitative analysis is designed to be flexible, and most people revisit their early work in any case.

The important thing is to start as soon as you have data. Don't delay because you're feeling uncertain (you can make changes later), and never allow documents to build up unprocessed.

'Chunking', fracturing, or slicing text

Unless you are simply indexing original sources, coding inevitably involves segmenting text or other source material, in so far as the code is applied to sections of the text only. Segmenting may occur as a preliminary step to coding and analysis, or during the process of coding, depending on the method you are using to apply codes. Some codes will be applied to longer 'chunks', but most will be used with shorter passages. Breaking the text into short paragraphs or even smaller

---

[7]For those using a grounded theory methodology, this question should not be asked too early (e.g., in the first two or three sources), assuming that the data are more or less relevant to the topic of investigation. This is so that you do not pre-empt possible new ways of thinking about the issues raised.

passages can be helpful in clarifying content and meaning in the text, especially in dealing with long, possibly poorly structured turns of conversation from a talkative participant. Each of these passages can then be coded with one or more relevant codes.

Coding is often seen as 'fracturing' the text (e.g., Strauss, 1987), with attention then being paid to each separate fragment.[8] This metaphor, with its strong connotation of breaking something into small pieces, suggests a consequent loss of connection between the fragments of data and hence connections to the immediate and larger context of the surrounding text. This has led to criticism of the practice of microanalysis (Hodgkinson, 2008). Fracturing of data into very small segments can be a problem with manual methods where copies of sources are cut up into pieces for sorting into piles. It was seen as a problem also in the early days of qualitative computing when, on retrieval, the coded segment was visually separated from the surrounding text. It is less of a problem with current software, in that the immediate and larger contexts of any coded segment are each available with a click of the mouse (cf. Figure 5.4), although the initial retrieval may still be of the decontextualised segment.

Apply all relevant codes to the whole 'meaning unit' (a sentence, a paragraph, several paragraphs), even if each doesn't apply to the whole passage. Codes will overlap, while the specific text that gave rise to the code is still readily apparent within the passage. Segmenting text, then, might be thought about more as slicing or layering rather than fracturing, and 'disconnect' issues with fracturing can largely be overcome. In slicing the text, multiple codes are used to capture the who, what, when, where, and how of what is being reported in a passage of text (Figure 5.5).

Using multiple overlapping codes on text has the advantage that patterns of connection between codes can be readily explored. Codes applied to the same or overlapping passages of text can be presumed to have some relationship; codes applied to adjacent passages of text may or may not have any association. As you code your way through data sources, patterns of association between codes will become apparent. To facilitate later analyses, it is important to note these associations in memos as you become aware of them, or if you are working on paper, then you need also to note the document, page, and line numbers where the associations were seen, so that they can be located again when needed for further analysis or as evidence for the pattern.

---

[8]It is important not to confuse coding detail (identifying specific subcategories of content in the text) with coding detailed (small) segments of data. They have different meanings, so while the two often go together, they do not necessarily do so.

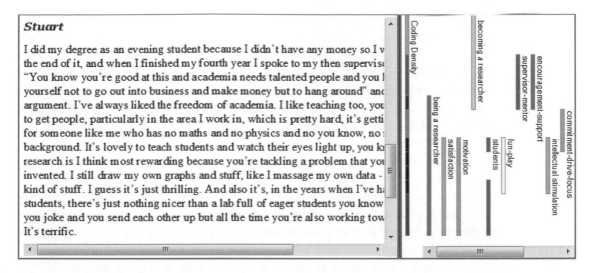

Figure 5.5   Coding stripes showing multiple overlapping codes applied to adjacent text in NVivo

Tips for coders:

✓ Apply codes to *meaning units* within the source. These might vary in size, depending on your current purpose, as well as the nature of the material being coded.

✓ Apply as many codes to a meaning unit as is necessary to capture all the dimensions of what is going on in that passage.

Coding different types of data

Qualitative data take many forms, with implications for coding practices. Data vary in their degree of structure; how openly ideas, experiences, and attitudes are recounted or discussed; whether they are descriptive or emotive; the style of language used; and so on.

Interview transcripts are typically complex in terms of the number of cross-cutting contexts, ideas, and concepts present in any one passage, as people express and respond to whatever thoughts are prompted by an interviewer's questions or comments. Consequently, coding of these is multifaceted in order to capture descriptive context and experience as well as interpreted rationales and responses, and memo writing associated with coding is likely to be extensive, focusing on both cases and concepts.

In contrast to coding an interview where you are focused directly on what is said by the interviewee in response to your questions, to effectively code *focus group data* you will pay more attention to the interaction within the group. View any individual's comments in the light of that interaction.

Field notes differ from interview transcripts in having been written, in most cases, by the person who is coding them. Like memos, field notes are more likely to be written around particular incidents or observations or topics, making coding more straightforward. Coding of field notes is likely to be more descriptive than coding of interview data, particularly if the observer's reflections are stored separately from his or her observations. Where events being observed have become familiar to the observer/coder, Charmaz (2006) suggests using an approach which compares one incident with another, rather than routinely working through the detail of each incident, as a way of 'breaking through' the ordinariness of each one.

Short responses to open-ended questions lack elaboration, particularly those provided in response to a self-completed questionnaire, and so they can leave open as many questions as they answer (some would question that these should be considered as qualitative data). Often these are suitable for semi-automated coding procedures, such as word searches, or they can be readily categorised – if they are coded at all. For interactive coding of short-answer responses, depending on the nature of the questions and to what extent the responses to different questions are interrelated, it can be more helpful (and efficient) to focus in turn on the issues for the study by coding all responses to each question, question-by-question, rather than the more usual procedure of working through all questions for each case, case-by-case. (This depends on how necessary it is to see each case as a whole.) Memo writing, in this type of project, is likely to be associated with important codes or with the project as a whole, rather than with individual cases.

Streaming data (audio, video) pose a mechanical difficulty for coding of content. By the time you realise you want to code a specific passage in a particular way, you have missed the marker (usually a time stamp) for the beginning of the passage. You will therefore need to be very familiar with the content of the source so that you know what is coming, have detailed notes to assist, or be prepared to do a lot of backtracking as you work through, all of which make the task very laborious and slow. Retrieval is also much more time consuming than for written text. If the reason for working with video is to capture non-verbal cues, then a parallel transcript or summary of the spoken words would be very helpful.

Epistemological frames, theoretical perspectives, and coding

Epistemological frameworks for understanding the social world influence the questions being asked, and consequently the ideas about what to code and how to code (or whether to code at all). Some will see and code only those things that have been directly observed and reported; others will seek to understand and code the speaker's interpretation or construction of their experience; and others again, their own interpretation or construction of what was said and done by the participant.

Different theoretical approaches to understanding the social world, similarly, lead to different questions being asked, and different concerns in coding. Those whose focus is on larger issues such as the causes, expressions, and impacts of power and domination throughout society will identify different features in their data from others who attend to the structure of a conversation. Cooper's (2008) description of how different social theorists would attend to quite different features in studying a door (Box 2.2) suggests that each would code using different labels, and would read different implications from those codes. These orientations influence decisions about coding right from the start of the process, even for something as apparently straightforward as 'clerical' and descriptive coding: do we pay attention to a person's gender? Their sexuality? Whether this event occurred before or after a change was introduced into office procedures? The presence or proximity and size of the photograph of the child?

Attending to the detail of our texts or other sources will facilitate openness to what those texts are saying, but reflexive awareness of the ways in which prior frameworks and pre-existing knowledge might influence interpretation and understanding is called for and their impact should be noted in memos as coding proceeds.

Methodological purposes and coding

Because each methodological approach seeks to meet different purposes and has different emphases, what is coded and how the coding is applied will vary. Is the emphasis on process, or structure, or emotion? Does the coder work holistically or focus on detail? Are the initial codes they create descriptive or interpretive? Examples of how different methodological approaches might impact on the coding of one interview are illustrated in Box 5.4.

┐ **Box 5.4** ┌

Different methodological emphases in coding a sample of text

Different methodological approaches to text can be illustrated from Shane's account of how he came to be interested in research.

- The grounded theorist, with an emphasis on *Shane's perspective* on the *process* of his becoming interested, would note his desire and capacity to pinpoint when this occurred; the circumstances, process, and consequences of his being encouraged and praised by others and the important role that encouragement played; the pleasure he gained from his engagement with the task; and

(Continued)

(Continued)

at a later stage of interpretation, perhaps the match between the tasks he undertook and his personality.
- An interpretive phenomenologist, concerned to identify the essential elements of the *experience* of becoming and being a researcher, might focus on Shane's passion, the pleasure of working in intimate contact with data; the satisfaction that comes from carefully completing a task and creating a product that can be held and admired; and the warmth of receiving interest and praise from others.
- Someone interested in discourse analysis would focus on the *language* of passion and romance in Shane's telling of his experience, and what that conveys about the meaning of that experience for him. It is a language which contrasts strongly with the language of performance, of duty, and of play that is found in other transcripts.

Issues of validity and reliability in coding

How you perceive, interpret, and code your data will be impacted intellectually and practically by:

- the perspectives learned through your disciplinary training;
- the focus of your study, the questions you are asking, and related or consequent choices regarding epistemology and methodology;
- the extent to which you have already explored these questions in previous studies or in the theoretical and research literature;
- your own level of involvement in data collection and preparation, and consequent familiarity with their contents;
- your mood at the time, the degree of pressure you are under to finish, and other personal factors.

How credible is my interpretation?

All of our observations, of numbers and visual images as well as text, involve interpretation – by us, *and* by the participants who provided the data. They represent one view among many. By making your perspective and your questions explicit, you can increase the consistency of your coding, and assist the reader to understand how and why you interpreted the data in a particular way. The issue is not whether you have discovered or developed a 'true' understanding of the data, but whether, in the eyes of the coder and those evaluating the coding, the interpretation makes sense *given the conceptual framework of the coder* (Kvale, 1996; see Box 5.5).

┐ **Box 5.5** ┌

Hamlet's interview

Kvale (1996: 151–3) uses Hamlet's interview of Polonius to illustrate how interview technique, the responses given, and interpretation of those responses are influenced by the purposes of both interviewer and interviewee. The interview is very short, comprising just three questions:

Hamlet: Do you see yonder cloud that's almost in shape of a camel?

Polonius: By th' mass, and 'tis like a camel indeed.

Hamlet: Methinks it is like a weasel.

Polonius: It is back'd like a weasel.

Hamlet: Or like a whale?

Polonius: Very like a whale.

Hamlet: … (Aside) They fool me to the top of my bent.

(*Hamlet*, Act III, Scene 2)

Kvale observes that this appears, at first, to be use of an unreliable interview technique, with its three leading questions leading to entirely different answers that tell us nothing of the shape of the cloud. But is the cloud the issue, or is it rather the personality of Polonius, and his trustworthiness? Now, Hamlet's sophisticated indirect interview technique provides 'reliable, thrice-checked knowledge about Polonius as an unreliable person' (1996: 151–2). This is confirmed in Hamlet's aside at the end of the interview.

  But then, if the interview is considered in the context of a royal court where a prince is questioning a courtier, it demonstrates the potency of power relations. Polonius was well versed in indirect interview techniques (drawing on evidence from an earlier scene), so perhaps he is simply playing up to Hamlet as a courtier?

  Finally, Kvale notes, the central theme of the play is 'a preoccupation with the frail nature of reality'; thus his interview may be seen as reflecting 'pervasive doubt about the appearance of the world, including the shape of a cloud and the personalities of fellow players' (1996: 153).

What if I get it wrong?

In discussing open coding and the anxiety that novices have about identifying the intended meaning of an interviewee's words, Strauss observed:

> The aim of the coding is to *open up* the inquiry. Every interpretation at this point is tentative. In a genuine sense, the analyst is not primarily concerned with this particular document, but for what it can do to further the next steps of the inquiry. Whatever is wrong in interpreting those lines and words will eventually be cancelled out through later steps of the inquiry. Concepts will then work or not work, distinctions will be useful or not useful – or modified, and so forth. (1987: 29)

Coding involves regular review and revision of concepts. If you are unsure about whether to apply a particular code you might review what text you have already coded there, to check if it matches. When you start to organise, group, or synthesise codes, you will inevitably review and revise what you have coded. These are opportunities to 'get it right' and to recode and/or remove irrelevant material. Finding missing gems is a little harder. I sometimes locate these also during the process of reviewing a code, when I check what else a particular passage is coded at and discover via the coding stripes that a concept present in the text is missing from that list (this would be difficult to do manually). I have also found missing codes during analysis, particularly when looking for exceptions to an association. For example, in my original coding of Stuart's document in the Researchers project, I had missed coding his passage where he talks about playing with graphs and massaging data as being about intellectual stimulation, as it should have been. This became evident when I was looking to see whether one could experience enjoyment or satisfaction in doing research without talking at all about being intellectually stimulated by it, and this passage came up. I added the additional code to the passage, and dismissed it as a valid result for this query – problem quickly solved!

Multiple coders and coding reliability

There is often an expectation in qualitative circles that coding should be checked for reliability. Coding for reliability usually means that a second person is asked to code a sample of material, to see if they arrive at the same codes for each passage as did the first person, or a sample might be recoded at a later stage to see if the coder has remained consistent in applying codes throughout the project. These kinds of checks are often seen also as contributing to the validity of the conclusions drawn from the codes. These practices derive from coding in surveys and other quantitative work designed for measurement or statistical analysis, where codes become separated from data and so clear definition and consistent application of a code is critical to being able to interpret statistical results.

In qualitative work, however, 'there is no single set of categories waiting to be discovered. There are as many ways of "seeing" the data as one can invent' (Dey, 1993: 110–11). Most samples of qualitative data have multiple stories to tell, and each person coming to the data brings with them their own purposes, perspectives, experiences, and knowledge. As indicated earlier, each of these influences what is seen in the data, their interpretation of what is seen, and hence what categories are developed from the data.

It is *not* reasonable to expect that two people coming to a sample of data, only for the purpose of coding, will code it using the same categories and in the same way, unless the second person is drilled in the purpose and framework for the project, and given a tightly defined set of codes to work with, with strict instructions and training in how to apply them. (I have been known to refer to this as the 'trained monkey' approach to coding reliability.) It *is* reasonable to expect some consistency in coding done by the same person across a whole project, and that any early vagueness in codes has been clarified and 'tidied up' by the time final analyses are undertaken.[9] Additionally, the categories developed should make sense (in the context of the project's purpose, etc.) to a second observer and potentially to those who provided the data, and it should be evident that the data have been appropriately fitted to the categories (Guba, 1978, reported in Patton, 2002).

What is more likely to convince an audience of the reliability and validity of your conclusions than an artificially created measure of reliability is the strength of your argument and the clarity and comprehensiveness of your evidence. What was it that convinced you of the conclusion you have reached? To take your audience through that process or argument as a means of convincing them, you will need to have recorded detailed memos of the process you went through, and you will need to be able to readily locate relevant supporting evidence from your data (more on this in later chapters). The implication, for now, is that reliability testing for coding does not, in itself, add to the strength of your conclusions. Rather, you need to keep a clear record (audit trail) of your coding decisions, linked to a strong evidentiary database (Yin, 2003).

Determining inter- and intra-coder agreement on coding *is* relevant in the context of a team and/or longitudinal project, where consistency between coders is clearly necessary. The real value of the exercise in producing a measure, though, is not the measure itself, but what can be learned in the process. Having additional people code the same document, especially while the codes are being developed, and then comparing that coding promotes some very worthwhile discussions about how the coding is being approached, based on the differences observed, leading to agreement about what is important (hopefully!) and clear definitions for categories. For a team project, this needs to occur relatively early in the coding process, and again at regular intervals throughout, to keep all coders 'on the same page'. For your individual project, comparing your coding on a sample of data with that done by someone else (with some guidance as to the purpose and orientation of the project) similarly can lead to valuable discussions (as with brainstorming more generally) about how the coding is proceeding; it's just not particularly useful in terms of 'reliability'.

For those working on computer, several qualitative software packages now support checking for inter-coder agreement by, first of all, tracking the contribution of each user to the project, including application of codes, and then showing comparison data where two have coded the same text. Figure 5.6 shows the output from NVivo. The main results pane shows measures of agreement (various percentages and the kappa statistic, calculated at the level of characters coded) for two researchers regarding the application of each code within one source. Double-clicking on any line in the results pane opens the actual text, with

---

[9]This is most easily achieved by reviewing the text stored under each code for consistency.

coding stripes showing lines of text where each coder applied that particular code (with a further option of showing exact characters), thereby providing a useful basis for discussion about how coding is being applied.

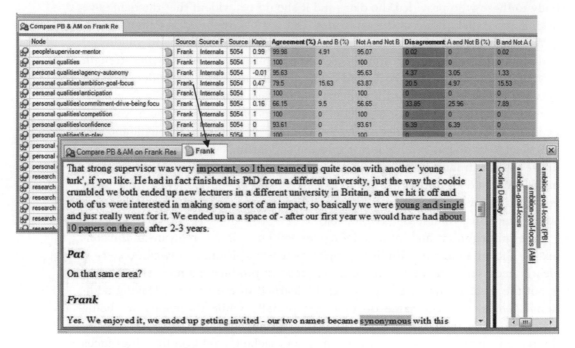

Figure 5.6   Results from checking inter-coder agreement in NVivo

Managing the process of coding

When am I done?

Codes always need revising as the work proceeds. Some will be changed, others deleted, new ones emerge. Generally speaking, coding and recoding are finished when all of the incidents can be readily classified, categories are 'saturated' and sufficient numbers of regularities emerge (Miles & Huberman, 1994). But what does saturation mean, in practice? It is commonly thought of as being when no new categories are 'emerging', that is, being found in the data (as seen in Box 2.8). Corbin and Strauss (2008) argue that, more than that, each category must be fully developed and described, with variations in each identified and preferably related to other concepts, before saturation is considered to have been reached and sampling (to extend categories and theoretical understanding) can cease. This could mean, of course, that one never finishes!

Once a category has been elaborated and refined, the question arises as to whether to code every instance where there is a reference to it in the remaining data. A related issue is whether to code every aspect of any category that is evident in any particular account, or just those that appear to be important or meaningful. I have seen gross examples of overcoding in some novices' projects using computer software, where every vague reference to a concept has been captured, often with extensive context, with the consequence that the meaning of the concept becomes clouded, and the patterns of association with other codes are more difficult to see.[10] (Perhaps this is not an issue with manual coding, where applying and using a code are more laborious.) Once again, how much to code is a question of methodology and purpose. If the goal of category creation is to reach a point where the category can be comprehensively described, then once no new information is forthcoming, there is little point in continuing and thereby adding redundant material. If the goal, however, is to go beyond description, and to identify the extent to which this category exists across the sample, or the extent to which it is associated with other particular categories (and when it isn't), and how it varies in relation to those, then it is useful to continue to code instances of a category for as long as data are being gathered and coded, that is, until sufficiency for the project as a whole is reached. This is implying that, when it comes time for analysis, it will be necessary not just to be able to identify associations and variations, but to be able to produce comprehensive evidence for those associations – and that, too, is an issue of methodology.

In some situations, especially where you are having to manage large volumes of textual sources, once categories are well established along with their variations and conditions, then techniques for rapid perusal of remaining recordings or texts can be applied appropriately. These techniques include listening carefully to non-transcribed audio for confirmation of or variations on what has already been established; or word searches through computer-based transcripts or documents to identify potentially relevant text. The passages so identified can then be perused in more detail.

Staying sane!

While novices working on computer may be at greater (though not exclusive) risk of becoming caught in an interminable coding trap, those working manually more often become overwhelmed with the volume and complexity of their data. Neither is a happy situation. If you are simply recording or organising rather than engaging in interpretive thinking, coding has the potential to become a headache, rather

---

[10]MAXQDA's solution is to allow each instance that a code is applied to be weighted, using a sliding scale of 0–100.

than a pathway to enlightenment. Helen Marshall noted that the source of this problem was coding rather than computers, quoting a contributor to an email discussion on the issue: 'I am a poor veteran of both methods and they both WRECK MY HEAD ... When I used paper and scissors I was constantly chasing scraps of paper – now I am a zombie in front of a confuser' (2002: 62, emphasis in original).

Coding must never become an end in itself. Practical strategies to avoid being either caught on a treadmill or lost in a pool of disconnected ideas include:

- Ensure you have efficient clerical systems for keeping track of relevant data and the ideas flowing from those.
- Automate whatever processes you can (such as routine coding of demographic data, or what structured question is being responded to), giving yourself more time for interpretive activity.
- Switch between coding and other tasks, such as reading and reflecting on a fresh item of data; reviewing the coding you have already done for one category; or checking what happens when you run a query using the data you have already coded.
- Regularly stop to write memos or draw models to capture ideas coming from the data. Lyn Richards' contribution to that same email discussion was that if you are coding for more than an hour or two without stopping to write a memo, you have 'lost the plot'.
- Focus on what you are wanting to achieve with your coding. You do not have to code every item of data, and you do not have to create a code for every idea contained within it! Remember to regularly ask the 'Why am I interested in that?' question.
- Once a category is taking shape, a process of refinement is taking place; so my recommendation, then, is to code only if the data provide a clear instance of the category, rather than a vague allusion to it. A helpful question to ask is whether you would want to find this passage of text each time you need to retrieve and review anything you know about this category – a consideration that is especially relevant if you already have a large amount of data relating to that category.
- Take regular time out from your data, walk right away from them (cleaning or weeding suddenly seem like remarkably attractive options!); give your brain a chance to move out of the rut and make fresh connections, and your unconscious creativity a chance to work.
- Take time also for discussions with colleagues about what you are doing. Research productivity is a direct consequence of doing so (Pelz & Andrews, 1976).

A final reminder: codes and coding in context

Remember that codes and coding are only one part of the process of qualitative analysis; they cannot exist in isolation. Codes will be used to link or test for associated ideas; they will need to become connected in various ways in order to build a metanarrative, a meaningful word picture, or a theory. Strategies for exploring and establishing or testing connections across data and links between codes will be covered in later chapters. Your more immediate tasks, however, are to determine what codes to use, and then how to create some order and structure in your coding system. These are the subjects of the next chapter.

Writing about coding processes

In the methods chapter

▶ Explain the approach you have taken to coding over the course of the project. For example, were the codes you used determined from your literature and theory, or did you create them from the data as you worked? Were they driven by any guiding philosophy or methodology (how)? Did you code in isolation, as part of a team, or were there regular discussions with others to provide some checks and balances?

▶ Provide an example that shows how a code originated and was developed and/or revised through the project.

▶ Describe the methods you used to record codes and to retrieve coded material, and also those for recording and making use of associated demographic or categorical data.

▶ Reflect on how or why your coding should be considered appropriate for your purpose.

Exercises

Exercise 1: Preliminary coding

▶ Read through Frank's account of his early career (Box 5.6), once he completed his PhD and began working with another new graduate – or select a magazine or newspaper article or a brief account from your own data. Underline significant words and phrases and use the margins to note the kinds of things you might want to index or code in that account. As an experiment, try working from the perspective of two (or more) of the following:

  ○ a grounded theorist who wants to understand the process of becoming established as a researcher;
  ○ a phenomenologist focusing on early career experience;
  ○ an ethnographer considering culturally based behaviours among younger, research-oriented academics; or
  ○ a narrative or discourse researcher looking at the structure or language of an account.

▶ Discuss your thoughts about codes and the notes you made with a colleague.

Box 5.6

Frank's early career development

Frank: I then teamed up quite soon with another 'young turk', if you like. He had in fact finished his PhD from a different university, just the way the cookie crumbled, we both ended up new lecturers in a different university in Britain, and we hit it off and both of us were interested in making some sort of an impact, so basically we were young and single and

(Continued)

(Continued)

> just really went for it. We ended up in a space of – after our first year we would have had about 10 papers on the go, after two to three years.
>
> *Pat*:   On that same area?
>
> *Frank*:   Yes. We enjoyed it, we ended up getting invited – our two names became synonymous with this certain approach, and we went around Britain and into Europe giving research papers and getting ourselves published.
>
> *Pat*:   So you've got a reputation?
>
> *Frank*:   Yes, it wasn't a – you've got to keep that going for basically 10 years before you build up a reputation. Those in the know in the area knew that we were up and coming and we knew that they knew that we were up and coming, because they'd start writing to us and asking us. We basically knew that it was us carving out a niche for ourselves in the research part of the profession and that was our key to success so we kept at it. Eventually we both went apart and our research paths have diverged.

Further reading

Saldaña (2009: Chapter 1) introduces his coding manual with an overview of codes and coding.

Coffey and Atkinson (1996: Chapter 2) provide a rationale for and approaches to coding with examples from anthropology.

Turner (1981) usefully describes the detail of his methods for using an index card system in his evolving approach to coding field notes in a grounded theory study.

Bernard and Ryan (2010: Chapter 4) describe, with examples, codebooks and manual coding processes.

Morse (1997), in a delightfully titled editorial, discusses how coding reliability processes can render interpretation of data 'perfectly healthy, but dead'.

6

Naming, organising, and refining codes

Coding is one of the best guarantees you have against losing sight of a valuable idea or item of data, as it ensures you will 'meet up' with it again during the course of analysis. It sounds like a straightforward activity (as indeed it is when coding highly structured survey data) until one is faced with paragraph after paragraph of complex discourse. Nuances in the text, intertwined thoughts, narrative twists and turns, mixed emotions, and competing rationalisations can all conspire to complicate the task and overwhelm the analyst.

In this chapter the focus is on the categories and concepts you will develop and use as you work through your sources, reflected in the labels you apply to the codes you create. Explore:

- the range of things going on in your data that you might capture with a code;
- strategies for seeing what is there in your data, and giving a name to it;
- how to structure your coding system to facilitate later interrogation of the concepts within it;
- ways to capture the context around what is happening; and
- ways to automate routine aspects of coding.

What's in a name?

Names given to things do matter! The name you give to something reflects your experience: seeing it evokes memories of previous encounters. It influences future ones. For example, if behaviour is labelled as deviant, this will bring forth different responses from the so-called deviant person and from those around that person than would occur in relation to the same behaviour occurring in a situation where it is not labelled as deviant (Becker, 1963). The labels Negro, Black, or African American carry very different associated meanings, and these will vary too for different groups: a term that would be considered derogatory if used by an outsider might be used as a term of defiance by an insider. The parents of a child diagnosed with, say, mild autism has to decide whether to accept the label, with the attendant benefits of government support for therapy, or to reject it so as to not predispose the behaviour of teachers and others in a negative way toward their child. When we name something, we give it a label; that label is cognitively and emotively evaluated, and it has action consequences (O'Brien, 2006).

Your labels will impact analysis

The kind of codes you create, reflected in the labels you give them, impacts on subsequent accessibility of evidence needed to support an argument. Use specific labels for passages of data, such as *dislike* and *carelessness*, rather than labels that just point to the general class of things being described, such as *attitudes* or *behaviour*. Coding with general class labels 'tells you little about the participant's meaning or action' and creates the danger of losing an insider view (Charmaz, 2006: 49). In practical terms, use of such categories means you are unable to even start to identify meaningful or clear patterns of association between what is at one code and what is at another without repetitive and detailed rereading, and possibly recoding.

At the same time, your labelling (and consequently, coding) can be too narrowly defined for some purposes; for example, in most cases it will be sufficient to create a code for *confidence* (for example) as one element or dimension of personality, rather than create separate codes for positive expressions of confidence and for lack of confidence (coding as *personality* would be too general). Very narrow codes limit analysis if they do not gather sufficient data to give a rounded or balanced sense of what is going on there and of what the critical dimensions are within that (e.g., there might be something other than just positive or negative ways of expressing confidence). If, however, you wanted to use your coding to test 'if–then' propositions about having or not having confidence (to continue the same example), then you might need to code for directional detail as well.

Keeping a balance between generality and specificity of labels and codes benefits from practice and experience. It involves judgements in relation to the purposes of the project, the nature of the data, and your anticipated analysis processes. As noted by Emerson et al.:

> While it is often useful to begin coding by focusing on a term in the notes – whether the fieldworker's or a member's – the fieldworker must transform that term so that it references a more general category. Yet, at the other extreme, it is not useful to use very general categories as codes. For example, it would not be helpful to code as 'social control' staff procedures for searching residents' rooms for 'buzzes' and other contraband in a reform school. This category is too general and without specific connection to the events described in the notes. But, a code like 'staff control – room searches' would categorise these staff activities as a specific kind of control and perhaps stimulate the field researcher to think about and identify other forms of 'staff control'. (1995: 150)[1]

---

[1]If using QDA software, two codes (room searches and staff control) would be applied to the same text to capture both the action (or strategy) and its purpose.

In practical terms, using qualitative analysis software for coding rather than coding on paper or using general purpose software will give you added flexibility to merge, split, rearrange, and recode coded material as your analysis (and your thought processes) develop.

Naming broad topic areas

Using broad topic codes that have been defined by your research questions is *one* way of getting started, especially if you are feeling a bit unsure just yet about the idea of interpreting data.[2] You are likely to use them (if at all) on larger chunks of data, and you can probably expect to rework them as you move further into your project. Sorting passages (large or small) into broad topic categories is seen as appropriate:

- as a starting strategy for organising your data and ideas, to be followed by more detailed coding of relevant sections (Box 6.1);
- when the text can be clearly divided into sections dealing with different topics, such as occurs with responses to open-ended questions from a survey, with data from a structured interview, or where a theory specifies specific features to look for;
- as a way to obtain an overview of the material you already have on various topics to determine whether you will need more data to extend or clarify any of them;
- to identify passages suitable for detailed analytic attention using narrative, discourse, or conversation analysis;
- to identify the structural elements of a narrative;
- if not all of the material you have is relevant to the current project. Using broadly defined categories allows you to 'park' things for later consideration; this reduces the obsessive need to code everything in detail without losing access, either presently or in the future, to potentially relevant passages.

                 ┐ **Box 6.1** ┌

Starting with topic codes

Katey de Gioia (2003) explored the continuity of infant care behaviours between home and child care for culturally diverse families for her PhD. She began by coding whole paragraphs relating to sleeping and feeding from within her transcripts, as presumed key concerns and contexts for infant care. Working, then, within these passages, she found parents' concerns were not so much about particular or culturally specific ways of managing sleeping or feeding, but rather about the quality of their communication with the staff of the child care centre – an issue that cut across all aspects of infant care. This then set the direction for further interviewing and analysis.

---

[2]The alternative is to start with one or another form of open coding (see later).

Coding context

This is not necessarily the most exciting kind of coding to be doing, but it can be very necessary.

In most of your projects there will be passages within the text that need to be specifically coded to capture the context of what is being said or done, such as a time period, the stage of development being referred to, the setting, who else is present, or perhaps the type of activity. For example, in coding children's behaviour, it may also be relevant to code whether this behaviour occurred in the classroom, the playground, the community, or at home. In coding Shane's and other researchers' documents, I included a code on almost every passage to identify whether they were talking about events and experiences related to *becoming* a researcher or *being* a researcher. Contextual codes then provide a basis for comparison when considering more specific aspects of what is occurring (Box 6.2).

Where an aspect of context applies to a whole source or case, for example, these interviews were conducted in a rural area whereas those were in the city, or where data were collected at different time periods, then this kind of contextual information will usually be recorded as attribute (variable) data relating to the source or case, and not as a code (cf. Chapter 3, section 'Recording sample details for analysis').

Box 6.2

Coding context

When James Hunter studied the decision to outsource the meter reading activities of a publicly listed Australian energy company (cf. Box 3.8), he coded what people filling different roles in the company (decision makers, decision implementers, employees, and contractors) said about actions taken, feelings evoked, and views developed, in relation to the change in systems. The stage in the process each was referring to was also coded throughout the same texts. This meant that all actions, feelings, and perspectives could be examined in relation to whether they occurred in the leadup to the decision to outsource, immediately after that decision (less than one year), or into the medium term after the commencement of outsourcing (two to four years – see Table 9.2) (Hunter & Cooksey, 2004).

Naming codes to capture substance and meaning

Many of the strategies related to working with the detail of a text are drawn from writing on grounded theory. This does *not* mean everyone using these strategies is using grounded theory methodology. Rather it has come about because grounded theorists have elaborated and discussed their coding strategies in more detail (and more transparently) than has occurred for most other approaches, and because many of these strategies are generic and equally applicable across a range of situations and approaches. From one of the more prolific writers on grounded theory methods:

> Techniques and procedures are tools to be used by the researcher as he or she sees fit to solve methodological problems. *They are not a set of directives to be rigidly adhered to.* No researcher should become so obsessed with following a set of coding procedures that the fluid and dynamic nature of qualitative analysis is lost. *The analytic process is first and foremost a thinking process.* It requires stepping into the shoes of the other and trying to see the world from their perspective. Analysis should be relaxed, flexible, and driven by insights gained through interaction with data rather than being structured and based on procedures. (Corbin, 2009: 40–1, emphasis added)

Using separate codes for each element of what is going on in a passage (each 'slice') rather than attempting to find a single comprehensive code often makes the task of naming codes easier, although this can be at the risk of losing a sense of the whole. Vigilance and strategies to maintain that perspective, such as recording thoughts about links between codes in memos, are therefore needed. Computer software, if it is used, makes reconstructing wholes more feasible. In whatever system you develop, flexibility is needed so that material can be recoded or combined as the project unfolds in order to reflect emerging understanding and facilitate further analysis.

As you work, keep a record of descriptions for codes used and categories developed. If you are working on paper, keep a codebook (cf. Chapter 5); if on computer, enter descriptions into the properties dialogue or memo field for each code, and print as a reference list. Descriptions assist in clarification of what you mean by the code, and set its boundaries. The record of how you were using that code is useful:

- for consistency in coding;
- as a refresher if you have a period away from the data and then come back to them;
- for developing consistent coding among team members in larger projects; and
- when people have very 'messy' coding systems, because the exercise of ensuring each code has a clear description sharpens thinking about that code, and helps with rationalisation (or elaboration) of codes.

Strategies to break open the data (open coding)

The terms 'microanalysis', 'open coding', and 'line-by-line coding' are used similarly to emphasise a close level of attention being given to the text during the initial phases of coding, with the purpose of *opening up* the data. Exactly how that is achieved varies for different analysts.

Open coding of these types is done selectively, and for a limited amount of data only – the first document, or selected passages from within documents as needed. None of those who developed these practices suggest working slavishly in this way through an entire set of texts. The purpose is to generate ideas and categories; further coding then involves exploring and applying those ideas or codes as the sample is purposively extended and further text is reviewed. In this process, the analyst is looking for confirmation and contradiction, dominance, patterns of association, or extension of the concepts being coded, while noting in detailed memos the variations in their use and the circumstances of those variations. If new concepts are seen at a later time, then these can be added, but these need also to be evaluated in the light of previous as well as later data and understandings.

Line-by-line coding

The popularised (but less often practised?) idea of *line-by-line coding* involves printing the text of a document with a wide margin and writing a word or phrase, preferably involving a gerund (an 'ing' word[3]), to 'name' each and every line of text. The value of the approach lies in ensuring the coder takes account of everything that is recorded in that item of data (Box 6.3). Charmaz (2006), Gibbs (2007), Saldaña (2009), and Hodgkinson (2008) provide examples which demonstrate both benefits in and problems of this approach. The approach is somewhat more disciplined and focused than off-the-top-of-your-head marginal words or phrases, but often appears to be more like annotating text as a way of noting detail and generating ideas, rather than coding, particularly where there has been no attempt to be consistent in the words or phrases that are applied to very similar passages. Furthermore, if this type of coding is being done as part of a grounded theory or other symbolic interactionist approach, it is critical that what is being said is viewed and interpreted (as much as is possible) from the perspective of the speaker, and that the phrases or codes used reflect that, rather than the perspective or experience of the analyst. Ask yourself: 'What were *they* meaning when they said that?' rather than, 'What am I seeing here in what they say?'

| Box 6.3 |

Line-by-line coding

Susan is here talking about being a scientist at a new university.

being involved; breadth of interest	I'm involved in a broad stream – a wide variety of
history of engagement	things. This is mainly because when I first came here
non-research environment	our emphasis wasn't on research, but I really enjoy
enjoying research, being a scientist	research, I think it is part of being a scientist and

---

[3]More technically, a noun formed from a verb.

lack of time and resources	because of the time constraints and the facilities I
making choices	decided to collaborate with another person – with
collaborating	Brian, and we worked together because two heads
making a choice	and four hands are better than less. So I decided to
staying with choice	work together and that's the way things have been,
	that's been more or less a loose umbrella over our
different backgrounds	projects. By training I'm an organic chemist and he is
	a co-ordination chemist. So our backgrounds aren't all
making difference work for benefit	that similar but it's been useful because we've been
benefiting from others' input	able to sort of benefit from other people's skills in that
	sort of a working relationship, so that's been good.
variety of projects	And because of that, we had a number of projects,
varying leadership	some of them are more Brian and some of them are
playing? enjoying?	more me, although we both dabble in them both.

Microanalysis

The analyst taking a *microanalytic* approach engages in an exhaustive examination of almost every word or phrase used in the passage(s) being considered, exploring all possible meanings, why the speaker might have used that word rather than an alternative, and how this word is similar to or different from others used (Corbin & Strauss, 2008: e.g., 60–3). The results of this exercise are recorded in memos and in codes which identify the dimensions embedded in the concepts represented by the words used (Box 6.4). *The purpose here is not to come up with a definitive set of codes that sums up what this person is saying, but to use what the person is saying to open up a wide range of issues that can be addressed in further interviews.* Through focusing on dimensions – the structure of the issues being investigated – questions to pursue are identified, leading to theoretical sampling, and codes are generated for application to further documents. You might simply create a code for each dimension, or you might create codes for the various positions along the dimensions, even though the current text is positioned at only one of them (Gibbs, 2007; Strauss, 1987).

Similarly, when coding for something quite specific within a more general category, one might think about other specific examples that could belong to the same general category, and either note these in a memo, or create 'anticipatory' codes for them. For example, 'latecomers' to a theatre are one type of audience, and recognising this generates thoughts about other audience types that might be considered; observation of a strategy used to manage latecomers leads to thinking about and watching for other strategies that might be used (Emerson et al., 1995; Gibbs, 2007). Working in detail like this will initially generate a large number of codes (and memos), not all of which will 'receive' text. (Hmmm, why did nobody talk in that way about that?) The list will be refined later.

| Box 6.4 |

Microanalysis

Annie was asked how she 'got started in research'. Her response, 'I can't say I ever really planned to get into research', triggers several ideas to consider:

- 'I can't say ...' carries an implication of honesty in responding to the question; others might be able to say they planned it. Is being enthusiastic and deliberate about research expected in this situation, so that one might be tempted to say what isn't true?
- 'Ever ... planned': when does the planning happen? How long does it take?
- Degrees of planning – from a carefully executed career plan to no planning. Where does 'really planned' fit into that scale? What would it mean to really plan? How does planning relate to agency and choice? Can someone else plan for you?
- The degree of agency one exercises in becoming involved in research: is it a deliberate choice? An inevitability? Or something, as Annie suggested elsewhere, that you can simply drift into, that just happens?
- 'Get into' – suggests being caught up in, enmeshed, a level of engagement that is different from just 'doing' (compare getting into dancing with casually going to a dance evening, or getting into cooking compared with doing cooking).

Use contrasts to clarify meaning

Thinking about opposites, perhaps substituting an opposite term in what someone says, can help to clarify meaning. Thinking about the opposite of 'fun' in the context of an interview about wellbeing at work suggested boredom or tedium, leading to the idea that what this participant meant by fun was being mentally stimulated (i.e., more than simply feeling pleasure or enjoying oneself), with boredom resulting from the absence of mental stimulation; thus the opportunity for mental stimulation could be seen as a condition for wellbeing at work (or at least, for this type of work). It is the issue being raised, rather than the individual's position on that issue, that is most relevant when creating codes for qualitative analysis.

Compare and contrast to identify dimensional structure

Dimensions are usually defined in terms of their polar opposites. Observing similarities and differences in how words, phrases, experiences, scenes, incidents, ideas, or pictures are used, viewed, or told in relation to an object or experience will alert you to dimensions that structure it (Box 6.5). If you don't have further examples in your data to use as a basis for comparison, compare with a theoretical example, an imaginary example, or with one drawn from other experience (Corbin & Strauss, 2008). How you use the dimensions you identify – whether you code for the dimension as a whole, or for position on it – will depend on the purpose it is designed to serve and the ways in which it will be used in further analyses.

Box 6.5

From comparisons to dimensions

Each of these statements says something about what it means to think of oneself (to identify) as a researcher, but each does so in a quite different way.

> When I started working for <university research centre> – that's when I started to feel like a researcher, because there was this – even though it was only one tiny little office which people used to think was this large bustling place with lots of researchers in it – it felt like I was part of something – it had a reason for being and it did have a purpose – so then I started to feel like a researcher.

> I haven't come from an academic research background at all … I've always been paid to be a researcher and I'm a researcher when I have a job to be a researcher. Before that I was just studying and bumming around.

> I think if anything I would see myself now as a writer rather than a researcher because I've been doing it so long and I've got so old that it's possible to delegate a lot of the hands-on work to others …

> I would do it anyway – paid or not. I feel immensely privileged to be one of the few people in the world who are getting paid to do what they love.

> So I guess for me [the inclination to research] has always been there.

Dimensions of identification as a researcher from these passages which may or may not prove useful for further investigation (and interrelationship) include:

- role definition: from being self-defined to being defined by others (also role adoption?);
- engagement: level of involvement in the day-to-day tasks of research;
- temporality: from beginning and ending to just going on, always there;
- perspective: from cognitive to emotive.

Sorting already coded data across demographic subgroups or different contexts in comparative analyses sometimes reveals additional dimensions of the coded concept as a useful by-product of the wider insights gained from such analyses (cf. Chapter 9). For example, when I compared scientists' with social scientists' expressions of satisfaction in relation to doing research in one particular set of data, I found that the source of their satisfaction differed in a consistent way: scientists' satisfaction was in response to having agency (i.e., making things happen) while social scientists expressed satisfaction in relation to achievement in conducting the research or as an outcome of their research. These differences in source of satisfaction, were not associated with any other demographic variables and had not previously been apparent or considered.

For situations where people, systems, or other phenomena are in direct conflict, Saldaña (2009: 95) suggested using 'versus codes' which are a special case of dimensional codes. Doing so alerts the user to three aspects of any conflict, with each warranting codes: one aspect identifies the stakeholders in the conflict (us–them); another captures how each side perceives and acts toward the conflict (your way versus our way); the third codes the central issue in the conflict (e.g., autonomy–control).

Use *in vivo* codes

Using words or phrases used by participants as labels for codes to capture the essence of what the participants are saying in their own terms is often associated with line-by-line coding and microanalysis, where they are termed *in vivo* codes. Saldaña (2009) recommends enclosing the names of these types of codes in quotation marks as an indication of their having been drawn directly from participants' speech. In current literature (and software), both the term and the practice have become somewhat overused and of less utility than in Strauss' original concept of *in vivo* codes, described as:

> the behaviours or processes which will explain to the analyst how the basic problem of the actors is resolved or processed ... [They] have two characteristics: analytic usefulness and imagery. Their analytic usefulness relates the given category to others, with specified meaning, and carries it forward easily in formulation of the theory. Imagery is useful insofar as the analyst does not have to keep illustrating the code in order to give it meaning. (1987: 33)[4]

Overdependence on *in vivo* codes as currently used 'can limit your ability to transcend to more conceptual and theoretical levels of analysis and insight' (Saldaña, 2009: 77). Where they are descriptive and unique to one person, the coder needs to move on from them quite quickly to generate a more analytical code. Thus, for example, 'drifted into it' and 'really went for it' are reasonably self-explanatory and could be more generally useful, but as an *in vivo* code 'sits under their skin' or 'stuffed as individuals' would require interpretation and modification to become useful for coding other participants' text or for analysis.

---

[4]Strauss did not distinguish between *in vivo* codes and emic codes.

Tag Indigenous (emic) terms

Indigenous codes, similarly, are drawn from terms used by participants. In contrast to the transitory nature of *in vivo* expressions, indigenous or emic terms are those used by participants to describe something familiar in the environment or group within which they move (refer to the discussion about *bludging* in Chapter 4, section 'Explore language'). They are most commonly used and discussed, therefore, in ethnographic research, where they can be seen as concepts that reveal tacit understandings of the cultural environment. For example, *supercrip* is a term that was used rather disparagingly by people with spinal injuries to describe someone who had become famous for some kind of special achievement developed consequent to their injury and who was constantly held up to them as a role model during their rehabilitation (Kemp, 1999). The tagging of indigenous and emic terms (including various synonyms or subcategories) serves also as a foundation for establishing folk taxonomies and domain analysis (Bernard & Ryan, 2010).

Note repetitions and patterns

Expressions that are repeated and themes that keep re-emerging within an interview are worthy of special attention. The tendency of people to repeat themselves has three implications for coding: if you miss something important, it will come up again; repeated words or ideas point to concepts that should be coded (Box 6.6); and variations in the use of a word or phrase provide an opportunity for comparison.

Box 6.6

Noting and interpreting repetitions

Interviews from the Researchers project data reveal informative examples of repetitive use of words or phrases:

- Frank repeats the term 'strong' when talking about both his thesis and his supervisor. His repeated use of the term is clearly linked with the importance of status to him (note his later ambition), and his inheritance of status as a graduate student from having a supervisor of high status.
- Shane repeats the words 'I decided' with respect to choosing to study history and to engage in a research project in history four times within the two initial paragraphs of his story. The words 'I decided' suggest a very deliberate choice on his part, yet there is a possible contradiction to his apparent instrumentality in choosing a career in that, each time, his decision was associated with an also repeated comment about being encouraged by significant others (lecturers).

Ask questions

Asking questions generates ideas, focuses attention, and increases sensitivity to what is going on in the data. The most obvious question to ask is, 'What is this all about?' to get at the major concern being expressed in the data. Having established a 'what', one might then ask 'who', 'when', 'where', 'how', 'why', and 'so what' questions around that. Or ask questions related to Strauss' (1987) 'coding paradigm': what actions, interactions, or strategies are occurring? Under what conditions? With what consequences (how does the person then construct the situation)? Questions such as these help to ensure thoroughness of coding and facilitate analysis by pointing to relationships in the data. Each of these questions will generate one or more codes.

As ethnographers, Emerson et al. emphasise questions for fieldwork data that focus on processes rather than causes or motives – on what is occurring rather than why:

- What are people doing? What are they trying to accomplish?
- How, exactly, do they do this? What specific means and/or strategies do they use?
- How do members talk about, characterize, and understand what is going on?
- What assumptions are they making? (1995: 146)

They note: 'These questions reflect a sensitivity to the *practical* concerns, conditions, and constraints that actors confront and deal with in their everyday lives and actions' and they 'help specify the meanings and points of view of those under study' (1995: 147).

Lyn Richards (2009) proposed that by asking three easy-to-remember questions about any passage in the data, you will be able to identify a topic of interest, and then abstract from that to a more general concept. Her first question is simply to ask 'What's interesting?' as a way of identifying a passage on which to focus. Then, 'Why is it interesting?' This leads to a descriptive code, and possibly a note in the margin or a memo. The third question in this sequence is the most critical, and in my experience, the most useful question one can ever ask while coding. The question 'Why am I interested in that?' will lift you 'off the page' and into thinking (and coding) at a more conceptual or abstract level (Box 6.7).

┌─────────┐ **Box 6.7** ┌─────────┐

Moving from description to abstraction

Why is Shane's report of being encouraged by a lecturer interesting? Initially, descriptively, because he was *encouraged*, because that encouragement came from a *lecturer*, and it was during his *undergraduate years* (generating three codes). Why am I interested in that? Clearly it points to a specific trigger and a motivator in the development of his interest in research and in so doing raises the more generally applicable issue of *the relevance of significant others in our development as researchers.* Then I observed that each time this comes up in Shane's story, he quickly goes on to point out his own enjoyment, implying that although this encouragement from significant others was influential, it was quickly superseded by his own pleasure. More abstractly, this whole sequence might then be developed as a memo about *internalisation of research as a valued activity*, with an additional code for *internalisation* (or *adoption* or *identification*).

Brainstorm interpretations

Sharing a brief sample of (de-identified) data with others in a 'brainstorming' session at various stages during the coding process has long been recognised as a highly productive way of breaking through barriers faced in interpreting and coding data (Boyatzis, 1998; Turner, 1981), and in locating 'buried treasure' (Saldaña, 2009). If one is a member of a team then this will occur naturally, but isolated graduate students might need to seek out others with whom they can do this from a wider field; a mix of disciplines is not a problem (Richards, 2009). The data sample from this session can then be compared with others, to see if the codes generated 'resonate' (Fielding, 2008; see Box 6.8).

Box 6.8

Catching ideas from others

I had asked Shane if he could identify a time when research became of particular interest to him. He responded, 'Yes I can, with precision', followed by an elaboration of when and how this occurred. I recorded this simply as indicating a critical turning point experience – until I was engaged in a discussion with some workshop participants around this sample of text. Their response to his reply, in contrast, was to see it as indicative of his personality, pointing to the careful, attention-to-detail way in which he thought about things. When reflecting on this characteristic, I noted how he later described going about his work of identifying and carefully piecing together archival snippets of information and photographs for analysis of social history, and saw why he, with this personality trait, might become so passionate about doing this particular kind of research.

Interpret linguistic features

How people say things can be as important as what they say; language is both symbolic and social. Interpretive analysis can benefit therefore from taking account of forms of expression used, and the way in which the accounts given or situations observed are structured. Linguistic features point to the meaning of events or experiences for the teller. Are they using metaphors and analogies; how do they use pronouns and articles; are they making statements, asking questions, or pronouncing declarations; do they suggest what they say is opinion or fact; and do the tenses they use for verbs refer to the past, the present, or the future (Fairclough, 2003; Morse, 1999; see Box 6.9)? For example, a school principal might variously refer to the staff of the school in which he works as *the* staff, *my* staff, or *our* staff, each of which has very different implications for interpreting his relationship with his staff. Pronouns such as 'my', 'we', and 'our' indicate level and type of ownership or involvement; articles ('a' or 'the') specify a generalised or a particularised object, event, or experience. Each of these pronouns or articles gives different meaning and intent to the words to which they are attached, with consequent significance for interpretation and coding of that text. (See also Chapter 7 for more on narrative and linguistic features.)

Box 6.9

Observing linguistic features in text

Janice Morse (1999) and her associates investigated the giving of comfort by nurses when dealing with trauma in the emergency department of a hospital. They found that when someone experienced trauma to a part of their body, they used objectified terms to disassociate from their experience of extreme pain. For example, a linesman struck by lightning while up a pole used 'the hand' when talking about the injury to his hand, but 'my hand' when mentioning the same body part immediately before the injury occurred, even within the same sentence: 'my right hand was up high – so naturally it entered *the right* the most' and reverting again to 'my hand' once he had recovered (Morse & Mitcham, 1998, quoted in Morse, 1999: 397).

Employ theoretical or a priori codes

As an alternative or addition to using codes derived directly from the data or your interpretation of them, if you have already undertaken a substantive review of the literature, or are building on previous studies, you will be able to generate a start list of codes covering the range of phenomena you expect to meet in your data; Miles and Huberman (1994) suggest as many as 50 to 60. These will assist in ensuring that your coding links with important research questions, and can be done without inhibiting you from capturing fresh ideas. Alternatively, generate a start list by brainstorming the issues and concerns raised by your questions, ensuring that all the terms included in your questions are represented in the coding system. These codes do not have to be treated as prescriptive, and data should not be 'forced' into them: no data are data, too. The chances are that you will end up modifying or adding to your list, in any case.

Patton (2002: 456) referred to codes brought to the data by the analyst as sensitising concepts. He noted the need to look at how these became manifest and were given meaning in the context of the data. Patton also raised the possibility of using such codes to prompt a fresh perspective by 'turning them around', citing the example provided by Conroy (1987). In this study the concept of victimisation was used to show how police officers experienced negative consequences such as isolation, detachment, cynicism, anger, and sadness through their job. Even within the process of developing grounded theory 'we do not have to discover all new categories nor ignore all categories in the literature that might apply' (Glaser, 1978: 148), as long as you don't 'force' the data into existing categories.

A number of disciplines have pre-existing protocols for coding which might be applied to new data, such as the Outline of Cultural Materials developed in anthropology, Bloom's taxonomy of educational terms, or a range of established dramaturgical, motif, and other literary codes (Saldaña, 2009). In others, a coding protocol might be developed specifically to test established practice or theoretical propositions (Box 6.10). Use of these specialised coding systems tends to be prescriptive, and they do not have general application beyond the specific purpose for which they were developed.

Box 6.10

Developing and using a theoretically based coding protocol

Butow and Lobb (2004) undertook a detailed examination of the process of initial genetic counselling sessions with women at high risk of breast cancer because of their family history. They based their coding system on established clinical practice guidelines, a semi-structured survey of practitioners in the field, literature covering both general genetic counselling and counselling for breast and ovarian cancer, and the broader doctor–patient communication literature. It was then piloted on transcribed audiotapes from a total of 14 sessions covering affected and unaffected women and each of seven clinicians or counsellors. Their slightly revised, detailed coding system and associated codebook covered important facts given and received during the exchange and behaviours designed to facilitate either active involvement in the consultation and/or expression of emotional concerns. A record of the presence or absence of each listed component in the coding system, applied across the entire sample of 158 consultations, revealed that the counsellors managed quite well to facilitate understanding through questions and analogies, but that they encouraged limited active involvement apart from initial agenda setting. It also revealed that most discussion of emotional concerns was initiated by the patient.

Code values

Bernard and Ryan (2010: 87) argue for the inclusion of (scalar) values within coding systems, as well as index (concept or theme) codes. These code for the amount of something as well as the mention of it. These might be as simple as yes/no values, or they might make up an ordinal scale from, say, very strong through to very weak, where each value is set up as a separate code.[5]

The recently developed Dedoose software,[6] which is a web-based tool designed for mixed methods applications, offers the capacity to add code-specific ratings or weights to any coded passage, with these then being available for data visualisation, filtering, and comparative analysis. MAXQDA provides a similar solution when value codes are needed. Each time a code is applied to a text segment, a strength score with a scale value of 0 to 100 can be applied. These scores can then be used to filter or sort retrieved passages.

Automating coding

Automating routine coding

If you are using computer software, most programs now offer ways of 'automatically' coding larger chunks of pre-processed text based on field delimiters (e.g., MAXQDA) or heading styles (e.g., NVivo). Headings or field delimiters

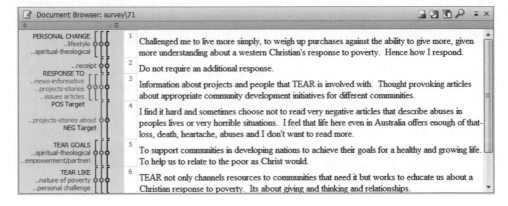

Figure 6.1   Open-ended survey questions auto coded for question asked (shown in CAPS) in MAXQDA

---

[5]To avoid creating a 'viral' coding system, rather than setting up repetitive value codes tied to each relevant concept or theme code, create a single set of codes for values separately from the concept and theme codes, and code relevant text with both the concept code *and* the value code. How strongly each concept was experienced or represented can then be ascertained by intersecting the concept codes with the value codes in a cross-tabulation.

[6]www.dedoose.com.

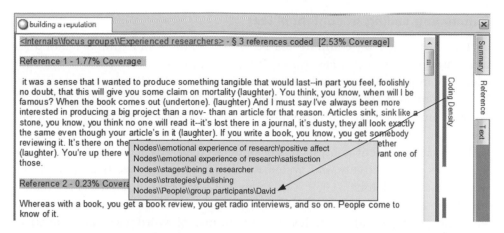

Figure 6.2   Checking which focus group speaker said what about 'building a reputation' in NVivo

Note: Hovering with the mouse pointer over the Coding Density bar (part of the Coding Stripes display) reveals what codes were used on the adjacent passage.

might relate to the questions that were asked (Figure 6.1), who was speaking in a group interview or discussion, the sections of a report or submission, or the site or timing of an event as recorded in field notes. Alternatively for structured survey data, both programs will now import a 'dataset' prepared in spreadsheet or database format, and auto code cases, attributes, and responses to questions, based on data in rows and columns.

Using the auto coding facilities offered by the software in this way makes good sense in that it deals very efficiently with the rather boring task of this routine type of coding, leaving you more time to work through and think in detail about the content of the data. When responses to questions have been auto coded, the coder then has a choice between coding content from the retrieved text for each question, in turn (i.e., coding the issues covered in one question at a time), or coding in the usual way from each source in turn. Automatically generated codes can be employed in comparative analyses, or used simply as a way of rapidly checking contextual information when you are reviewing a particular category of responses (Figure 6.2).

Data in variable form (e.g., categorical or numeric or date) that apply to entire sources or cases in a project can be set up in your computer database as attributes of those sources or cases. This can be done interactively, one value at a time, or a whole set of variable data can be imported as attributes (rather than text) from a spreadsheet such that it is then applied to the relevant sources or cases. This allows data to be classified in multiple ways, to facilitate sorting coded data into comparative tables based on the values of each attribute (cf. Chapter 9).

Automating coding of content in text

Earlier (in Chapter 4), computer-based word counting and similar techniques were suggested as one of several exploratory strategies. Now we will consider using a computer to automatically identify and count all instances of occurrence of one or more words or phrases in a body of text as a strategy for coding and analysing text – a procedure that is generally referred to as content analysis.

Historically, content analysis has been defined as 'any technique for making inferences by objectively and systematically identifying specified characteristics of messages' (Holsti, 1969: 14). Today the term content analysis is broadly applied to a range of strategies for text analysis, almost always involving use of a computer, large-scale samples of text, counts of word use, and statistical analysis of the results. Results are then interpreted in the light of the research questions and the cultural or political environment of the sample. It has been applied, most commonly, to analysis of large bodies of data such as newspaper editorials and articles, business and legal reports, and short, descriptive, survey responses.

There are now numerous automated content analysis software options available to researchers who have digitised data, as well as word frequency and text searching facilities within most QDA software. These produce coding or codable finds of words or phrases from a body of data without the researcher's needing to work through each separate text. Most programs offer keyword-in-context (KWIC) options, providing either the full line of text surrounding the word, or a specified number or words either side of the keyword. They also allow you to specify stop words (words that you do not want to count, such as 'are', 'be', 'and', 'the', 'this'), and some provide options for collating words with the same stem (so that, for example, 'help', 'helper', and 'helping' are treated as a single unit; cf. Figure 4.5).

Text search facilities within QDA software usually allow you to search for either particular or alternative words within the same query, such that you find all instances of that word (or related words), in context, either throughout your data or in a specified subset of your data. You then have the option of saving the finds as a coding category, but typically you will need to 'clean up' what is saved, because some finds will prove to be irrelevant. Some software will allow a query for nearby occurrence of more than one word, so as to make the search more targeted. For example, a search for *enjoy** in the same paragraph as *research*, using a compound query in NVivo, will limit finds for 'enjoy', 'enjoys', 'enjoyed', 'enjoying', or 'enjoyment' to when these are used in the same linguistic context as 'research' rather than 'sport' or 'business'.

Although it can be used with any kind of text, and finds can be reviewed in context, coding using word counting or text search facilities is not an appropriate substitute for the kind of interpretive, interactive coding of text described earlier. It *might* be appropriate and useful when all that is needed is rapid location, review, coding, or counting of:

- topics covered in short-answer responses from survey data, where it will give you an overview of the most commonly reported issues or experiences, or it can point to interesting ideas to explore further (Box 6.11);
- specific terms used, such as technical terms, or metaphors or emic terms;
- long documents such as reports, interviews, or articles, to sift through and identify passages most relevant to the study, perhaps for further coding using more traditional coding techniques (Box 6.12);
- interviews or other data where conclusions have been established on a subset of available data, and you simply want to check the remainder to ensure there are no contrary instances described;
- as a means of checking the thoroughness of coding (search for instances of a word or words, less ['AND NOT'] what has been coded already); and
- for comparative analysis of texts, for example, to compare changes in a report since a previous enquiry, or as a test of common authorship.

🛈 The principal problem with using text search or word lists as a basis for coding is that potentially relevant passages where the keyword is not used will be missed, and many irrelevant passages might be found. Spelling and typing errors will cause 'misses' as well. Accuracy can be improved if some interactive coding has already been done, to identify key concepts and the alternative words that have been used to express those concepts.

Box 6.11

Using qualitative software to explore and code survey responses

MAXDictio, an add-on module for MAXQDA, was used to explore the words used by respondents to five open-ended questions in a supporter survey for TEAR Australia, an overseas aid organisation (Figure 6.3). Selecting a found word allows the user to explore the words as they appear in their original context, and if wished, to then code them. Marking words as stop words will ensure that if the query is rerun, these words will not be listed in further searches through this type of data. (Specific dictionaries and stop lists can be created for future use in different datasets.)

(Continued)

(Continued)

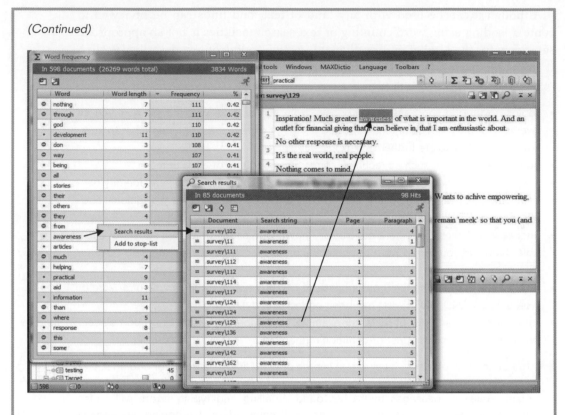

Figure 6.3   Word counts and associated content for one question in a survey, using MAXDictio

---

| Box 6.12 |

Coping with cancer: sport or war?

Clive Seale (2001) used a combination of computer-based content analysis and qualitative coding to study the use of 'struggle' language and sporting metaphors in media stories about people with cancer. He extracted 358 texts specifically depicting a person with cancer from the articles, separately for each gender. Using content analysis software,[7] he created a profile of words used, from which linguistic terms associated with military, sports, and other metaphors were identified. Further coding of the context in which the words appeared drew on this sensitisation to language to provide a review of the different ways in which struggle language was applied, with and without sporting connotations. Reports of people experiencing different types of cancer and in differing situations were compared. Subsets of these coded texts were further analysed to provide a quantification of

---

[7]At the time he used Concordance software (www.concordancesoftware.co.uk) for the content analysis component of his project, and NVivo for the qualitative coding. He could now use MAXQDA or NVivo for the entire analysis.

terms used in those different situations. This iterative procedure, drawing on the strengths of both discourse analysis and content analysis, enabled Seale to dispute previous theory and argue that the language used to describe people's experience with cancer was more sporting than militaristic in orientation. Seale suggests that sport, seen as a life and death struggle, is more acceptable to contemporary (Western) sensibilities than militaristic images. Those who heroically display courage and determination to win on the sports field are recorded on a roll of honour, for example lauding psychological (or other) gains along the way, even if the physical struggle is ultimately lost.

Commercial, general purpose content analysis software, designed to replace interactive coding, is customisable. At the simplest level, customisable programs have a facility to identify stop words and/or create custom dictionaries, so that only words of interest to the researcher at the time are found and alternative words for the same concept (synonyms) can be treated as a single entity. In languages such as English, the existence of homonyms creates considerable difficulty for automatic categorisation; words can have different meanings depending on whether they are used as a verb or an adjective (such as *appropriate*) or if they appear at the beginning or end of a sentence, for example. More advanced programs can discern different meanings for the same word depending on the context, through using paired words, and they have dictionaries in which synonyms have been defined.[8] A typical content analysis dictionary will involve around 500 to 5000 terms, with the larger dictionaries used to process, for example, many thousands of newspaper articles per second. Context specific programs examine co-occurrences of a smaller number of terms and include complex syntactical rules to determine relationships between the concepts that are embodied within statements (e.g., Carley, 1993).

Another type of content analysis program will group or categorise the data for the researcher, with categories based initially on the regularity of co-occurrence of words. These, too, can be modified by the user. The text analysis component of the Statistical Package for the Social Sciences (SPSS), for example, will categorise short-answer responses to open-ended questions in order that they can be incorporated into the statistical analysis with pre-categorised or scaled responses. Other programs will show words or categories in diagrammatic relationship to each other, with or without access to surrounding text (e.g., Box 6.13).

Developing a coding system

Typically, as you work through your data, you will develop your codes in three ways:

1 To start with, unless you are working with theoretically derived *a priori* codes, you will be creating codes to catch ideas as they happen. The list grows, and it becomes more difficult to remember if you've already seen and labelled a particular concept, and if so, how you labelled it. (I generated 60 codes from just the first two three-page sources in the Researchers project.) Management becomes an issue.

---

[8]For example, the *General Inquirer*, at www.wjh.harvard.edu/~inquirer.

| Box 6.13 |

Mapping and interpreting concepts with Leximancer

Leximancer (www.leximancer.com) is an example of commercially available software that will display found concepts in a series of overlapping concentric circles to show the relationship between them (Figure 6.4). The size of the word in the display is representative of its frequency of occurrence, and its location shows its proximity in the text to surrounding words. Double-clicking on a word will open occurrences of the word in the original text; text where two or more words occur in proximity can be requested. The qualities identified by Leximancer (for this very descriptive project) broadly concurred with those identified through coding and interpretive analysis (cf. Chapter 8).

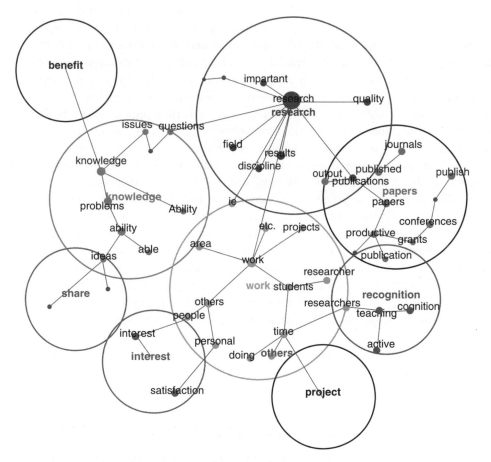

Figure 6.4   Qualities of high-performing researchers, identified using Leximancer

2   Next, you start to sort and connect both existing and new codes into categories and subcategories. These reflect the structure of the data, that is, the kinds of things that are being considered.

3 Additionally (perhaps later), you will construct metacodes or more abstract codes to reflect either overarching ideas or higher-order concepts, or to identify broader, more complex themes running through the data (cf. Chapter 8).

If you are now at the stage where you have been working for a while, it will help if you organise the codes you are creating into some kind of taxonomy or catalogue or hierarchical system – a system of categories and subcategories. In such systems, a category at a higher level describes the contents, in general terms, of the items below it. Everything that is true about the code at the top level must also be true about any codes below it, and similarly as one moves down the levels. Each layer in the hierarchy contains more specific types or subgroups of the item above, and may be 'parent' to more specific items below. Think about how plants or animals are ordered according to family, genus, and species. Within the plant kingdom, the Myrtaceae (myrtle) family includes the genus *Eucalyptus* (commonly known as gum trees), defined by the nature of their flowers and fruit. *Citriodora* (the lemon-scented gum) is one of many species of *Eucalyptus*. All *citriodora* are eucalypts, and but not all eucalypts are lemon scented. We are all used to this kind of cataloguing system, not only though plants and animals, but in libraries, and (perhaps!) in our own filing systems.

Applying this kind of hierarchically organised catalogue or taxonomy to your coding system brings several benefits:

- It creates order: you know where to look to place or find a particular code.
- It brings conceptual clarity to your project: the *kinds of things* you are considering become clearly evident, both to yourself and to anyone else reviewing your work.
- It provides a prompt to code additional aspects of your data as you work, in two ways:

  o you are reminded to code for context as well as content – for emotions or other responses as well as an event or action – because you have grouped codes for each of these types of things;
  o you will be encouraged to think about additional subcategories that might arise in your data.

- It will assist you to identify patterns of relationships in your data. Not only will you be able to ask questions about a particular category or concept through exploring relationships between it and other categories, you will be able to look at the patterns of association between one group of codes and another (e.g., between emotions and events, to see if particular events regularly bring forth particular emotions).

When you build a hierarchical coding system, the items in a particular branch of the system are similar in that they represent the same kind of thing, but they do not necessarily have any other association with each other (Box 6.14). For example, enjoyment and frustration are both emotions but they are not similar in other ways; they are likely to occur in different circumstances and they have different effects. A catalogue or coding system of this type, therefore, is atheoretical in the sense that there is no necessary relationship between the items that are grouped together in the same branch. You will use other methods for identifying and recording theoretical connections as these usually go across branches.

| Box 6.14 |

Shopping for women's clothing

Department stores selling women's clothing use two different methods for arranging their wares. In some, the clothing is organised by brand name, so that all Country Road blouses, skirts, dresses, and suits will be together, all Esprit items will be together, all Sportscraft, Anthea Crawford, Carla Zampatti will be each in their own area, and so on. In other stores, all the shirts and blouses are together, all the skirts together, all the slacks together, and all the suits together. This doesn't mean that the different blouses bear any particular relation to each other, or that this dress is worn with that dress – only that those in the same section are the same kind of thing, and it is useful for clarity and comparison of their respective features to have them all located together. Furthermore, if a new brand of shirt comes along, the store assistant will know exactly where to locate it. By having all the shirts together, I can review all the options, compare sizes, quality, and prices, and basically learn all I might want to know about available shirts. None of these things is easily done when the shirts are distributed across the store according to brand.

    After scanning the various sections, I might then put together a coordinated outfit that comprises a shirt, a pair of slacks, a jacket, and a pair of shoes, each selected out of their respective section. Putting together the outfit is more like making theoretical connections between the codes: these things go together to build a 'smart casual' concept; they are colour coordinated; or they set each other off in some interesting way. When you work with your data, these kinds of connections will not be made evident through the coding system but will be recorded in another way as a set of codes that have been identified as regularly co-occurring or that 'hang together' in some other respect (cf. Chapters 8 and 10).

Filing systems can be arranged in multiple ways: for example, you might file your tax return for 2012 with all your financial statements for 2012, or it might be filed with previous tax returns. The indexes of some recipe books have individual recipes organised by type of ingredient; others are organised by class of final product. Which is more helpful at a particular time will depend on whether you are looking for some way of using a surplus of zucchini, or a cake of some sort to bake for afternoon tea, but if you know the criteria by which the index is organised, you will know where to look. If there is a change in the critical variables around which an index – or your coding system – is built, the final content might look different, *but it will have been constructed using the same principles.* Codebooks should be logical, so that when you need to find a code, it will be obvious which higher-level code it will be under; each item within the catalogue will have a particular location, based on what kind of item it is; and each item will appear *once only* within the catalogue, with all associated data accessible from that one place.

Strategies for seeing structure

For some studies, it is possible to predict in advance the kinds of groupings, or hierarchical trees, that you will use; in others, you will need to experiment and explore. Even if you can predict the broad structure, locating all the specific concepts will not occur automatically; some might remain difficult to catalogue until late in the study. Your coding system will not remain fixed, it will be a work in progress. You will, nevertheless, be able to start developing it once you have a clear idea of where your project is going, and you have established a number of codes. Strategies you might use to help organise your coding system include:

▶ List all the codes you have created, each on a separate piece of paper, and push them around a table until you have them in groups that make sense to you. Provide a label for each group. Alternatively, if you are using software, place all the codes into a model, and push them around the screen until they are in groups (Figure 6.5). Label each group with a name that can be used as a parent or top-level code in the coding hierarchy.

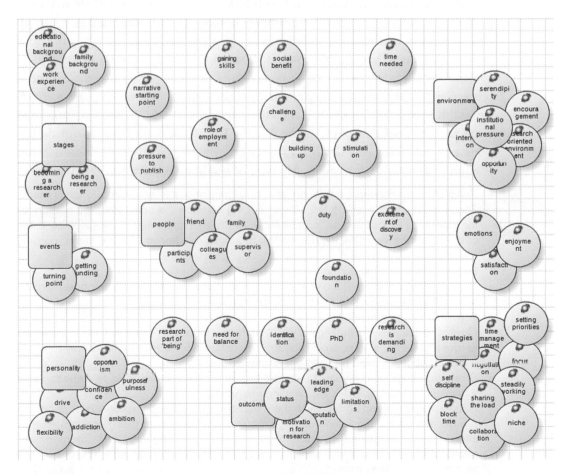

Figure 6.5   Sorting codes into groups using QDA modelling software

▶ Tell your project to someone else. They will hear the *kinds of things* you are talking about, and will help you to identify them.

▶ If you have sorted codes into hierarchical 'trees' using software with visualisation capacity, experiment with putting codes from the same tree into a cluster analysis (e.g., based on words used in the coded material) as a way of seeing which ones don't fit so well (cf. Chapter 10). This is not a definitive test, but it may help you think about how you have grouped them. For example, I had a tree in the Researchers project that I defined as intellectual experience, but uncertainty and passion clustered separately from creativity, challenge, stimulation, fascination, immersion, and curiosity based on the kind of material coded there. On further reflection and examination of the coded text, I decided to reassign those two codes to a tree that was about emotional rather than intellectual experience.

Several authors provide suggestions about the grouping of codes you are likely to use in your coding system. For research projects which deal with the lives and interactions of people, the kinds of labels that most appropriately act as parent codes tend to be general terms that are often quite predictable from the start of the coding process. For example, Lofland (1971) suggested *acts, activities, meanings, participation, relationships,* and *settings* as groupings for codes generated in an ethnographic context. Bogdan and Biklen (1992) listed *setting/context, definition of the situation, perspectives, understandings of people/objects, process, activities, events, strategies, relationships and social structure,* and *methods* (research process). The kinds of headings used by Clarke (2009) in situational maps may be useful also (cf. Figure 10.13). The list of code groups with definitions I provided for users of NVivo software (Bazeley, 2007: 106–7) – a list that is equally applicable for use in any type of qualitative software – included:

- *People/Actors/Players*: people, groups, or organisations to whom reference is made. These are rarely, if ever, coded without coding also (on the same text) the reason for the reference to that person, organisation, or group. Depending on the project, these codes might be very specific (Dr Smith), or simply role based (doctor, nurse, partner, friend).
- *Events*: things that happen at a point in time.
- *Actions*: things that are done at a point in time. These would usually be coded also by an Actor code (unless it is an action of the speaker).
- *Activities*: ongoing actions.
- *Context (situation)*: the settings in which actions, etc. occur. This may include branches to identify phases, stages, timing, location (note that if contextual factors apply to whole cases, attributes should be used rather than codes).
- *Strategies*: purposeful activity to achieve a goal or deal with an issue. In some projects this might be more specific, e.g., coping strategies.
- *Issues*: matters raised about which there may be some debate. Typically both 'sides' of the debate are included under a single code. If the number of these proliferates they might later be grouped into types of issues, e.g., political, structural, interpersonal, personal, environmental, with each of these being represented by branches, or perhaps as separate top-level trees.

- *Attitudes*: listing the type of attitude, rather than the focus of the attitude (that gets coded separately).
- *Beliefs/Ideological position/Frameworks*: intellectual positions (or discourses) which are evident in thinking and action.
- *Cultural context*: likely to have a number of branches, depending on the setting being considered (e.g., cultural, organisational, social).
- *Emotional responses or states* (feelings).
- *Personal characteristics*: descriptors of the person.
- *Impact/Outcomes*: e.g., facilitator/barrier, help/hinder, etc. In general there should not be further codes under these specifying particular facilitators or barriers; rather the passage or item should be coded additionally with whatever is acting as the facilitator or barrier.

If you have a typical project of moderate complexity it should require no more than 10 top-level (parent) categories to cover the topic; that is, you will have 10 or fewer 'sorts' of codes. No one project is likely to include all the kinds of codes suggested above. Furthermore, most code systems do not go more than two to three levels deep. If they do, it is likely that the categories being used are no longer true subcategories of the higher-order categories they are under; and, on a practical level, it becomes inconvenient for the coder to remember, locate, and effectively use them.

The coding system for the Researchers project has gone through a number of iterations as the project has developed. It is set out in its current form, to provide just one example, in Figure 6.6.[9]

Tips for coders:

✓ Organise your structure based on conceptual similarities (the same sorts or classes of things), not observed or theoretical associations, nor according to how you think you will want to write the results chapters of your dissertation (the latter is likely to preclude your discovering anything new).

✓ Something that is a consequence from one process can become a condition for another. This also reinforces the need to organise your coding hierarchy under headings describing kinds of items (i.e., taxonomically), not what role they play in any emerging theory.

✓ Use a separate code for each element (who, what, how, when, etc.) of what the text is about, thus:

   o each code should encompass one concept only; and
   o a particular passage of text will be coded using multiple codes.

✓ Each concept or code appears only once in the whole system.

✓ Don't worry if not all your codes can be immediately sorted into the hierarchy. Be prepared to modify it as you gain further understanding of your data.

✓ Record ideas prompted by your sorting activity in your project journal.

---

[9]Other examples are available at www.researchsupport.com.au.

environment / stages / strategies (left panel)

Name	Source	Reference	Description
environment		1	10
serendipity	11	13	
interpersonal	0	0	
encouragement-support	19	36	includes recognition and reward
loneliness-isolation	4	7	incl isolation
research culture	8	10	
role model	5	6	
institutional	0	0	
insecurity	4	6	
funding	8	9	
opportunity	10	13	
autonomy	7	8	
competing demands	5	8	
working conditions-demands	16	46	includes institutional demands
time issues	11	23	merge of block time (value of) and time needed/spending
strategies	0	0	
collaboration	10	12	includes 'sharing the load'
collegial contact	11	28	peer interaction and networking
niche	5	7	making an area yours (and being known for it)
publishing	6	16	view broadly as producing something tangible from rese
setting priorities	5	5	
time management	3	4	being organised, ensuring time for research, self-discipli
stages	0	0	
becoming a researcher	20	36	
being a researcher	18	47	
research pathway	1	1	
identification	15	24	recognition of being a researcher - or not
interruption	5	5	
turning point	6	8	critical experience setting the person on a path to being
drifting into research	4	4	link with serendipity? Opposite of being purposeful?
gaining skills	11	18	includes competence
building a reputation	11	18	includes gaining recognition
working as a researcher	7	10	
making choices	3	6	
PhD experience	10	21	
undergraduate experience	5	7	
obsession	10	16	driven passion: shifted from emotions to pathway - can o

personal qualities / experience of research (right panel)

Name	Source	Reference	Description
personal qualities-doing responses	2	8	
ambitious - goal oriented	11	20	having a goal one is working toward
confidence	8	10	
opportunism	7	10	
research part of 'being'	6	7	combine with identification?
commitment-drive-focus	17	39	thisis about being focused and committed etc; i.e. the doi
open to ideas	5	8	maybe = curiosity?
agency	13	21	about taking control
fun-play	4	6	
anticipation	5	5	includes having imagination and foresight
other experience	0	0	
education-training	7	14	
family-childhood background	4	5	
work experience	5	8	
intellectual experience of research	0	0	
fascination	6	10	link with stimulation and/or enjoyment?
intellectual stimulation	14	18	
creativity-originality	12	31	
curiosity	9	28	
immersion	10	26	experience of total involvement in the task - differs from f
challenge	14	31	includes 'research is demanding'
emotional experience of research	0	0	
positive affect	24	167	
enjoyment	13	28	sense of having fun
excitement	6	14	includes 'research highs'
passion	10	17	emotional or intellectual experience? - strong kind of inte
satisfaction	17	40	
negative affect	14	67	
stress	4	8	includes self-doubt;
frustration	8	18	
feeling low	4	6	
uncertainty	5	5	all related to dealing with research issues, so fairly intelle
people referred to	0	0	
colleagues-peers	7	9	
family	5	6	
lecturer	3	6	
supervisor-mentor	11	18	

Figure 6.6 Coding structure for the Researchers project

Reviewing and refining codes and the coding structure

As noted at the beginning of this chapter, the focus so far has been on early coding strategies. Inevitably, not all the codes you produce will continue to prove useful. Some will be too general, others too specific to one or two segments of data. With the exception of contextual codes, a category that is so broad or so vaguely defined that it codes a very large number of passages or very lengthy passages is less likely to be useful in analysis. Similarly, a category that codes only one or a very small number of passages will generally not be useful in analysis (unless, of course, it captures an exceptionally insightful thought), and too many of these will create a proliferating coding system that becomes unmanageable.

Strategies are needed, therefore, for refining the codes you have been creating. Typically you will begin to refine codes after going through your first few sources, and as you begin to define your coding system; the processes of refining and sorting go hand in hand.

▶ Review your list of codes, as a whole, simple list. How well does it reflect the concerns of your project? Show the list to someone not familiar with your project. Can they tell what your project is about, from your list of codes? Underline those that appear to be especially germane to your project; query those that are unclear or that may not be needed. The latter will attract special attention (renaming, recoding, deletion, or archiving) in the review process.

▶ Where a code is too broad to be analytically useful, review its contents and code it on to finer categories, or simply refine it by removing less relevant material.

▶ Define each code, by identifying its properties or as part of creating a codebook, as a first step in refining detailed codes. In defining the code, you are forced to clarify what data the code represents. Recode segments that are not relevant to a more appropriate category and remove the original code from all irrelevant material.

▶ Merge codes that have a common (or quite similar) meaning into a single code, such that each of the original codes is replaced by the new synthesised code.

▶ As you go through the process of sorting codes into a hierarchically organised system, you will find yourself often reviewing coded data, in order to decide where that code belongs in the system. This process is never concluded in one step: not only do some codes resist early cataloguing, but you will see some differently as further data and later reflection lead to fresh understanding.

Refining codes in these ways is greatly simplified when specialised QDAS is used for coding. Such programs are designed to cater for the flexibility required in coding qualitative data; hence they facilitate the sorting, merging, and renaming of codes, the recoding of coded material, or the removal of codes from data.

Writing about codes

In the methods chapter

▶ Describe the way in which you went about creating, developing, and structuring your coding system, as a way of helping the reader to understand your approach to early data analysis, what informed it, and the process by which you arrived at those codes (cf. Chapter 5, section 'Writing about coding processes').

▶ Provide a summary list of the kinds of things being coded, rather than a full list of codes. The full list, with frequencies and/or brief definitions, might be placed in an appendix to a report or thesis, if doing so would aid the reader's understanding of the process of your analysis and its outcomes.

▶ If you used any automated or rapid coding techniques, describe these and note any benefits or limitations that arose from using them.

Exercises

Exercise 1: Generating codes

Three mothers tell about their experience of having their youngest child immunised (Box 6.15). Use the various strategies outlined above to generate codes from these three accounts, for example:

▶ Compare and contrast experiences with needles; note repetitions; note Vivien's use of pronouns (you might write a memo about the latter).

▶ Identify attitudes to both the process and the outcome of immunisation and strategies for managing the process. (As this was the point of the study, this would definitely warrant another memo.)

▶ What kinds of codes are you generating? Try organising them into groups.

Box 6.15

Three immunisation stories

Vivien's story

Interviewer: So the last immunisation would have been the 18-month-old?

Vivien: Yeah. I've always, half an hour before on the day give them a good dose of Panadol, the maximum that you can give them and I hate needles at the best of times, but I have to psych myself up to get them. I mean, I know they have to have them and I'll get them, but I have to psych myself up, I get really, really upset when they have needles. I absolutely hate needles, but I know it's going to do them good and they have to have it. And the day he had it, he wasn't all that well and I thought they wouldn't give it to him.

Interviewer: He had a cold or something?

Vivien: Yeah, he had a little bit of a cold. Not a heavy cold, just a little bit of a cold, but they gave it to him. He had the boosters so it was two needles. He didn't like them. He knew straight away. I mean, 'cause all day I'm going, 'Oh god, I've got to have these needles, we've got to have them done,' so he sort of picked up off me and <sister> was upset because she said, 'Oh, poor thing, he's got to have needles,' so he was sort of like, going, 'What's going on mum?' you know. So when we got to the doctor's, he knew straight away and he just started. I just, you know, try and convince him that everything was okay and we have to have these needles. So we had them done, but we had a good dose of Panadol and he cried for oh, I think ten minutes, ten minutes I think he went for.

Angela's story

Angela: I was a bit worried because I knew what he was like with needles and there was a little girl there who was having hers done at the same time. She went in before Nigel and she screamed and screamed and screamed and yeah, it really concerned me because I thought he would be pretty upset. But I went in and I was very nervous and I held him and he had his little injection and he was fine, he screamed a little bit and then stopped and fell asleep by the time I got to the car.

Interviewer: Oh, that was wonderful. And beforehand, was it hard to make that decision?

Angela: Well, it was really easy for me because I basically just thought that if I didn't immunise him, other things could happen that would be worse.

Felicity's story

<<Felicity is separated from the children's father>>

Felicity: Well, I didn't take her, her father did. I chickened out at that. She just cried and everything was fine. She got a lump under the skin, but other than that, she was doing fine.

Interviewer: So what is it that you chicken out of?

Felicity: The pain. I had enough pain giving birth to her, I don't see I should put her through pain because she put me through enough. (Laughter)

Interviewer: Ah, that's why it's father's turn, is it?

Felicity: I've got three children and like, the father's taken them every time. I'm just, I don't know, it just makes my heart go out to them, you know? [Int.: Yeah] You know, so and then they can't get the cranks with me, they can get the cranks with him.

Interviewer: Oh, okay. So it's just the pain, seeing them in pain that worries you?

Felicity: Yes. I don't like needles very much, so you know, and they're younger so it really hurts.

Further reading

Saldaña's (2009) *Coding manual for qualitative researchers* is a comprehensive review of specific first- and second-cycle coding strategies for qualitative data, with practical suggestions for working with the coded data.

Bernard and Ryan (2010: Chapter 3) review a number of methods for identifying 'themes', with a summary table and decision tree to identify practical, expertise, stage, and outcome factors relating to each method. Chapter 13 covers both manual and automated content analysis of texts.

Gibbs (2007: Chapter 4) provides a brief but useful overview of issues and strategies for coding.

Richards (2009: Chapter 6) reviews ways of managing and organising codes and ideas generated through coding, including developing a category system.

Authors writing on grounded theory approaches to analysis usually dedicate a chapter to coding strategies, as used in their particular approach.

7

Alternative approaches to breaking open and connecting data

At the beginning of this book I proposed that qualitative research is inherently case based. This chapter focuses on methods that give a central place to connections within and across cases. In most projects, the cases are people who are being considered individually, although each can also be one of many that together comprise a case. This chapter is designed to provide a counterbalance to the previous two, with their focus on coding strategies, by offering alternative ways to think about and work with your data. Some strategies are drawn from established methodologies, such as phenomenology, narrative, and discourse analysis; others from common practice. Assess the usefulness of each for your own project, pick up ideas, or explore more deeply through further reading if you want to pursue a particular pathway.

In this chapter:

- discover additional strategies for building on individual case analyses;
- review various approaches to thematic analysis, and the limitations of simply 'identifying themes' (as commonly understood) as an approach to data analysis;
- discover the range of strategies for analysis offered by those who write about narrative methods, and how you might apply these to the stories and accounts within your data;
- from a brief introduction to various approaches to the analysis of conversations and other forms of discourse, assess their potential relevance for your research purposes.

Because coding serves as an indexing process, it remains relevant to – but not the focus of – many of the approaches outlined in this chapter. Use of software also remains relevant, particularly specialised qualitative analysis software, because these programs provide extensive linking and modelling tools as well as those for coding.

Building on cases

Not all analysis methods rely on the kind of detailed coding strategies described in the last two chapters. Indeed, one of the dangers for those who rely heavily on coding as a form of analysis is that the perspective of the case(s) can be lost. Without understanding the dynamics of each of the cases in a study, analysis across cases is in danger of being superficial. Aggregation of fragments from across cases risks an artificiality that does not truly represent any case.

Case descriptions, profiles, and summaries serve a much wider range of analytic purposes than case study research alone. In small-sample studies, or for studies with a methodological or substantive focus on particular cases, preparation of a profile for each case is a most useful early step for both within-case and cross-case analysis. Additionally, case descriptions sit within and add to the contextual framework for qualitative research. A *case study*, therefore, can be both an analysis process and a product of analysis (Stake, 2000).

Robert Stake emphasises the intrinsic value of the particular in a case study, seeing it as more important to adequately represent (describe) the case than to draw generalisations. 'Damage occurs when the commitment to generalize or to theorize runs so strong that the researcher's attention is drawn away from features important for understanding the case itself' (2000: 439), and, 'the understanding of human experience is a matter of chronologies more than of causes and effects' (1995: 39). Stake sees it as the task of the reader to draw his or her own conclusions on the basis of the information provided. While Yin (2003) also sees case studies as a research strategy with a strong descriptive purpose, he is more inclined to emphasise the role of theory in designing a case study, and the exploratory and evaluative role of case studies in developing explanations of complex causal events. He points to a number of classic case studies which have focused on developing descriptive theory, however, including Whyte's ([1943] 1993) *Street corner society* and Brinton's (1938) *Anatomy of a revolution*. Regardless of the type of case study design or its ultimate purpose, Yin asserts the absolute need for a careful descriptive analysis of each case and the context for the cases. (Approaches to comparative analyses using cases (cross-case analyses) will be covered in Chapter 9.)

Strategies for working with cases include:

▶ Write the story of each case, organised into chapters based on significant time periods or events.
▶ Prepare a case as a vignette to illustrate and contextualise particular points or themes.
▶ Use the case as a structure to bring together data from multiple sources.
▶ Prepare a summary of each case, giving attention to each of a series of points of interest for your study.
▶ Create a profile of each case under headings reflecting those points of interest in an Excel spreadsheet, to allow for further work using comparative analyses.
▶ Create a visual model of a case or cases:

  ○ based on the key processes or issues for that case;
  ○ to 'reintegrate' the case from the categories used to code it;
  ○ as a timeline showing critical events with supplementary contextual information.

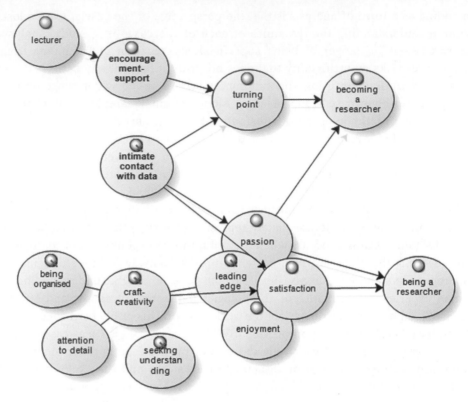

Figure 7.1   Case model for Shane, based on categories used to code his interview

My model for Shane (Figure 7.1) was built around the most critical factors in his becoming and remaining a researcher: the encouragement he received during his undergraduate career, and the pleasure and satisfaction derived from immersion in archival data.[1] Creating this model forced consideration of how different aspects of Shane's history and dialogue fitted together, and of what was 'core' to the process under consideration as far as he was concerned.

Themes as an alternative to codes?

The term 'theme' is best used to describe an integrating, relational statement derived from the data that identifies both content and meaning. 'A theme is an outcome of coding, categorization, and analytic reflection' (Saldaña, 2009: 13). 'A significant part of the aims of thematized analysis involve [sic] working out the

---

[1]The crosses on some coding categories indicate that these categories were moved and/or renamed in later arrangements of the NVivo coding system.

relationships *between* code categories, and the significance of such relationships for the development of theoretical conceptions and statements' (Gibson & Brown, 2009: 138). For example, Saldaña described a study in which two categories of oppression between elementary school children were identified: oppression through physical force, and oppression through hurting others' feelings. One of the themes developed from this coding was that 'peer oppression is gendered' (2009: 12).

Thematic analysis is sometimes presented as an alternative to coding, especially by those who indicate concern about fracturing or segmenting data in a way that doesn't allow for reconnection of fractured elements. The consensus among those who seek to interpret, analyse, and theorise qualitative data, however, is that the development of themes depends on data having been coded already.

Themes are just a step on the way

Braun and Clarke argue that thematic analysis provides a 'rich and detailed, yet complex, account of the data' (2006: 78) and therefore constitutes a method in its own right. Many others who write about thematic analysis, however, see it as a tool to use within other methodological traditions (e.g., Boyatzis, 1998; Ryan & Bernard, 2000), rather than having the status of a methodological approach in itself. Much depends, of course, on what is understood by thematic analysis; the adjectives used by Braun and Clarke ('rich', 'detailed', 'complex') are important qualifiers.

The problem in much current practice is that thematic analysis has become a label applied to very descriptive writing about a list of ideas (or concepts or categories), supported by limited evidence. In dissertation and funding proposals, an applicant might provide a detailed description of how qualitative data are going to be gathered, but then simply declare that 'themes will be identified in the data' as an approach to analysis. Similarly, when people talk about having identified themes in the data as their method of analysis, they often describe for their results four or five key categories that were 'discovered in' or 'emerged from' the data, providing just a quote or two as evidence for each and with little or no attempt to justify those categories or link them into a more comprehensive model. Such reports are rarely acceptable to journal reviewers.

Description of 'thematic' codes and categories identified in the data provides a useful starting point in developing a report of findings from a study, but effective analysis requires using data to build a comprehensive, contextualised, and integrated understanding or theoretical model of what has been found, with an argument drawn from across the data that establishes the conclusions drawn. Identifying themes, at best, falls somewhere in the process between coding and theory development (Figure 7.2). Strength of analysis will be recognised even by those who may work differently, while disconnected, descriptive reporting with a few illustrative quotes for evidence is likely to be unconvincing even to those familiar with qualitative methods.

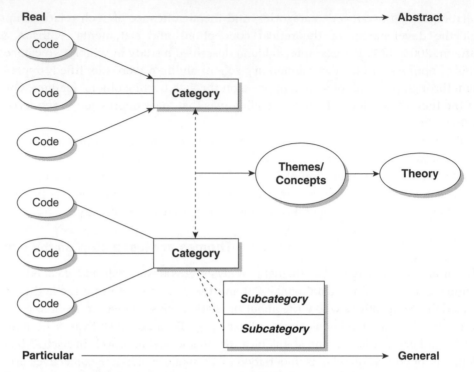

Figure 7.2   A streamlined codes-to-theory model for qualitative inquiry

Source: Saldaña, 2009: 12, Figure 1.1

Constructing themes

There are various strategies for generating themes that you might explore:

▶ If you become aware of a pattern or trend (a theme) while you are reading or working through your data, note it in an analytic memo supported by whatever prompted the awareness, and then ensure that your coding or alternative recording system will capture necessary information to test its generality across the data.

▶ Cut out (physically or electronically) exemplar quotes or expressions and arrange these into piles of things that go together. Name the piles to generate themes. If you have other people doing the sorting, have them 'think aloud', and tape them as they work to see what criteria they are using.

▶ Develop assertions based on what you are seeing in your data (then seek to test their validity).

▶ Note repetitive or patterned relationships between identified elements in the data (Chapter 10 will provide ways of reviewing these).

▶ Create thematic connections based on the relationship between a set of conditions, actions/interactions, and consequences (see Chapter 8, section 'Learning from grounded theory').

▶ Write a vignette about a particular aspect of your data, and then create a summary (thematic) statement for it.

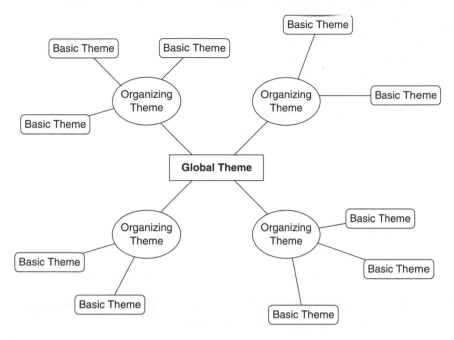

Figure 7.3   Structure of a thematic network

Source: Attride-Stirling, 2001: 388, Figure 1

▶ Go beyond identifying or constructing simple thematic statements to consider how the various themes intersect to create a constellation. Explore their context and their inter-relationships to build a coordinated network of understanding (Figure 7.3).

Learning from phenomenology: building thematic understanding

Phenomenology aims to identify the 'essence' of a phenomenon through an individual's experience of that phenomenon. Original (e.g., Husserlian) forms of phenomenology sought objective description of an object through first-person experience ('intentionality') with the individual's particularistic perspectives set aside ('bracketed'). Existential phenomenologists (e.g., Heidegger, Merleau-Ponty, Sartre) recognised the intersubjectivity or embeddedness of our experience of the world of people, objects, relationships, and language, and attempted to interpret the original intentions and meanings held by a person in relation to a phenomenon. More recently, interpretative phenomenologists (led by Jonathan Smith) have developed a more subjective (psychological) approach in which they seek to understand a particular 'lived experience', something that will have already been the subject of reflection, thinking, and feeling by the experiencing person. They distinguish between experience in general and 'an experience' of some significance in which the experiencing person is aware of each element of what is happening, with these elements linked by common meaning even if they are not sequential. The phenomenological task involves a 'double hermeneutic because the researcher is trying to make sense of the participant trying to make sense of what is happening to [her or himself]' (Smith, Flowers, & Larkin, 2009: 3).

Phenomenologists generally work with transcripts of interviews, using thematic statements rather than codes to identify those things that make a phenomenon what it is. A theme was defined by Smith et al. as a 'concise and pithy statement of what was important in the various comments attached to a piece of transcript ... usually expressed as phrases ... [that] contain enough particularity to be grounded and enough abstraction to be conceptual' (2009: 92). Themes reflecting detail are then clustered and combined into 'superordinate' themes that describe the essential (and more general) aspects of the experience being studied (Box 7.1).

Box 7.1

An example of themes and superordinate themes developed through interpretative phenomenological analysis (IPA)

Jonathan Smith and Mike Osborn (2003) illustrated the process of developing phenomenological themes using a study they had conducted on the psychological aspects of living with chronic lower back pain. They listed themes and superordinate themes developed from their first participant as an example, along with keywords or phrases from the text to support them (2003: 74).

1   *Living with an unwanted self*

Undesirable behaviour ascribed to pain	*it's the pain*
Struggle to accept self and identity – unwanted self	*who I am*
Unwanted self rejected as true self	*hateful bit*
Struggle to accept new self	*hard to believe*
Undesirable, destructive self	*mean*
Conflict of selves, me versus not me	*me not me*
Living with a new self	*new me*

2   *A self that cannot be understood or controlled*

Lack of control over self	*can't help*
Rejection of change	*still same*
Avoidance of implications	*no different*
Responsibility, self versus pain	*understand*

3   *Undesirable feelings*

Shame	*disgusting*
Anger and pain	*snappy*
Lack of compassion	*don't care*
Confusion, lack of control	*no idea*
Ranking duress, self versus pain	*cope*
Shame of disclosure	*talk*

Suggested steps[2] in thematic analysis start with:

▶ Answering the questions you are asking of your participants yourself so that you can analyse your own response. This will help you to bracket (or understand) your own experience. Engaging strongly and skilfully with the participant (both during the interview and during analysis) will also facilitate your bracketing of prior experience.

▶ Reading a transcript to get a sense of the whole.

Continue, as you work to condense the essential characteristics of an object or experience, *from the perspective of those experiencing it*, by moving from particular to shared experience, and from descriptive to interpretive analysis.

▶ Break your data into statements or 'natural meaning units', with each meaning unit entered into a row of a table or typed with a very wide margin. If you use a table, set it out with an additional column to allow for your interpretation of the meaning of each statement, and perhaps also a third that will be used for a more abstract rendering of the essence of the statement (a thematic statement or code; Figure 7.4).

▶ State the central theme of each meaning unit in the right-hand column, simply, and without interpretation. Record this generically, rather than in the specific terms of the interviewee, in the second column.

▶ Interrogate the central theme of each meaning unit in terms of the study's purpose and questions (the third column is used for recording the results of this step).

▶ Cluster the thematic statements, checking back against the original transcripts while doing so. The transcript and themes must each account for the other, but don't ignore data or themes which don't fit: attempt to integrate discrepancies and contradictions into your description or theory. Work iteratively toward a composite picture to capture all essential themes regarding the structure and meaning of the experience, ignoring redundancies.

▶ Interrogate each cluster to determine its 'essence' or essential meaning.

▶ Integrate these clusters into an exhaustive description of the investigated topic.

▶ Validate your description through member checking of the results. Work any relevant new data from this process into the final results.

✓ Focus your analysis intensively on individual cases before seeking common themes across cases. The entire process may be repeated for each case; alternatively use the combined themes from all cases for the clustering process.

Box 7.2 shows an example of a study carried out using interpretative phenomenological analysis that illustrates both the strengths and weaknesses of much of the work done using this approach.

---

[2]These steps draw on the methods of phenomenologists including Colaizzi (1978), Giorgi and Giorgi (2003), Hycner (1999), Smith et al. (2009), and Wojnar and Swanson (2007).

Being a research student

My thoughts about my current experience are completely different to my initial experiences at Masters level and on my previous research projects.	*PhD research differs from earlier research experiences.*	
This project began as a self-directed study of a topic that I am passionate about. I appreciate the freedom to take the project in whatever direction I choose and at the same time fearful that such freedom could lead to academic peril.	*Choice about direction is a positive experience but also generates fear.*	*emotional tension: autonomy- fearfulness*
It is wonderful to find precious literature that contributes to the understanding of the project and very frustrating finding fascinating literature that has nothing to do with the study and yet you would like to weave it in somehow. From the perspective of discipline, it is comforting to have someone who will put barricades around the knowledge base for the study; cut off those long alleys that will lead nowhere; and put covers on the bottomless pits of information that will not adequately inform or direct the study.	*Reading literature is always enjoyable, but it is not always relevant to this project (leading also to mixed emotions). Having another person assist in setting limits is helpful.*	*enjoyment- frustration freedom to explore- need to set limits*
...	...	...

Descriptive statement:

As a research student one experiences mixed emotions that arise from the tension between the freedom of having autonomy to explore the topic and fear of becoming lost, leading to failure.

Figure 7.4   Phenomenological (thematic) analysis of meaning units in written text

---

Box 7.2

Interpretative phenomenological analysis of experience of loss following spinal cord injury

Adele Dickson interviewed a homogeneous sample of eight people with spinal cord injury at C5/C6 level, asking general questions relating to their experience of living with their injury (Dickson, Allan, & O'Carroll, 2008). She read, highlighted, and clustered emerging themes for each participant, then explored similarities and differences to develop her thematic categories. Reflecting an 'insider per-spective' on living with spinal cord injury, she identified three recurrent themes regarding the experi-ence of loss, described as loss of control, including bodily control and emotional control; loss of independence; and loss (or change) of identity. The most critical impact for these participants was the psychological impact of double incontinence, which necessitated a daily invasion of their body and their privacy by an assistant. As a consequence of this, they experienced helplessness, frustra-tion, embarrassment, and a sense of shame. A perpetual risk of 'accidents' contributed to a loss of spontaneity and independence, and altogether, to a change or loss of identity and deterioration of quality of life.

Three of the eight did not experience a change of identity despite their experiences – but apparently this warranted just two brief paragraphs of coverage in 16 pages of text (including 10 of results and discussion), considerably less than the one person who experienced a 'total' loss of identity.

Using a computer for phenomenological (thematic) analysis

Phenomenologists generally have been slow to adopt QDA software as a tool for assisting phenomenological analysis. In response to a recent question about how one might use NVivo for interpretative phenomenological analysis,[3] I suggested:

▶ Use annotations or see also links to record comments or memos on passages of particular interest.

▶ Use codes to attach thematic style labels to sense or meaning units in the text (i.e., passages generally ranging from a sentence to a paragraph in length).

▶ Sort themes into clusters, for example, using the modeller to do so, to create superordinate themes. These clusters might then be recorded using sets[4] (allowing a taxonomic code system to be separately maintained), or by rearranging the codes into a hierarchical list based on the thematic structure.

✓ For some versions of IPA, the above steps would be carried out independently for each participant, before synthesising them, by creating a thematic code list for each participant in a separate folder (these can be merged later). Others would code and reflect on all participants by creating a common list of codes, and then cluster the codes.

▶ Use the code clusters (e.g., as sets or aggregated nodes) in a case-by-themes matrix, to illuminate commonalities and differences across the cases. Check which cases are exceptions for a particular aspect of experience (then explore why they are different).

For the clustering stage (cf. Chapter 10):

▶ You might also consider looking at themes (as rows) against the same themes (as columns) in a matrix query as a way of seeing which themes co-occur with which other ones (using AND or NEAR-in-the-same-source depending on how much your themes intersect).

▶ You could try clustering your themes using the cluster analysis visualisation strategy, to see which of the themes you have created are based either on similar words or on shared cross-codes.

❗ The problem with both of the latter strategies is that they can be based on associations or similarities that are coincidental rather than being conceptually based, so they might simply confuse rather than assist you!

---

[3]An equivalent strategy could be used with MAXQDA or other qualitative software; the main difference is the terminology used.

[4]Sets hold aliases for items within them, so that they update as those items are updated. Sets are usually treated as single items in queries (although the 'members' can be itemised if wanted); they can be imported into a model as a single item or with their members also showing.

Focus on interaction: working with focus group data

Focus groups are used as a source of data where the interaction between participants is expected to generate additional or different information from that obtained when someone is interviewed alone. This might be in community settings, when private and public values and beliefs intersect; in exploratory and evaluation studies; or in commercial settings for product evaluation. Data from the discussion may be analysed to gain an understanding of particular experiences, issues, or processes, but often focus group data are under-analysed, for example, where they are used simply to generate relevant questions for a fixed-format questionnaire, or to produce a descriptive report illustrated by participant quotes for market research. In these, the interactive component of the group discussion is ignored, along with much of the deeper meaning of what is said.

Group dynamics operating in a focus group are affected by the heterogeneity or homogeneity of its participants, and by whether the group was brought together (constructed) especially for the purpose of the research or was an existing (naturally occurring) group. These factors can affect the freedom of participants to speak, the patterns of influence regarding expressed opinions, the level of consensus in a group discussion, and the shape of the information obtained. From the point of view of analysis, therefore, it is important to ascertain how the composition of a focus group has impacted on both individual contributions and the nature of the interaction that occurred in the group discussion.

The unique interactive element of focus groups is worthy of special analytic attention:

> Brief intense discussion of an issue may be as, or more important, as lengthy, negotiated but superficial coverage. Frequency of discussion of specific topics may not be as relevant as diversity of opinions. The task of the analyst is constantly to question how interaction may indicate consensus, negotiated understanding, or disagreement. For example, did participants have clear views that were consistently held throughout the discussion or did their views change as a result of listening to others? Group dynamics are important and constitute data to be analysed. (Willis, Green, Daly, Williamson, & Bandyopadhyay, 2009: 134)

Karen Willis and colleagues go so far as to say:

> In interpreting the data (both content and interaction), the analyst is less concerned with whether the information presented by participants is 'objectively true', and more interested in the way that such information is presented and received within the group and how group interaction may challenge or confirm people's stated views. (2009: 134)

While Carey and Asbury (2012) agree with an emphasis on exploring the way interaction within a group fashions expressed content and opinions, they see the interaction as an integral part of understanding the data – as an essential element of context that is necessary to interpret the data – rather than parallel information. To resolve this issue of the relative importance of the content of the information versus the way participants interacted in relation to the content, consider the purpose of your study and your reasons for gathering data from groups rather than individuals.

Identify individual participants as they contribute to a focus group so that you can explore the sequence of input by any one participant. This allows you to explore whether particular opinions are being expressed across the group, or by one or two within the group. Changes in opinion during the session become evident also, and are especially interesting; these can be explored in relation to the ongoing conversation, to see what might have prompted the change. Discontinuities in conversation, use of humour, discord between participants, and the silence of some members are all indicative of interactive influences within the group. Table 7.1 outlines a framework for analysis that focuses on the interactive qualities of a focus group; the application of these principles to analysis is illustrated in Box 7.3.

Table 7.1 Analysing group interaction

Group component	Aspect of interaction for analysis
What?	What topics/opinions produced consensus?
	What statements seemed to evoke conflict?
	What were the contradictions in the discussion?
	What common experiences were expressed?
	Did the collective interaction generate new insights or precipitate an exchange of information among participants?
Who?	Whose interests were being represented in the group?
	Were alliances formed among group members?
	Was a particular member or viewpoint silenced?
How?	How closely did the group adhere to the issues presented for discussion?
	How did group members respond to the ideas of others?
	How did the group resolve disagreements?
	How were emotions handled?
	How were non-verbal signs and behaviours used to contribute to the discussion?

Source: Willis et al., 2009: 133, adapted from Stevens, 1996: 172

Box 7.3

Analysing interaction in a focus group

Deborah Warr, in her study of young people, gender roles, and intimacy that was based on exist-ing 'naturally occurring' groups, observed that participants were able to challenge and push each other in ways that a researcher would not have dared to do, as in the following exchange:

Shane:　You've got to be kidding! You'll never catch me going into a woman's shop by myself!

Meagan:　My Dad does.

Shane:　Is there something wrong with him?

Caitlin:　No, but. You can't sort of say there's something wrong with someone because they're walking into a shop. It's more like you're getting embarrassed for doing it.

Shane:　I'd walk in one door and I'd be out the other!

Meagan:　But wait on, if your missus or someone asks you to go and buy, you know, personal stuff?

Shane:　What? Singlets?

Meagan:　Yeah, or tampons?

Shane:　I wouldn't buy them.

Meagan:　My boyfriend is different.

Caitlin:　Say your girlfriend asks for you to get her some tampons at the store, you wouldn't do it?

Shane:　You've got to be kidding me! [The women are astonished with this and there are lots of comments on top of one another.]

Meagan:　You are disgusting!

Shane:　She goes, 'Go and get these,' and I go, 'Arg, arg, no way.'

Meagan:　Why though?

Shane:　My face would go that red that I'd have to walk out of the shop, like a beetroot. That's a woman's thing. (2005: 215–16)

Through the expression and testing of divergent opinions, Warr was able to discern in this group the contradictory impact of circumstance (e.g., unemployment) on breaking down traditional expectations of gender roles while gender differences were sustained in the more private areas of intimate relations.

Focus on stories and accounts: identifying structure, interpreting meaning

Narratives, stories, and accounts occur within almost all data forms. Even if you are not doing narrative analysis as such, you will gain analytic insights from these various ways in which narrative researchers analyse stories and/or accounts of experiences that comprise or are embedded within text, audio, or video sources. The considerable variety of approaches taken in analysing narratives provides you with a set of strategies that rely less on coding and more on seeing the connections within and across each of your cases.

Perhaps a single narrative flows across a whole interview, or you might locate one or more stories or accounts or parts of stories within a longer text. If segments of a particular narrative are scattered through a text, arrange them so that they form a sequenced story, building it around a plot that conveys the significance of the story *from the perspective of the teller* (Maxwell & Miller, 2008).

People tell stories

People organise even non-systematic experiences into coherent stories (McCance, McKenna, & Boore, 2001). Plot, character, voice, and other features of the story are arranged to convey the implicit meaning of an experience for the teller (Poirier & Ayres, 1997). It is often easier for a participant to tell the story of an experience than to respond to questions, provide explanations, or proffer opinions. Narratives therefore provide a useful way of working with ill-defined concepts or with sensitive or controversial topics (Coffey & Atkinson, 1996; McCance et al., 2001). They are also useful in the study of process (*how* this situation came about), as a way of avoiding direct 'why?' questions yet still arriving at relevant information.

Narratives of many different types are found in varied contexts (Box 7.4), but they cluster into three primary forms:

- Narratives as stories are structured sequentially around a plot, with a beginning, a middle, and an end, and in the telling they reveal how the speaker understands experiences or events and interprets them. Content of and linguistic expression in narrative are coloured by both immediate and wider context, including the wider socio-political discourses in society. Narrative is distinguished from other forms of discourse such as chronicles, reports, arguments, and question and answer exchanges by its concern with sequence and consequence (Riessman, 2008: 5).
- Narratives of personal experience are a naturally occurring language form in which a single speaker recounts a real experience that has occurred in the past. The temporal sequence in the narrative follows the sequence in which they became known to the narrator. Typically they are 'performed', to be emotionally and socially evaluated by an audience, but in an interview situation they might be provided in response to an open question. Life stories might be gathered over several interviews, supplemented by other documents.
- Alternatively, stories to give an account of events and experiences are provided in response to specific questions or they are framed and constructed jointly by the interviewer and interviewee. A large amount of unstructured or semistructured interview text is likely to be in the form of 'accounts' rather than longer or more comprehensive narratives or stories.

Box 7.4

Contexts for and types of stories

- Oral histories or life stories:

  o may be organised in chapters or told as a 'career' (in terms of social roles as well as work roles);

  o reveal an individual's perspective on self and on the wider social and cultural setting, including key social actors in the life of that person;

  o give meaning in the present through events of the past.

- These take the form of:

  o biographies and autobiographies;

  o life histories and personal experience stories;

  o oral history – personal reflections from people.

- Cultural stories include:

  o heritage narratives – defining the identity of country or community or family;

  o folk tales, folk songs;

  o myths, legends, fairy tales – usually with an implied moral;

  o morality plays and fables.

- Organisational stories:

  o stories of success, stories about leaders;

  o atrocity stories – stories to warn the listeners about people or situations.

- Accounts:

  o provide a short explanation, perhaps for unanticipated or unusual behaviour; or to make excuses for or justify questionable behaviour.

- Humour:

  o stories of unanticipated misfortune (mostly others', sometimes one's own) that rely on incongruities or an unexpected turn.

- Literature:
  o novels, epic dramas.

Narratives, stories, and accounts as subjects for analysis

Narratives, as sequentially told stories composed for a particular audience at a particular time, do not speak for themselves. They are influenced by culturally and demographically based discursive practices. When told in the context of an interview, they are co-constructed with the interviewer (Riessman, 2008). They require interpretation. Even the shape and style of transcription involves analysis and influences the course of further analysis – and more so if the transcription involves translation.

You can analyse narratives and stories, like other kinds of qualitative data, in terms of both form and function. Narrative analysis is case centred; therefore study a narrative holistically prior to any more detailed consideration. Then, narrative analysis distinctively focuses on elements of purpose, plot, setting, structure, linguistic features, and language, to derive the meanings embedded in these for the teller and for his or her audience. This range of possibilities makes for considerable diversity in approaches to narrative analysis.

Where stories and accounts are embedded within longer interviews, you might combine coding with narrative techniques to analyse both the substantive content of the interviews and the embedded stories (Riessman, 2008). Like any other data, you can code and analyse narratives to support the development of theoretical understanding, or the particulars of an experience can be used to create contextual understanding (Polkinghorne, 1988). Jane Elliott (2005) described several studies in which coded variable and/or narrative data were used to construct longitudinal profiles of individuals (real or typical or unusual) in a way that gave life to the drier statistical reporting of trends and patterns. Riessman and Quinney, in their somewhat critical review of narrative strategies in social work research, warned against confusing narrative analysis with thematic analysis, however:

> Social work authors said they applied 'narrative analysis', but on closer inspection findings were constructed by inductive thematic coding ('we looked for themes'). Snippets of talk (mostly non-narrative, stripped of sequence and consequence) were presented to illustrate common thematic elements across interviews. (2005: 397)

Hermeneutics

Hermeneutics is the theory of interpretation of text. It arose from biblical exegesis, where a puzzling text would be interpreted in the light of the biblical corpus as a whole. Hermeneutic theory, with its focus on methods and purposes of interpretation, was then applied to other written texts to discern the original intentions of the author within that author's context. The concept of the hermeneutic circle was developed by Friedrich Schleiermacher to describe the dynamic, iterative process of understanding the meaning of the whole and of the parts within it as interdependent activities. Later philosophers (Heidegger, Gadamer) saw the hermeneutic circle as applying to all knowledge in so far as all knowing involves a circularity of interpretation. Hermeneutic methods have been applied to both phenomenology and narrative analysis (Smith et al., 2009).

Paul Ricoeur (1970) described two types of hermeneutic interpretation:

- the hermeneutics of meaning recollection (of empathy), designed to understand and faithfully disclose aspects of the author's lifeworld or experience; and
- the hermeneutics of suspicion (of questioning), designed to reveal a deeper understanding that deconstructs and challenges the surface account.

As an analyst of people's narratives, you will move between striving for an inside view, where you see things from the perspective of the participant, and taking an outside view, standing alongside the participant, questioning, assessing, and interpreting latent meanings in what is being said. Narrative analysis is quintessentially qualitative, as you apply an interpretivist approach to others' constructions of their lifeworlds. Like phenomenological analysis, narrative analysis therefore involves a double hermeneutic.

A story or account is purposeful

The act of telling a story can serve many purposes: to remember, argue, justify, persuade, engage, entertain, perhaps even to mislead an audience (Riessman & Quinney, 2005). Stories are told of successful and unsuccessful experiences in the form of a moral tale for the listeners, perhaps teaching the value of hard work, or the need to take advice. A story can be told in different ways so as to attribute blame differently – to the person, or to something in their situation (Coffey & Atkinson, 1996). Stories are told to pass on cultural heritage. Story-telling can be used as a therapeutic tool – first in diagnosis, and then in reframing a person's perspective on life events or to shape new coping behaviours (Box 7.5). Stories are told strategically to create organisational change, or for knowledge management (Denning, 2001; Patton, 2002). Identifying the purpose of the story will assist with determining how the teller makes (or made) sense of the world they live in, and of his or her place or experience in it.

┐ **Box 7.5** ┌

Purposes of illness narratives

Arthur Frank sees story-telling in the medical context as a way of caring rather than being cared for – of becoming healers: 'Stories repair the damage that illness has done' to people's sense of self, and where they are in their lives (1995: 54–5). He identifies three genres of illness narrative, each serving a different purpose.

- The restitution narrative has three movements: physical misery or social default; the remedy; and restoration of physical comfort and social duties. The restitution narrative is seen as a preoccupation of the West.
- The chaos narrative is a non-story, often unheard, about bad things that will never get better. It signals a loss or lack of control, so that the overwhelmed person can't speak coherently and the listener struggles to keep listening. In order to start to tell the story, the teller has to be able to stand outside of themselves. Frank calls it 'the anti-narrative of time without sequence, telling without mediation and speaking about oneself without being fully able to reflect on oneself' (1995: 98).
- In the quest narrative, the teller is in control, having met illness head on and gained from it; it is a journey with a departure (symptoms recognised), an initiation (suffering), and a return with strength and a manifesto (insight for others to share).

Stories as socio-political process

Stories are embedded in cultural and social processes. Illness narratives typically occur within the micro-society of family and friends; other stories, such as those linked with the abortion debate in the United States or the refugee and asylum seeker debate in Australia, become embedded within the larger socio-political context of the day and are used as tools to achieve a social or political purpose. Persecuted Argentinians developed the testimonio as a way of retelling personally experienced historical events, often through literary and visual means, in a way that was designed to bring about social change through an appeal to the emotions of the listeners. Such use of emotive narrative is not always directed to promoting social justice, however (Box 7.6).

Box 7.6

Story as a political tool

In Jannet Pendleton's exploration of a pharmaceutical company's PR campaign to persuade public opinion and gain government support for a new vaccine (cf. Box 3.4), she analysed the case narratives that provided part of the campaign materials. She found the narratives comprised several variations on the sad story of a child with the targeted disease, all written to a formula in which a healthy, happy child becomes ill; is diagnosed with the serious but vaccine-preventable disease; recovers (perhaps) after a considerable battle; but then (potentially or actually) suffers severe long-term consequences – all of which could have been prevented had the child had the newly developed vaccine. These narratives were used to support media releases and create news items in a press and television campaign that eventually had the desired effect.

When you are exploring the purpose of a story or account, ask:

▶ What was the context in which it was produced?
▶ What effect was the story designed to have on the audience or setting in which it was told?
▶ Who was allowed to tell this particular story?
▶ What did the telling achieve for the teller?

Plot

The purpose of a story is made evident through its plot – 'the organizing theme that identifies the significance and the role of the individual events', weaving them together 'into a schematic whole' (Polkinghorne, 1988: 18). The plot of a story focuses around a protagonist (or hero), usually supported by other characters who are viewed in relationship to the protagonist. The narrator relates events involving the protagonist and other characters in temporal succession, so that prior events and choices tend to be seen as influencing later events, in a causal sequence. The audience constructs the plot through a process of abduction as conjectures are made about how events fit together; as understanding grows the interpretation changes until a 'best fit' is reached and the meaning of the story is discerned.

Plots were classified by Kenneth and Mary Gergen (1988) as progressive, regressive, or stable, based on whether the protagonist advances toward his or her goal, remains in the same position with regard to the goal, or becomes further removed. They note, however, that it is possible to be both progressive and steady; for example, when a person has to be innovative but is also reliable.

Plot is more evident in narrated stories than in narratives of personal experience or short accounts. To explore the plot of a story, and its significance:[5]

▶ Examine the physical and cognitive nature of the protagonist – the main character in the story.
▶ Identify relationships between the protagonist and significant others.
▶ Explore the choices and actions the protagonist takes in achieving his or her goals.
▶ Map the development of the plot along a timeline, showing significant events, twists, and turns, with contextual information indicated as well.
▶ Trace the development of the story, from beginning, through middle, to end. What is it that gives the story coherence?
▶ Chart the life course (as a graph), with its patterns of ascent, decline, and stability.
▶ Compare stories about similar events in different settings (cf. Box 4.6). How do the events vary in the stories from different settings?

Genre

When narratives have a common pattern to the unfolding of their plot such that members of the audience can anticipate what will happen to the main characters, then those narratives can be said to belong to a particular genre. The genre of a narrative describes its distinctive structure and contents, and sets it within a socially and culturally recognised framework. This facilitates communication of events and experiences for the author and assists the audience to make sense of the events being portrayed (Andrews, Day Sclater, Squire, & Tamboukou, 2004; Elliott, 2005).

Stories in Western literature fit within four main genres:

• romance, where the hero faces a series of personal challenges but eventually reaches his or her goal;
• comedy, in which the (often exaggerated) anti-hero has, or acquires, the social skills needed to overcome the hazards that threaten the social order and ensure a happy ending;
• tragedy, in which the hero is defeated by the forces of evil and suffers great sorrow; and
• satire, a form of ironic comedy, which expresses a cynical view on people of authority, often exposing them as inept or corrupt.

---

[5]See Elliott (2005), McCance et al. (2001).

Other commonly recognised genres include the epic, fable, horror story, melo-drama, and detective story (Elliott, 2005; Gibbs, 2007). Additional genres might be defined for specific cultures or subcultural groups (Box 7.7).

To identify genre:

▶ View the story within its social and cultural context.
▶ Look for patterns in the ways the stories are told, particularly for predictability in the plot.
▶ Explore the purposes served by the different patterns found.

┐ **Box 7.7** ┌

The genre of HIV narratives

Corinne Squire (in Andrews et al., 2004) analysed the genre of HIV narratives in two countries. These narratives positioned the tellers 'as creative interpreters and constructors of their places within cultures', able to 'remake events and experiences into their lived cultures' (2004: 118).

Two genres were dominant in the United Kingdom: 'coming-out' stories that mirrored those of gay and lesbian coming-out stories were told by gay men and by heterosexual men and women; and heterosexual romance stories were told by some women. In South Africa, the genre of the stories took several forms, each reflecting a different response to the silence that accompanied HIV in South Africa for many years. These were identified by Squire as an 'Oprification' disclosure genre (named after the format of the Oprah Winfrey show); religious (conversion and witnessing) stories; and a 'speaking-out' genre that reflected the tradition of nation building in South Africa.

Narrative structure

Exploring the structure of a narrative takes you beyond a focus on the content. Structural analysis draws attention to the way people portray events and, in so doing, reveals something of the teller, their cognitive schema, and their purpose in recounting the narrative. Structural analysis can reveal differences in how people experience an event which, thematically, appears to be common across cases (Riessman, 2008).

People from different cultural and linguistic backgrounds structure their nar-ratives differently. These vary, for example, from the typical Western pattern of a story that is cohesive, sequential, and focused, to a non-Western pattern of thematically associated episodes without a clearly enunciated point. Such differ-ences can create disenfranchisement, misunderstanding, or even conflict in international meetings where these differences are not recognised and accepted. Riessman compared the structural analysis of narrative with the structural analysis of a musical composition:

When we go to a concert, unless we are musicians, we typically just experience the work; the performers, on the other hand, have done considerable 'unpacking' [of the score, its instrumentation, and its phraseology] in rehearsal to construct the unity we hear. Structural analysis of oral narrative requires the same level of scrutiny; we slow down a narrative account … to notice how a narrator uses form and language to achieve particular effects. (2008: 81)

Labov's structural model

Labov and Waletzky's (1967) 'evaluation' model of structural analysis, comprising six elements, is the most often described and applied form of structural analysis. It is best applied to relatively short narratives of personal experience (Labov, 1997). Labov applied it primarily to incidents of violence recounted by people across different cultures.

The six elements in the model are:

- abstract – a summary of the sequence of events in the narrative;
- orientation – sets up the time, place, situation, participants, and initial behaviour;
- complicating actions – reports a sequence of events, each given in response to a potential question, 'And what happened [then]?';
- evaluation – consequences for the needs and desires of the narrator;
- resolution – what finally happened;
- coda – a final return to the present in a way that precludes the question, 'And what happened then?'

Structural analysis of this style provides an understanding of the temporal organisation of a narrative, with the complicating action giving the chronology of events. The ordering of the structural elements is not fixed, nor are all elements always present. Although complicating actions are necessarily sequential, evaluative elements may occur throughout the narrative. Critically, 'it is the evaluation that conveys to an audience how they are to understand the *meaning* of the events that constitute the narrative, and simultaneously indicates what type of response is required' (Elliott, 2005: 9).

In a study exploring nursing culture, and the role of nursing culture in relation to staff retention and patient care, Jan Savage (2000) compared thematic analysis of interview data based on coding with an analysis of the nurse's narratives using Labov's structural approach. She found the structural approach retained a holistic view of the moral core of the story, whereas the thematic approach focused more on the relationship between time, space, role, and knowledge; both revealed a concern with issues of professional identity. Savage concluded that each approach offered 'different emphases on meaning … glimpsing different kinds of "truths"' (2000: 1499).

By applying Labov's structural elements to Elizabeth's somewhat disjointed story of how she became involved in research (Table 7.2), I found the identification of evaluative elements throughout the story brought a coherence to it that was otherwise not so evident. Deciding the exact boundaries of some of the elements in a personal narrative is not always easy, but perhaps this doesn't matter in so far as the exercise of attempting to do so helps you to better understand the story and the teller's perspective on the experience(s) being described.

Table 7.2 The structure of Elizabeth's account of becoming involved in research

Element	Narrative
Orientation: inclusive of *abstract*	My parents are professor and associate professor of psychology … so I have grown up in this sort of very academic background, *research has been just one of the things that people do as long as I remember*, and it was always presented as something that was interesting and exciting because you actually found out new things and people passed through our home who had discovered new things, which we talked about over the dinner tables so –
Complicating actions with *evaluative statements*	And my first job, I did mathematics, *not with a view to doing research*, it was just my best subject at school, I did a maths degree and I did a little bit of psychology … there was not really a lot I could do with that so I got a job in the public service as a clerk …
	and then I got a job in crime research *and that gave me a whole new focus on research because here people were doing research that really affected people's lives* and legislation and working on things like bail reform and [aboriginal legal rights] … We did a whole range of things, looked at homosexual offences as they were then, back in the mid seventies I guess. *That was good in what was a sense that research really can change people's lives through legislation.*
	Then I went off and had children and became a depressed housewife, and my friend said why don't you get a part-time job Elizabeth, lots of women feel better with a part-time job. Places like [town] and [regional centre] have the highest unemployment in Australia, don't be silly, there aren't any jobs, and certainly none that would be any less boring than being at home with the kids.
	But nevertheless to prove the point I had to buy Saturday's paper and sure enough there was a job for a research assistant, with experience in research, preferably an honours degree, not necessarily, make your own hours and the topic was disability and I had a child that was disabled, so there I was experienced with disability as well, I mean talk about made to measure job.
Resolution	So that was good, I got back into that and my boss was very encouraging and the other women I worked with were encouraging and I was back at uni within a year with a view to doing honours and PhD on account I wanted to be a researcher instead of a research assistant.
Coda (evaluative)	*So I guess for me it has always been there.*

Using poetic structure for units of discourse

James Gee (1986; 1991) developed an alternative way of structuring narrative that does not depend on temporal sequence, a single focal point, or a resolving plot. The text is organised into fluent thematic stanzas with the interviewer's interjections or prompts removed, reflecting the units of speech of the narrator. Intonation and other prosodic features provide cues as to what is important; hence it is critical to work with constant reference to the original recording. Line and stanza breaks reflect pauses and changes in pitch, with each stanza being about a single topic within the story (often captured in a heading for the stanza). Already, a level of interpretation has been applied to the text in defining textual boundaries and in designing the stanza-based transcript of the narrative.

Catherine Kohler Riessman (2008) has provided several examples of text arranged in this way, applied to stories told in research on the meaning and management of infertility, and in research on divorce. She described her work on one very difficult passage, Rick's description of 'bleak depression' following separation – a passage that might otherwise have simply been divided into thematically coded segments: 'Meanings became clear only after repeatedly listening to the tape for relevant units of discourse and recurrent figurative language. When I finally constructed a textual representation that displayed my understandings from the raw material, it felt liberating' (2008: 100). From this passage, and others like it, she was then able to identify some of the subtle ways in which men expressed distress following separation: their approach–avoidance form of speaking about feelings, along with their emphasis on doing rather than feeling.

Transitional and linguistic features in narrative

In free-flowing narrative, shifts in content, pauses, changes in tone of voice, or repeated phrases are each significant for interpretation of the narrative. Gaps and inconsistencies, for example, might suggest alternative counter-narratives (Bernard & Ryan, 2010). Narratives often contain features that prompt surprise or curiosity or that suggest particular meaning, such as sudden shifts of direction, contradictions, omissions, repetitions, critical events, or unexpected endings. Why does Mr Brown never say anything about his son, despite his obvious presence in the house where Mr Brown has been caring for and regularly turning his vegetative wife every two hours for the past 10 years (Poirier & Ayres, 1997: 552–4)? Why does he continue his seven-times repeated mantra of 'She took care of me for 45 years, and now I'll take care of her' when he also comments that 'I ain't doin'' her no favors 'cause if she knew what she was goin'' through, she, one way or the other, she wouldn't put up with it'? Perhaps it is the anticipated ending of mastery in not allowing her need to be the death of him that gives meaning to the current plot? These are not questions that can be answered with coding; rather, the reader 'must *listen to and hear the silence*' (Laub, 1991: 58, quoted by Poirier & Ayres, 1997) to discern a story that is often not heard even by the narrator.

▶ Use highlighters and marginal notes or, if you are working on computer, colour, annotations, memos, and/or codes to identify features of the telling, such as sudden shifts in the narrative, critical events, key statements, repetitions.

▶ Look for what is not present in the narrative, as well as what is, and record those omissions using annotations or memos.

▶ Use links to point to developments or contradictions in a story or explanation (Figure 7.5).

▶ For each linguistic feature, note also (in memo or code) the purpose of the element – whether intentional or not. Ask and note what the teller is achieving by its use (Box 7.8).

▶ Observe whether participants are telling of a real or hypothetical experience, offering fact or opinion, and if they are speaking for themselves or for others.

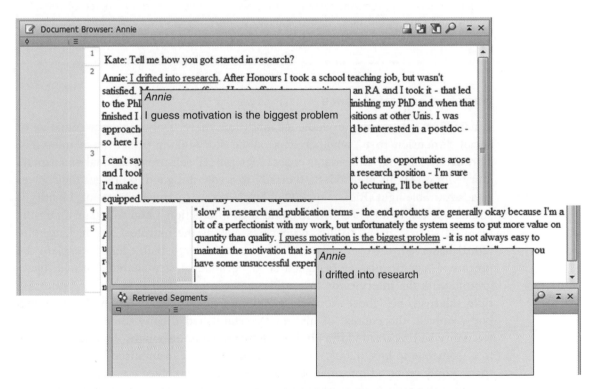

Figure 7.5   Using the two-way links feature of MAXQDA to point to a development within the text

Note: hovering over a link reveals the linked text; Ctrl+click takes you to the linked text.

Box 7.8

Exploring the meaning of inconsistencies in language

Changes in tense provide clues as to important issues for the interviewee or story-teller. Jonathan Smith (Smith et al., 2009: 104–5) provides an example from a woman suffering chronic back pain, who says:

> I just think I'm the fittest because there are three girls … and I thought well I'm the fittest and I used to work like a horse and I thought I was the strongest.

Smith suggests that her shift from present tense to past reflects 'the heart of the psychological battle for Linda, as her sense of identity is ravaged by her back pain'; she clings to her past identity of being super-fit while also recognising that she has now lost this with her current physical limitations. His interpretation is based on 'a close reading of what is already within the passage, helped by analysis of what the participant said elsewhere in the interview'. This interpretation might, more speculatively, be related to more formal theoretical positions, but only at a later time.

Similarly, think back to Vivien's account of taking her son for vaccination (Box 6.15), and her 'confused' use of pronouns when she reported (in multiple ways) thinking about how 'I've got to have these needles, we've got to have them done.' Was she projecting her own fears onto her child, or did her confusion of pronouns reflect a strong level of bonding and the degree of empathy she felt for him? One would need further data to provide context for and allow adequate interpretation of statements such as these.

Narrative as performance

A narrative has to have an audience, and thus there is always a performative or social dimension to it, whether it is public story-telling or narrative interview. Through the telling, 'informants enact biographical, self-presentational and explanatory work' (Atkinson, 2005: 8), typically in a way designed to present themselves in a favourable light (Riessman, 2008). From a constructivist viewpoint, identity is situated, social reality is constructed through interaction – and so, when analysing people's stories, attend to the audience as well as the narrator. Kristin Langellier (2001) observed, for example, that her interviewee felt better able to explain the (negative) significance of being tattooed because of her shared Catholic background with the interviewer. When Riessman interviewed Burt, a man with multiple sclerosis, he 'chose to disclose intimate details about his [malfunctioning] body' only in the context of his having established a connection with her as a woman who represented the kind of companionship he sought – 'someone to talk to … someone to love' (2008: 112). She argued that he dramatised his story, rather than simply reported information, because of that perceived connection.

A narrator who is particularly conscious of his or her audience will use characteristic linguistic features directed to creating a closeness between performer and audience. These include using direct speech to build credibility; asides to engage with the audience; repetition to mark key moments; expressive sounds to signal pivotal turning points in the action; and a combination of both past and historical present verb tenses that underscore the agency of the narrator (Riessman, 2008). These features were evident in the way Burt constructed his identity through the story of his last day at work.

Each narrative is a product of telling and hearing (or reading). Each telling of a story can vary, each reading of a text can bring different meaning, and readings by different audiences will have different meanings. An interviewee may speak with multiple voices – perhaps representing another's viewpoint and then counterbalancing that with their personal view. Or, they might position themselves in several roles: 'Speaking as a politician ... [perhaps something about national finances imposing limitations on government support for child care], but then, as the mother of a young child ... [the need to have reliable and adequately financed child care services], and as an activist ... [the implications of child care for gender equality].' The opportunity is there for you to compare and contextualise such differences, rather than treat them as a problem.

A story does not speak for itself, it is performed by a narrator. Ask, therefore:

▶ For whom was the story constructed? What was it designed to accomplish?
▶ Was there a common cultural understanding between narrator and audience? What cultural resources does the narration draw on or take for granted?
▶ Is the story told in the style of a report, or is the narrator 'losing the plot' to communicate their own emotions? Explore other linguistic features used by the narrator to retain attention.
▶ A narration can be seen as a dramaturgical production that can be analysed (and coded) in terms of intrapersonal and interpersonal experiences and actions including conflicts, strategies, attitudes, emotions, and subtexts (Saldaña, 2009).

Deconstruct the storyline

In the view of postmodernists, truth is illusory, multifaceted, and subject to individual and local interpretation. Accepted values and conventional social structures are to be interrogated and challenged to expose the ways in which they have been mediated by power relations inherent in the metanarratives of society, religion, or economic theory (Crotty, 1998; Richardson, 2000). Individual, public, and official discourses, time and context bound, are deconstructed (disaggregated; disassembled; disarranged) and the signs and symbols within those discourses given free play to allow new possibilities of meaning to emerge (Grbich, 2007). Particular attention is paid to exposing dichotomies in social values, through exploring silences, disruptions, contractions, and contradictions (Box 7.9).

▶ Record links between dispersed words or statements within and across texts to reflect the development of a particular thread of meaning.
▶ Within that thread, identify hierarchies, dichotomies, and opposites for specific attention.

▶ Look for what is not said, and what (or whom) is minimised, considering how this is so, and what it means in the context of the thread.

▶ Examine generalisations and assumptions inherent in the text, consider their social-cultural-historical roots, and explore how these influence the flow of argument.

❗ Formalising an approach to deconstruction is dangerous: treat these simply as transitional strategies to help open up the text. Consequently, they will provide (ambiguous) insights, not definitive conclusions.

Box 7.9

Deconstructing media portrayal of children who kill

Ruth Webber (1997) explored the twin themes of good and evil in cases involving child murderers, as portrayed in the Australian print media. In one, a 13- and a 14-year-old boy robbed and stabbed a taxi driver. Each of the boys pleaded 'not guilty' and accused the other of the actual murder. Initial media reports portrayed the two boys in a similar way. Then, during the committal hearing, the older one changed his plea to manslaughter and became the primary witness against the other. From that point, reports changed so that the younger boy became the 'evil' ruthless killer and the older boy an easily led child 'victim'. Increasingly, journalists ascribed positive attributes to one, and negative to the other. Parents of both boys attended court with them, but while parents of one were described 'hugging him' and 'whispering assurances', the other was 'flanked' by his family. The older boy, 'blonde and fair skinned with fleshy features', despite having a criminal record and admitting to initiating the idea of the robbery, was depicted as remorseful, and from an unfortunate but caring family who were having family counselling to remediate a few problems. The younger boy, 'short, [with] dark hair and thin, angular features', was portrayed in contrast as the product of a 'bad' (uncaring) single-parent family, a cold and callous ringleader (despite having no criminal record) who, having fathered a child, sought adult status for himself. The first was charged with armed robbery and manslaughter and sentenced to three years' detention in a youth training centre; the second with murder and 13 years' imprisonment in an adult prison.

In each of the cases studied, the voices of law and order and of the professional expert prevailed with their message that a dysfunctional family (or the state as substitute parent) is the root of evil. Readers were left in no doubt as to the joint guilt of the accused *and* his or her family by the dominant but simplistic confrontation between evil and goodness in the reports of these cases. The voices of the children and their families were never heard.

Discerning meaning making in narrative analysis

Perhaps the most critical element of all in narrative analysis for the social scientist is that narrative conveys the participant's understanding of the events or experiences they describe – how they make meaning of them (Box 7.10). As analyst, you will seek to understand the author as well as the text – to develop empathy with your story-tellers, to see the world they describe from their perspective, but also to challenge and question their perspectives, seeking deeper or latent meanings.

Discerning and understanding these meanings bring together insights gained from your analyses of purpose, plot, genre, structure, linguistic features, and audience.

Box 7.10

Caregivers making meaning of their lives

Lioness Ayres (2000a; 2000b) used narrative inquiry methods to study 36 family caregivers. Her starting assumption, based on previous research, was that the meaning that caregivers gave to their experience was more relevant to understanding the stress of caregiving than to the objective features of that experience. She sought, therefore, to identify how caregivers made meaning of their situations, and to explore the contexts in which these meanings occurred. Because each story was unique, even when circumstances were similar, each had first to be studied as a self-contained whole. Texts were read for implicit as well as explicit meaning – a technique referred to as 'overreading'. Caregivers used expectations, explanations, and strategies to interpret their circumstances in the context of their lives, to identify those circumstances that required interventions, to select strategies to manage those circumstances, to predict the outcome of a strategy, and to make sense of the events that occurred. She worked back and forth within each case in a 'hermeneutic spiral' and then combined this with thematic analysis to extend her hermeneutic understanding across cases. From this she identified four distinct story types, revealed through the iterative interaction of caregivers' expectations, explanations, and strategies: stories of ideal lives, stories of ordinary lives, stories of compromised lives, and ambiguous stories that comprised a conflicted mix of these.

▶ Interpret the purpose and context for the telling of a story to provide a mechanism for exploring how the teller makes sense of a particular experience.

▶ If you undertake a structural analysis of a story or an account, look especially to the evaluative component in that story to discern meaning.

▶ Narratives may involve distortions of facts, but these distortions convey meanings given to events which provide valid understandings of lives in social contexts. Explore distortions for what they can tell you about how the teller makes meaning.

▶ 'Overread' your texts by examining repetitions, omissions, distractions from the topic, and contradictions within the text.

Applying lessons from narrative approaches

This review of narrative approaches, as extensive as it is, will not turn you into a narrative researcher. If you wish to pursue that pathway, you will need to study in more detail the sources quoted, and further examples of the application of these strategies (Riessman, 2008, would provide an excellent starting point). They are included here to alert you to alternative ways of thinking about your data, to remind you of the importance of seeing and understanding the storyline that connects your data segments, to help you to recognise some of the features within your data in a way that will enrich your understanding of them, and perhaps to encourage you to go on to explore and apply some of these narrative strategies in your own study.

Focus on discourse: the intersubjective space

Discourse analytic methods derive generally from social semiotics – the analysis of signs and symbols. Analysis of signs involves studying the rules or forms of language, and the relationship between language and behaviour. Hepburn and Potter (2004: 181) describe discourse analysis as having a 'varied intellectual geography' covering an ever-changing collection of subspecialties. For the purposes of this review, these will be grouped into two major strands: those that focus on the structure of talk or text, with little or no reference to other contextual factors; and those that explore issues associated with power and control as they are expressed through language within the wider context of society and culture.

Like narrative, the various approaches taken and methods used in discourse analysis derive from a constructivist perspective. And, as with narrative methods, the idea here is for you to become aware of these methods as an alternative approach to research and data analysis: you may wish to go further in exploring their relevance to your questions, or you might simply use this awareness to sharpen your analytic focus as you review data that were not specifically designed for this purpose. In particular, you will become aware of the influence of language in shaping all social interaction from your individual interview through to major social movements.

Structure in talk and text

Conversation analysis and discursive psychology each draw primarily on recordings made in natural settings in order to determine how a conversation develops and is maintained, and/or how ideas are jointly constructed through conversation. Analysis is facilitated by working with both the recording and a detailed transcript of it. Segments of text that are of focal interest will typically be transcribed using standardised symbols to mark inflections, volume, pauses, co-occurring sequences, and other vocal features, to facilitate detailed interpretation (cf. Box 3.5).

Researchers engaged in *conversation analysis* examine the structural aspects of turn-taking and other 'rules' in naturally occurring conversation, for example, whether a request is direct or indirect and whether it offers a way out (Drew, 2003; Peräkylä, 2004). Conversation analysts don't explain a turn by using speaker's intentions, or by reference to role or status. They look at the spoken words, rather than making assumptions about orientations and motives (Box 7.11). This type of analysis is not concerned with details of contextual or other social information, but rather examines the way the conversation develops around a particular type of interaction such as the beginning of a clinical interview, or the response to a cold call on the telephone. Data for this type of analysis are usually quite short excerpts of recorded conversation, transcribed in detail to include expression as well as content.

▶ Identify sequences of related talk.

▶ Examine how speakers take on particular roles or identities, for example, as client or questioner.

▶ Look for outcomes in the talk – a repair, request for clarification, laughter. How were these produced?

▶ Consider deviant cases where something that is expected does not happen. Why were those different?

✓ Computer-based coding can be used to label the nature of each element or turn in the conversation, with patterns in the sequencing of these then identified using the query functions, to allow interpretation by the researcher.

Box 7.11

The structure of an inconsistency in conversation

Paul Drew (2003) described how an inconsistency in what someone says (such as a strong denial followed by an exception) might at first be interpreted as attributable to some psychological variable in the speaker, but when a collection of extracts with this feature are considered, it begins to appear less as a psychological attribute and more like something generated by the interaction. Thus a pattern is revealed where the initial version of the retracted statement is always strongly or categorically stated; the recipient avoids endorsing the initial version (by silence or a minimal acknowledgement); and the subsequent retraction is given with the same lexical form but in explicit contrast to the initial version. These subsequent versions, then, are designed to be consistent with the initial version, but to allow an exception. Analysis of the setting in which these statements arise indicates that the initial overstated versions are necessary to achieve a social purpose which would not have been achieved with the weaker version if it had been given straight away. The latter can, however, be given safely once the moment requiring the stronger version has passed.

Discursive psychology is 'concerned with the role of talk and texts in social practices' (Hepburn & Potter, 2004: 185). Discourse is seen to be the primary medium of human action and interaction through which ideas are constructed.

Rather than seeing such discursive constructions as expressions of the speaker's underlying cognitive states, they are examined in the context of their occurrence as situated and occasioned constructions whose precise nature makes sense to participants and analysts alike in terms of the social action these descriptions accomplish. (Potter & Edwards, 1992: 2)

Turn-taking in naturally occurring conversation may be explored, as in conversation analysis, but with attention given to the way critical concepts are introduced and developed in the conversation. Hepburn and Potter (2004) provide an example from their research in which they analysed the expression of 'concern' in initial calls to a child protection agency. They recognised standard ways in which concern might be expressed by the caller, and several ways in which it was implied if not expressed. The expression or recognition of concern was found to 'soften' the initial interactions between the caller and the child protection officer, whereas starting straight into a direct report of abuse would then require the officer to immediately ask for evidence. In addition to contributing to theory on the way cognition is understood in psychology, this research was able to provide practical help to the agency by providing an understanding of how problems can arise in interacting with callers, with suggestions for how to counter them.

▶ Explore patterns in how conversations (or texts) develop in relation to an issue or a situation of interest.
▶ Look at deviant cases to identify alternative approaches and their consequences.
▶ Think about the conversation in your interviews:
  ○ How has the way you introduced topics for discussion influenced the kinds of responses you obtained?
  ○ How have you responded to what was said by the interviewee, and what impact has that had on maintaining the conversation?
  ○ How have your responses and prompts through the course of the interview influenced the development of ideas around the topics being discussed? Your 'mmms' will have a reinforcing effect, for example, encouraging further contribution in the same vein from the interviewee.
▶ Use this awareness of methods described in conversation analysis and discursive psychology when you explore interactions within a focus group.

Discourse in social context

The defining feature of *critical discourse analysis* is 'its concern with power as a central condition in social life ... Not only the notion of struggles for power and control, but also the intertextuality and recontextualization of competing discourses in various public spaces and genres, are closely attended to' (Wodak, 2004: 199). Critical discourse analysis is typically multidisciplinary, and is primarily problem oriented – with a focus on social inequality as expressed in language. The analyst pays more attention than those working in discursive psychology to the social setting and historical context, incorporating fieldwork and ethnography as part of the method (Hepburn & Potter, 2004; Wodak, 2004). Texts are analysed for the way in which the discourses within them construct people and situations, for arguments used to legitimate particular viewpoints, and for the way in which those viewpoints and arguments are expressed. For example, the construction of 'us' and 'them' is fundamental in discourses of identity and difference. Analyses are informed by theory.

Ruth Wodak (2004: 210) suggests the following steps in undertaking critical discourse analysis. These steps are taken recursively, moving between text, ethnographic data, theories, and analysis. She provides a brief worked example (taken from a much more extensive analysis) based on a political interview during the emergence of an extremist right-wing party in Austria.

▶ Select text to analyse.
▶ Review other sources that provide concurrent contextual information.
▶ Identify the genre and type of discourse, as a basis for seeking more background information such as texts on similar topics, using similar arguments, of similar genres.
▶ Determine precise research questions. Seek out explanatory theories relevant to the questions.
▶ Operationalise the questions, developing categories that will capture relevant data.
▶ Review and code the text, using the categories determined in the previous step.
▶ Draw up a context diagram for the text.
▶ Interpret the text in relation to the research questions.

Foucaultian discourse analysis similarly focuses on a problem, and asks how this issue or problem came to be, rather than why (Kendall & Wickham, 2004). The analyst seeks to find the beginnings of related practices in historical archives, focusing on their discursive (linguistic) features, rather than institutions or people. The past is used to understand the present, and as a springboard into the future: what provided the (now long past) foundations that allowed the emergence of ideas that shape ways of responding to a current social issue? Discontinuities in the historical archive are of particular interest, but they are surprisingly rare in comparison to the continuity of discourse.

Foucault studied historically created discourses – of science, medicine, and sexuality, for example – and showed how they served prevailing institutional structures through the integration of power and knowledge. The availability of discursive resources to a society – the variety of ways in which objects and subjects might be constructed – either facilitates or constrains conversation and thus social life and so discourses impact on the distribution and exercise of power. Reversal of dominant discourses requires resistance that recognises the legitimacy of alternative or counter-discourses (Willig, 2003).

In taking a topic, such as obesity, feminism, or professionalism, to investigate through a study of discourse, one would work through the following issues and questions:

▶ Investigate how this topic emerged within discourse.
▶ Delimit and specify what is to be included in considering the topic.

▶ Investigate, through a sample of texts, who talks and writes about this topic; where it is talked and written about; and how it is talked and written about, focusing especially on statements that recur or regularly co-occur.

▶ What new concepts have arisen? Under what conditions did they arise?

▶ What are the dominant forms of discourse that define the substance of the topic?

▶ What power relations are involved? How do individuals and groups watch and normalise or manage these?

Applying lessons from discourse analysis

Qualitative analysts might wish to take note of the ways in which various styles of discourse analysts (or narrative researchers) approach their task and draw on these strategies to enrich their analysis, but they are warned against regarding simple summaries, quotes, interpretive labels, or references to discursive features as evidence of having done a fully fledged discourse (or narrative) analysis:

> Original analysis should seek to show how established discursive devices are used, in new sets of material, to manage the speakers' interactional business. What is required is to show what the feature does, how it is used, what it is used to do, how it is handled sequentially and rhetorically, and so on. (Antaki et al., 2003: 29)

As with strategies and lessons drawn from any established methodology, read, learn, practise, and apply – but do so recognising both the full requirements of the methodology, and the limitations of the way in which you have applied it.

The value of case-based approaches

Bent Flyvbjerg made an impassioned plea for the value of case-based research by suggesting it generates 'the type of context-dependent knowledge that research on learning shows to be necessary to allow people to develop from rule-based beginners [relying on analytical rationality] to virtuoso experts [offering a fluid performance of tacit skills]' (2004: 421). He notes, further, that all experts 'operate on the basis of intimate knowledge of several thousand concrete cases in their areas of expertise. Context-dependent knowledge and experience are at the very heart of expert activity. Such knowledge and expertise also lie at the centre of the case study as a … method of learning' (2004: 421).

While the methods described in this chapter are not specifically designed or presented as case study methods in the sense that Yin or Stake or Flyvbjerg might describe them, many of those reviewed do emphasise the importance of seeing each case in your study as a complete entity within a context. For the methods that have been reviewed, cases have typically been individuals, although some of the principles could be applied to collective cases such as work groups or organisations, or even cultures.

Writing about your use of case-based, thematic, and narrative methods

In the methods chapter

▶ Explain your rationale for the methods you have chosen – what they were intended to achieve in relation to your research goals and questions. Reference the source(s) of your ideas.

▶ Describe what you actually did (the steps you took), and provide an example of the process.

▶ Discuss any limitations you experienced in applying your chosen methods, as well as noting where they worked particularly well.

Exercises

Exercise 1: From categories to themes

▶ Identify two or three significant categories or themes in your data that relate together in some way. Express that *relationship* as a higher-level (superordinate) thematic statement (i.e., not as a category!).

Exercise 2: Structure and plot

▶ Explore the structure and plot of two or three classic children's stories. How are they similar and different? If possible, compare these with the structure and plot of a children's story from a different culture.

Exercise 3: Purpose in an account

▶ Identify a brief account within your data. What purpose does it serve for the teller?

Exercise 4: A double hermeneutic

▶ Watch or read a life story, told in film or biography or even a novel. How does the central character make meaning of the events of their life?

Exercise 5: Linguistic features

▶ Review your data to identify linguistic features, e.g., turning points, hesitations, use of pronouns. What do these tell you about the speaker?

Further reading

Smith et al. (2009) comprehensively and clearly present background and theory, methods and examples for interpretative phenomenological analysis.
Colaizzi (1978) details a classical approach to phenomenology from a psychologist's viewpoint.

Attride-Stirling (2001) and Braun and Clarke (2006) each write about taking thematic analysis beyond identification of simple themes.

Farnsworth and Boon (2010) describe the high level of group interaction and conflictual dynamics running parallel to information gathering that operated in their focus groups exploring the experience of poverty and deprivation. This interaction was analysed from the perspective of focal conflict theory.

Riessman (2008) covers several approaches to narrative analysis, amply supported by examples primarily drawn from the author's own research that illustrate a thought-provoking depth of analysis.

Elliott (2005) provides an overview of narrative analysis, from both quantitative and qualitative perspectives.

Poirier and Ayres (2002) used stories from life and stories from fiction to address issues raised in theories of nursing care and in feminist theories, as they relate to family caregiving.

Gilligan, Spencer, Weinberg, and Bertsch (2003) describe their 'listening guide' for interview data that suggests three readings of the text: for plot, as an 'I poem', and to categorise. Rogers (2005) similarly describes using four (interconnected) readings of children's narratives to discern the unsayable as well as the overt content.

Gee (2011) explains and illustrates 27 tools (questions to ask of data) for learning how humans make meaning and communicate (i.e., for doing discourse analysis).

Van Maanen (1979) outlines a range of ways in which 'fictions' are created in ethnographic research, and how these might contribute to an interpretation of culture.

Silverman (2010) draws a very large proportion of his examples from discursive and conversation analysis projects, presenting them in a very readable style.

Bernard and Ryan (2010: Chapter 10) provide detail on discourse analysis, supported by multiple examples. Chapters 8 on domain analysis and 16 on decision modelling cover alternative methods of gathering and analysing culturally relevant data, not included here.

Friese (2012) explains use of hyperlinking and the network tool in Atlas.ti for showing connections in data.

PART 3

DESCRIBE, COMPARE, AND RELATE: MOVING ON FROM CODES AND THEMES

These next three chapters are loosely based on a repetitive cycle of analysis that will inexorably lead you toward building rich description and explanatory theory. In Chapter 1 of this book I described the *Describe, Compare, Relate* sequence of analytic steps as a kind of 'formula' for moving beyond piles of coded data and simple thematic analysis. This sequence has a history, and perhaps that history will help to contextualise this approach to thinking your way through an analysis.

That history goes back to the 1980s – not that I saw it so clearly then. The dominant fashion in practice-based social research and evaluation at the time was to run surveys comprising mainly 'closed' questions (questions with pre-categorised response options) supplemented by a small number of 'open' questions, usually of the 'please explain', 'provide an example', or 'any other comments' varieties. Traditionally, one approached statistical analysis of the closed variables with a routine series of steps:

- Obtain the frequencies and/or 'descriptives' (depending on whether it was a categorical or continuous variable) to get a picture of the spread of responses, i.e., the number of people who chose a particular alternative, or the average rating or score given in response to a proposition, along with the level of variability in those scores.
- Run comparative analyses using cross-tabs, *t*-tests, or one-way ANOVAs (again depending on whether the dependent variable was categorical or continuous) systematically across all variables, to assess whether each varied for different (usually demographic, occasionally experimental) subgroups in the sample. This step might then be supplemented by analyses that took two (rarely more) grouping variables into account at the same time (e.g., gender and education) in order to determine which had the stronger relationship with the outcome.

Many reports done at that time went no further than this – simply reporting frequencies and differences between groups. Taking things a step or two further, however, is what I found made the whole exercise more productive. Patterns of response demanded an explanation that was not satisfied, necessarily, by simple association with or partitioning by demographic or similar variables. And so to the third step:

- For any variable of interest, look for any other variables across the dataset that might help one to understand the variety of responses given, and test the association with each of those other variables. Occasionally, one might also run a factor or regression analysis, to cluster a set of variables or to predict an outcome variable.

Jump forward now, across several decades. I am now less often analysing survey data; rather, I am spending my time working primarily with academics and students engaged in analysing qualitative or mixed methods data. All too often, I am asked the question: 'Now I've coded all my data, what do I do next?', or similarly, 'How can I print off all the text for each of my codes?' Both of these questions are symptomatic of problems that can 'cripple' analysis (if not the analyst). Borrowing those three steps and translating them for qualitative analysis has become a constructive pathway to take novice researchers through the mental barrier that 'analysis' can create.

If you've been following the suggestions in this book, you've actually already done a lot of analysis and writing as you've coded and connected your data. Even so, this step marks a new phase in your research, where you have piles of data, a bundle of concepts, stories, and scattered ideas about how codes might connect. The strategies outlined in the three chapters that comprise this part of the book are designed to open the way from working with discrete information 'bits' to the kind of relational thinking that can form the basis of rich, interpretive description, modelling, and theory building.

The value of reflective writing and visualisation in tables, charts, and diagrams has been a constant theme of this book, and continues to be so here. Indeed, writing and visualisation are integral components of this whole stage of analysis:

- ✓ Recording analysis prompts further thoughts and further questions – a 'continual internal dialogue' prompting more reflective writing that eventually moves you toward theoretical integration (Strauss, 1987: 110).
- ✓ Attempting to put your ideas into a visual diagram forces you to think about relationships between concepts and also generates the kind of thinking that will move you toward theoretical integration.

Miles and Huberman visualised and described it this way (see figure):

Looking at [a chart, table, network diagram] helps you to summarize and begin to see themes, patterns, and clusters. You write analytic text that clarifies and formalizes these first findings, helps make sense of the display, and may suggest additional comparisons to be made via the display.

Those new comparisons, in turn, help you discover new relationships and propose explanations. The resulting analytic text then may suggest ways of elaborating the display, integrating or rearranging it to permit what amounts to a reanalysis. The reanalysis helps deepen the initial explanations. (1994: 101)

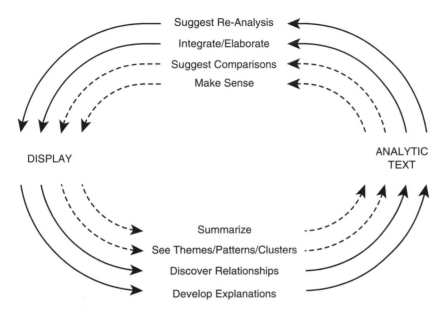

Interaction between display and analytic text

Source: Miles and Huberman, 1994: 101, Figure 5.4

8

Describing, evolving, and theorising concepts

Concepts are the building blocks from which theory is constructed. A concept at any level is a labelled phenomenon – a representation of something (or a class of somethings) that exists (in critical realist terms, either physically or mentally). 'Concepts give us a basis for discourse and arriving at shared understandings' (Corbin, 2009: 40). This chapter focuses particularly on the development of coded categories, although those working with more generalised themes will also find strategies to think about and apply, and the principle of describing before going into deeper comparative and relational analyses is relevant for all approaches to analytic work.

In this chapter:

- learn how reviewing, describing and writing about the categories and concepts you have identified through coding will move your analysis forward;
- combine or abstract from your initial coded concepts to develop more analytically useful focused codes, metacodes, or pattern codes.

And for those for whom it is relevant:

- Explore and review a range of approaches to theorising and developing the composition and structure of concepts.

Describing categories and concepts (or themes) as a step in analysis

After steadily growing knowledge of your data through developing, organising, and refining codes, many will feel uncertain about how to move on. This is especially a problem if you have been doggedly working away at coding without regularly pausing to reflect, write memos, and develop conceptual linkages between categories.

Beginning to write about the codes and concepts you are working with is one way forward.

Why describe?

Description provides you with a non-threatening entry point to the process of writing and further analysis. It is a beginning step toward completing that looming final report that even the most uncertain of us can take, but even more importantly for now, thorough, carefully executed qualitative description is foundational to further analysis – an argument Michael Quinn Patton (2002) repeated multiple times in his chapter on analysis. 'Even at the highest levels of abstract science, there could be no scientific hypotheses and theoretical or laboratory activity without prior or accompanying descriptions. Though description is clearly not theory, description is basic to theorizing' (Corbin & Strauss, 2008: 54). Not all the descriptive analysis and writing you do at the moment will necessarily end up in your final dissertation or report, but it will move you toward that goal.

Description fills several important roles in qualitative research:

- description of context and sample situates the study;
- the process of describing assists in refining ideas about what the data are saying;
- describing specific categories, concepts, or themes assists in clarifying their relevance, variations, dimensions, and parameters, as a basis for further comparative and relational analysis; and
- description facilitates generalisation to other settings.

In the context of analytic interpretation, therefore, description can serve as both means and outcome. Here, I will be focusing on description as a *means* of enhancing the quality of analysis. Description as an *outcome* of analysis is reviewed in Chapter 12.

Describing coded categories

Move to the first of your substantive concept or theme codes, to describe its characteristics and boundaries. *How* did people talk about this phenomenon, and *how many* talked about it? Who *didn't* talk about it? What's *not* included? What else did they refer to when they talked about this? Description is about making complicated things understandable by reducing them to their component parts (Miles & Huberman, 1994). Patton suggests that this 'detailed, hard work' of description should be completed before launching into the 'creative work of interpreting the data' (2002: 438). Others would argue that interpretation is happening all along, but all agree that you need to clarify (i.e., carefully describe) the social phenomena that are represented by your codes or concepts before you attempt to investigate interrelationships between them. If you are working in an emergent approach involving theoretical sampling, this process of conceptualisation and description of the dimensions and properties of concepts will have been going on progressively as you worked with your data. For others, it will become part of the process of review once data are recontextualised in codes. An intermediate position where you are both reviewing and clarifying as you go and reviewing and clarifying again once everything is coded is, of course, most likely.

This process of describing categories, concepts, or themes in the context of analytical writing involves specifying their relevance, variations, dimensions, and parameters, as a basis for further comparative and relational analysis (Box 8.1). Do not become overconcerned at this stage if working through codes in this way at first is lacking order. As you progress through this and the next steps, you will begin to see connections between the various concepts you are working with, allowing you to sequence presentation and build toward a conclusion. And although description does need to precede further analysis, once the context and sample have been adequately described and codes have been refined, I find it can be quite practical and efficient to then proceed from description of a particular substantive category or concept directly through to running comparisons and exploring other interrelationships for that particular concept, before describing the next one. Focusing attention on one particular aspect and following it through as far as possible before moving on to another allows time to digest and explore it, prompting insights about it and its place in the larger picture. Each will, in any case, lead you to others to work through. You might treat this stage as an exercise in disciplined, methodical analysis, remembering Thomas Edison's adage about writing (and analysis!) being 99 per cent perspiration and just 1 per cent inspiration!

Box 8.1

Description contributes to analysis

Jennifer was looking at coordination of care across primary health services, particularly general practitioners' communication and linkages with other health professionals. She had developed a list of factors leading to health professionals' propensity to engage in collaborative care across services, and had started to try to write some conclusions about this. The first code in this group she had listed was *previous experience* and she had moved directly into attempting to show how this impacted on coordination of services. She had then worked on through each item in her list in this way, but she felt very unsatisfied with the result as nothing seemed to tie together and she was unable to reach any overall conclusions.

Jennifer had moved directly into attempting to relate categories to outcomes, but she hadn't stopped to identify and describe the characteristics (or as grounded theorists might refer to them, the properties and dimensions) of each. When we sat down to read what she had coded as *previous experience*, several dimensions became apparent. The coded text was about the type (personal/professional), duration, and quality of *relationships* with other service providers. This led to two important considerations: (a) previous experience could be seen in terms of those aspects of relationships, rather than as a separate code, and (b) this now allowed her to ask how each of these dimensions of previous experience (or more broadly now, of relationships) impacted

(Continued)

(Continued)

on a particular health professional's likelihood of working in a coordinated way with other professionals. This significantly enriched the analysis on the one hand by breaking the concept down into its component dimensions, but also reduced overall complexity on the other, by linking this category to a broader concept. Jennifer continued the process of working through her codes by describing each of them first, and reported considerable relief and much more satisfaction with the progress of her analysis.

Strategies to help with describing concepts

Choose a concept or category to work with, either by working methodically through a set of codes (or themes), or maybe starting with one that seems to be particularly interesting for your study. Then:

▶ Note where this concept sits within your coding system and/or current analysis framework. This will help to put it into context and to see what its role might be in your analysis.

▶ Read through text coded for the concept you are considering. Make a summary by listing the points you observe as you read (Box 8.2).

▶ Check any notes or memos you have already written about this concept, along with any links between its code and others that you have recorded. Use these memos and links and compare with similar codes in order to clarify the description.

▶ Follow this by reviewing the summary and then identifying dimensions that capture the main features of this concept.

▶ Define the boundaries of the code and the concept it represents – what it includes, what it doesn't include.

▶ Consider how widely this concept was raised in your data, for how many cases it was relevant, and who or which these cases were. Identify also where it was absent, or was discussed in negative terms. Do those who discussed it differ from those who didn't in any obvious way?

▶ Confirm the distinctiveness of this concept. Is it different from others, or could it incorporate others within it? As well as providing clarification of this concept, this may also point to linkages with other concepts – in which case preliminary modelling of those linkages might prove useful here.

▶ Write a 'job description' for the concept.

Box 8.2

Dimensions and summary description of 'obsession'

These are the notes I made when reviewing and describing the concept of obsession in my Researchers project (originally recorded as part of my memo for obsession).

Characteristics of obsession from reviewing coded text:

- o oblivious to others when talking about research (David) ((more about passion than obsession?))
- o something that all [genuine] researchers have (Ange)
- o curious and clever (Paul)
- o not necessarily good communicators or attractive to others (Paul)
- o capacity to ignore or stand up against prevailing society (Paul) ((= driven?))
- o balanced humanity vs compartmentalised or isolated-destructive (but productive) life (David)
- o total absorption, as in a relationship with a partner (Ange)
- o 'stuffed' as individuals – unbalanced – but totally dedicated to making an impact (which has a self-serving quality in it as well) (several experienced researchers)
- o addictive qualities – research absorbs full attention, day and night (Frank)
- o good research 'requires obsession' = passion, doggedness and conviction (re value and direction) (Stephen)
- o research is always present – sitting under the skin – but not necessarily permanent (Stephen, also Frank)
- o drivenness – oblivious to (destructive) consequences (Reeves)
- o being 'sucked in' to try to understand something; totally focused on the challenge of the quest and ignoring more personal issues (Susan + memo)

→ *Dimensions:*

- o balance/imbalance of activity (research–work–life) – between work and other relationships // focus–commitment – persistence // oblivious to other elements of life ((= drivenness))
- o destructiveness productivity
- o (self-serving) passion
- o temporality – may be for a period only

Possible consequences of obsession:

- o productivity (necessary for high levels of)
- o ego-enhancement
- o 'stuffed' personal relationships

I then considered how the text I had coded as obsession compared with other similar codes – again, recorded in the memo:

Reviewed *passion* – a couple of overlapping segments, but generally is a lesser phenomenon than obsession – not so unbalanced, and perhaps not so productive.

Fascination is a lesser phenomenon again, and has a more intellectual rather than emotive quality to it. Perhaps obsession is more emotive than intellectual?

Reviewed *immersion* – this also feeds into obsession but is less than full obsession – lacks the drivenness.

Excitement seems to be more of a *consequence* of passion/immersion/obsession than something that feeds into it.

(Continued)

(Continued)

And finally, a summary (so far) recorded in a draft report:

> The concept of obsession describes a kind of *driven passion* that was raised as a characteristic of researchers almost entirely by those already experienced as researchers. (The two people at an earlier career stage who raised it have since become directors of major university research centres.) It involves almost total commitment of time and mental energy to research – a 'superstrength' version of passion resulting in complete immersion, at least for a period of time. While it involves a high level of intellectual activity, obsession itself is more of an emotional than an intellectual response. It can lead to high levels of achievement and a sense of excitement and personal fulfilment, but potentially at the cost of a balanced life and maintaining personal relationships.

Evolving concepts with analytic, meta-, or pattern codes

At the risk of pushing the department store analogy (Box 6.14) too far, think about the ways in which various separate items of women's clothing (blouse, slacks, jacket, shoes, etc.) might be put together to make an outfit. Selected items might be brought together as a coordinated outfit (together they make for a larger concept); you might choose a combination because it's something you've seen together often (they regularly co-occur); you could choose a particular scarf to go with this blouse because the colouring of the scarf will bring out (i.e., impact on) the highlights in the pattern on the blouse; or, having bought a particular dress, you go looking for a matching pair of shoes. These kinds of connections are more conceptual or theoretical than organisational or taxonomic. You are focusing more on how things connect and what things mean in relation to each other, rather than simply on sorting them into the types of thing they are.

Many researchers employ a second level of coding – referred to variously as focused coding, or as using metacodes or pattern codes – that is applied to data more frequently as a project progresses, to capture these kinds of connections.[1] Such codes tend to be more abstract or analytical than descriptive. They might move you from specific or unique detail to a more general concept; encompass thematic statements describing patterns or rules or relationships among codes; link codes that suggest causes or explanations; or name constructs that represent or otherwise bind a group of codes. Analytic codes that abstract from the data are useful *across* documents; they link also to the broader field of knowledge.

Focused coding is a general description of a process that is designed to reduce and focus the number of codes created through the initial, detailed coding process,

---

[1] Interpretative phenomenologists, similarly, develop superordinate themes, usually *after* they have completed their initial thematic analysis; cf. Chapter 7.

espccially where that has resulted in a large number of specific codes (Saldaña, 2009). You would do this with a view to identifying the primary elements of or processes related to 'what is going on here' to arrive at those categories likely to be most salient as a foundation for theoretical integration. Focused codes (a) are potentially relevant across all sources of data, (b) are able to be woven together as a statement that summarises the data, and (c) often end in 'ing' because they capture processes. To create focused codes:

▶ Review your codes, and see which of your initial codes are based around a similar concept or process.

▶ Combine these, naming them now for the common concept or process they represent.

▶ Evaluate remaining categories that are isolates, or that code only one or two passages, to see if they are still needed and whether they can be combined with others. Remove any codes that are no longer relevant or needed (create an archive folder if you can't bear to throw them out).

▶ Memo the process as you make choices and think about labels.

▶ Use the focused codes for any further coding that you might do.

Metacodes represent a number of codes pulled together into a 'higher-level' (more abstract) conceptual category or construct – something like that which is achieved with a factor analysis of numeric variables. If you become aware of categories or concepts that focus around or point to the same idea – that 'hang together' – while you are doing your initial coding (or later), a metacode will help you record this as you work, and you can modify it as the idea becomes more refined. Metacodes will help you to see the larger picture in your data, the key constructs that could frame your results. Use of metacodes does not mean you neglect all the original codes, however, as these provide specificity for the higher-level concept, and reflect different dimensions of it. For example, in my coding of accounts about the development of researchers, I created the metacode *purposeful commitment* to link together the more detailed codes I had created for ambition, drive, commitment, focus, time management, purposefulness, developing a niche, and agency (some of which had been classified in my coding system as personality factors and some as strategies). These were all associated with the more general idea of being purposeful and committed in research, and could be seen as dimensions of it.

What's needed, then, is a way of recording metacodes and working with them that does not obliterate their contributing categories. If you are working with paper copies of coded material, this would involve grouping records (or copies) associated with member codes in some way – and adding notes to your journal about what you are seeing. Because I was using NVivo for analysis of the data, I was able to create a *code set* holding aliases for the detailed codes to serve as the metacode (Figure 8.1). In this way, the integrity of the coding system was preserved, the set was updated as additional material was added to member codes, and the set could be used also as a composite element in further analyses.

Figure 8.1   Using a set to identify a metacode in NVivo

MAXQDA also has a sets function for codes, while Atlas.ti allows codes to be clustered in families or visualised as semantic nets.

Abstracting, developing and recording metacodes builds on the strategies you are already applying as you tidy up and refine your first codes (cf. Chapter 6). In addition:

▶ Challenge each of your codes by asking, 'What am I learning from the material in this code?' You may find you have several codes that are different expressions of the same concept. For example, codes for moving from supported to independent accommodation, finding a job, and developing a relationship, in the context of a study about people who have a mental illness, might all turn out to be about the more abstract concept of *demonstrating improvement*. By abstracting from the data, you develop analytic concepts that help you move forward from the data. In a strategic sense, these questions also help to keep you 'on target', to bring your focus to issues relevant to your research questions.

▶ Develop a system for recording codes that seem to you to be focused around a common idea or purpose (to 'hang together'): lists with memos if you are working on paper or a word processor; sets (or an equivalent) if you are using QDA software; diagrams or models if you prefer to work visually.[2]

✅ Keep writing memos for codes as the writing process is most often what triggers ideas about a concept or metacode.

✅ Keep working through new data with your more detailed codes.[3] If you move too soon to a small number of more general codes, you are likely to miss observing some of the nuances in the data that become apparent as you tease out the different elements of

---

[2]If you are using the sets function in QDA software to record a metacode, coding using the detailed code will automatically update the metacode. If you are using a coding hierarchy, you can optionally aggregate or combine the subcodes at a higher-level code.

[3]This suggestion assumes you have a 'reasonable' number of detailed codes – not the 1000+ I have sometimes encountered where the researchers continued to record every nuance of how an idea was expressed as a new code.

what is going on there. Additionally, working only with broader categories or themes encourages a tendency to descriptive reporting of each category or theme, without deeper analysis.

 Apply the suggestions for describing concepts (above) to your metacodes.

Pattern coding describes a level of coding that is more inferential and explanatory. It is applied in the analysis process when the significance of particular comments or observational notes becomes evident to the researcher (Miles and Huberman, 1994, also include as pattern codes those that I have described as metacodes). If you become sensitive to a pattern of co-occurrence of codes as you are coding, or when you become aware of other relational connections between codes, write a memo or draw a model to record that – even for those that might not appear to be of great significance at this stage. This will prompt further questions, early analysis, and increasing sensitivity to the data (cf. Box 8.3). Later, you will map these pattern codes to explore their interconnections, to build on the conceptual framework for your study and contribute to theory building.

Box 8.3

A possible pattern code?

In the Researchers project, I created a simple model (Figure 8.2) to record an idea about the way chance events can become opportunities. This was crystallised by a lifetime pattern of operation described by Barbara, one of the very experienced researchers who ran a successful technical consulting business:

> I describe myself as an opportunist really. I rarely try to make a thing happen. I look around for what's going to happen and then I exploit it. For instance I wouldn't want to try and decide that the world wanted a certain kind of [chemical] analysis and then push them to have it. Rather I look around and see what's developing and I think ah yes, we can do that, and then we hop onto that bandwagon.

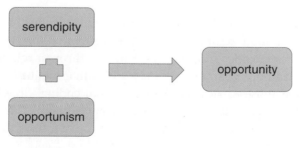

Figure 8.2 Opportunism creates opportunity from chance events

(Continued)

(Continued)

How would this translate from a research business environment to an academic research environment? Having created the model, I am now sensitised to the issue and can look to see whether it applies in an academic setting and, if so, what shape it might take. Is the academic researcher proactive in 'making a thing happen', for example, or do they wait for opportunities to present themselves? Based on Barbara's account, and recollections of discussions with and data from other researchers, I was then led to explore the relationship of this concept to the concept of agency, being open to ideas, perhaps obsession, and so on. For example, although Barbara described herself as an opportunist, she also demonstrated early initiative, for example, in learning to use new analytic techniques and then using that knowledge to train others and establish her business, which then placed her in a position to exploit new opportunities. Academics looking for research funding might take up an unexpected opportunity that comes along (an evaluation consultancy, for example), but they are likely to also be steadily working at building a research profile in a particular area that then allows them to apply for funding from a general pool to use for their area of interest. As a consequence, I recorded the now extended association between these ideas with a pattern code *making opportunity*, linking the codes opportunity, serendipity, opportunism, open to ideas, anticipation, and agency, to emphasise the instrumentality of these researchers in creating their own opportunities out of events or experiences which happen along.

Learning from grounded theory: building focused categories

Important intermediate tasks in developing a grounded theory are:

- to link concepts generated through open coding (cf. Chapter 6) into more significant clusters (categories); and
- to generate initial propositions about processes.

These are tasks that share similarity with the development of metacodes or pattern codes, described above.[4] As well as providing concepts and links to support a theoretical framework, each of these will guide further theoretical sampling that is designed to explore variations in these concepts or processes under different conditions.

Traditionally, *axial coding* was the term used by Strauss and Corbin for purposefully reintegrating fractured data or codes generated through initial coding into a systematic explanatory framework – typically through relating process categories (actions, interactions, strategies) to categories that identify conditions and/or consequences of those processes. The term 'axial coding' draws from the metaphor of the hub or axis around which other connected items turn. In the latest edition of their *Basics* text (Corbin & Strauss, 2008), Corbin used the term in a historical

---

[4]I have not included Glaser's (1978) idea of coding families in this discussion because these are more akin to taxonomic categories (as discussed in Chapter 6) than to conceptually based metacodes or pattern codes.

sense only, emphasising rather that the actions of breaking data apart (open coding) and relating concepts to each other (formerly axial coding) co-occur in the analysis process, with the latter occurring as connections observed in the data are reflected on and elaborated through a memo-writing process (Box 8.4).

Box 8.4

Bringing concepts together

The pattern code *making opportunity* (described above) provides a simple illustration of this process of relating concepts: a chance event (condition) and a strategy (opportunism) lead to the creation of opportunity (consequence). On further reflection, I note that the code for agency is a common element in both *purposeful commitment* and *making opportunity*. These two meta-codes can be seen to describe two dimensions of agency that together work to create a person capable of becoming, or being, an involved and effective researcher – or businessperson. Thinking this way leads to further related (sensitising) questions: under what conditions might someone with those qualities go into research rather than business, where the same qualities are valuable; and are there other dimensions critical to agency? It also sends me back to review an early interview with Andrew who, after completing a first-class honours degree, decided to go into business (where he also excelled) because a research career offered an uncertain future, but who then reported a few years later being 'lured' back into doctoral study and research because 'my passion for research cannot be extinguished'.

Rather than axial coding, Kathy Charmaz prefers to use the term and draw on the principles (as outlined above) of *focused coding* as a second phase in coding.[5] In her hands, focused codes are 'more directive, selective and conceptual' than initial codes. They are then used to 'sift through' and 'synthesize and explain' larger amounts of data (2006: 57). Charmaz described, for example, how she developed a code for 'identifying moment' to capture the events and emotions that were associated when a significant personal identity (often negative, such as with disability, but also potentially positive) was conferred by another person. To help refine focused codes:

▶ Compare incidents or cases where a code might apply with those where it does not.
▶ Compare incidents where the code applies, for intensity and impact.
▶ Compare coded data with codes. Does the code fit, or should it be elaborated?

---

[5]Charmaz' (2006) criticism of axial coding was that it imposed too rigid a frame on analysis; she recommended a more flexible approach emphasising careful comparison as being as effective as axial coding. Comparison is a different process, however, from the connecting process implied by axial coding or Corbin's memo writing.

What can we learn from grounded theorists about second-, intermediate-, and higher-order stages and types of coding?

- First and most obviously: that you need to go beyond initial descriptive or context-specific codes in order to develop substantive theory.
- The importance of maintaining a constant comparative orientation at all levels of data analysis – from initial comparison of incidents and comparisons of codes to comparison of groups of codes (categories). 'Ultimately is it this iterative analytical method of constantly comparing and collecting or generating data that results in high-level conceptually abstract categories rich with meaning, possessive of properties and providing an explanation of variance through categorical dimensionalization' (Birks & Mills, 2011: 94).
- The recursive nature of analysis means that different phases of coding (initial, intermediate, advanced) occur both concurrently and iteratively. Even at advanced stages of data analysis it is sometimes necessary to return to initial open coding techniques to extend or clarify an issue in analysis.
- Intermediate- and higher-level codes are multidimensional.
- Refining codes is a process that continues throughout a project. Elaborating a code may involve theoretical sampling to gather more relevant data.
- The salience, for analysis, of particular dimensions of a phenomenon or an experience will be impacted by the perspective of the analyst.
- Memo writing to support observation of co-occurrences of or similarities between concepts is critical for generating higher-order codes.

Moving forward

You have been describing lower-level concepts or themes (represented by coding categories) and now you are combining coded categories into higher-order focused codes, metacodes, or pattern codes. With a refined set of codes to work with, and beginning ideas about how various codes might relate to each other, you are able to move forward in a more constructive and efficient way. At this stage you might well move to the next chapter, where comparative analyses will tell you whether people from different groups within society talk or write about experiences or issues in similar or different ways, to see what you learn from those to help with answering your research questions and to guiding further analysis.

Or, you might continue to work through the remainder of this chapter, to focus on the further analytical and theoretical development of particular concepts *if* concept clarification or development is a focus for your study.

Theorising concepts

'The capacity to conceptualize has been described as that which makes us uniquely human, and that which allows us to handle knowledge in the manner that we do … [Concepts] shape the vast majority of what we experience as well as our capacity to reason' (Thorne, 2008: 170). Whereas refining and describing the range of codes and concepts used in your study was an essentially practical exercise, analysing and theorising concepts is an exercise in deep, reflective thinking, aided by practical strategies (Box 8.5). The approach you take to theorising concepts, as well, will be impacted by your ontological perspective – your view of what constitutes reality.

Box 8.5

Reflecting on a concept

When a student wrote up her theoretical analysis of a particular concept, I was rather disparaging of her first efforts: 'Sounds a bit motherhood' was my response. Later, I began to write an article on developing a concept I'd been working on statistically for some years, but now wanted to look at more theoretically. That's when I discovered, as I reviewed relevant data and juggled the various dimensions and indicators I was working with, that the task was indeed far more difficult than I had anticipated. My results also seemed rather 'motherhood', once completed, although the apparent simplicity of the concepts veiled the complexity they contained.[6]

In the sense being used here, a concept is a theoretical construction, based on empirical analysis, that captures the substance of an object or idea (Becker, 1998; Goertz, 2006). Without the empirical base for a concept, you are left with a definitional argument over semantic signs (arbitrary words).

> Concepts are theories about ontology: they are theories about the fundamental constitutive elements of a phenomenon … In short, I propose a causal, ontological, and realist view of concepts. It is an ontological view because it focuses on what constitutes a phenomenon. It is causal because it identifies ontological attributes that play a key role in causal hypotheses, explanations, and mechanisms. It is realist because it involves an empirical analysis of the phenomenon. (Goertz, 2006: 5)

The problem in much social science literature (and therefore practice) is that concepts are often operationalised before they have been theorised, with the concept then being defined by what is used to measure it. Drawing on the concept of democracy to illustrate his approach, Gary Goertz argued that both conceptualisation and measurement are important, but that theory should drive measurement.

As pattern-recognition devices, concepts allow us to draw inferences about an object in particular settings without our always having to check all properties. Our confidence in doing so, however, is dependent on both the pre-definition and current presence of sufficient conditions for that concept to be evident. Context

---

[6]Close familiarity with the material you are analysing, over an extended period of working with it, can sometimes lead to your thinking you have nothing new to say from your data, when in fact you do. Test this by presenting your work to, or at least by discussing it with, colleagues who are less familiar with what you are doing.

and function assist in this process; we can usually interpret gender, for example, from ancillary features when people are wearing clothes, without needing to examine the naked body (Smith & Medin, 1981).

The relational context also impacts, explicitly or tacitly, on the inferred meaning of concepts (Becker, 1998). The meaning of poverty, for example, is relational: poverty in one setting is relative wealth in another. As noted in Chapter 4, even the physical concept of tallness, for a person, is relational: a person who is tall in one country (or era) would be seen as medium or perhaps short in another. For concepts like retardation, or lower class, or underdevelopment, the problem of relativity may be less obvious but is potentially more important. Importance, of course, is also determined by social context. Thus, while we might agree on core characteristics of poverty, or tallness, or even 'lower class', how those concepts find expression and what serves to indicate them will vary in different settings and from the perspective of different people.

The structure of concepts

Concepts are multidimensional and multilevel. They are described using multiple criteria. It is possible, therefore, to analyse concepts by how many levels they have, how many dimensions there are in each level, what is the substantive content of each dimension at each level, and what might serve as indicators for those. Typically concepts are theorised with a three-level structure:

- The basic level, usually a noun, is what is used in theoretical propositions. Goertz focused on democracy; Nussbaum (1992) on the essential characteristics of being human; Putnam (2000) and others on the concept of social capital. I was interested in theorising about what constitutes research performance; one of my students, as an organisational psychologist, is analysing localised concepts of wellbeing in the workplace; another is looking at how people understand self-management in relation to chronic disease.
- The secondary level comprises the dimensions that constitute the concept; for example, in the case of democracy, these include civil rights and competitive elections. For social capital, they might include embeddedness and autonomy, and social cohesion evidenced in reciprocity and trust. Each dimension varies along a continuum (although some might usually assume only the values of 0 or 1). These dimensions play a central role in causal mechanisms when the concept they comprise is applied to particular situations.
- The third or indicator level is the level at which the dimensions are operationalised (defined in terms of the evidence that might point to their presence) so that they can be identified, coded, and potentially measured. These are designed to be used to guide data gathering, to determine if a concept is present or not. Substitutability is acceptable at the indicator level; substitutability of indicators is essential for functional equivalence in comparative cross-national or longitudinal research.

There are two primary approaches to thinking about the composition of the dimensional structure of a concept, with a third that is less useful (Goertz, 2006;

Smith & Medin, 1981). Which is most appropriate in any situation can be determined by the answers to two fundamental questions:

1 Is there a single set of criteria for all examples of this phenomenon?
2 Are the properties specified in that set of criteria all true for all examples of the phenomenon?

The approaches are as follows:

- The first is to take an (Aristotelian) *essentialist* or *classical* view that says that all instances of a concept have to exhibit a complete set of common properties and that these characteristics alone provide both necessary and sufficient conditions to be able to declare this to be an example of the concept.[7] A square, for example, has four essential properties: it is always a closed figure with four sides of equal lengths and with equal angles. In the research activity component of the model I developed of research performance, I have suggested that a positive value must exist on each of four dimensions (engagement; task orientation; research practice; and intellectual processes) for research performance to become evident (see Figure 8.3).
- The second approach is to recognise that not all examples will always exhibit all the criteria for the concept, even though they are still recognisable as fitting that concept. Wittgenstein referred to such examples as having a family resemblance that allows them to be considered together under one rubric. The *family resemblance model* or *probabilistic* view contains no essential conditions; there just has to be sufficient of a range of defining properties to be able to say the concept is present (i.e., what makes for sufficiency has to be defined). Compare the concept of a cup with the concept of a square. In the case of the cup, which usually, but not always, is a concave object with a handle out of which you can drink hot liquids, you have a concept with properties that fit most objects we refer to as cups, but not all (e.g., the cups used for Chinese tea, which don't have a handle). In the performing component of research performance, I have suggested (rather controversially) that research might be communicated and made visible *either* through formal channels of dissemination (typically publication) *or* through informal channels of collegial engagement – with one or other (or both) making for sufficiency.
- A third approach to concepts, used primarily in psychology, is based on *exemplars*. In this approach the concept is best represented by descriptions of cases that are known to be prototypes of the phenomenon of interest, even though they might have quite varied properties (e.g., a suicidal psychiatric patient).

How much can a concept be tightened or stretched before it is too exclusive or too inclusive? An ideal type of most essentialist concepts will be likely to describe no, or a very limited number of, empirical examples. The problem is, natural language concepts have fuzzy boundaries so that membership of a category is often a matter of degree. To return to the idea of being tall: how high do you have to be to be considered tall in Australia, or America, or France, or Japan today? If

---

[7]This perspective parallels the process of analytic induction for developing theory; cf. Chapter 11. There are some who doubt that it is possible to define essentialist concepts in social science. Note, for example, that I resort to a mathematical concept to illustrate this type of structure.

you are 170 cm, is that tall? What about if you are 175, or 178, or 180 cm? Where does the boundary lie? Goertz sees the essentialist view of concepts and the family resemblance model as anchor points on a continuum, thus allowing, for example, for a degree of substitutability within a necessary condition as one moves along the continuum.

The structure of a concept that is designed to be measured is therefore best represented using the mathematics of fuzzy logic (which allows for overlapping ranges of values) and set theory, rather than arithmetic and statistical theory. Using set theory, necessary and sufficient dimensions are modelled using AND (intersections), and family resemblances are modelled using OR (unions). Statistical measures use means and correlations, which generate a different kind of model. Figure 8.3 illustrates the way the multilevel, multidimensional structure of a concept can be represented, using my model of research performance as an example.[8]

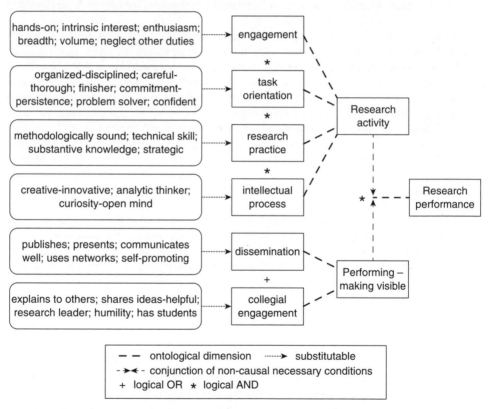

Figure 8.3   Conceptual model of the dimensions of research performance

Source: Bazeley, 2010b: 897, Figure 2

---

[8]Not shown in the model are two necessary conditions for research performance (education with training; and opportunity that includes resources), and three broad categories of outcomes from (consequences of) research performance (publications, impact, and recognition).

The consequences of concept meaning and structure

The model chosen for structuring a concept and the intension and extension of its dimensional structure have important ramifications for selecting cases that instantiate the concept – which means (in more colloquial terms) that it has implications for who or what gets to claim the concept (where it's a 'good' thing) or who gets branded with it (if it's a 'bad' thing). For the essentialist view, as more attributes are specified (an increase in intension), coverage (extension) is reduced (and vice versa). The opposite is true for a family resemblance model of concepts where an increase in intension also increases extension (assuming no increase in the total number of properties required for sufficiency). Depending on the decisions made, samples will be either impossible to find, or at the other extreme, will include too many marginal cases. A non-concept needs to be defined as well, as selecting non-concept cases (for comparative analyses) will involve separating irrelevant from negative cases: what you want is those where it might have occurred, but didn't. Cases selected on the basis of the definition of the concept will, of course, influence the conclusions drawn and the theories developed from any consequent investigation.

The dimensional structure has consequences potentially not only for the research process, but in relation to labelling of people and other phenomena. Additionally, the relational nature of concepts, described above, brings to attention their causal implications. When a concept has a different meaning or significance in a different setting, it will have different consequences. The notion that the dimensions included in concepts have consequences within their context is central to Goertz' approach to analysing concepts:

> My approach stresses that concept analysis involves ascertaining the constitutive characteristics of a phenomenon that have central causal powers. These causal powers and their related causal mechanisms play a role in our theories. A purely semantic analysis of concepts, words, and their definitions is never adequate by itself. (Goertz, 2006: 5).

If, for example, you include the school setting as a criterion for where the concept of *education* can be observed, then you will miss the fact that a lot of education actually occurs outside a school. Similarly, if education involves a formal relationship between a knowledgeable person (a teacher) and a novice (a student), you will limit examples. Howard Becker (1998) would include, as rather extreme examples in his concept of education, the way a drug user will teach a novice how to smoke or inject drugs, or the way thieves might pass on knowledge of techniques for being more effective (and avoiding arrest) within their peer group. This enlarges the reach of the concept, but it also refines it by clarifying the core dimensions of what comprises education (such as passing on knowledge and skills to someone who learns). Widening the view of education from teacher–pupil education to include peer learning, along with adding a dimension about the relationship being mandated or voluntary, has implications for theory regarding the distribution of power in education.

Similarly, a concept of *compliance* in medicine suggests a power dynamic between health professionals and patients. Simply changing the name of the concept to *adherence* did nothing to change that, but new emphases on *self-management* in health service delivery are now taking shape and taking hold, particularly with respect to chronic disease management. 'Merely fiddling with the packaging of an idea is rarely sufficient to enact any meaningful result in knowledge development, while finding an original conceptual approach [and setting it within a changed organising structure] that forces rethinking an old problem may be quite powerful' (Thorne, 2008: 171).

Finally, something that is considered to be a concept might be regarded in another setting simply as a dimension of a broader concept. There is no *a priori* way to determine whether something is a concept or a dimension, it is best determined empirically: components or dimensions are those things that allow you to distinguish between concepts (Smith & Medin, 1981). The dimensions of research activity (each of which, in turn, could be analysed as a concept) allow you to distinguish between research performance expressed via some form of dissemination (which could include within a newspaper) and journalism.

Strategies for analysing and theorising concepts

Analysis of concepts might start from different points and can take a variety of routes. These are simply a collection of suggestions that might help your thinking processes as you grapple with the meaning and structure of a concept. The critical factor in any of these approaches is to *keep challenging your data*. By that I mean, use any idea that comes from your working with the data as a springboard for further questions that will send you back into the data for additional clarification or evidence. Set in motion a chain reaction of: question – information – question – idea – question – check evidence – clarification.

Working from coded (indicator) data:

▶ Concepts are developed in 'continuous dialogue with empirical data' (Becker, 1998: 109) because they are a way of summarising data. Use the kinds of strategies noted earlier – noting relationships, memoing, grouping. Often these processes are going on at the same time as you are coding, especially if you have the flexibility of being able to review coded passages in context and rearrange codes as you work.

▶ A code acquires meaning as the researcher works with it. Gradually build up understanding from informants and through team discussions, as you learn about each other's frames of meaning (Mishler, 1986).

▶ Sort codes into groups that together suggest a common dimension (so the codes will then represent potential indicators), using the cards on table method or a computer model. This will involve a great deal of trial and error as you arrange and rearrange the codes, deep thought, and continual review of the content of your codes to check 'fit'.

▶ If you are working on computer, explore the way various pairs or groups of codes 'behave' in relation to other variables to see what they have in common, and how they differ. Ask questions about those differences to explore how they are expressed and the context for them.

Working from cases:

▶ Start with a case example and identify dimensions and/or indicators present in the case. Add contrasting cases. Refine dimensions through a process of comparative quizzing of the data.

▶ Take a statement you have made about a particular case, and restate it without using any of the terms specific to that case by giving a more general class for each term. This will lead to a more generalised statement describing the concept (Becker, 1998).

Comparative analyses with negative examples:

▶ Contrast with something similar but which is not the concept to identify differences that make your concept distinct.

▶ Defining a negative case is useful in refining the definition of a positive case of the concept; try then taking the negative and defining its opposite. Does it match where you started?

Structuring the concept:

▶ Identify dimensions that are co-related – ones that always appear together – to create a network of dimensions or features rather than just a list. For example, being animate and feathered contribute together to distinguishing a bird: note that flying is not essential to that concept. If substantive knowledge and technical or methodological skill are applied for sufficient time to derive a creative solution to a problem arising out of intellectual curiosity or strategic need, then we would probably recognise that activity as research.

▶ Create a model of the concept, showing its component parts or dimensions, and showing also how you see it relating to the primary concern of your study.

▶ Explore what is left of the concept if you take something away: is it still the concept?

▶ Use the mathematics of logic (i.e., set theory) as the most appropriate way to model the dimensional structure of concepts based on either an essentialist model (with necessary and sufficient conditions) or a family resemblance model (defining how many of a set of conditions makes for sufficiency).

Exploring defined concepts:

▶ Set concepts into the set of relations they imply, e.g., where is it found; what else is going on there? How is that set of relations organised (e.g., as conditions and consequences; product or input or both; in a repetitive/iterative pattern)? Has it always been so, and is it always so in other places?

▶ Identify the concept and its dimensions with labels that effectively convey its and their conceptual meaning, as the labels will shape the accessibility of the concept.

Alternative approaches to theorising and developing concepts

Dimensional analysis

Dimensional analysis (Schatzman, 1991) has its roots in pragmatism and symbolic interactionism. This means that concepts are seen as being socially constructed, and therefore highly dependent on the social context and perspective of individual sources. 'It does not make sense, in using dimensional analysis, to look for the essence of a concept since dimensional analysis defines concepts as being contextually embedded' (Caron & Bowers, 2000: 295). The many ways a concept is used by different participants or in different sources are examined to reveal implicit dimensions, and to attribute relevance and salience to those dimensions (e.g., Box 8.6).

▶ Begin with a review and analysis of what you know already, to identify your own assumptions and to avoid 'recognition–recall' impacting when you examine new data. Make your perspective explicit and use it as a basis for comparison with others' perspectives.

▶ Sample from multiple sources, guided by ongoing analysis.

▶ Identify as many dimensions as possible in your data, without attributing meaning to them. This involves a very detailed form of open coding that is more descriptive than interpretive. It is designed to ensure that you remain open to all possibilities that might come from others' perspectives. It also helps to break down unquestioned assumptions about the concept.

▶ Examine the relationships between these and challenge each of your interim conclusions. Explore how dimensions vary in different contexts and from different participants' perspectives, using comparative, pattern, and relational analyses. Create dimensional matrices to represent visually how the various dimensions found in the data interrelate.

▶ Seek and analyse further data to investigate uncertainties and discrepancies.

▶ Describe the concept in terms of these integrated dimensions, taking account of multiple perspectives and different contexts. Identify under what conditions a concept varies in meaning and how it shifts in definition and use under those different conditions.

| Box 8.6 |

A dimensional analysis of trust

Chantal Caron and Barbara Bowers (2000) used the concept of *trust* in the context of nurse–client relationships as an example to demonstrate the application of dimensional analysis for concept development, drawing on just a small number of journal articles to do so.

Time (duration) was found to be a central condition of trust. This prompted further questions (2000: 304):

- Is duration always a condition for the development of trust?
- How does this condition relate to the development of trust?
- What other conditions facilitate the development of trust?
- (How) does time influence trusting from the client's perspective?
- Is trust possible without duration of time?
- Are there other conditions that substitute for duration of time?

In their search for evidence they found that *time* allows the nurse and clients to:

- take things slowly;
- be consistent;
- be persistent;

- be supportive;
- go at the client's pace.

This led to more questions about the when and how of consistency and persistence, and about pacing work; for example, consistency of timing was not useful for a client who did not need regular appointments. Under what conditions, then, is what kind of consistency (continuous time versus repeated contacts) seen as beneficial?

Working similarly through dimensions of further reported experiences of time in relation to trust, they found that time can be subdimensionalised by amount, uses, meanings, and purposes. Additional (non-time) dimensions of trust, revealed as they worked, included competence and sharing the same goal.

The next task in dimensional analysis is to attempt to relate the various subdimensions, for example, by gathering evidence of dimensions and subdimensions over multiple sources (no one source will have all) and examining their pattern of co-occurrence using a dimensional matrix (cf. Chapter 10).

Phenomenography

Phenomenography is an empirically based methodology that seeks 'description, analysis, and understanding of experiences ... to find and systematize forms of thought in terms of which people interpret [socially significant] aspects of reality' (Marton, 1981: 180). Perceptions of experience obtained from others are sorted into logically related categories of description, typically arranged in hierarchically inclusive relationships. These structured categories of description create a coherent framework, from the perspective of the participants as a whole, for understanding the 'outcome space'. This outcome space describes the common, intersubjective meanings of the phenomenon that are stable and generalisable across situations. In 'mapping' collective understanding of a phenomenon, the phenomenographer is concerned not with the influence of individual differences on conceptions, but rather with what is common between them – the superordinate categories under which variation might occur (Marton, 1981).

The process of phenomenographic analysis 'is a strongly iterative and comparative one, involving the continual sorting and resorting of data, plus ongoing comparisons between data and the developing categories of description, as well as between the categories themselves' (Åkerlind, 2005: 324). Suggested steps in this process are based on Åkerlind (2005), Marton (1981), and Sin (2010):

▶ Within the limits of the topic, select a maximum-variation sample to interview, to facilitate comparative analyses.

▶ Ask questions about the phenomenon being studied. Follow up questions by asking interviewees to reflect on terms they have used (even those that seem obvious).

▶ Once all interviews are completed and transcribed, read all the transcripts to become familiar with the data.

▶ Identify different conceptions of the phenomenon, taking into account both its referential (meaning) aspect and its structural aspect, and code into a collective scheme to maximise similarities within categories and differences between categories. Data will now be reconceptualised in terms of the category, rather than the individuals who provided them, although the individual context will be checked to confirm interpretation.

▶ Revise, recode, and review as necessary in an iterative process to identify global meanings (those that are supported by evidence of being widely held), along with associated structural features. The idea is to separate forms of thought from the process of thinking and the thinker so as to discern categories of description held by the collective mind.

▶ Report findings by describing the qualitatively different categories of conception of the phenomenon. Each conception should offer something distinctive, but the goal also is to be parsimonious: 'we have repeatedly found that phenomena, aspects of reality, are experienced (or conceptualized) in a relatively limited number of qualitatively different ways' (Marton, 1981: 181). Use quotations to support and clarify these conceptions, ensuring that they have been selected to correctly convey the interviewees' intended meanings.

Box 8.7

Phenomenographic description of academics' conceptions of research

Angela Brew (2001) interviewed 57 successful researchers in Australian universities from across the three disciplinary groupings of science and technology, social sciences, and arts and humanities, in order to discover how they conceptualised research. Her analysis revealed four different ways in which academic researchers conceptualised research, with some individuals embracing more than one. Differences in conception were not related to disciplinary differences. In summary, these conceptions were described as:

- *Domino conception*: research is a series of separate elements (tasks, events, ideas, etc.), each of which is viewed as distinct but which may be combined in a number of ways with others and which could have consequences for other elements.
- *Trading conception*: research is a social phenomenon, occurring in a social marketplace, and often described in terms of relationships with or some other form of connection to other people. Publications, grants, and networks are traded for money or prestige.
- *Layer conception*: research in this conception is internally oriented, emphasising the activity of bringing ideas, truth, or knowledge to light. The focus is on the process rather than on the researcher.
- *Journey conception*: in this conception the everyday life issues of the researcher coalesce with issues being investigated in research. Personal transformation goes hand in hand with research processes and outcomes.

Rather than having a hierarchical structure, relationships between the conceptions hinged around whether there was an external or internal project orientation, and whether the researcher was present or absent in awareness. Each conception fitted a different cell in the four-cell matrix defined by intersecting these two factors.

Repertory grid technique

The repertory grid technique, based on the personal construct theory of George Kelly (1955), provides a method – a cognitive mapping tool – for ascertaining how people construe an element or a phenomenon such as an object, an event, an experience, an idea.[9] Participants compare similarities and differences between items, making judgements about dimensions of difference that are linked into an overall personal construct system. Particular constructs become meaningful within an entire network in which some constructs are more important than others – and evolve into a form of 'idiographic cartography' (Fransella, Bell, & Bannister, 2003).

There are a number of variations in how the repertory grid might be used in research – qualitative or quantitative; idiographic or nomothetic; with a focus on elements, participants, or constructs – with the choice of technique depending on the purpose (Tan & Hunter, 2002). In the current context of developing concepts, it can be used to identify and structure the dimensions (bipolar constructs) that people use to describe a concept. For example:

▶ Select several examples of the concept (e.g., five or so), or ask your participants to provide examples.

▶ Either randomly or systematically, generate triads from the examples (five examples generates 10 triads; four examples generates four triads).

▶ Ask your participants to say how, within any triad, two members might be considered alike in a way that differentiates them from the third. Repeat for each triad. Each comparison will result in one or more bipolar dimensions.

▶ Create a table in which the examples identify columns and the dimensions identify rows. Ask your participants to score each example on each dimension using either dichotomous scoring or a five- or seven-point rating scale.

Recording qualitative commentary during the task can help to elucidate the concept and its dimensions. Statistical analyses can be used to compare the relative importance of the dimensions, and/or to assess the degree of differentiation (complexity) or similarity (integration) between the scales, as an aid in structuring the dimensions of the concept. Shared dimensions can be developed either by having a group work on the task together, or by statistically amalgamating individuals' dimensions and/or by having the group rate those that occurred in several of the individual responses.

What about constructs?

Researchers working in psychology and education have a long history of actively seeking ways to make inferences about abstract concepts, such as intelligence or prejudice, usually employing factor analytic (or similar) statistical techniques. Their goal is to identify or hypothesise a common factor or latent variable that

---

[9]Kelly referred to his underlying philosophy as *constructive alternativism*, holding to a position that would now be referred to as critical realism.

underlies and causes their measurements (a reflective model), or alternatively to ensure that their measurements coherently capture a composite factor that is defined or determined by a particular combination of observable variables (a formative model) (Schmittmann, Cramer, Waldorp, Epskamp, Kievit, & Borsboom, 2011). Either way, this factor is usually referred to as a construct – something that *represents*, linguistically, an *inferred* entity or trait or process. Historically, there has been considerable confusion and debate over the concept of a 'construct' (Slaney & Racine, 2011). Additionally, those who write about constructs appear at times to use the terms 'construct' and 'concept' interchangeably, with a number of parallels being evident between a formative view of constructs and Goertz' (2006) conceptualisation of concepts.

Models of what constitutes a construct differ with regard to whether observable variables are causally related to the construct or constitutive of it; the degree and direction of causal relationships; whether mechanisms connecting different components can be articulated; the substitutability of indicators; and the kinds of mathematical models that might be applied to their structures. Additionally, whereas concepts are typically theorised with a three-level (or greater) structure with constituent dimensions and observable indicators, constructs are typically discussed only in terms of their indicators (observable or measurable variables).

Schmittmann et al. (2011) proposed an alternative (third) view of constructs as a network of dynamically related observable variables that constitute the construct rather than measure it. The architecture and causal dynamics of the system are therefore best visualised and analysed using network analysis. For example, the symptoms of depression are not passive variables that can be added to give a score, but are autonomously functioning indicators that can be connected in a developmental pathway (e.g., lack of sleep → fatigue → loss of concentration). The system (i.e., the construct) is identified through the structure of connections between the observable variables that serve as its constituents, and the state of the system is analysable in terms of its network dynamics (e.g., by employing tools for social network analysis, cf. Chapter 10).

Overview

In describing, analysing, and theorising concepts, 'constant comparison' has a central role in terms of process, and dimensions have a role in most perspectives as structural components of concepts. That people construct (or construe) concepts in their own way is generally agreed, but the extent to which we can determine the essence of a concept, and how universally that essence would hold, are sources of difference between realist or critical realist and constructivist theorists.

In practical terms, clarification of the meaning of categories and concepts for a particular project is an essential step toward further analysis. Some may wish to take that clarification and analysis of a particular concept further, making it a focus of their current research – one that will contribute to their own and others' further understanding and theorising about essential elements and causative mechanisms related to the broader topic for which that concept is central.

Writing about describing and analysing concepts

In the methods chapter

Describe, in practical terms and with an example or two:

▶ The steps you took in reviewing, particularising, and describing the codes, concepts, or themes that you developed through your coding work or alternative analyses of your data.

▶ The process you engaged in to identify and record higher-level focused, pattern, or metacodes. For example, did you rely on memos; check for co-occurrences or other associations in some way; or invite colleagues to help you sort them?

If you have been working on theorising a concept, then:

▶ Explain your understanding of how your philosophical approach contributes to or otherwise impacts on your understanding of what makes for the substance and structure of a concept, and to identifying indicators for it.

▶ Identify the process by which you have derived the structural components of the concept, and the extent to which any component is essential to that concept.

▶ Attempt to visually represent your concept, showing the structure of the linkages between the central core, the various dimensions, and their indicators.

As part of the presentation of results

Clarifying critical concepts and their component dimensions along the way contributes greatly to your being able to put together a thesis at the end of your project, one that is supported by adequate empirically based, theoretically oriented explanation. In my own doctoral experience, my having clarified concepts of mental health in a community context, disadvantage in the context of mental health, and community development (each on the basis of both literature and data as I progressed through stages of the project) was critical to my being able to bind these diverse strands together in a thesis supported by a theoretical model and research evidence from the studied community (cf. Chapter 12).

Exercises

The four brief stories recorded in Box 8.8 were written by students in response to being asked to describe a time when they felt they were part of a community.

Exercise 1: Dimensions of community

▶ Let's say you have developed a code or theme to capture the idea of interdependence as a component of being a part of a community. Review how each person talks about interdependence, and describe the key elements in their understanding or experience of it. Now use that to identify potential dimensions of interdependence or to describe it in some other way that will facilitate your further analysis.

▶ Interdependence can be seen as one of several dimensions that might be used in describing the overarching concept of community. What others can you identify and describe from these brief stories? Are there any you would suggest, on the basis of this (very small) set of data, that could be considered essential to a concept of community?

Box 8.8

Stories of community

Alison: The time was Clean Up Australia Day, 1994. Two flatmates and I went to uni to collect our gloves and garbage bags and I hate to get dirty so was kind of begrudgingly going. When I got there and had to enrol I felt as though I had just joined the army. I had a job to do, a purpose, a reason for doing it, and I suddenly became 'inspired'. The atmosphere was what did it. Lots of other people, the radios on saying it was 'Clean Up Australia Day, do your bit for your country' etc. So I did what I thought I never would and collected garbage for three hours and felt a sense of goodness and purpose. The real effect of community spirit hit later when I saw on the news the thousands of people all helping, helping our country. I felt in awe of the people joining forces and helping what usually gets neglected (the environment). It was then I realised what people, as a country, really had the power to achieve.

Anthony: I feel a sense of being a part of a community when I think about my present living arrangements. I live in a house with five other people. Only one of the people I live with was a previous acquaintance of mine, hence, I have only come to know the other four people I live with through living with them. The reason I sense being a part of a community is that each person in the house where I live is in some ways dependent upon the other members of the household. For example, we all contribute to paying bills, cooking meals, washing up, etc. In this way our household is like a system, but a community system. Also, what makes my living arrangement seem like a community is that we have all come to know one another's living habits. In this sense, we have nothing to hide from each other. Lastly if members in our household do not contribute or make any effort to make ends meet, our household will break down. For this matter, I feel that being part of a community is a feeling of being dependent upon, and actively affecting the living arrangement of, each member of our household.

Bernice: I was part of a team of nine people who were brought together to design a new system for an organisation which would increase productivity (the goal of many companies at the time) but which would also consider occupational and safety issues as well. The sense of community was felt by all because we talked about how well we worked together, how much we stimulated each other's thinking and how much we achieved together. The culmination of this teamwork was in a presentation to senior management which aimed at getting funding for the project of $50,000. This we achieved – apparently a first for anyone to get senior management to fund so much. This situation was probably the culmination of the sense of being part of a community but the feeling of being part of the community (the team) evolved over mutually shared experiences over time.

Colin: I went on a trip to Africa for an eight-week truck safari. There were 10 people on board the truck. We had to organise duties for everyone. We all had to pitch in and help everyone else for eight weeks. Any tensions had to be resolved within the groups. Everyone had to rely on everyone else to survive. If an enjoyable time was to be had it was up to all the members of the group to cooperate together to ensure this happened. We had to ensure we developed a community spirit within the group in order for the trip to be a success. We had to ensure that everything was shared evenly among the group. It forced you to cooperate with people while living with them in extremely close quarters for eight weeks. To think more of other people than yourself. You had to do this if the group was to survive and enjoy the trip.

Further reading

Follow up on the references used in this chapter for further details of their authors' various approaches. For those exploring concepts in depth, the first half of Goertz (2006) and Becker's (1998) chapter on concepts are particularly helpful.

9

Comparative analyses as a means of furthering analysis

Comparison is something we do every day, all the time. Whenever we have to make a decision, we consider and compare options, laying out the features for each and evaluating which is best for our purpose. When a new baby is born, we instantly seek to compare his or her features with those of the parents – and perhaps notice for the first time that one of the parents has long delicate fingers, or a mole behind the left ear.

Comparative analyses in research occur at many levels, from initial reflection and coding onwards. Comparison can be seen as a goal in itself, an end point of analysis, but when analysis stops with comparison I am often left suspended and waiting for the climax – and like anything half-baked, it could have been so much better. Routine comparative analyses are being viewed here primarily as a step in the analytic process. Obtaining benefit depends on your stopping to *record* what you have learned from the comparison you have just run and to *reflect* on what you are seeing as you go, prompting further interrogation of your data.

In this chapter I first focus on strategies and tools you can use to undertake comparative analyses, and then show where and how these strategies and tools might be applied to advance your analytic understanding of your data through:

- comparisons of concepts across subgroups in your sample;
- comparisons across different contexts for action;
- comparisons within or across cases in a variety of formats; and
- use of a variety of display formats for the results of comparative analyses.

Why compare?

Right from the starting point of analysis, qualitative researchers are encouraged to engage in a 'constant comparative process': to consider various possible meanings of words by imaginatively comparing them with others that might have been used; to compare incident against incident for similarities and differences; to consider opposites and extremes; or to think through what an absolute expression would mean if it wasn't treated as absolute. When things are thought to be conceptually similar, they are given the same code; yet it may be known, or later found, that they reflect different dimensions of that concept, or different positions along a dimension. The process of comparison, like no other, brings into sharp focus the distinguishing features of whatever it is you are considering. Comparison can have a 'wow' factor, the power to surprise and excite your interest, to set your brain racing. Comparison generates interesting information in itself that will enrich your descriptions and provide data to report, but also, as these differences become apparent, they spark further questions: why are these different? Or indeed: why are these more or less similar in this way? And so, by questioning when and where and why those differences were expressed, you will be led on to explore possible relationships with other contexts, experiences, emotions, interactions, and so on. So, why compare? Four reasons, at least, suggest themselves:

- for what the comparisons will tell you about the phenomena you are studying by sharpening your observation and helping you to see detail and variations (new dimensions) previously missed; and
- to prompt further questioning of the data as you seek to understand what is behind the similarities and differences you have found; or
- those involved in an evaluation (or similar) study with a comparative question will need to report comparative outcomes (without forgetting to consider process!);
- and finally, undertaking comparisons will enhance your capacity to generalise from your data – as will be discussed in Chapter 13.

In practical strategy terms, once you have developed, organised, refined, and described a set of codes, to compare coded material across individual cases or groups of cases will help progress your analysis – taking you beyond a description of 'themes'. At its most basic level, you can take things that have been said about just one topic; observations or accounts of a particular incident; an expression of an attitude or an emotion; or whatever data have been sorted into a pile or coded at a category or given in answer to the same prompt; and start asking straightforward questions like: does gender, or age, or location, or role relate to the way in which different people experience this phenomenon or express this emotion (or whatever it is) – or indeed, to whether they report it at all? Doing so may reveal that some demographically or contextually defined groups experience or express things more or less frequently than others, or that the phenomenon being considered actually varies in its expression across a number of dimensions, as revealed by different subgroups (Box 9.1). With the assistance of software, you might consider several topics or behaviours or emotions at the same time, so that you can examine patterns across these, as well as differences within each. Comparison can occur within a case as well; for example, one might consider how the same woman acts and responds when playing out different roles in her life, such as wife, mother, employee, friend.

| Box 9.1

A simple comparison

A small sample of mothers of young children were asked, as part of a survey, what was the main thing that they think about in relation to immunisation. When their responses were compared across educational groups it was noted that those who had left school before completing secondary school (i.e., at 15 or 16 years of age) focused on the experience of needles and pain for their child (not necessarily negatively) while those who had completed secondary school or had tertiary qualifications referred to the general health of their child or to the possibility of adverse reactions. In an additional sample who were interviewed (cf. Box 6.15), mothers in the lowest educational group also focused on the needles/pain issue, to the extent that they had others either go with them when a vaccination was due or take the child for them. One dimension in the way mothers think about immunisation suggested by these very brief responses has therefore to do with their time perspective – their level of concern with the immediate or longer-term consequences of vaccination. A second possibility is whether their focus is on the immediate process (vaccination) or the outcome (immunisation). The educational comparison served primarily to point up these possibilities (which would need to be confirmed with a larger sample), but it also suggests that further data gathering and analysis of the significance of these dimensions and of their association with educational background could have practical implications for designing strategies for promoting immunisation compliance amongst particular target audiences.

The comparative process

'Compare and contrast ...' has always been a favourite question starter for teachers designing a school examination in almost any subject. The skills you learned and exercised then, in responding to such questions, are the skills you need to apply now to comparisons. 'Compare and contrast the French and Russian revolutions.' So, what were the similarities between them? And how did they differ? Now, no longer a school student, you are carrying out research at site A and site B. So, what do your observations at site A reveal that is different from site B? What aspects are common to both? You begin your analysis, as you probably did in your history class, by documenting the characteristics of each case being compared (as noted in the previous chapter). With the features of each case made clear, now you can see which features are unique to A or B, and which are common to both. To take your analysis further, your next task is to attempt to discern whether those patterns of similarity and difference relate only to these cases, or whether they point to something more significant about the underlying processes that produce such similarities and differences. If the latter, you would predict that these contexts and processes (and the patterns they produce) might then be reflected in further cases.

Many of your comparisons will involve looking at a particular concept or category (rather than cases), perhaps representing an experience, event, attitude, or emotion – something that is usually captured in a code – from two or more different perspectives. How do people talk about that event now it's happened, compared to the way they were talking about it beforehand? How does the worker's perspective on the efficiency of work practices at the factory differ from that of management? Similarities and differences revealed by these comparisons help you to discern specific features or dimensions of that experience, event, attitude, or emotion. These features are then considered in the context of the attribute that revealed the differences – gender, education, or age; culture, environment, or time – to describe a pattern, to identify a possible explanation. In addition, such comparisons often reveal anomalies, or identify extreme or negative cases. Following up anomalies or unusual cases allows you to explore and understand more of the dynamics that created them.

In what follows I will build on these two ways of thinking about the process of comparison:

- comparison of a concept or category (represented by a code) from the perspective of two or more groups or under two or more different conditions; and
- comparison within or across cases (sites, organisations, people, incidents, or events) that differ in some (usually descriptive) regard.

Each of these can be extended in microscopic or macroscopic directions: one can compare perspectives on dimensions within a concept, or across a range of related concepts. Within-case comparisons are possible, while cross-case comparisons are commonplace. The analysis of a single concept or case is likely to be more intensely detailed than for a larger set, but in broad terms the processes of analysis are similar whether one is considering one concept or several, one case or several.

Corbin and Strauss (2008) raise a third type of comparison which they refer to as 'theoretical comparison' – something you do when you come across an event or incident or idea but you are having a problem conceptualising it from the participant's perspective, perhaps because the participant mentions it in passing without further explanation. In order to understand and define the meaning of these events or incidents, we draw upon what we already know, and compare with that in order to make sense of or help imagine what we don't know. What we already know might be from our own life experience, it could be from the literature, it could be a 'way-out' comparison. Corbin and Strauss caution that this theoretical understanding isn't then applied to the data (as it didn't come from there), but it is used to increase sensitivity to the data, and (if judged to be sufficiently important) to guide further theoretical sampling.

Comparison of cases requires thorough understanding of the case. Comparison of concepts or categories across subgroups or from different perspectives requires thorough understanding of the category or concept being compared. Both rely, therefore, on having effectively described the cases and/or concepts being considered. The actual process of comparison then involves three steps:

- sorting or sifting the data about the cases or concepts being compared, to identify and separate those that come from each alternative perspective, context, or subgroup;

- identifying and summarising the key points for each comparative group – often set out in a table, especially if more than one case or concept is being compared;
- interpretation of the sorted and summarised data to identify (a) if there are any differences and if so, what those differences are, and (b) what these point to in terms of underlying experiences or processes, potentially for further analysis.

Strategies to manage these steps will vary depending on what tools you have available. I will describe these possibilities before going on to discuss how you might apply them to your data.

Managing data to make subgroup, contextual, or case comparisons

Comparative analyses, especially, are where your choice of data management tools (paper, general purpose program, or specialised software) really makes a difference to your efficiency and effectiveness – that is, to the way in which you operate, and to what it will be possible for you to achieve. The first of the three steps outlined above, the sorting and sifting of data, is very greatly assisted by having used computer software for coding and for recording attributes of sources or cases in your research. The second step of summarising and displaying differences can also be assisted by working with tables in your regular computer programs (such as Word or Excel), to allow for flexible editing of text and rearrangement of displays. Sifting and sorting and drawing up tabular displays can be undertaken using paper-based methods (this is how Matthew Miles and Michael Huberman did all their original work with matrices in the 1970s), but simply reading and even rereading text or re-viewing images or video data without any of these additional steps will not reliably get you there in terms of making effective comparisons.

Tools for sifting and sorting

- If you are working with photocopied segments, or paper output from coding, then you will need to literally sort the material for one code at a time into physical heaps for each subgroup, for comparative review.
- If you have used marginal or colour codes on the original documents, you will need to go through *all* the relevant documents for each subgroup, locating and carefully recording what has been observed or what is said by those in the different groups about the issue being compared – a very tedious and laborious approach (this would be easier if you have also recorded codes with page numbers as indexes on paper or in Excel).
- Tabular summaries or comparative checklists can be created on paper or in a Word or Excel table, filling information while you review text, or as a follow-on to either of the above approaches (see below for advice on the design of tables).
- If you have recorded summary data or short-answer responses for each of your cases across a range of topics in an Excel table, including categorised attributes, use the sort function to make a comparison based on the values for the categorised attribute

(Figure 9.1; see also Figure 9.6).[1] This will sort all the data in the table, allowing you to compare text data within each of any number of other columns. Use either the split pane tool (located in the lower right corner of the window) or hide columns (right-click at the top of one or more selected columns > Hide) to place the text-based items (concepts or categories) that you want to compare adjacent to the column used for sorting. All the responses for each subgroup of interest will appear consecutively, making it easier to see commonalities where they exist. Summarise the pattern for each group (rather than each individual entry) as your basis for further interpretation.

- When you use Excel (or a table in Word), you can insert extra columns anywhere within the table; these columns can be used, say, to add in a *post hoc* rating based on text in an adjacent column. This, then, allows for further sorting and additional pattern analysis on the basis of content that was originally entered as text.
- If you have data coded using QDA software, you will be able to retrieve full text and/or relevant notes or images for any code for each of the subgroups (identified by values of attributes) you are comparing, using the query functions of the software. Data management tools that allow you to consider comparisons for multiple coding categories at the same time, using a matrix to display the results, are more efficient in terms of steps needed to generate the data displays. More importantly, by making both numbers and text available for perusal these facilitate both detection of patterns of response across that range of categories, *and* detection of differences in the forms of expression used by different groups with regard to the same category (Figure 9.2).

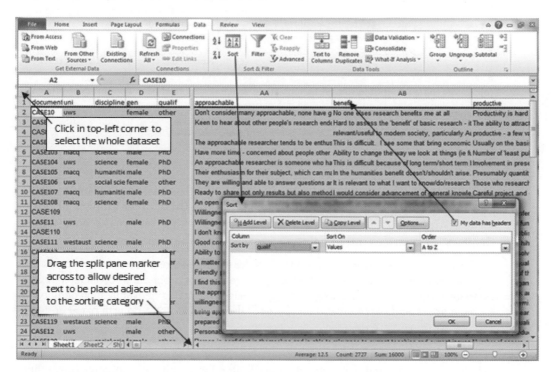

Figure 9.1   Using Excel to sort data, based on a categorical variable

---

[1] Alternatively use a Word table, but Excel provides more functionality.

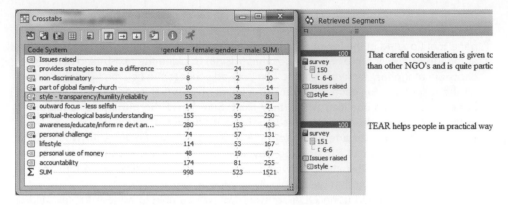

(a) Screen display of cross-tabulated output for a range of issues raised by people of different genders, with access to retrieved segments for females talking about the agency's style of working

Issues raised	gender = female	gender = male
provides strategies to make a difference	My outlook has not changed but I enjoy being informed about the world both in Christian circles and other so I can pray and find other opportunities to contribute. survey\107, 1 encouraged me to participate in an overseas volunteer program survey\111, 1	more aware of good way of supporting those in need survey\106, 1 Broadened awareness of the developing world and what we can do in response to the many needs. survey\112, 1 And an outlet for financial giving that I can

(b) 'Quote matrix' output from a cross-tabulation, which is exported as a word processor file. Up to four columns of data can be included in a quote matrix

Figure 9.2   MAXQDA output options for comparative analysis

Designing comparative displays

When you are comparing one or more coded categories across subgroups, regardless of whether it is on paper or using a computer, there are a number of design issues, strategies, and accepted practices to apply that will make your tabular displays, or matrices, more helpful for answering your questions.[2]

- The first and most obvious point is to consider what questions you want the comparison to answer, and what aspects of the project are most appropriate to consider in relation to each other. So, for example, if you are looking at a series of events, then perhaps the most appropriate attributes to compare for those would be to do with place or time; if

---

[2]The terms 'matrix' and 'table' are often used interchangeably by qualitative researchers. A matrix refers here to a tabular display in which rows and columns each define a set of items that are of interest, and the combination of values on any pair of those items is found in the cell where those values intersect.

you are considering strategies employed, then perhaps consider those in relation to role or level of experience of people who might employ those strategies.

- It is usually best to restrict your choices to one kind of thing (one set or type of codes, such as specific examples of feelings; or strategies; or management issues) considered in relation to the values of one attribute (such as male and female as values of gender; or senior manager, middle manager, supervisor, shop floor worker as values of position in the company), for any single-pattern matrix display. Similarly, don't make your table too big or overload it with minor categories; as an alternative, you might want to group minor categories into domains. There is a limit to how much you can absorb in one sitting!

- Assuming you live in a culture with a language that is read from left to right, then the standard approach to building (row by column) comparative tables for concepts is to use the codes representing the concepts or categories you want to have compared (known more formally as the dependent variables) to define the rows, and the values of the attribute being used to define the subgroups being compared (i.e., the independent variables) to define the columns. Each cell in a row will then contain information for the concept for that row, for one subgroup as defined by the column. This arrangement works best because we naturally tend to read across the rows to make the comparisons.

- For comparisons of individual cases, the cases would usually be placed in the rows, and the attribute or concepts on which they are being compared define the columns.

- Where the table contains information relating to individual sources, ensure the source of each item is identified, so that the origin and the broader context of the summary or quote can be tracked and checked (computer software does this automatically).

- When you have multiple raw data entries for a particular coded category for each subgroup or set of cases, make a summary table (e.g., Table 9.1). Each cell contains counts (where relevant) and brief wording to draw together the essence of what was recorded about each category for each group.

- Alternatively, one of the 'tricks' I employ when using QDA software, for matrix results that appear to be fruitful, is to copy and paste the table with its numeric counts into Word, and then insert a text summary of the coded segments into each cell.

- For those creating summary matrix displays, whether from paper or computer sources, Miles and Huberman (1994) recommend:

  o Only include items (specific actions or occurrences) mentioned by a participant in a cell if they are not denied or disconfirmed by someone else.
  o If more than one person (or a larger proportion, depending on numbers being considered) emphasised the importance of something, give that item an asterisk to make it stand out.
  o If you are making 'don't know' entries, then do so in three versions: DK1 for the question was not asked; DK2 for when the question was asked but not answered; or DK3 for an ambiguous answer.

- When you are designing matrix displays, don't expect to necessarily get it right first go: 'It usually takes several alternative cuts before a workable and productive set of partitions and/or clusters emerges' (Miles & Huberman, 1994: 182).

- Keep a record of any decision rules you employ as you select data for your matrix, and as you summarise data.

Table 9.1 Summary table comparing changes in emotion over time for researchers at different career stages

Career stage	Stage of development being described*	
	Becoming a researcher	**Being a researcher**
Beginner or early career (n = 24)	*Enjoyment (8 cases, 9 passages):* just expressed as interest in something, sometimes with career implications	*Enjoyment (3 cases, 3 passages):* always something new, interacting with people, students learning
	Satisfaction (5 cases, 7 passages): personal learning, having time to read/think, helping others, connecting with participants or audience	*Satisfaction (4 cases, 7 passages):* having an impact, helping others, achieving a goal
Experienced, established (n = 18)	*Enjoyment (3 cases, 6 passages):* success (recognition), handling data	*Enjoyment (4 cases, 4 passages):* intensive/challenging work, autonomy
	Satisfaction (2 cases, 3 passages): immersion and discovery	*Satisfaction (11 cases, 17 passages):* crafting something lasting, making a difference to people's lives, absorption in something you find fascinating, connections with students, people are interested in your work

*'Cases' refers to the number of people who were coded as expressing this emotion; 'passages' refers to the number of separate text segments where this emotion was expressed.

The next step

Use both counts and text to draw conclusions from the pattern of results and comparisons within them:

- Counts will tell you *how many* in each group talked about that aspect or item, or *how often* each kind of event occurred in each setting (make sure you are aware of how many there were in each group to start with).
- The text will tell you *in what ways* members of each group talked about that aspect or item, or *how* the form of that event varied in each setting.

🛈 Beware reading too much into small comparative differences between groups. Some variation can be expected from 'chance' factors including inconsistencies in sampling, data gathering, and coding.

Finally, record what you learn from each comparison *straight away*, even if it is just to note that you did not learn anything new, *before* you move on to do another. It will be much more difficult to do later when you don't have the reason for doing it and the data found by it fresh in your mind. You need to add explanatory text (not just a summary) to give meaning to the results shown in the table, in terms of your project goals. Thus for Table 9.1, for example, I would comment on the possibility of a trend to shift in emphasis from enjoyment to satisfaction as a researcher matures, where satisfaction is less about personal pleasure and more about a deeper emotion stemming from intense involvement in a purposeful task that has meaning beyond the self. This would need to be checked through further theoretical sampling.

Comparing concepts or categories across groups or situations

Comparing perspectives on a concept or category follows on directly from the work you have done in describing these. The first thing you need to decide is what to compare, as it is unlikely that you will be able to compare *every* coding category you have created across every attribute or contextual situation that you have data for – and nor should you (although use of software can make at least a brief scanning of many categories more feasible). As part of reviewing and refining your categories, earlier on, you will have identified those that are definitely of interest to analyse further, and perhaps also some further 'possibles', depending on what you learn from the first set of comparisons (and how soon the report is due).

If you are studying the process of implementing a decision over time, if you have deliberately chosen two contrasting research sites, or if you have deliberately included people who have different roles or genders or ages in your sample because you suspect those factors will matter, then comparison is inherent in your research question. Or, you might choose to frame your comparisons based on a theoretical understanding of the issues: you could have good theoretical or sociological reasons – perhaps even formal propositions – for examining the influence of gender or status or religion on aspects of your topic, as evidenced in the things you have read or observed or that participants have said. Alternatively, purely exploratory comparisons satisfy curiosity and may, opportunistically, help to clarify features and dimensions or components of the experience or concept that is being compared.

- ✓ Regard the notes you make as a consequence of running these kinds of comparisons as working documents, not final text for your report. Add insights from what you are seeing to your existing descriptive notes about the categories and concepts you are examining.

- ✓ You can approach this kind of comparative work with your data in a very methodical way, as a stage in processing your data, especially if you are using computer software which makes it very easy to run multiple comparative analyses. Beware getting trapped into doing so without stopping to reflect on and record what you have learned from each comparison along the way! Use what you are seeing from this particular comparison as a jumping-off point for exploring wider relationships. Then come back to the next comparison, and so on, iteratively working through your data, describing, comparing, reflecting, relating.

Comparing concepts across demographically defined subgroups

Gender, age, and indicators of status are obvious (and classically sociological) bases for comparison, but in your project you will have other demographic attributes to consider that are specifically related to your topic and questions. Discipline (e.g., science, social science, or humanities) is an important one in my studies of researchers (even more so than gender). Management researchers would be interested in the roles participants have within the company or organisation they represent.

▶ To compare across a category or concept requires that you sort the coded material by value of the attribute (i.e., each subgroup) being considered, using any of the methods outlined earlier. Thus, for example: *here is all the coded material on pre-operative anxiety, now I'll sort it for those who come from different cultural backgrounds.*

▶ Having sorted it, your next task is to review the material for each subgroup, noting similarities and differences in aspects covered, forms of expression, emotions expressed – whatever elements are relevant to your research questions *and any others you notice* (Box 9.2).

▶ Record what you are learning about patterns of similarity and difference as you go, and ask further questions: *what is it about this particular culture, or their refugee history, that adds to the anxiety of this cultural group about having an operation?* Hints for relevant further questions will be embedded within the comparative text.

⌐ Box 9.2 ⌐

Using comparison to prompt questions: independent versus collaborative management of chronic illness

Jeremy Yorgason and colleagues (2010) interviewed 28 older couples in which one spouse was diagnosed with both diabetes and osteoarthritis to explore the relationship between family resiliency, coping strategies, and adjustment in managing life with multiple chronic illnesses. As part of this exploration, they compared actions taken independently and together as couples. They identified three patterns of couple interaction regarding daily routines – ranging from the ill person managing all aspects independently of his or her spouse, through partial assistance from a spouse, to full collaboration between couples. Yorgason et al. went on to summarise and then discuss these patterns of coping with chronic disease in relation to the literature, with ambiguous references to the relationship between them and positive outcomes for management of multiple chronic illnesses.

Fifteen couples included references to exercise and diet as important to maintaining their health, even though these were not always easy to maintain – especially where exercise for diabetes created issues for arthritis. With regard to exercise, the authors noted:

A similar pattern [to that for diet] was found with regard to exercising, in that some exercised alone (10), some couples exercised together (6), and some exercised both as individuals and couples (2). One husband stated, 'We go out down on the trail here and we get in anywhere between 2 and 3 miles there just walking, and she's outdoing me now.' It is interesting to note that five of the six references to exercising together involved walking. In contrast, reports of individual exercising involved activities such as walking, swimming, or aerobics, as well as activities to keep joints moving. (2010: 40)

Having identified comparative differences in exercise routines between individuals and couples, Yorgason et al. might then have looked at *how* the couples talked about their chosen forms of exercise, asking (of their data), for example:

- Were the differences in the type of exercise undertaken by individuals and couples because:
  - the nature of the exercise facilitated or precluded doing it together;
  - walking was selected by couples especially as something they could both manage to do?

- Did sharing exercise with a partner encourage persistence with it?
- What kind of exercise was engaged in by the couple who didn't walk? How else did they differ from the walkers, in talking about exercise?
- Did those who walked (or exercised more generally) independently of their partner do so alone or regularly with someone else? How did they talk about walking, specifically, compared with those who walked together?
- For those who sometimes exercised together and sometimes independently:
  - Did they engage in different kinds of exercise at those times?
  - Were there other factors that determined whether they exercised together or alone on any given occasion?

Comparison always prompts further questions like these, leading to the identification of relevant dimensions and deeper understanding of the issues being investigated – in this case (potentially):

- Dimensions of exercise as it relates to engagement by older chronically ill people, e.g., level of exertion required, social interactivity, skill required, accessibility, persistence.
- Dimensions and understanding related to the nature of collaboration between couples in exercising, whether they actually did the activity together or not (with potential relevance to other coping strategies), e.g., who initiates the activity, who ensures maintenance of it, pressure applied (application of power/coercion), pride in or celebration of the other's achievements.
- These could then be investigated in relation to the outcomes of interest, i.e., family resilience, coping, and healthy management of chronic disease.

Comparing coded data across times and contexts

Many studies are carried out across different sites or settings or times, or in contexts that vary in some other way. This is usually a deliberate choice of the researcher, as it allows for the kinds of comparisons that facilitate reaching an understanding of underlying processes, and for making generalisations beyond those immediate settings. If there are no differences in patterns across varying contexts, this will suggest a process that is likely to apply in a wider range of settings. Where differences occur, this prompts questions about the aspects of the context that make a difference, the mechanisms behind them, and the implications of those.

Most comparisons suggested here can be applied either within or across cases. Where entire sources of data come from different settings or times, then those differences can be recorded as attribute data attached to those sources, and treated in the same way as demographic data as far as the processing of the data is concerned. But in Chapter 6, I wrote also about situations in which context might be recorded in codes, because it varied throughout the source. Field observations, in particular, are likely to have multiple (mini)contexts recorded within each set of observations. Even if the overall setting for the observations is uniform throughout the source, variations could be recorded based on time of day, location within a site, who else was present at the time, and so on. As noted earlier, if one is studying children's behaviour, it could be important to know whether the behaviour occurred in the home, the classroom, the playground, the community, at a friend's house, or at mum's workplace, and whether it was morning, midday, or in the late afternoon when children are tired and tend to hyperactivity. Retrospective interviews cover different time periods or places; a woman talks about aspects of her life as she plays out her different roles as wife, mother, scout leader, and scientist. Again, the sorting is done in much the same way; it is just that you are now using additional codes as the basis for the comparisons, rather than comparing subgroups based on attribute data.

Comparisons involving time might be set out according to phases of a process or significant events in a process, or simply in terms of chronological time (Box 9.3). Time-ordered comparisons, which can include both variable and process data, help to ground understanding of a complex flow of events and lay a basis for further causal analysis. As well as having obvious application to historical data, they are especially useful for narrative data, field notes, or longitudinal data.

Box 9.3

Comparing a set of concept codes across different coded contexts

In his study of the decision to outsource the meter reading activities of a publicly listed Australian energy company (cf. Boxes 3.8 and 6.2), James Hunter generated a series of tables through undertaking comparative analyses of (coded) issues raised by managers, employees, and contractors across the pre-announcement, pre-implementation, immediate post-implementation, and medium-term periods, made possible by his having coded the period being referred to by each interviewee throughout each of his interview transcripts. This analysis was conducted separately for each role-based group, as each of these needed first to be understood on its own (Hunter & Cooksey, 2004). Table 9.2 shows one of several comparative tables he generated to facilitate his analysis. By putting these analyses for each role together he was able to show how and why an initial positive impact from outsourcing, in this company, became negative within a relatively short time.

Table 9.2 Time-ordered matrix of issues raised by a decision to outsource meter reading activity: summary analysis for the decision maker role

Outsourcing dimensions	Critical stages in the outsourcing process			
	Pre-announcement	Pre-implementation	Post-implementation (0–1 year)	Post-implementation (2–4 years)
Critical issues				
– Economic factors	Inefficient and ineffective	Inefficient and ineffective	Efficient and effective	Efficient and effective
– Strategic factors	Poor work culture Uncompetitive Careful planning	Poor work culture Careful implementation	Improved control Careful implementation Rising competitive pressures	Looking for synergies Rising competitive pressures
– Behavioural factors	Bad attitude and low commitment Concern for employees Good communication	Increased power for management Concern for employees Good communication	Motivated meter readers Good communication	Good communication
Views developed	Need for significant change	Need for significant change	Wouldn't change anything	Question understanding of activity
Actions taken	High absenteeism and turnover Low-quality meter reading	High absenteeism and turnover Contract development	Professional meter reading Focused quality meter reading Ongoing contract modification	Exploitation of contract by service providers
Feelings evoked	Frustration with poor operations Enough is enough Deserved to be dealt with	Frustration with negotiations Confidence in the decision	Enthusiasm for the new model Very confident in the decision Accepted the outcomes	Less confident about the results

Source: Hunter and Cooksey, 2004: 31, Table 1

Evaluating impact and outcomes

Effective evaluation of a social change process or intervention requires knowledge of the immediate impact and longer-term outcomes of the change, as well as understanding of the processes through which these came about. Comparison provides one basis for assessing impact or outcomes, and contributes also to understanding process. These comparisons usually take one or other (but sometimes both) of two different forms:

- Comparisons based on group assignment (e.g., experimental or control; condition 1 or condition 2). These follow the same format as other comparisons of coded experiences or responses across groups based on attributes.
- Comparisons of responses to particular interventions, events, conditions, or experiences.

The latter, like those involving context, rely on the coder having recorded not only what is happening, but also and at the same time, the response to whatever that was. Thus, if help was provided or a coping strategy employed following a crisis event, the analyst needs to note the nature of the event, the kind of help given or coping strategy employed, and whether that assistance or strategy was found to be helpful or not helpful in those circumstances – each with a code that is applied to the same text. This is so that intersections between specific events, strategies, and evaluations of those strategies can be most easily detected.

Alternative ways of describing impacts include barrier/facilitator or positive/negative as well as helpful/not-helpful and, thinking along other dimensions, direct/indirect or proximal/distal. Analysis, then (for these examples), would take the form of using a matrix display or series of displays to look at the patterns of what strategies were used for what situations, and then for which were found to be helpful or not helpful, under what circumstances, and perhaps also whether that was assessed with reference to the short or longer term.

Comparing free text on the basis of responses to survey questions or scaled scores

Survey researchers often include open-ended questions in their questionnaires or interview schedules, with an option for the respondent to make additional comments at the end of the survey. Sometimes respondents are followed up for a further semi-structured interview. As well as demographic information, the survey will include questions with pre-categorised responses, and sometimes also responses to scaled items, various kinds of ratings, or other measured outcomes.

Each of these numeric responses or scores can be used in the same way as demographic data, as a basis for comparing coded responses to the open-ended questions from the same survey, or coded data from a matched follow-up interview.[3] Where

---

[3]For additional detail on the use of computer programs for combining qualitative and quantitative data in this way, see Bazeley (2006a; 2010a).

the numeric data are continuous or there are a large number of categories, they will need to be regrouped into a manageable number of categories – that number depending in part on how big the sample is altogether (Box 9.4).

⌐ Box 9.4 ⌐

Using comparative analysis to interpret or validate scaled scores

Surgery and pain

Patients recovering from day surgery were asked to complete a visual analogue scale to record the level of pain they were experiencing, and were interviewed also about their experience of surgery and pain (Coll, n.d.). Their descriptions of their experience of pain could be sorted by the rating they had given for the level of pain experienced (reduced to a 10-point scale). In this way, it could be determined what each point on a pain scale of this type meant for people experiencing it, thus making use of the scale more meaningful for further research.

Healthcare in emotional circumstances

Prospective parents whose unborn baby was diagnosed with a serious abnormality were inter-viewed regarding their satisfaction with care from various health service providers, and at the same time they provided ratings of their satisfaction on five-point scales (Green, Statham, & Solomou, 2008). When Green et al. compared the content of the concurrently conducted inter-view and the ratings, they found a range of discrepancies. For example, in the interview, com-pared to the scaled measure:

- the parents' focus was on emotional rather than the practical aspects;
- individual care they happened to receive was satisfactory, but the system had problems;
- they were unsure how to rate absence of care (including if it was not wanted);
- they spoke of having to ask for care rather than having it offered, and of whether care offered became care received.

Satisfaction, in the context of emotionally laden healthcare, was found through this exercise to be coloured by people's expectations of what care should be (when they might not have relevant experi-ence to base that on), and by what had happened since the event being discussed. By combining and comparing text with scaled data, the study demonstrated the questionable value of scaled (0–5 numeric) ratings of satisfaction, especially in the context of a complex and emotive issue.

Two-factor comparisons

Not all 'independent' variables are as independent as that label might suggest. Being a female in a science department can be a very different experience from being a female in a social science or a humanities department, for example. You can sort to make this type of comparison by hand (if you are patient and well organised); or, using software, you can cross-tabulate gender by discipline, with data in the cells 'scoped' to include only the experience you are interested in comparing – a relatively simple operation to run (Figure 9.3).

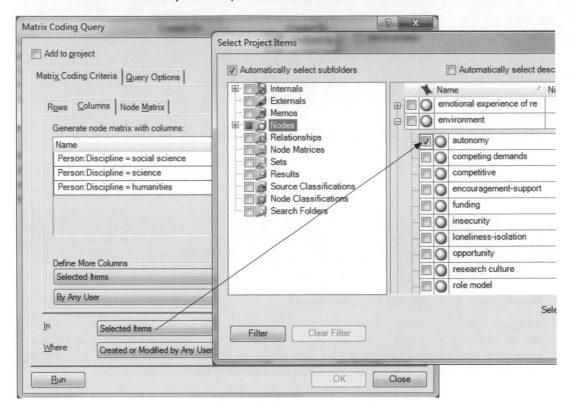

Figure 9.3 Using NVivo to compare what was said about autonomy in research, based on a combination of gender (in rows) and discipline (in columns)[4]

Similarly, some aspect of experience might vary over time in relation to some other factor, such as the role a person has within the family unit, or within a company. Thus, if you are considering something like how anxiety was expressed by different family members over time, you would set out items representing different family roles in rows (these might be cases, codes, or sets of sources, depending on the arrangement of your data), with the time sequence defining columns, and coded data about anxiety as the selected item in the cells for each role at each time period. Simply repeat the procedure for any other emotion or concern you wish to investigate by changing the content of the cells. The entries in each cell for a final summary table might contain the frequency and/or a summary of responses for the cases represented by that cell, or they could be presented in a graph where this will show differences more dramatically than they appear in a list or table (Box 9.5). Table 9.1 was similarly created by running a two-factor analysis.

---

[4]It is advisable to run a query like this for all sources first, to give you a total number of 'possible' cases for each cell, so that you can assess the significance of counts obtained when you run it for a selected code.

Box 9.5

Exploring different partners' changes in emotions over time

People who had experienced a heart attack and their partners (35 couples) were interviewed at two, three, and four weeks post-hospitalisation. Table 9.3 records their comparative levels of anxiety and confidence over time as reflected in the number of passages coded for each person at each time period. The table clearly shows it is the partners, more than those who had the heart attack, who experience higher levels of anxiety and lower confidence to start with. It also shows, for both partners, that confidence rose dramatically in the short term, appearing to drop off somewhat by the following week.

Table 9.3 Changes in expression of anxiety and confidence over time for couples following hospitalisation of one partner for heart attack (number of passages coded)

| | Time post-hospitalisation for heart attack | | |
	2 weeks	3 weeks	4 weeks
Experience of worry/fear/anxiety			
Heart attack victim	39	48	41
Partner	62	46	44
Expression of confidence			
Heart attack victim	18	55	36
Partner	8	31	13

Review of which cases were coded and of the detailed text in each cell in the matrix to investigate this later decline in confidence revealed that those expressing confidence at three and four weeks largely comprised different couples, however. Additionally, couples were more cautious in the way they expressed confidence at three weeks than were those expressing confidence at four weeks. *These additional observations point to the absolute importance of not relying on numbers alone, but always checking the text as well.* They also point to further questions to investigate:

- Is there potential danger in becoming confident too early?
- How does level of confidence relate to the kinds of activities in which the survivor engaged as the weeks went by?

If I were to present the data in Table 9.3 in a report rather than using it as a step in analysis, I would present it as a line graph with all four lines shown together (Figure 9.4).

(Continued)

(Continued)

🛈 It is very easy, when using graphical representations of data, to do so in such a way that the impression made on the reader (e.g., of differences) is distorted. If you are using a bar graph, for example, caution is needed regarding relative scaling of the *x* and *y* axes.

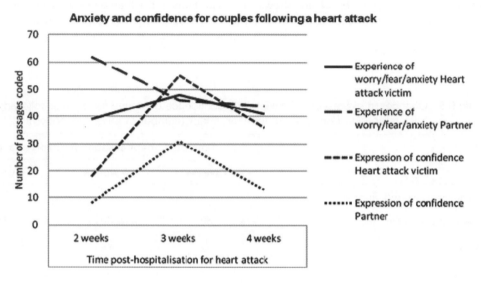

Figure 9.4   Using a graph to view or present comparative data*

* This graph was prepared in Excel from a data table created in NVivo. While NVivo will display results graphically, Excel provides more flexibility in formatting the display for presentation.

Comparing cases

We will now turn our attention to comparative techniques that focus on cases rather than concepts, although many of the ideas are similar and the data management tools and strategies you learned in working with concepts will be of benefit here, too. As with concepts, thorough (descriptive) knowledge of each case is a necessary precursor to successful comparison.

Case comparisons can be used to further explore and describe your data, or you might use them as a tool for explaining and predicting (Miles & Huberman, 1994). The focus here continues to be on deepening your knowledge and understanding of your data, but in the process you will be learning strategies and picking up ideas for ways of working with your data that will carry across into more complex, end-product analyses.

Comparing cases with theory

Comparing cases with theory increases your sensitivity to the data. It might also create some surprises if you find your cases don't fit as expected, prompting a change in theory or practice. Barbara Bowers explains:

> Dimensional Analysis [of the literature] … becomes a mechanism to do a comparative analysis with what is developed from interviews. So for example, in my study of caregiving, it allowed me to say that the researchers and professionals conceptualize and study caregiving in this way, the concept of caregiving (in the literature) has the following dimensions, integrates the following assumptions. In contrast, interviews with caregivers suggested that the concept of caregiving was understood as a fundamentally different thing. So then you are in a position to say that the professionals may design interventions based on their understanding of caregiving, but since it is at odds with the experience of caregiving, the intervention is likely to miss the mark. (personal communication, 2 August 2006)

The literature defined caregiving in terms of assistance with daily tasks, but what she found was that caregivers defined caregiving in psychosocial terms (Bowers, 1989).

Contextual comparative analyses *within* cases

Detailed case analysis, whether the case comprises a single person or a cluster of people or other items bound together in some way, can include comparative analyses. As suggested earlier, you might compare some aspects of life and experience for someone with respect to a range of different roles that they fulfil within their family and society (husband, father, lawyer, president of the local Rotary group), the settings in which they live and work or, in a longitudinal study, changes in attitude or experience over a period of time.

Similar principles apply to a case comprising a number of people, such as for a family, an organisation, a community, or a historical event, in that you can compare the attitudes and experiences of those various persons who are part of the family, organisation, or event, as James Hunter did (cf. Box 9.3). Cases defined by events or programmes or policies typically involve data from a variety of sources, including documents as well as interviews and other media, and these, as with most single case studies, often also involve a time element or some form of sequential activity or events (Box 9.6). Comparisons of what is done in public with what is said or done in private offer another possibility (Hammersley & Atkinson, 2007).

▶ Within-case comparison requires that you have a common set of behaviours, issues, or events that you want to explore from the different perspectives, contexts, or times available for your case. Your analysis begins with deciding what those are, as a first step.

▶ Prepare a brief summary of each identified behaviour, issue, etc., from the different perspectives or as they appear in different contexts.

▶ Use matrices, flow charts, or other visual tools to compare how these behaviours or issues vary, noting patterns that suggest relationships between them and also in relation to time or other contextual variations (Figure 9.5).

▶ Use the within-case comparison to sharpen awareness of features of the case, to refine concepts, to increase sensitivity to contextual factors impacting on the case, and so to lead into further, relational analyses.

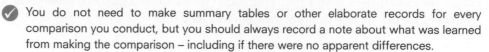 You do not need to make summary tables or other elaborate records for every comparison you conduct, but you should always record a note about what was learned from making the comparison – including if there were no apparent differences.

Box 9.6

Mapping shifts in a public relations campaign

In her case analysis of a pharmaceutical company's use of public media for political influence (Boxes 3.4 and 7.6), Jannet Pendleton used a time series analysis of (coded) media materials to show that different message strategies were deployed at various times during the campaign to build toward a push for government action (Figure 9.5).[5] Early in the campaign, the focus was on the severity of the disease. In mid-campaign, the importance of immunisation gained emphasis, but then the need for government funding for the vaccine became a focus along with continuing attention to the severity of the disease.

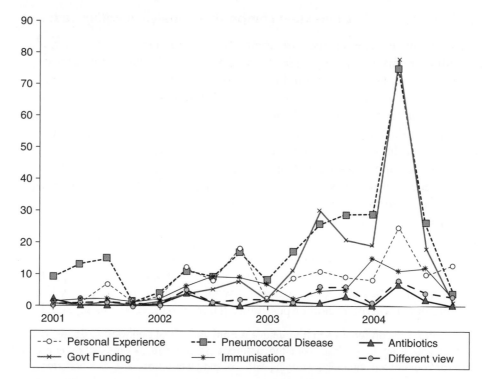

Figure 9.5   Story elements appearing in media discourse over time

---

[5]In QDAS, run a matrix of codes representing content by attributes (or codes) for time periods.

Cross-case comparisons

Knowledge of individual cases is a necessary precursor to considering these in cross-case analysis. Cross-case comparisons might then begin with comparisons of pairs of cases, selected deliberately on the basis of either similarity or contrast. Similarities and differences between the pairs are listed as a way of identifying more subtle features of the cases. Comparisons involving a wider sample extend single and paired case analyses in ways that parallel many of the approaches already considered, employing the same kind of sifting and sorting and display strategies that are used when comparing concepts across subgroups.

When cases are compared together such that each still retains its uniqueness, samples are usually relatively small. The purpose is to explore similarities and differences across cases, with a view to increasing understanding of the processes that shape each case and the hope of identifying more general patterns and processes that can then assist in understanding experience or explaining behaviour across a wider population.

Most cross-case analyses, like other comparative analyses, rely on some form of pattern matching as one of the steps, with matrix or tabular displays being the primary tool used. The difference here, from the kinds of matrices shown earlier, are that the rows are typically defined by individual cases rather than groups, with the columns then showing variables or issues of interest. Cases may be arranged in the rows in some sort of demographically defined or conceptual order. Alternatively, they are arranged randomly to start with, with a view to reordering them on some criterion of interest as some clustering or pattern of association becomes more apparent – something that is quite easy to do using a spreadsheet or word processor table (Box 9.7).[6]

Box 9.7

Research opportunities for new academic staff

A spreadsheet was filled using brief notes and key comments derived from semi-structured interviews about research career opportunities for new academic staff that were conducted with the heads of 56 academic departments covering six discipline areas in 12 Australian universities (Bazeley et al., 1996). Figure 9.6 shows data relating to structural aspects of departmental research life (six of a total of 26 aspects), with additional categorical variables classifying discipline of the department and university status (referred to as Sandstone, Greenfield, and New, numbered 1, 2, and 3 respectively),

(Continued)

---

[6]NVivo's framework matrix function provides an attribute-ordered display of case data for selected codes that allows users to create, save, and print summary cross-case matrices within the software.

(Continued)

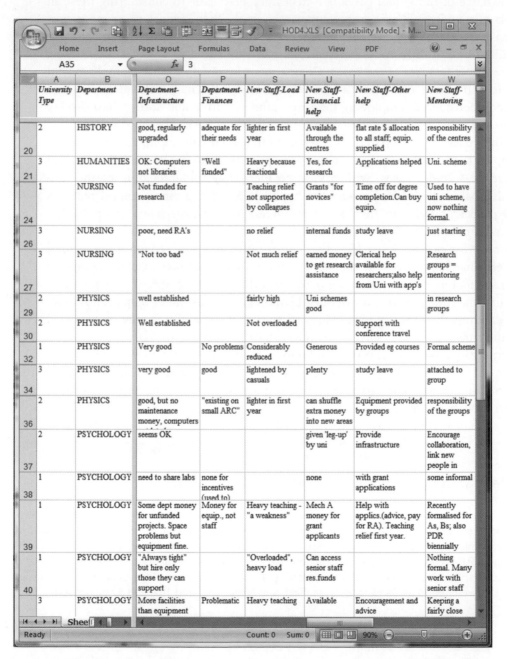

University Type	Department	Department-Infrastructure	Department-Finances	New Staff-Load	New Staff-Financial help	New Staff-Other help	New Staff-Mentoring
2	HISTORY	good, regularly upgraded	adequate for their needs	lighter in first year	Available through the centres	flat rate $ allocation to all staff; equip. supplied	responsibility of the centres
3	HUMANITIES	OK: Computers not libraries	"Well funded"	Heavy because fractional	Yes, for research	Applications helped	Uni. scheme
1	NURSING	Not funded for research		Teaching relief not supported by colleagues	Grants "for novices"	Time off for degree completion.Can buy equip.	Used to have uni scheme, now nothing formal.
3	NURSING	poor, need RA's		no relief	internal funds	study leave	just starting
3	NURSING	"Not too bad"		Not much relief	earned money to get research assistance	Clerical help available for researchers;also help from Uni with app's	Research groups = mentoring
2	PHYSICS	well established		fairly high	Uni schemes good		in research groups
2	PHYSICS	Well established		Not overloaded		Support with conference travel	
1	PHYSICS	Very good	No problems	Considerably reduced	Generous	Provided eg courses	Formal scheme
3	PHYSICS	very good	good	lightened by casuals	plenty	study leave	attached to group
2	PHYSICS	good, but no maintenance money, computers	"existing on small ARC"	lighter in first year	can shuffle extra money into new areas	Equipment provided by groups	responsibility of the groups
2	PSYCHOLOGY	seems OK			given 'leg-up' by uni	Provide infrastructure	Encourage collaboration, link new people in
1	PSYCHOLOGY	need to share labs	none for incentives (used to)		none	with grant applications	some informal
1	PSYCHOLOGY	Some dept money for unfunded projects. Space problems but equipment fine.	Money for equip., not staff	Heavy teaching - "a weakness"	Mech A money for grant applicants	Help with applics.(advice, pay for RA). Teaching relief first year.	Recently formalised for As, Bs; also PDR biennially
1	PSYCHOLOGY	"Always tight" but hire only those they can support		"Overloaded", heavy load	Can access senior staff res.funds		Nothing formal. Many work with senior staff
3	PSYCHOLOGY	More facilities than equipment	Problematic	Heavy teaching	Available	Encouragement and advice	Keeping a fairly close

Figure 9.6   Using sorted data in Excel to compare patterns of response across subgroups of cases

Cases (departments) could be sorted using the categorical variables. Sorting and then examining the patterns in related columns showed that discipline was more significant than university status in determining the pattern of opportunity for new researchers:

- Research activity was expected in physics and new academic staff were provided with 'honeymoon periods' from teaching as well as computer facilities and financial support.
- Research was supported in psychology with money and equipment, but teaching loads were a problem.
- Most new academic staff (in 1995) in nursing (and social work) were still undergoing research training; high teaching demands and patchy support for research hampered progress.
- Physics and history (both 'pure' disciplines) had more in common with each other than with others; similarly the applied disciplines of nursing and social work were more similar to each other than to others.

Options for developing cross-case comparative matrices include, but are not limited to:

▶ Using theory as a basis for selecting dimensions for comparing the cases, with the theoretical orientation or conceptual model helping to focus and guide both data collection and analysis (Yin, 2003).

▶ For an exploratory study, or a study designed to inductively build theory, treating the ordering of the cases and the dimensions on which to compare them experimentally, with dimensions in columns based on issues raised in earlier coding and descriptive analyses (as in the example in Box 9.7).

▶ Working from narratives based on a sequence of events to allow comparison; for example, you might identify common stages in the unfolding plots of life stories, narratives of events, or the process and progress of a project group, noting how each case progresses through these (Box 9.8; see also Box 10.3).

Looking across cases deepens our understanding and can increase generalisability. Simply summarising superficially across some themes or main variables by itself tells us little, however. Combining 'process' and 'variable' approaches is needed (Miles & Huberman, 1994: 205–6). We have to look carefully at the complex configurations of processes within each case to understand the local (individual) dynamics, as did Laudel and Gläser (2008; see Box 9.8), before we can begin to see a patterning of experience that transcends particular cases.

| Box 9.8

Narrative-based cross-case comparative analysis

Grit Laudel and Jochen Gläser (2008) traced the development of 16 early career researchers in Australia as they progressed from apprentice to colleague in an attempt to capture the mechanisms that underlie the transition from dependent to independent researcher. They saw this transition as

(Continued)

(Continued)

occurring primarily in the immediate postdoctoral period, and involving three interrelated but independent 'careers': the cognitive, the community, and the organisational. These involved, respectively, development of the researcher's knowledge base; increasing participation in a scientific (disciplinary) community; and acquiring adequate hosting through provision of material resources.

To achieve their goal, Laudel and Gläser drew on biographical interviews with 16 academics who had completed their doctorate in the past eight years, supplementing these interviews with detailed bibliometric data (i.e., publications and citations) for each researcher. They analysed each of their 16 cases in detail first, mapping the intersection of their three careers (Figure 9.7), and then compared those who had successfully made the transition to independent researcher (i.e., they were still actively engaged in research and publishing) with those who had not, tabulating details from each case. The career of the academic in Figure 9.7, for example, lacked synchronisation between his (or her) community and organisational careers, given the 'postdoctoral phase' began three years before the PhD was awarded.

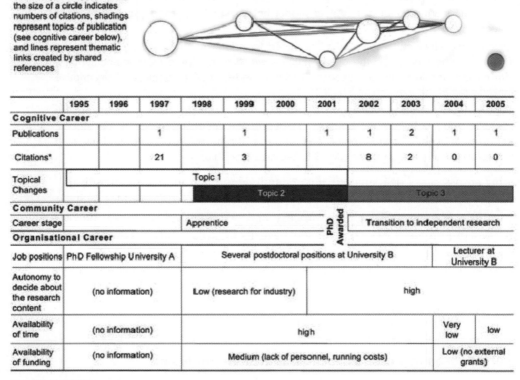

Figure 9.7   Career profile of an early career researcher and main influencing conditions

Source: Laudel & Gläser, 2008: 394, Figure 2 Reprinted with kind permission from Springer Science and Business Media.

From their analysis, Laudel and Gläser concluded:

The transition [from dependent to independent researcher] usually builds on a successful PhD, whose topic is expanded and supplemented by new topics. To begin a career as an independent researcher requires more time for research than is provided by the standard academic position. Therefore, it occurs within extended PhD phases or in research-intensive phases prior to academic standard employment. It is only in exceptional cases that this transition appears to be possible under conditions of standard teaching and research employment at universities. (2008: 402)

Interpreting comparative analyses

Strategies to assist in interpreting comparative analyses, tables, and displays, *beyond simply describing differences*, include the following:

▶ Aggregate or cluster cases to aid in clarifying patterns.

▶ Identify common themes across cases, overriding individual case dynamics, leading to the identification of key variables or core concepts.

▶ Turn comments into ratings and/or counts. Symbols (or colours) can be used instead of or as well as text entries in cells, or as a next-stage table, in order to make patterns more obvious.

▶ Condense case synopses into a generalised cross-case narrative (interpretive synthesis). Check against original synopses to see and show how points in the narrative are exemplified, then describe the essential elements of whatever experience is being examined.

▶ Note relations between variables, concepts, and/or issues that become apparent when they are listed side-by-side in a table. Memoing these will provide starting points to prompt relational analyses.

▶ Note exceptions, and prepare to investigate these to identify reasons for and implications of the differences they show. Similarly, explore extreme cases to see what they reveal. The exception or extreme case can reveal a 'hidden' variable that ends up explaining what is happening across the data more generally.

Throughout all of this comparative work involving case, group, and contextual differences, it is your writing about what you are finding – the conclusions reached and the questions arising – that will have most impact on the path your analysis takes. You only know what you know, and discover what you don't know, when you try to write about it. At this pre-reporting stage, this might be something as simple as adding notes to your descriptions for each of the categories and concepts you are working with, while you traverse back and forth through the describing, comparing, and relating stages of analysis, but that will be sufficient to keep you thinking about connections and further differences to investigate. A greater sense of integration will follow as you move on to do more to relate categories to other categories.

Comparison as end or means?

Each of the types of comparison that have been outlined here can be written up descriptively for the different subgroups or clusters or settings, but each naturally leads you on to want to understand what generated those differences or patterns, to explore how and why the observations made through the comparisons have come about. While comparisons can be, and indeed often are, provided as primary results, the argument of this book is that *comparative analyses are rarely an end point, rather they are just one tool among many on the analytic journey*, to be supplemented by reflective writing and followed by relational analyses. The next step on that path therefore will take you into identifying, exploring, and describing relationships between the concepts, categories, and dimensions of your data to which you have become increasingly sensitised through the descriptive and comparative processes used so far. And (in a later chapter) your comparative skills will become useful again when I review different approaches to the question of establishing causation.

Writing about comparisons

In the methods chapter

▶ Describe when and how you used comparative strategies in your analysis, including:
  ○ your purpose in making comparisons
  ○ your strategy for choosing what to compare
  ○ the tools you used to assist your comparative analyses
  ○ what you considered in the results (e.g., numbers, text, patterns)
  ○ how you went about interpreting and making use of the results (e.g., patterns, relationships, anomalies).

As part of the presentation of results

▶ Use data derived from comparisons to demonstrate how you developed your understanding of the issues for your study.

▶ Use tables or graphs rather than long and complex (and boring!) prose descriptions if you need to present details of comparative differences.

✓ Provide displays from your comparative analyses *selectively* to convey important information to the reader. Don't overload your presentation with tables – place additional tables in an appendix if it is necessary for the reader to consult your evidence.

❗ Don't expect the reader to do the analysis for you! You need to explain the significance of the material that is in the table.

Exercises

Exercise 1: Case comparison

▶ Using the four stories about being in community from Box 8.8, fill out a case comparison summary such as that set out in Table 9.4. Add two more columns to include two dimensions you came up with from your previous work in Chapter 8.

▶ What do you learn about the characteristics of community in modern times from comparing these cases? Can you, from your table, identify any potential relationships between different aspects of community?

Table 9.4

Person	Gender	Membership	Interdependence	Nature of interactions	Time span	Physical proximity
		Characteristics and dimensions of experience of community				
Alison	F					
Bernice	F					
Anthony	M					
Colin	M					

Further reading

Miles and Huberman (1994): case-based comparative analyses using matrix displays of summary data form the backbone of these authors' strategy for qualitative analysis.

10

Relational analyses

Comparisons across sample subgroups don't usually provide a complete answer in themselves. The astute researcher will be propelled into asking further questions: what are the implications of these similarities (or differences)? What was it about this group's experience that meant their response was so different from the others? And then there are the questions you noted as you worked through your data: what happens if ...? Did everyone respond that way? Weren't some of them also talking about having gained a new perspective on that issue?

In this chapter you will choose from a variety of strategies designed to help you see associations between various elements of your data. Some rely on your having a comprehensive coding system for your data, others do not. All benefit from your having noted possible connections as you worked through your data. Some allow you to directly assess the strength of a relationship; others point to those relationships you might need to consider further. Some benefit from or depend on use of specialised software, others do not. Each one that you employ will set you thinking more deeply about your data, will enrich your analysis, and will help you communicate what you are doing and finding. Strategies covered include:

- identifying patterns of association through cross-case analyses, pattern analyses, and proximity analyses;
- strategies for visualising patterned relationships through various kinds of maps, plots, and models; and
- ways to visualise and investigate relationships between specific concepts, categories, or themes.

Coding and connecting working together

Categorising data (in codes) and connecting data (e.g., through juxtaposition, linkages, and memos) are generally seen as alternative or parallel approaches to working with data, with the former based on similarities identified through comparative processes, and the latter based on contiguities of data in context. Maxwell and Miller (2008), presenting evidence of the complementarity of categorisation and contiguity from scientific studies in language and memory, argued for their complementarity also in analysis of qualitative data. Researchers using either approach begin with thorough reading of and familiarity with the text; in both approaches they implicitly or explicitly unitise or segment data; and both rely heavily on memoing. Although there are these similarities, and context is attended to in both approaches, there are differences in how context is understood, as there are with how data are segmented, and how they are reconnected.

Coding strategies are generally well understood, but connecting strategies are often misunderstood as preserving data in their original form. Rather, 'they are ways to analyse and reduce data. This is generally done by identifying key relationships that tie the data together into a narrative or sequence and eliminating information that is not germane to these relationships' (Maxwell & Miller, 2008: 467). Such strategies often involve categorisation, for example, of themes that appear throughout a story. Structural elements in a narrative might be identified and then reconnected to show time-based or other functional links between particular segments (as distinct from the content-based connections associated with coding). And while coding strategies are criticised for decontextualising data, connecting strategies can create 'imprisonment in the story' where data are seen only within their fixed contextual frameworks. How then might coding and connecting strategies be combined to allow benefit from both in a more rounded approach to data analysis?

As you work through your data (a reminder!):

▶ While you are comparing and contrasting, look also for antecedents and consequences (to reveal systems, relationships, and process, the flow of events over time).
▶ Create profiles and vignettes as well as codes.
▶ Create case-based models from the codes used for each case.
▶ Create narrative summaries of the data for each case (record these in a linked memo).
▶ Use tools for linking within and across data sources, as well as coding data; both NVivo and MAXQDA provide for in-text links (one-way and two-way respectively, the former being better for sequencing, the latter for pairing).
▶ Record observed linkages – between codes and with context – in memos.

As part of further analysis, moving between coding and connecting strategies, sometimes integrating them, and using manual or computer-based tools:

▶ Link categories together into larger patterns, themes, or more abstract concepts.
▶ Establish linkages between codes *within* cases rather than across them to retain closer connection to context, before considering linkages across cases.

▶ Identify the 'prime narrative' for each case (the thematic category that holds it together and gives it meaning), and from the coding for that category, determine the structure, plot, and genre of the narrative.

▶ Review categories within the context of the narratives from which they came; review narratives with the additional understanding that comes from studying the categories derived from them.

▶ Connect codes via 'the paradigm' enunciated by Strauss (Corbin & Strauss, 2008; Strauss, 1987), in which a phenomenon (category) is viewed in terms of the conditions giving rise to it, the action and interactional strategies associated with it, and the consequences of those strategies under different conditions and within different contexts.

▶ Build a visual model that incorporates relational sequencing or causal linkages between codes to create a holistic interdependent network of events, accompanied by a discussion of the embedded linkages.

▶ Build a storyline from one or another of the previous two strategies: 'An explanation, after all, tells a story about the relations among things or people and events' (Schatzman, 1991: 308).

▶ If you are using QDA software, always check back from numerically tabulated cells of a matrix to the coded data, and often from a particular coded segment to the context from which that came.

▶ Develop theoretical connections between a series of field note (or reported) incidents, and link them in an integrative memo by writing connecting sentences (Emerson et al., 1995).

▶ Explore the immediate context of words that connect ideas, such as *because* and *if*.[1]

▶ Gilligan's second step in her 'listening guide' for analysing interviews suggests you create an 'I poem' by extracting all the first-person (I) statements from an interview, with their associated verb and other important words, and listing them in sequence. The I poem captures the 'associated stream of consciousness' (Gilligan et al., 2003: 260). Categorising then linking the I statements in this way foregrounds the voice of self while preserving the sequential links between the statements.

Some of the strategies detailed in the remainder of this chapter are based more on categorisation than on contiguity; all are designed to help you see associations and connections of one sort or another in your data.

Investigating relational patterns

From the comparative analyses you have been doing, you have a good idea of which groups talked more or less about particular things, of when and where different things were more or less likely to occur, and of how those things looked or sounded in different circumstances. And, you have a bundle of questions that came out of those analyses. Some of these will be answered by exploring specific

---

[1] A reminder: If you are using software, these words are often specified as 'stop words' and so you will need to access the list of stop words and delete them from it.

connections between pairs of codes in your data, some by building a data narrative, and others by examining the patterning of relationships between categories in your data, based on cross-case and matrix displays of potential interrelationships. It is the patterning of relationships to which I will turn first, as the practical strategies and tools are similar to those you used for comparative analyses. And like comparative analyses, pattern analysis can generate almost as many questions as it answers.

- You might have designed your data collection or coding structure deliberately to investigate the association between two sets of phenomena, for example, between behavioural problems and the strategies used to solve them.
- Perhaps the idea to investigate a connection has come out of your analysis so far – something you have recorded in a memo about an association you were noting along the way.
- Alternatively, you might have some theoretically derived criteria for assessing relationships in your data, and you are trawling through your data to see how they stack up in relation to those criteria.

Setting up relational analyses follows the same general guidelines as for comparative analyses (cf. Chapter 9, section 'Designing comparative displays'), with the primary difference being in the content that is generated. Visual displays will prove useful for relational analyses also. And, as with all previous strategies, it will remain your task to interpret the results generated by any analytic strategy.

Cross-case analyses

With cross-case analyses you are generally looking at the patterning and interrelationship of two or more concepts or processes across the set of cases, often as an extension of the comparative analyses you have already done. The goal is to establish if there are patterns of association within cases that hold true across cases, without losing sight of the particularities of each case.

Strategies for a cross-case analysis, in broad terms, include three steps:

▶ Identify concepts, themes, or issues that go across cases (related to your research question).
▶ Group cases into families or types, based on similar configurations of characteristics.
▶ Synthesise interpretations across cases by looking for commonalities and noting differences.

Cross-case analysis using summary data

A conceptually clustered matrix brings together items that 'belong together' for each of the cases in your study (Miles & Huberman, 1994: 127). You can construct this type of matrix without specialist software for a small to moderate sample by going through the data you have for each case and recording a categorical or brief text summary of relevant data for that case for each of the columns of the matrix (Box 10.1). The purpose of doing so is to identify what kind of relationships exist between those items, if any, and possibly also to cluster the cases into groups with similar responses.

▶ Working on paper or using an Excel or a Word table, first create a case-based table, similar to that in Figure 10.1 (this table is drawn from the same data as Figure 9.6):
  ○ Define columns based on the questions being asked (and the data available). Base these on some standardised content analytic themes related to the question.
  ○ Enter each case in a new row, and enter summary information for each case – labels, summary phrases, ratings, brief quotes – relevant to each of the columns, across the cells.
  ○ It helps if cases are sequenced according to how they relate to one of the themes of interest (you might insert an additional column, categorise adjacent text, and sort it to achieve this), or perhaps sequence or sort them according to some other attribute (Miles and Huberman referred to this as a case-ordered matrix).
▶ Review adjacent cells to determine if there is a pattern of association between responses (note that I have hidden some columns in the Excel table for this analysis in order to bring relevant columns together).

Tactics for trying to make sense of the table include:

▶ See if the data support your conceptual framework.
▶ Review only a few items (columns) at a time, selecting them on the basis of your questions.
▶ Collapse columns to reduce complexity. For example, with Figure 10.1, I could reduce the six columns to three by combining columns H, J, and K as being about professional interaction, combining columns I and L as research orientation, and leaving column AC as is, reflecting the funding sources for the departments.
▶ Compare cases to see what makes them similar or different.
▶ Sort and combine rows of the table, especially if a pattern is similar for cases that have a common classification (university type or discipline in this instance), or that share some common feature identified in the columns (e.g., all those departments with a strong research orientation).
▶ Create a brief summary table from the display, categorising responses and amalgamating similar cases where possible (i.e., drawing on previous strategies to 'collapse' both rows and columns into a lesser number), in order to see the pattern of association more clearly.
▶ See if you can come up with one or more statements to pull together the ideas generated by the matrix.

Box 10.1

Creating a case-based matrix using brief summaries

In our study of early career researchers (Bazeley et al., 1996), we understood that the climate of the department where an early career researcher began their academic career was a critical factor for their further development as a researcher. We have already compared a cross-section of departments to look at the opportunities they presented for early career researchers in terms of openings for them, the resources available, and the pressures applied if they started work there (cf. Box 9.7). Figure 10.1 shows the data entered for a number of departments for variables associated with research climate and professional interactions. This allowed us to consider the relationship between these and the department's external funding sources as an indicator of the extent to which resources for research might be available, and as a further indicator of (or outcome of) the strength of the research culture.

A	B	H	I	J	K	L	AC
University Type	Department	Department-Cohesiveness/ stability	Department-Research ethos	Department-Collegial interactions	Departmental research-Teams, groups	Department-Support for research	Departmental research - funding
1	HISTORY	Established:"A tolerably friendly dept"	"Extremely high priority";traditionally strong	Team teaching + "a lot of talking to each other"	"Most of us are loner researchers"	"Taking research v.seriously" eg relief post-study leave	Uni and ARC - good
2	HISTORY	generally good, one outsider	University policy	Good deal of contact, only one who does not fit in	Individual within the centres	expected	ARC and internal - "success rate pretty good"
3	HUMANITIES	OK, on one campus	"Not systematic"	"Normal", some resist	Solo	Encouraged	Only ARC small
1	NURSING	Tall poppy syndrome exists, loyalty to faculty not dept	Developing, but only handful of active	Tearoom not used but some mixing	Both; collab. encouraged	Dean supportive, not uni	Only one ARC. Staff don't apply, burnt out by failure.
3	NURSING	not cohesive	strong focus - creating environment	no	collab. outside uni	compulsory-cannot only teach	Gov't, commercial; no ARC
3	NURSING		New but v. important. Staff committed.	Only at weekly meetings	Inter-dept research group; most dept research	"Nothing prescribed", not saying all have to do it	Dept, uni; one NHMRC
2	PHYSICS	Stable	Very important		Two groups in department	Support	Most from the ARC
1	PHYSICS	High	"Dominant",v. competitive	"Absolutely crucial"	All research collabor.	Very strong	ARC, uni - high
3	PHYSICS	yes	Everybody expected to research	yes	2 groups	expected	ARC small CSIRO Gov't
2	PHYSICS	cohesive within centres but not between centres	Expected, uni policy for promotion	No	teams in centres	expected	having trouble with large ARC, existing on small
2	PSYCHOLOGY	positive tone	high	informal groups, focus around labs	solo and collab.	Good-Try to support anyone who is productive	very good, esp NHMRC
1	PSYCHOLOGY	Staff in 3 buildings - some friction but OK	"V.Important"; quantum effect	Lacks tearoom; dept "not as social as some"	Collab. encouraged but solo goes on. Res. grps. fostered.	Teaching relief to help res.; Prof. appted. for research development	Recently industry grants.

Figure 10.1   Case-based table to explore associations between professional relationships, departmental ethos and support, and research funding outcomes, using Excel

Cross-case analysis using coded data

If your data are coded, then cross-case analyses can be readily arranged:

▶ Either enter relevant codes derived from case analysis into a case by variable table using a spreadsheet and sort (Box 10.2).

▶ Or generate a case-by-code matrix directly from the coded data in QDA software.

Then:

▶ Look for relationships in the patterns of distribution across columns, employing much the same tactics as for the example above.

✅ It is important to retain access to the original data throughout this process; this is where access via a double-click in QDA software has a distinct advantage over codes in a spreadsheet or on paper.

Box 10.2

Employing coded case summaries in relational analysis

In a longitudinal study of the configuration of family members' responses to a child's chronic illness, Knafl and Ayres (1996) prepared case summaries for each family. Each case summary reduced 100–150 pages of transcript to approximately 20 pages of ordered information covering topics related to the conceptual framework for the study and to emergent categories. Coded case summaries were then used in a matrix to compare and sort patterns of response across members within families (Table 10.1). They were able to identify five family management styles – thriving, accommodating, enduring, struggling, and floundering – and, from the family summaries and transcripts, 'to describe the content of each style in a way that communicated the complexity of the families' experiences' (Ayres, Kavanaugh, & Knafl, 2003: 10).

Table 10.1   Examples of thematically coded data sorted by family management style (FMS)

ID number	Child identity mother	Child identity father	Identity self	View of illness mother	View of illness father	View of illness self	Mutuality mother	Mutuality father	FMS
8	Normal	Normal	Same	Life goes on	Life goes on	No big deal	Yes	Yes	Thriving
14	Normal	Normal	Same	Serious	Life goes on	Intrusive	Yes	Yes	Thriving
58	Tragic	Normal	More	Hateful	Life goes on	Intrusive	No	No	Struggling
49	Normal	Normal	More	Life goes on	Uninformed	Intrusive	No	No	Struggling

Source: Knafl & Ayres, 1996: 360, Table 4 (partial)

Cross-case synthesis: creating a common narrative

Synthesising case studies to build a common narrative allows the researcher to see essential relationships between circumstances, events, and responses that go beyond single instances to become evident for multiple cases.

▶ Gain an intimate knowledge of each of several individual cases as an essential first step, with each case being understood on its own terms.

▶ Create a common history that builds on the narratives of individual cases, to better see a core or explanatory process (Box 10.3).

▶ Where there is not a single narrative, you might create types or families that show particular patterns or configurations of relationships.

Perhaps there are comparative relationships that change over time?

▶ Explore the relationships embedded in a sequence of events as they respond to changing conditions. You can do this visually with annotated timelines and then amalgamate them into a 'composite sequence analysis, a process-oriented approach showing how different cases take diverse pathways through a generally-framed flow of events and states' (Miles & Huberman, 1994: 177, 204–5).

⌐ **Box 10.3** ⌐

Creating a common narrative from individual cases

For her dissertation research, Connie Gersick (1988) studied the content and process of group development for eight naturally occurring teams that were undertaking projects for someone external to the group. She recorded the entire proceedings of each group (a total of 72 meetings), along with her observations of the group process, to trace what an organisational work group does over its entire lifespan to create a final product by its last meeting. Working from detailed transcripts through three stages of condensation to lists of events which allowed an overall view of the team's progress, she produced detailed case studies for each group.

Her first surprise occurred when she realised that the first four groups studied did not progress through an anticipated series of stages (as the literature would have predicted), but rather moved through 'alternating inertia and revolution' toward their goal, all with a critical 'midpoint transition'. At this predictable point, the group reviewed its progress, became conscious of time, and made fresh strategic decisions about the direction to take for the rest of its life cycle, a direction it then maintained until the end. Gersick had promised the first teams a record of how their product had developed; this forced her to note progress in the *content* of their project, not just to record the group process (as was common practice), and in so doing, she noted a critical point where they 'turned the corner' or 'began a new era' in their work. After some prompting through reading

(Continued)

(Continued)

completely unrelated literature on the concept of midlife transition in adult education, she recognised this midpoint transition as something that occurred in similar fashion in all four groups. This idea was then confirmed through studying the progress of four more diverse project groups, where the same phenomenon was recorded.

She then needed to place her findings in a theoretical context. She found that context serendipitously through some recreational reading in natural history, an idea that was then developed through a re-examination of her data and careful comparison with traditional paradigms of group process. She concluded that 'groups develop through the sudden formation, maintenance, and sudden revision of a framework for performance; the developmental process is a punctuated equilibrium' (1988: 32).[2]

Visual strategies for cross-case analyses

Visual displays involving cross-case analyses are, as always, a particularly effective aid to both analysis and presentation of data. Approaches to producing and using visual displays to explore and investigate relationships in data are best demonstrated by recourse to some examples.

Mapping the location of cases

John Snow's pioneering use of epidemiological mapping is a classic in public health literature. Soho, London, in 1854, was the site of a major outbreak of cholera that caused many deaths. At that time, water was delivered to London households via neighbourhood wells which drew from the River Thames. Dr John Snow, already exploring a possible link between water supply sources and cholera, plotted the location of the water pumps and of each recorded death on a street map (Figure 10.2). He interviewed each family where a death had occurred, to eliminate other possible causes of death, and he talked to people across the areas affected about their understanding of the outbreak and their knowledge of those who had died. From the combination of frequencies on his map and his interviews, he was able to establish that the outbreak was focused around the Broad Street Pump and to argue that the pump handle should be removed (Frerichs, www.ph.ucla.edu/epi/snow.html). Frerichs demonstrates that mapping techniques such as these, combined with interviews, have had continued relevance in disease control, for example, in isolating the cause of an outbreak of cholera in Haiti in 2010.

---

[2]Extracts from Gersick's article, along with commentary by her, her thesis supervisor, and the editor of *The Academy of Management Journal*, were recorded in Frost and Stablein (1992).

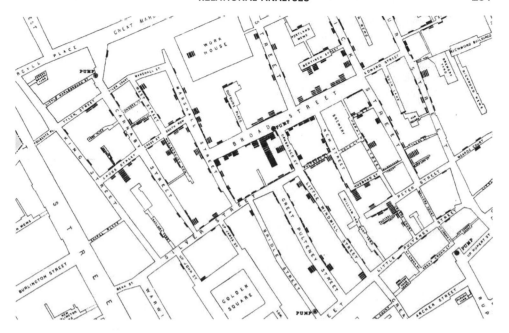

Figure 10.2   Portion of John Snow's map

Source: Frerichs, www.ph.ucla.edu/epi/snow/snowmap1_1854_lge.htm

Using a scatterplot

Miles and Huberman (1994: 198–9) plotted cases against axes representing two orthogonal (i.e., unrelated) dimensions of interest as a way of visually comparing the relative position of their cases on those two dimensions (Figure 10.3). They were able to incorporate an additional time element into their display by showing also how particular cases had 'moved' over time with regard to either of the two dimensions. They were testing whether pressure from administrators to adopt an innovation was being 'softened' by their allowing teachers a high degree of latitude about the final shape of the innovation as it was implemented. Their conclusion was that, in fact, the opposite seemed to be the case, although where there was high pressure to adopt, latitude increased somewhat once the innovation was being implemented.

Exploring overlapping sets of cases

This approach is made possible by the use of NVivo software. Two sets of cases, each defined by the cases having been coded at different but potentially related concepts of interest, are placed into a model at the same time. The cases for each concept are arrayed in such a way that it is easily possible to see how many, and which ones, are coded only at concept A, how many at both A and B, and how

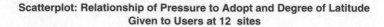

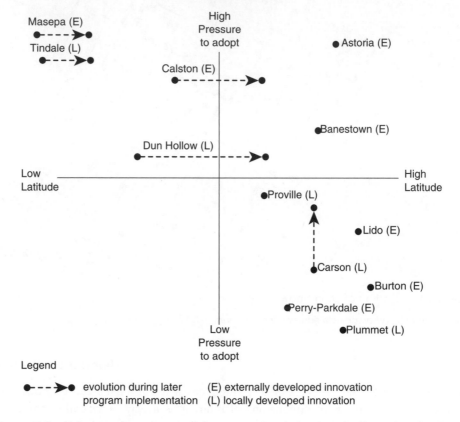

Figure 10.3   Using a scatterplot to explore cases in relation to two dimensionalised axes
Source: Miles and Huberman, 1994: 199, Figure 7.7

many at concept B only. The display is interactive, in so far as there are attributes associated with the cases, and this allows for cases in the display to be visually linked to attribute information and/or for cases to be 'turned off' in the display. Thus it is also possible to quickly assess whether cases that are A only, A + B, or B only have particular demographic (or other quantitative) characteristics.

Figure 10.4 shows use of this technique to examine whether researchers who talk about being stimulated intellectually by their research have also talked about having gained satisfaction from their engagement in research. The aim is to see if intellectual stimulation might be one factor that contributes to satisfaction and hence motivation. Immediately one can observe from the display that: career stage made minimal difference to the patterns of association between these concepts across cases; early career researchers were less likely to be coded at either concept than later career researchers; and scientists (unlike social scientists) did not express satisfaction in the absence of intellectual stimulation.

Following steps in the analysis process would then be:

▶ Investigate the four cases who spoke of intellectual stimulation but not satisfaction (their text is directly accessible from the model).

▶ Check out the ways those who were coded for both actually talked about each, to ascertain the validity and nature of the link between them (use a *near* coding query, or a case by variable matrix for the 11 cases and two variables).

▶ Investigate what had provided satisfaction to those not talking about intellectual stimulation (review satisfaction in *cases* not coded at stimulation).

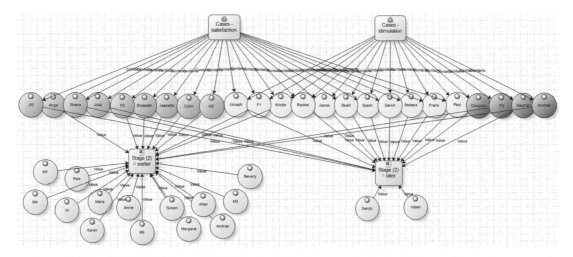

(a) All cases with coding at satisfaction and/or intellectual stimulation

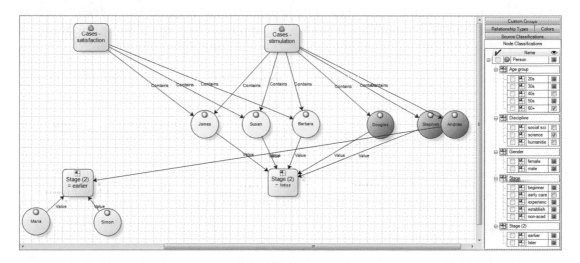

(b) Scientists with coding at satisfaction and/or stimulation

Figure 10.4   Using interactive modelling to investigate the association of codes across cases

Social network analysis (SNA)

Sociograms – drawing links to show connections between people – were a classic way for anthropologists, sociologists, and social psychologists to explore community, work, and friendship networks. Now, in combination with graph theory and developments in spatial statistics, social network analysis has developed into a quintessential way of combining qualitative with numerical and statistical data and analyses. With its emphasis on relationships and relatedness, SNA is a useful counter to the individual focus of much social research.

The focus of social network analysis is on ties between people (or other social objects), these ties being ascertained through interviews, observation, or analysis of relevant lists, archival documents, secondary sources such as diaries and letters, and, more recently, connections through social networking sites. You might study all of the ties within a defined population (a complete network); ties for a specific person (an egonet); ties between 'blocks' of complete networks (block modelling); or, ties between, say, actors and events (two-mode networks). Often more than one kind of relational data is obtained for the same network; for example, in a study of academic collegial research groups I asked with whom members (a) collaborated, (b) discussed their research, (c) went for coffee, and (d) from whom they sought advice about their research. Contextualising qualitative data and attribute data for the actors or elements in the network are usually recorded also (Box 10.4).

The presence or absence of ties between each possible pair of elements (directly reported, or ascertained via participation in a common event, group, setting, etc.) are recorded in an adjacency or incidence matrix (directly in the software, or in Excel).[3] The matrix is transformed by specialised software such as UCINET[4] into a network diagram accompanied by a range of statistical measures describing network characteristics. These include:

- A visual display of network linkages, created from the adjacency or incidence data (e.g., Figure 10.5):

  - ties can be shown as directional or non-directional, weighted for strength or frequency, and/or signed (+ or –);

---

[3]An adjacency matrix is one where, say, the same list of people heads both rows and columns, with connections between people recorded in cells; an incidence matrix would place, say, events in columns with people in rows, and participation recorded in cells as 1s or 0s.

[4]Software and tutorials for UCINET are available from www.analytictech.com/.

o each node in the network can be sized to reflect the number of links it has, or an attribute (such as income), or it can be given a shape and/or colour to indicate one or two attributes (such as gender);

o the position of any node in the network is visible from its pattern of connections, e.g., indirected and outdirected centrality, isolation, clique membership, whether it acts as a bridge between blocks.

- Mathematical and statistical analyses of the nodes in the network and their connections include, for example:

  o distance – the number of connections needed to travel between any two nodes;

  o density – percentage of possible ties that are actualised;

  o centrality: degree centrality – number of connections; closeness centrality – shortest distances to other nodes; betweenness centrality – who most often lies in the path connecting other nodes.

Qualitative data relating to network connections and the way the network operates add explanatory detail to the visual connections and measures provided by the network analysis software. Indeed, network relations are 'embedded in particular social, cultural, temporal, and spatial contexts', and these are ignored at the peril of missing vital clues regarding the significance of the relationships (Clark, 2007: 20).

┐ **Box 10.4** ┌

Using SNA to analyse the emergence of the punk scene in London

Nick Crossley (2008; 2011) drew on archival and secondary sources to study the role of network dynamics in the emergence of punk culture in London in the mid 1970s. The high density, low diameter, and closed edges of the London network suggested a high degree of cohesion among those involved in the 'punk revolution' such that they were successfully able to launch a deviant subculture (Figure 10.5). In Manchester, by comparison, this level of cohesion took longer to develop, and hence the 'punk scene' was slower to emerge.

Qualitative analysis of the archival records pointed to a high level of cooperation, but also to the operation of power and influence within the London scene. Three actors in the punk network stood out as being central on every available measure. McClaren and Rhodes, as agents who held financial, knowledge, and contact resources, had exploited that centrality and were indeed 'key movers and shakers in the network', but Vicious had not, despite being well known and popular from having played in several bands. Crossley combined qualitative data

(Continued)

(Continued)

with block modelling to assist his exploration of the power dynamics and subgroup cohesion in the network.

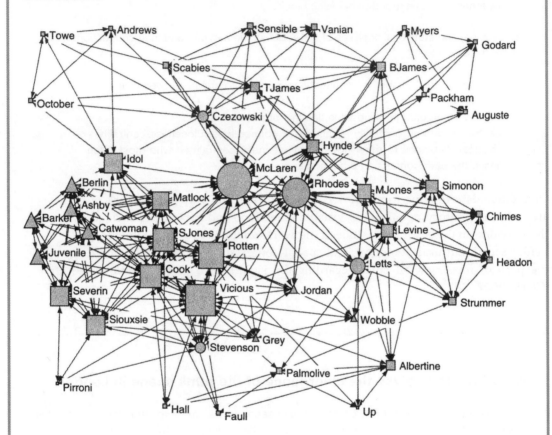

Figure 10.5   Network of punk pioneers in London visualised through social network analysis

Source: Crossley, 2011: 84, Figure 5.1

Identifying patterns of association between sets of related phenomena, using coded data

When you were coding, I suggested that you should use separate codes for each element of what was going on in the passage you were considering at the time – something which, I'm sure, made some of you rather anxious about the level to which you were slicing up your data. Perhaps you were noting relationships between categories along the way as you worked through your data. The problem is, unless you knew what you were looking for and were very consistent about noting instances (bits of evidence) as you went, you will not have a strong basis for any conclusions you draw from those notes. The strategies described in this section recombine categories in ways that will reveal the existence and strength of patterns of association across data.

Pattern analysis

Pattern analysis[5] will tell you how often different categories you have used code the same passage or are present in the same case. The patterning comes from your looking at cross-tabulating each of one set of codes (e.g., problems faced) with each of another set of codes (e.g., coping strategies), all at the same time. You might look at patterns of association also between things like issues and responses; actions and feelings; sources of inspiration and consequent actions; or communication flows and content within a business. These kinds of analyses are more theoretically based, in that you will be looking to identify meaningful relationships between two sets of codes, rather than simply describing codes or sorting coded material based on subgroup membership.

Matrices designed to show patterns have a similar appearance to those you've done before, but if you are not using software they can be more complex to construct as you have now moved beyond a simple sorting task based on group membership. Now you are looking for when two (or more) kinds of things are present for the same case and/or in the same data context, in order to determine whether they bear any relationship to each other. These relationships are most clearly evident when two codes intersect or overlap on a passage (or other segment) of data, but sometimes it is sufficient that they are near each other within a source, or just that both are present for the same case.

In general, pattern analyses should be theoretically driven: you will have a reason for wanting to see where and how the items you place in the rows and columns are associated based on your existing (and ever-deepening) knowledge of your data. You can use them also in a purely exploratory way, but the complexity of the data display, if you're not sure what you're looking for, mitigates against this. Once you have generated the matrix, for some analyses it is just the

---

[5]Those working within a grounded theory or dimensional analysis framework might think of conditional matrices or dimensional matrices as a form of pattern analysis.

patterning that you need to see; for others, you will want to drill down into the supporting text to understand better why it might be that these two elements were found together. Within that patterning, it is important to realise that not all cases within a cell will necessarily experience the combination of factors represented by that cell similarly. Having access to the supporting text is critical to interpretation therefore.

Pattern analysis without QDA software

Box 10.5 provides an example of a pattern analysis based on manual data entry, drawn from Matthew Miles' work with introducing a change process in schools. Generating this kind of display from paper-based data can be very time consuming. You will benefit from thorough preparation in terms of being familiar with the content of each of the categories or concepts being tabulated.

▶ Design the row and column headers (categories) for your table, and set these out on a large sheet of paper or in an Excel spreadsheet.

▶ Scan through your coded data, looking for passages of text or segments of visual material where both a row and a column category are present.

▶ Keep a tally of finds for cell entries, or better, put in case identifiers (as Miles did).

▶ To gain full benefit, make notes of your observations based on the associated text as you identify the connections you are recording in the cells. Record these in memos, and/ or briefly as a note in the cell of the table.

Box 10.5

Displaying data for pattern analysis

The data for this analysis were drawn from a study of a change process to reform a number of urban high schools, with the specific question for this analysis asking what strategies the schools used to cope with problems associated with the change process (Louis & Miles, 1990, reported in Miles & Huberman, 1994). The researchers categorised the types of problems encountered and rated each for difficulty, and they developed and clustered a list of the coping strategies used in the schools. These then defined the columns and rows of the matrix, with case identifiers for the schools entered in relevant cells, based on the knowledge of and data available to the research team (Table 10.2).

Careful ordering of the two main variables being displayed was important for interpreting this table. The researchers noted, for example, a pattern in which successful schools not only used a broader array of coping strategies, but tailored the depth of their coping strategies to the difficulty of the problem encountered.

Table 10.2 Variable-by-variable matrix: coping strategies and problems, by case

STYLE	Coping Strategies	Program process	Program content	Target pop.	Skill lacks	Attitudes	Crises	Competing demands
	Can't determine	B	A2					
DO NOTHING	None	C2			C1	C2		
TEMPORIZE	Delaying/avoiding		C1			C2		
DO IT THE USUAL WAY	Short-run coping	C1 C2	C1					
	Using existing meetings/	A2 B	C2					
	roles	C1 C2						
	Action-taking	C1						
	People-shuffling		C1?			A1	C1 C2	
EASE OFF	Program modification		B	A1 B C1	B?	B	B	
DO IT HARDER	Symbolic support					A1 C1 C2		A1
	Rewards/incentives					A1 A2 B C2		
	Negotiating							
	Pressuring/requiring					B C2		
BUILD PERSONAL CAPACITY	Person-changing	A2		A1 A2 B?	A1			
BUILD SYSTEM CAPACITY	New orchestration structure	A2 C1	C1		A2			
	New interaction arenas			B				
	Vision-building/sharing		A1			A1 A2 B		
	Monitoring		C1					
	Rolling planning							
	Ongoing assistance		A1			A2		
ADD NEW PEOPLE	Re-staffing					A2 B		
REDESIGN THE SYSTEM	Increasing control							A1
	Empowering	A1 A2 B?				A1 A2		
	Role redesign							
	Organization redesign							

Legend:
A1 Agassiz   [more successful]
A2 Alameda
B   Burroughs   [moderately successful]
C1 Caruso   [less successful]
C2 Chester
?   items with less researcher certainty

Source: Miles and Huberman, 1994: 221, Table 8.8 (partial)

Pattern analysis using QDA software

Using QDA software offers the advantages of speed and flexibility in creating these more complex arrangements of data. Once the work of coding the data is completed, especially if the codes are arranged in a hierarchical structure, the computer is able to create a table for pattern analysis in a matter of seconds. In doing so, it provides source data for each 'hit' as well as numbers of sources or cases coded in each cell (Box 10.6). Because it is so quick to generate and/or modify a table using software, pattern analyses can be used more freely for exploratory work as well as to confirm (or dismiss) suspected patterns. As with comparative analyses, exploring a pattern can raise as many questions as it answers, and as always, the interpretation is up to you; the computer simply facilitates this by locating all relevant co-occurring data.

Box 10.6

Using QDA software for pattern analysis

Most current types of QDA software will generate matrix displays based on coding, but they vary as to how flexibly they can do this, and they vary in the ways the results are displayed and in what additional information they provide for each cell.

MAXQDA will construct a *code relations browser* showing the number of sources with *intersections* between pairs of selected codes (Figure 10.6). It offers options to modify the basis of the display to show pairing of codes that are *near* each other (within a specified number of paragraphs) rather than intersecting; to activate a subset only of sources to be included in the analysis; to display numbers of intersections rather than a scaled symbol; to retrieve the coded passages represented by each cell by double-clicking on the relevant symbol, and to auto code retrieved passages at a new code for further analysis. Clicking on any particular retrieved passage shows it in its original context.

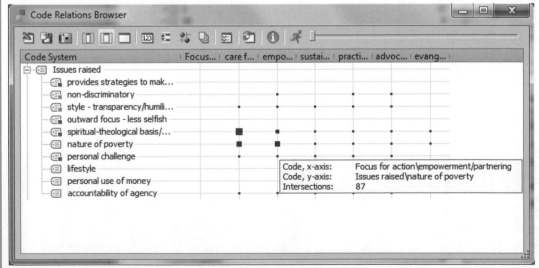

Figure 10.6　Code relations browser display in MAXQDA

NVivo's *matrix coding query* (cf. Figures 9.3 and 10.7) similarly can be used with selected codes in rows and columns, using intersections between pairs of row and column codes as the basis for selecting data. NVivo has a range of *near* and other options to choose from as the basis for defining cell content; a variety of cell display and visualisation options; the option to retrieve coded segments for any cell and to view those in context; the option to save the query specifications for reuse; and the option to save query results for reviewing or for reuse in a further query.

Interpretation of a matrix display involves consideration of the frequency and patterning of linkages from the numerical or visual display, and review of the text associated with each cell. Both NVivo and MAXQDA allow export and/or copying of the numeric results as a table that can be used in Excel or Word to record summaries of cell contents, where that would facilitate interpretation or presentation of the pattern and content of the display.

Matrix data of this nature from either program can be exported into statistical software to further explore the pattern of association, for example, through correspondence analysis.[6] While multivariate exploratory techniques can be used,[7] it is not appropriate to use chi-square and similar statistics to test patterns of association using this kind of data, as these assume independence of the variables, that is, that no-one has been coded for more than one row category, or for more than one column category.

Using a proximity matrix to cluster or dimensionalise codes

A proximity matrix (Bernard & Ryan, 2010) is a particular kind of pattern analysis that parallels a correlation matrix, but for qualitative coding. The same codes are placed in both rows and columns, usually with frequency of co-occurrence (a measure of similarity) in the cells. The matrix provides the basis for a range of exploratory multivariate statistical analyses, the results from which are most often presented and read visually (Bazeley, 2010a). Data for the cells can be obtained by:

▶ Asking a number of people to sort codes into groups and counting the frequency with which codes are put together.

▶ Using a triad test in which people are asked to identify which of three items is least like the other two – again counting the frequency with which items are paired.

▶ Finding all the times codes identifying rows and columns co-occur within the same context across a set of data – most easily accomplished using QDA software (Figure 10.7).

---

[6] QDAS identifies intersections present for particular segments of text, whereas a statistical program can identify only that both codes are present for the same case. Data transferred from QDAS to a statistical database therefore provides the basis for a more credible assessment of the pattern of association between the categories than could be obtained through, say, analysis of survey data.

[7] One advantage of these exploratory techniques is that they do not make assumptions about normality of distribution for each of the included variables, so they can be used with data generated through qualitative coding from non-random samples.

	commitment...	organised, ...	strategic	methodologi...	technical skill	substantive ...	analytic, thi...	creative, inn...
commitment, persist...	133	20	8	7	4	15	27	22
organised, disciplined	20	74	8	7	4	7	16	11
strategic	8	8	63	5	4	7	12	10
methodologically so...	7	7	5	96	12	19	37	27
technical skill	4	4	4	12	44	6	9	8
substantive knowled...	15	7	7	19	6	86	33	15
analytic, thinker	27	16	12	37	9	33	151	43
creative, innovative	22	11	10	27	8	15	43	138

Figure 10.7   Similarity matrix, based on the co-occurrence of codes in answering the same question

Note: the cell entries on the diagonal show the total number of participants using each concept to describe high-performing researchers; for example, 63 participants in total provided a description that was coded with *strategic*. Other cells show the number of participants who used that row–column combination when describing researchers who performed in particular ways; for example, *strategic* was used in the same context as *commitment* by eight participants.

Even though you are using statistical techniques to ascertain patterns, if you are working in QDA software, the qualitative data on which these patterns are based remain accessible along with the visualisations, to facilitate complementary interpretation of text and visual data. The primary output from the visualisation of a similarity matrix is either a cluster diagram (known as a dendrogram) showing when and how items cluster into groups (e.g., Figures 10.8 and 10.9), or a multidimensional (MDS) plot showing strength of connections between codes (e.g., Figure 10.10). Rather than seeing the results of these visual analyses as something that provides the definitive answer to your research questions, view them as providing clues about how things might be associated or not – setting off another train of exploration. For example, these tools might help to rationalise an extensive code list, or to build a dimensionalised model showing how one aspect of experience is related to another (Box 10.7). If these strategies all seem a bit mathematical and non-qualitative for you, be encouraged by the thoughts of Russell Bernard and Gery Ryan, who use them extensively in their anthropological work:

> Analysis is the essential qualitative act. Many methods for quantitative analysis – things like regression analysis, cluster analysis, factor analysis, and so on – are really methods for data processing. They are tools for finding patterns in data. Interpreting those patterns – deciding what they mean and linking your findings to those of other research – that's real analysis. (2010: 109)

Several qualitative programs now provide data visualisation tools based on multivariate exploratory analyses (e.g., Figures 10.9 and 10.10). Despite different programs and different approaches, each of the visualisations from the data in

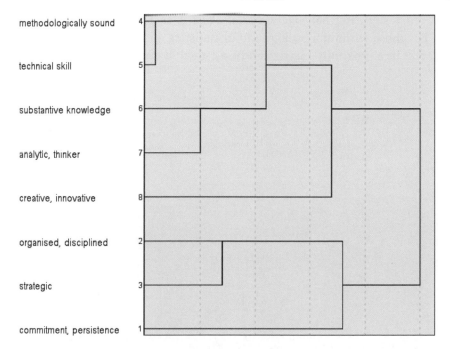

Figure 10.8   Cluster analysis (average linkage, based on frequency counts), using SPSS

Note: joining closer to the left margin indicates more closely associated characteristics.

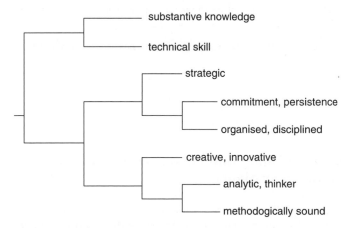

Figure 10.9   Cluster analysis based on the frequency with which words are shared in the coded text, using NVivo

Note: double-clicking on any code takes you to the text for that code.

Figure 10.7 suggests that *application of skills* is distinct from *types of research skills*. For those without a background in statistics, just reviewing text from cells of interest in a proximity matrix can be a valuable exercise.

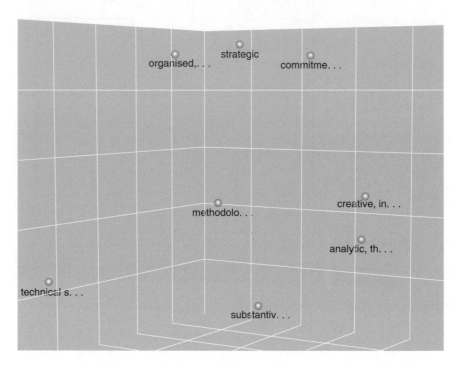

Figure 10.10　Multidimensional plot based on shared words in the coded text, using NVivo

Note: MDS plots can be rotated to more clearly discern dimensions and clusters.

▌ Box 10.7 ▐

Using multidimensional scaling and cluster analysis to develop a cultural model of domestic violence

Do diverse human service providers (welfare workers, domestic violence workers, nurses, and the general public) share an understanding of issues related to domestic violence, sufficient to facilitate communication between them? Cyleste Collins and William Dressler

(2008) drew on theory and methods from cultural anthropology to examine the cultural models of different service providers to see if they shared a single model for the domain of domestic violence. Beginning with cultural domain analysis (Bernard & Ryan, 2010) they had various service providers identify and sort the terms they use to describe the causes of domestic violence, recording their comments as they did so. Multidimensional scaling (MDS) was applied to the similarity matrices resulting from the sorts of the 32 identified terms for each group of service providers. These were then amalgamated into a general model showing controllability (dimension 1) and location within victim–perpetrator (dimension 2) as two perceived causal dimensions for domestic violence (Figure 10.11). Cluster analysis was used to identify the boundaries between groups of items, and analysis of participant commentaries was used to label the common dimensions of meaning for participants. The extent to which individuals were consonant with the shared model was assessed also using quantitative measures, with child welfare workers exhibiting highest levels of agreement within their own group and with the model, and domestic violence workers being most distinctive and most dissonant.

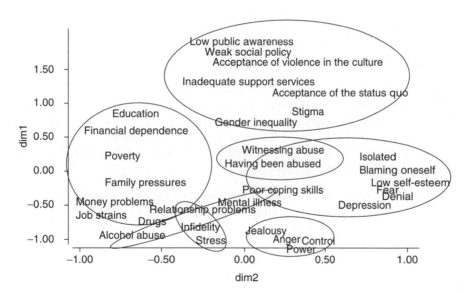

Figure 10.11   MDS and cluster analysis of causes of domestic violence

Source: Collins and Dressler, 2008: 372, Figure 1

Original authors' note: *N* =110, stress in two dimensions = 0.184. Items closer together in space and within the confines of the identified clusters were more likely to have been placed together during pile sorting.

Relating data to a theoretical model

If you have a model developed from theory or literature as a component of your research, then an important element of your analysis will be to relate your data to that model, asking either whether your data support it, or how you might develop the model so that it better fits with what you have found. Setting out the propositions of the model and recording your findings alongside is a way of doing this (Box 10.8).

Box 10.8

Testing and developing a literature-based model

Gerlese Åkerlind (2008) reviewed 10 studies that considered academic researchers' perspectives on the nature of research, and from these identified four dimensions describing the nature of research. These were (2008: 22):

- research intentions – who is affected by the research;
- research outcomes – the anticipated impact of the research;
- research questions – the nature of the object of study;
- research process – how research is undertaken.

In her own phenomenographic study in which she asked 28 active researchers to describe their research experience and provide examples of their own research activity, Åkerlind had similarly identified three of these dimensions (initially omitting *questions*, but then seeing evidence of it once she was alerted to it by the literature), and also an affective dimension not included in other studies. Additionally, she identified four different ways of understanding what it meant to be a university researcher (2008: 24):

- fulfilling academic requirements, with research experienced as an academic duty;
- establishing oneself in the field, with research experienced as a personal achievement;
- developing oneself personally, with research experienced as a route to personal understanding; and
- enabling broader change, with research experienced as an impetus for change to benefit a larger community.

With a goal of examining how the dimensions and experiences identified through these different sources might relate to each other to form an integrated model, she constructed the matrix shown in Table 10.3, and concluded from this that 'these different ways of experiencing are seen as related to each other through an expanding hierarchy of inclusive awareness' (2008: 24).

Table 10.3 Dimensions of research process and research experience: being a university researcher

Dimensions [literature based]	Categories [of experience]			
	1 Fulfilling requirements	2 Establishing oneself	3 Developing personally	4 Enabling change
Researcher intentions	Fulfil academic role	Become well known	Solve a puzzle	Make a contribution
Research process	Identify and solve a problem	Discover something new	Investigate an interesting question	Address community issues
Anticipated outcomes	Concrete products	Academic standing	Personal understanding	Benefits to community
Object of study	Independent research questions, bounded by a field of study	Integrated research questions, related to a field of study	Integrated research questions, related to field and personal issues	Integrated research questions, related to field/social issues
Underlying feelings	Anxiety to satisfaction	Frustration to joy	Interest and enthusiasm	Passionate engagement

Source: Åkerlind, 2008: 25, Table 4

Investigating relationships between specific categories and concepts

Ian Dey referred to the process of investigating specific relationships, carried out after having coded data, as 'the analytic equivalent of putting mortar between the building blocks' (1993: 47). The process of asking questions and setting up queries to check possibilities is not limited to questions arising from comparative and pattern searches; you will probably have a bundle of recorded hunches to test and questions to follow up already, perhaps with notes indicating where to find supporting data.

What follows are a number of specific strategies for identifying, testing, or better understanding specific associations in your data. Many of the strategies are visual and these particularly rely for their construction on your earlier work with data. Visual strategies won't confirm or negate linkages between concepts in your data in themselves, but they are a powerful way of helping you to identify and think about those relationships, as a foundation for going back to your evidentiary database for confirmation, rejection, or specification of necessary conditions.

To a large extent, if you are not using a computer, your going back to the database for evidence of specific associations will depend for its thoroughness on the adequacy of your data management system and your notes. For those using QDA software, checking associations between codes in your database relies on your moving on from a simple code-and-retrieve approach to discovering just what kinds of questions the software can help you answer. It also depends on the adequacy of your coding strategies and coding system. Those who master both will be richly rewarded.

'Jumping off' from comparative and pattern analyses

In reviewing comparative analyses and pattern analyses, I emphasised that while these analyses can give you results of direct relevance for your final project report, they could also generate as many questions as they answered. They prompt you to check other associations within your available data (Box 10.9). For example, if females report differently from males with respect to experience X:

▶ Review the content of what each of these groups says about experience X.
▶ Check what other demographic variables are associated with gender and make sure the association has more to do with gender than the other variables.
▶ Ask what it is about being female, as compared to being male, that might explain this difference in experience. Develop 'hypotheses' about possible associated factors, guided by the things said by each group and/or other experience and knowledge you have of your data: 'I wonder if it is because ....'
▶ Review your data for codes or other information that will help you to check out these ideas about potential associations with other factors.
▶ If you have appropriate software, use the query and search functions to test these associations (and when they are absent).

▶ The usefulness (or validity) of these ideas and associations can be further tested in theoretically sampled data collection, by developing if–then proposals, or by checking out rival explanations. This will lead to their being confirmed, needing to be qualified (e.g., for different conditions), or discounted.

Box 10.9

Exploring and testing associated ideas following comparative analyses

Scott Marsh, from William Clarke College in New South Wales and a doctoral student at Macquarie University, is using mixed methods to research the concept, practice, and impact of 'leadership for learning' in four schools – the kind of leadership that instigates a whole-school coordinated approach to learning for all members of the school community. From his reading, he became particularly interested in the notion of authoritative leadership (AL) as one of several possible styles of leadership, a style which combines firm direction with attention to relationships.

Throughout the process of coding interviews, he noticed that all four principals were regarded by their staff as being demanding and having high expectations, particularly for strong academic results, but the notion of relationships (the second component of AL) was discussed regularly and positively by both staff and principals in only two schools. In the other two schools the theme of relationships (between staff and principal) was discussed negatively by staff, and was mentioned barely at all by the principals.

From the coded text, Scott identified two relevant dimensions of relationship, communication, and trust. Using coding queries in NVivo to check associations, he found that when staff talked about vertical trust, they also talked about communication with their principal as being open and honest; when vertical trust was absent, communication was perceived as directive, one-way, and agenda based. The differences he had found between schools were confirmed in his statistical data, with the two schools where principals discussed relationships in terms of knowing their staff, communicating with them, and valuing them being significantly different on measures of AL than those where the principals and staff were more negative about or neglectful of relationships.

Conceptual mapping and modelling

Conceptual mapping was valuable early in a project to assist in initial conceptualisation and planning, and eventually the models you develop might be used in the presentation of your data, or incorporated into a final model depicting conclusions from an analysis. In the interim, your models will go through multiple iterations and become more refined as you learn from new data, and from exploring the relationships between those concepts you are identifying in your data (Box 10.10).

┐ **Box 10.10** ┌

Mapping interrelated concepts

Lynn Kemp (Director of the Centre for Health Equity Training, Research, and Evaluation at the University of New South Wales) investigated the community service needs of people with a spinal injury in NSW for her doctoral research (Kemp, 1999). She used multiple methods to dismiss as inappropriate six commonly held concepts of how need should be understood and measured. In an attempt to find a more satisfactory model of need, using a grounded approach to her qualitative data, Lynn identified five interrelated discourses for people with spinal injuries, the most central of which focused on dimensions of dependency. With the assistance of code retrieval and coding queries (in the predecessor to NVivo), she was able to clarify the nature of these concerns and their interrelationships and to represent those in a series of models (including Figure 10.12). This allowed her to see that the only way the need for community services by people with spinal injuries could be understood was in the extent to which services contributed to their plan for life, that plan being to be ordinary. Being ordinary meant engaging in interdependent relationships, participating meaningfully in society, and not being special or different.

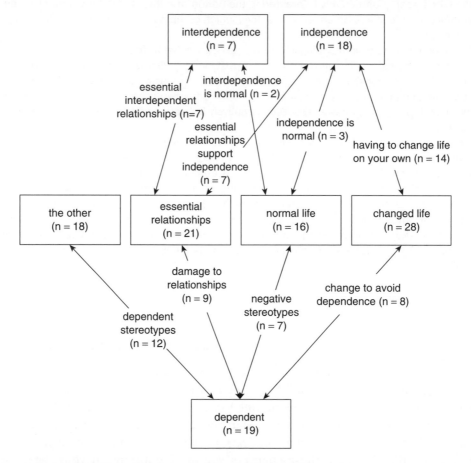

Figure 10.12   Mapping the relationship between dimensions of dependency and other central concerns for people with a spinal injury

Source: Kemp, 1999: 142, Figure 23

Situational analysis: an alternative approach to developing grounded theory

Situational maps, as developed by Adele Clarke (2005; 2009), 'map' elements of a situation as a tool for planning, developing, and clarifying the direction of an analysis, following on from open coding in the grounded theory tradition. The situation being mapped is placed within a wider social arena, where (collective) social worlds constructed through and defined by (often contested) shared discourses act to establish boundaries and gain social legitimation within the situation.

Clarke employs three main kinds of maps during the analysis process:

- The first 'situational map' begins with a messy 'dumping' of descriptive labels for all the human and non-human elements that matter in the situation being studied. These labels are organised into categories, and at the same time, relations between each possible pair of items are explored and described from the data. Ideas generated through this are recorded in memos. Some of these relationships will be worth pursuing, leading to 'exciting and creative moments of intellectual work' (2009: 219); others will not.[8] Not all elements are necessarily present in any given analysis, but Clarke notes that having these elements listed leads to more systematic analysis of data. Figure 10.13 combines an abstract template for a situational map with a research example from Clarke's study of the situation surrounding the introduction of RU486 (the 'abortion pill') in the United States.
- The second type of map developed is a 'social worlds/arenas map' which recognises the social worlds engaged in collective actions of relevance to the situation, and the discourses that mark those. These come together to give a picture of intersecting and often conflicting discourses, commitments, and ideologies in the arena surrounding the situation. Size is used to indicate relative power. An actor might participate in several (therefore overlapping) social worlds within one or more arenas. Mapping social worlds prompts questions like: what are the characteristics and components of each social world, and why and how do these interact? What variations exist within and between worlds? Each social world is described in a memo, leading to a picture of how action is structured in the situation. Figure 10.14 shows an abstract version of a social worlds/arenas map. Completed maps show the kinds of collective agents that may be present, negotiations between them, relative power and placement, and the intersecting and sometimes porous nature of their boundaries.
- Dimensions of key discursive issues become axes for a 'positional map'. Points on the map represent positions on discourses, rather than particular individuals or social collectives.

Questions arising can lead to more theoretical sampling, and the maps go through multiple iterations before saturation occurs. Saturation is reached when the researcher has an adequate understanding of the situation, and no further changes need to be made. Final project maps each present part or all of the analysis to an audience.

---

[8]Rather like social network analysis, the pattern of relationships supported by data potentially demonstrates which elements in the map are dominant in this situation.

INDIVIDUAL HUMAN ELEMENTS/ACTORS
e.g., key individuals and significant
(unorganized) people in the situation
   Etienne-Emile Baulieu [developer of and
   advocate for RU486]

COLLECTIVE HUMAN ELEMENTS/ACTORS
e.g., particular groups; specific organizations
   U.S. FDA
   U.S. Congress
   Pro-choice groups
   Anti-choice/anti-abortion groups
   Birth control advocacy groups
   Women's health movement groups
   Abortion services providers
   National Abortion Federation
   Professional medical groups

DISCURSIVE CONSTRUCTIONS OF
INDIVIDUAL AND/OR COLLECTIVE HUMAN
ACTORS
  As found in the situation
  Social world constructions of others
  Social world constructions of Baulieu
  Social world construction of FDA

POLITICAL/ECONOMIC ELEMENTS
e.g., the state; particular industry/ies; local/
regional/global orders; political parties; NGOs;
politicized issues
  Access to abortion
  Costs of abortion
  Political party concerns re abortion

TEMPORAL ELEMENTS
e.g. historical, seasonal, crisis, and/or trajectory
aspects
  Lateness of approval compared to Europe
  Rise of religious right in U.S. politics since
  1970s

MAJOR ISSUES/DEBATES (USUALLY
CONTESTED)
As found in the situation
  Safety of RU486
  Safety of abortion
  Morality of abortion
  Morality of unwanted children

OTHER KINDS OF ELEMENTS
As found in the situation
 (none present in this example)

NONHUMAN ELEMENTS/ACTANTS
e.g., technologies; material infrastructures;
specialized information and/or knowledges;
material "things"
  RU486
  Surgical abortion technologies
  FDA regulations for approval
  FDA regulations for use

IMPLICATED/SILENT ACTORS/ACTANTS
As found in the situation
  Women as users
  Genetic/genomic scientists
  Stem cell researchers
  Anti-abortion terrorists
  [Unborn foetuses]

DISCURSIVE CONSTRUCTION OF
NONHUMAN ACTANTS
As found in the situation
  Social world constructions of RU486
  Social world construction of abortion
  Construction of approval regulations
  Construction of use regulations

SOCIOCULTURAL/SYMBOLIC ELEMENTS
e.g., religion; race; sexuality; gender; ethnicity;
nationality; logos; icons; other visual and/or
aural symbols
  Morality of abortion
  Morality of unwanted children
  Pill for abortion as "magic bullet"

SPATIAL ELEMENTS
e.g., spaces in the situation, geographical
aspects, local, regional, national, global spatial
issues
  Potential ease of wide geographic availability
  of RU486
  Lack of abortion services in 84% of U.S.
  counties

RELATED DISCOURSES (HISTORICAL,
NARRATIVE, AND/OR VISUAL)
e.g., normative expectations of actors, actants,
and/or other specified elements; moral/ethical
elements; mass media and other popular
cultural discourses; situation-specific
discourses
  Abortion discourses
  Birth control discourses
  Sex/gender/feminism discourses
  Sexuality discourses

Figure 10.13   Clarke's abstract situational map, incorporating an example

Source: adapted from Clarke, 2009: 213, 218, Figures 7.6 and 7.7

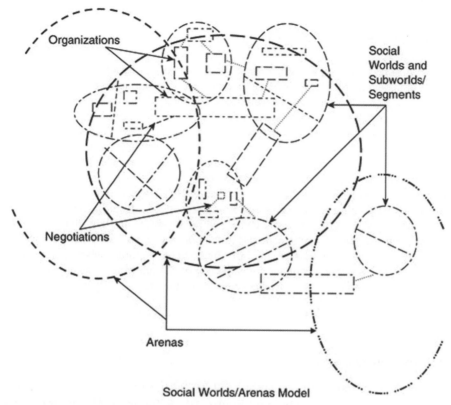

Figure 10.14   Abstract map of social worlds in arenas

Source: Clarke, 2005: 112, Figure 3.11

Work with divergent views and alternative understandings

Divergent views, negative cases, or outliers – however you choose to label them – provide a rich source for further analytic thinking; learn from them and grow your understanding so that your emerging theory can incorporate them. While they might be dismissed in statistical analyses, in qualitative work they cannot be ignored. More than that, at times they provide the hint that explains what is happening for the larger sample: 'In the interplay between theory and data as both are generated in the field, it is the empirical exception that often displays the analytic rule' (Van Maanen, 1979: 547).

Work at proposing alternative explanations of what is going on in your data, drawing on negative cases as one source of ideas, then check the elements of these explanations against other data. How widely are they supported? Can they be refined and developed? Record these verifying strategies and their results, even if they prove to be false leads, as this will help you build a case for the understanding of your data that you finally put forward (Box 10.11).

Box 10.11

Exploring negative cases

A doctoral student at a rural university in Australia was studying professional and administrative staff responses to amalgamations of administrative regions within government health services in low-density rural areas. Communication issues were assuming a central focus in her analysis (primarily, the lack of communication with employees throughout the process of amalgamation). Two of her 20 interviewees stood out, however, as having positive views about the amalgamations. So what was special about these two? One had taken a redundancy and established a new career; another had been given a senior position in the new system, with more power. Thus, those who were positive in their attitude had personally benefited from the amalgamations. This raised the question of whether those who were negative were so more because they were now worse off personally, rather than because the service had deteriorated (as they suggested). The student then checked for evidence of selfish versus altruistic thinking in her interview and questionnaire data. This challenged her generalisation about the centrality of the communication issue alone in explaining interviewees' responses, and eventually pointed to a much richer picture in which communication issues, specifically lack of engagement and transparency by the hierarchy, created a sense of uncertainty which fostered in employees a focus on their own interests.

Construct a typology

A typology is a classification system built by taking two (or more) dimensions to make an orthogonal display (e.g., Figure 10.15; Table 10.4). The logic of the pattern so made is then examined against the data to see if this makes for meaningful subgroups, classes, or ideal types, and for whether the pattern holds in different settings. Labels for cells often draw on indigenous terms – those used by the participants in their everyday conversations. Patton (2002) sees this as an abductive thinking process, while warning against manipulating the matrix in an attempt to fill out all cells: all new ideas generated must be tested and confirmed by the data. In that sense the typology is created as a working tool, as a means of seeing and testing relationships across dimensions, but a well-developed typology might be used also as a final presentation tool (cf. Box 12.6).

Table 10.4 is the result of my cross-classifying two important dimensions in researchers' lives, derived from interview, focus group, and participant observation data. Once I created it, I realised there must be at least one additional dimension needed (perhaps resources?), as low orientation to research in the institution could equally well result in the researcher's experiencing moderate or high levels of frustration – something that is not captured in this table. I am also unsure about some of the labels I've used. As a working model, nevertheless, it serves a purpose in helping me to think further about the relationships between personal and environmental factors in fostering research activity.

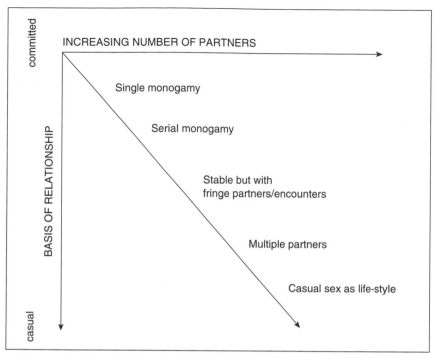

Figure 10.15   A typology of sexual lifestyles

Source: Ritchie & Spencer, 1994: 189, Figure 9.8

Table 10.4   A typology of academics' responses to institutional research orientation

Level of personal commitment to research	Research orientation of the institution	
	Low	**High**
Low	Non-researcher: neither need nor opportunity	Reluctant researcher: only does what is required
Moderate	Distracted researcher: always something more important to do	Small 'r' researcher: engages in data gathering, team projects, or pedagogical projects of local significance
High	Addicted researcher: will do it anyway, but is likely to suffer in their personal life as a consequence	Big 'R' researcher: harmony between personal and institutional goals creating possibility of major interpretive breakthroughs

Relate through sequence and context

Comparing composition of a timeline to composing music, Sheridan, Chamberlain and Dupuis (2011) describe their use of timelining as both a graphic elicitation and analysis strategy in their narrative study of weight loss over the lifetimes of four previously very obese women. For each, a plot of changes in weight over time was elaborated by photographs and notes of incidents and feelings recorded in diaries, and information from other documentary sources. These ensured both rich narrative data and more informed analysis in which turning points and epiphanies in the lives of their participants were highlighted. The exercise of composing the timelines proved to be a reflexive process for both participants and researchers, as the 'participants [could] effectively become researchers of their own lives' (2011: 566).

▶ Use tables and diagrams to map and hence clarify the interaction of events through history, development through a life course, or the pathway of a narrative. Add detail to the timeline showing things influencing those events, or relate events on one side of the line and responses to those events on the other side.

As part of her analysis of the process of 'reinventing' the secondary girls' school of which she was principal (cf. Box 2.10), Leoni Degenhardt (2006) prepared a time-delineated table matching the development of the new student growth model, in one column, with the process of creating change in the school, in a parallel column. Doing so in combination with creation of a diagram of the implementation process helped her to see and show the connections between events over time.

Using qualitative analysis software tools for exploring or testing relationships between coded concepts

Several strategies outlined earlier in this part of the book have relied on a three-step process:

▶ Reflective assessment of data based on careful reading and notetaking.

▶ Building models and diagrams based on ideas developed from that assessment.

▶ Then, using both notes and diagrams, identifying potential links between concepts or their subcategories or dimensions.

If you are relying primarily on your reading and notes, you will then need to work back through those, seeking evidence for or against any specific linkages you might have identified. If you have used software to code data, you can use the retrieval and query functions of the software to locate relevant data for assessing your hypothesised linkages, and additionally, for assessing how the nature of those linkages changes under different conditions.

Giving a full outline of how to use the query functions of specific programs is beyond the scope of this book. Instead, I will focus here on the generic kinds of queries you might use to assess associations between specific pairs of codes in most programs, and illustrate some of these with reference to NVivo and MAXQDA. Query functions in NVivo, complex retrievals in MAXQDA, and analysis tools in QDA software generally rely on logical (set-theory-based) operations carried out with coded data, so that you are able to ask the computer to retrieve for you all coded passages that meet the criteria specified in the query. Although you will be able to draw some conclusions quite quickly from the patterning of responses (e.g., when only those who had experienced a cyclone in the past spoke of fear in response to a storm), most analytical work will require that you scan the actual data found by the query, and interpret the meaning and significance of those passages. The computer helps by locating all relevant passages, but it cannot interpret the retrieved passages for you. The point is, however, that the computer can do complex sorting and sifting in a fraction of the time, and with greater accuracy, than you could ever hope to do any other way.

The logical functions employed by most coding-based programs are, first of all, the standard Boolean operators that you should already be familiar with through library searches (AND; OR; NOT); and second, proximity searches, including OVERLAPPING, NEAR, and PRECEDING or FOLLOWING. These work as follows (using the association between *storm* and *fear* as an example):

- AND (intersection) finds all passages coded at *both* storm and fear, allowing you to assess how they interact.
- OVERLAPPING finds complete passages coded at storm or fear *provided that* part of each passage is coded at both; this provides more context than an intersection.
- OR (union) finds all passages coded at *either* storm or fear, allowing you to see when one or other or both are present for any source.
- AND NOT can find all passages coded at storm that are *not also coded* at fear (or alternatively, at fear and not storm), to find when one is present without the other being there at the same time.[9]
- NEAR finds all passages coded at storm or fear *that co-occur within a specified context*, such as within one or a number of paragraphs, within a specified number of words (or minutes of video/audio, etc.), selected sources, or selected coded passages (options vary in different programs, e.g., Figure 10.16). Both have to be present within that context to be found.
- PRECEDING or FOLLOWED BY, for example, will find fear only if it comes *after* storm within a specified distance (with the same range of options as for NEAR).
- All queries can be optionally scoped to search through a subset of data. This will allow you to find, as well as where both are mentioned, instances of fear in, say, the set of sources or cases where storms are not mentioned at all (or vice versa) – useful for locating 'negative cases'.[10]

---

[9]If coding has been too fractured, this query could find passages that distort the intention of the question because the second code was on adjacent rather than intersecting text.

[10]At the time of writing, few QDA programs deal adequately and easily with (a) finding *cases not coded anywhere* with a particular code where cases comprise multiple sources or part only of a source, or (b) finding proximity relationships between codes within multi-source or part-source cases where those codes might be in different sources or different parts of sources. It can be done, but usually requires a 'workaround'.

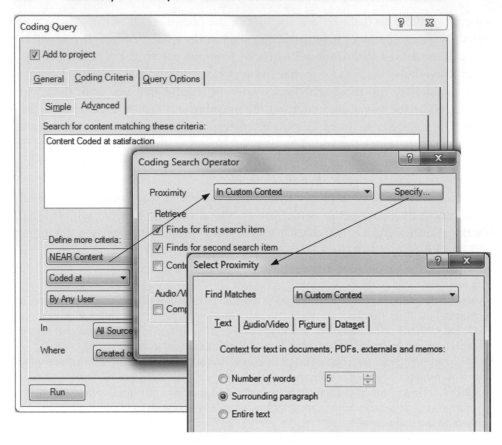

Figure 10.16   Setup dialogue for NEAR coding query using NVivo

- Results of queries can be exported, or saved in the software for later review or to include as items in further queries. NVivo will save the query specifications for rerunning as well (e.g., when more data have been coded, or with a different subset of data).

✅ Successful use of query functions in software will depend on the adequacy of your coding, and in particular, on your having remembered to use multiple codes to identify the multiple aspects or dimensions of what is going on within any passage.

Working through a query process using software: an example

A number of those for whom I have interview data have one or more passages coded with *identification*, capturing whether or not they saw themselves as being a researcher. The issue of personal or role identification was purposively followed up in focus groups. What did it mean to identify as a researcher, and is that something that came about at a particular time (*turning point*), was it a gradual awareness, or was it always there in some form (*part of being*)? I can show you the steps I took as an example of one way of tackling these questions, but with the warning that the results are very much limited by the brief and secondary nature of the data samples (especially the interview extracts).

Step 1. *Describing*. I reviewed all the text coded at *identification* and noted points of interest. From this I learned:

o The most striking thing was that most participants did *not* identify themselves as researchers, unless they were specifically asked about it. Identifying as a researcher was mostly to do with being directly engaged in research, may not be a permanent state, and was likely to be subordinate to other roles (like teaching, or just generally being an academic).

o Whether one 'owned up' to being a researcher or not depended on one's immediate social context. Several noted that the label 'shut off' conversations in a social setting, or had negative connotations for some groups.

o For some, research was a specific, separate activity, whereas for others, it infiltrated all they did and was part of who they were, and/or was integrated with their role and daily activities.

o Seeing oneself as a researcher could be an ongoing process, a phase, or a point in development. Once the 'bug' had 'bitten', it was rarely set aside completely.

Step 2. *Comparison*. The most obvious next step was to compare what was said about identification in relation to career stage, and across disciplines. This was done by creating a matrix which separated out all the text at *identification* according to values of those attributes. This showed me:

o The lone scientist who was in one of the focus groups referred to himself as a scientist rather than a researcher. This made me wonder if being a researcher was taken for granted by scientists, so I followed up by running a text search within the interview and media data for 'scientist'. This located just one more interviewee who described herself that way, and there were several in the very brief media stories, which were all with scientists.

o None of the experienced researchers (including those for whom the topic was raised in focus groups) identified themselves specifically as a researcher; they more commonly described themselves as academics who did research as part of that. Even some of those who would be considered by others in the system to be primarily researchers noted that they were more likely to engage in research-related roles while more junior staff did the 'real' day-to-day work of research.

o I checked what some of those not coded at identification had said (at this stage, just working from my knowledge of who of these might be interesting): for example, Stephen did not identify as a researcher because that required obsession and at present there were too many distractions.

Step 3. *Relating.* Now to look at the process of identifying a researcher – or not (using a range of coding queries to check):

o   Not everyone coded at either *turning point* or *research as part of being* was coded for identification (including Shane). Usually people who talked about a turning point did so in connection with a particular point of engagement in research, several at undergraduate level, i.e., their focus was on activity rather than identity.

o   Of those who gave an indication that research was part of 'being', three suggested being a researcher was their primary identity; all others referred to more differentiated roles or identities.

o   For two, part of the turning point experience was recognising that research was always there as part of who they were (Elizabeth and Andrew).

o   Nineteen people (out of 27) who talked about identification as a researcher but who were not coded (anywhere) for either *turning point* or *research as part of being*, usually linked it to (a period of) specific engagement with research, especially if they were employed as a researcher (e.g., in market research, or as a research assistant). In this sense what they said about *identification* was not particularly different from those who had talked about a *turning point*.

o   I rechecked the text at identification with coding stripes showing (in order of frequency of intersection). This alerted me to the relevance of working conditions in so far as they impact on engagement in research, and consequently identification with the research part of an academic role.

Conclusions. My (immediate) conclusions from this exercise:

o   Identifying oneself as a researcher was more often a function of employment (I must be a researcher because that's what I'm paid to do) or specific (periodic) engagement in research activity, than a primary attribute of identity.

o   Academic researchers rarely described themselves as such, even if research (rather than teaching) was a primary activity; they were inclined to see their role and identity as more differentiated than that. In part this points to a rather 'woolly' understanding (for both me and them) and brings into question the value of *identification as a researcher* as a concept.

o   This was not a fruitful line of enquiry in terms of understanding steps in the process of how one might come to be a researcher, or remain active as a researcher, especially within an academic context. Understanding the process of engagement in research is more relevant.

Data processing. Additional note:

o   During this process, there were several times when I found I needed to add coding to passages, or go back to some of the original sources to code broader passages. I find this is a quite common experience when running queries, where the examination of data in a detailed way in a specific context will point up issues in coding (often minor). I do not regard it as something to particularly worry about in the sense that at least you will find them under these circumstances. Adding (or removing) additional coding was a straightforward task, as was rerunning the queries based on revised coding, where necessary.

 Expect a lot of dead ends, twists, and turns on your path to great insights!

Writing about exploring and testing relationships in data

In the methods chapter

▶ As with comparative analyses, be explicit about how and why you are choosing particular strategies for analysis, and your rationale for choosing components within each strategy, the tools you used, and any principles you applied in choosing and using the results of your analyses.

Analytic writing 'as you go'

The value of what you have been doing as a data analyst as you worked through these last three chapters is predicated on your writing about what you are learning from your analysis *as you are doing it.* This material won't end up unchanged, but it will contribute to your final write-up. Writing as you go has multiple benefits, ranging from the pragmatic to the profound:

- You are less likely to be overwhelmed by a mass of printed or otherwise stored raw results from running analytic procedures.
- You are prompted to deal with, interpret, record, and reflect on the results of each analytic procedure as you complete it, while it is fresh in your mind.
- As part of that interpretation and reflection, you will be led to pursue further questions, and perhaps even further data, until you are satisfied that your understanding is both comprehensive and sound.
- You are less likely to suffer writer's block, because you will have already recorded a substantial amount of your results. Organising and adding to already written material is much easier than starting from scribbled notes on scraps of paper.[11]

As part of the final presentation of results

▶ Structure your material to tell the story of your research, building from basic elements progressively to complex interrelationships, always ensuring that the reader has necessary prior information to understand details of the relationship currently being discussed.

▶ Present material visually where that will assist the reader to comprehend what you have found. Avoid long or congested prose descriptions where a concise visual will do the job for you.

---

[11]As noted in an earlier chapter, you will benefit significantly from using styled headings and a document map (navigation pane) while you are writing about the analyses you are doing – in terms of locating where to 'drop in' new material, and later, for organising it into a sensible sequence.

▶ Tables or figures should be clear within themselves so that you don't need to repeat the details of your table or visual in the text, but at the same time, they need to be fully contextualised and interpreted within your text.

Exercises

Exercise 1: Using a summary table

▶ Create a summary table as a means to review the data in Figure 10.1. Ignoring, for the moment, that it is a small and unrepresentative sample, what conclusions might you draw from these data regarding the relationship between professional interaction of academics within a department, departmental ethos and support, and research funding outcomes?

Exercise 2: Mapping a network

▶ List up to 10 'friends' from your online social network in both the columns and the rows of a table (omitting yourself). Working across the cells, use 1 or 0 to indicate those who are connected within that group other than through you. Try creating a network map from the table by plotting the people on a piece of paper and drawing in the links. Who is at the centre of that group? Is anyone isolated? Are there subgroups (cliques)? Use symbols on the map to indicate gender or some other attribute of the people. Does that change your perception or tell you more about the network at all? (Those who are more adventurous might download a trial copy of UCINET from www.analytictech.com, along with a tutorial in how to use it.)

Exercise 3: Combine codes?

▶ When I coded the community data (cf. Box 8.8) I created separate codes for *working together* and *cooperation*. Sometimes just one of these codes was applied to a data sample, sometimes both. But then I asked myself, do these two codes really represent separate concepts or are they really much the same thing, i.e., should I keep both codes, or combine them? What steps would you take to assess the data (presumably a larger set of data than the four brief examples provided earlier) so you could answer that question? Which specific software query functions might you employ in the process?

Exercise 4: Your own project

▶ If you're like me when I read something, you would have been thinking on your way through this chapter about how each strategy described might be applied in your own project. Take time to experiment (in your imagination if not in practice) with the different ideas, exploring possibilities. Follow up on any that appear fruitful.

Further reading

Bernard and Ryan (2010) describe a number of additional (traditionally ethnographic) strategies for collecting and analysing relational data, including using free lists and pile sorts for cultural domain analysis (Chapter 8); cultural schema analysis (Chapter 14); and ethnographic decision modelling (Chapter 16). These can be found in Miles and Huberman (1994) also.

Clarke (2005) makes situational analysis clear, and is well illustrated with examples.

Corbin and Strauss (2008) illustrate the use of memos and diagrams in developing an understanding of the relationships between conditions; actions, strategies, and/or emotions; and consequences.

Sheridan, Chamberlain, and Dupuis (2011) present timelining as a strategy for both elicitation (co-construction) and analysis of narrative data.

Bazeley (2007: Chapter 8) details strategies using NVivo software for conducting queries of various types to answer questions raised by a variety of methodological approaches.

Friese (2012) explains the use of the query tool and other analysis strategies for Atlas.ti.

Richards (2009: Chapter 8) covers use of coding and text searches to explore patterns and relationships in data (assuming use of QDA software).

Scott (2012) provides a non-mathematical explanation of the theory and practice of SNA as a method.

Prell (2012) outlines theory and methods for the newcomer to SNA, with a practical (albeit quantitative) focus, walking you through projects of increasing complexity using UCINET.

Print resources and web-based tutorials are available for most major QDA software packages, some providing detail on when and how to conduct advanced queries; check developers' websites.

PART 4

BRINGING IT TOGETHER: MOVING TOWARD CLIMAX AND CLOSURE

You've been working through your data, exploring concepts, linking ideas, asking questions, writing reflections. Now you have a number of hunches to follow up, as well as some solid data to work from. Which ideas and what analyses will serve best to integrate and explain your observations and experience through this project?

It is difficult, if not impossible, to prescribe a pathway that will take you right to the specific point where things come together and you have a conclusion to your project. I can do no better than suggest that three activities, already themes throughout this book, are core processes underlying all strategies for 'getting there': write it, draw it, and tell it.

- As you attempt to write what you have been thinking about, you will be forced to clarify your ideas, to see and to fill in gaps. Your jottings will become a foundation for your final product.

  The goal of writing every day not only helps to avoid writing blocks, but gives regular practice to the qualitative researcher in externalising thoughts about the issues and evidence of the research in hand. Regular writing for oneself avoids the anxiety associated with having to write a paper for a seminar or a journal. Also it demonstrates practically that writing is a skill which can be acquired and improved by practice. (Gherardi & Turner, 2002: 04)

- Similarly, as you attempt to record what you have learned in a visual model, you will have to make decisions about what stays and what goes, and the relationships between items.

  You know what you display. Valid analysis requires, and is driven by, displays that are focused enough to permit a viewing of a full data set in the same location, and are arranged systematically to answer the research questions at hand. (Miles and Huberman, 1994: 91–2)

- Telling others about your project will test your conclusions and drive you toward coherence.

  If it makes sense to [others], it probably makes sense ... That dreaded question, 'What's your study about?', can [now] be answered in five minutes, not 50. (Richards, 2009: 146)

The chapters in this part capitalise on the work you have done already in moving beyond a simple thematic analysis. They take you further into opportunities to build soundly based and coherent description and explanation with your data, such that you can defend your conclusions. Perhaps, then, others will assess their value and extend their relevance to other settings.

11

If ... then ... is it because? Developing explanatory models and theories

In his brief review of causal analysis, Thomas Schwandt concluded that 'postmodern approaches to social inquiry aim to deconstruct all language of cause and effect' (2007: 30). In the everyday world, however, we 'naturally' ascribe cause and effect to the events, emotions, actions, and other experiences that make up our lives and the lives of those around us: 'Fred's feeling down because he lost his job.' And every day we use theory about physical and interpersonal processes to predict consequences and so modify our actions accordingly. Historically, interpreting theory, testing theory, and generating new theory have been core activities in sociology, psychology, and many other disciplines relying on social science research methods.

Not all projects are designed to produce explanatory theory, but whenever you are looking at processes or experiences within context(s) you will, inevitably, be considering how those processes or experiences change as contexts vary, and what that means for following events, further processes, or consequent emotions. At a basic level, you are 'doing theory' whenever you suggest a relationship between ideas or between categories.

This chapter begins with some backgrounding of ways of thinking about logic and theory before going on to describe perspectives on and strategies for developing *causal explanations* through qualitative analysis. (I will address the issue of developing theoretical coherence more generally in the next chapter.) It builds on strategies learned in previous chapters, where you connected, compared, and related data elements to deepen understanding of the situations, experiences, and processes that are the stuff of your research. It is a chapter that contains a collection of strategies, making it one to dip into without the expectation that you will use more than one or two. Read it through, initially simply to get the brain cells connecting and an idea of what's possible, and then select and apply whatever seems most appropriate to your purposes.

Analytic progression

Miles and Huberman (1994: 91) described analysis as progressing naturally from:

- telling a first 'story' about a specified situation (what happened, and then what happened), to
- constructing a 'map' (formalizing the elements of the story, locating key variables), to
- building a theory or model (how the variables are connected, how they influence each other).

Concluding with:

- [having] constructed a deeper story, in effect, that is both variable-oriented and process-oriented.

They add:

> Naturally there is no clear or clean boundary between describing and explaining; the researcher typically moves through a series of analysis episodes that condense more and more data into a more and more coherent understanding of what, how, and why. (Miles & Huberman, 1994: 91)

Cognitive progression in analysis

Theorising was included as the third of four more or less sequential cognitive processes for analysis described by Janice Morse (1994) – processes that she claimed are common across methodologies, although the specifics of how they are applied might vary for different methodological approaches. The four processes, which Morse described as comprehending, synthesising, theorising, and recontextualising, bear considerable resemblance to the stages outlined (above) by Miles and Huberman:

- *Comprehending*: learn everything you can about what is going on, from both the literature and your research site, but hold off from making judgements at this stage, so you will recognise when you are seeing something new. Comprehending provides the basis for rich description.
- *Synthesising*: sift and merge instances or events to describe typical or composite patterns; sifting 'shakes off' less important facets as you consider each additional case and move to a more aggregated, abstract picture. You need to compare cases *and* to analyse categories.
- *Theorising*: a stage of developing 'best guesses' about explanations (recognising that theory is not fact), and in the process, asking additional questions of the data and considering other sources so as to connect to a wider body of knowledge:

> Unfortunately theory is not acquired passively in moments of blinding insight. It is earned through an active, continuous, and rigorous process of viewing data as a puzzle as large as life: a puzzle that is life, a board game of wits … It is a process of speculation

and conjecture, of falsification and verification, of selecting, revising, and discarding ... it is the systematic selection and 'fitting' of alternative models to the data ... [a best fit] explains the data most simply. (Morse, 1994: 32–3)

- *Recontextualising*: now shape what has been synthesised for applicability to other settings and contexts (its practical application). Link what you have found with established knowledge.

Comprehending and synthesising (as Morse describes it) have been covered in earlier chapters. Our attention, here, is focused on strategies for theorising from qualitative data in the context of a rich historical legacy of logic, philosophy, and methods, while recontextualising for other settings will be addressed in the final chapter.

Explanatory theory as a goal of research

The idea that human behaviour can be summed up in general explanatory theories based on the patterning of experience and behaviour is anathema to many qualitative researchers, who insist that, because human behaviour is intentional and meaningful, it is necessary to understand each individual's interpretation of their experience of particular events. Robert Stake (2010), for example, supported the idea that there is an epistemological differentiation between developing an informal appreciation (*understanding*) of human experience, and identifying cause–effect *explanatory* relationships. My more pragmatic approach is to interpret any kind of understanding of human experience that necessarily involves seeing relationships between aspects of that experience as involving theory.

There is, indeed, widespread consensus regarding the importance of developing theory at some level as a goal for social science research. In order to apply what has been learned from the local setting to any other situation, you need to abstract from it to more general concepts and to identify relationships between those concepts. 'If theory building is indeed the research goal, then findings should be presented as a set of interrelated concepts, not just a listing of themes. It is the overall unifying explanatory scheme that raises findings to the level of theory' (Corbin & Strauss, 2008: 104). Whenever you describe your purpose in specifically relational, explanatory, or predictive terms, the process of getting there is likely to require (implicitly, if not explicitly) the application of logic and relational understanding and the outcome can be described as embracing theory.

Defining theory

In the broader natural and social sciences, formal or general theory is defined as 'a unified, systematic causal *explanation* of a diverse range of social phenomena' (Schwandt, 2007: 292, emphasis in original). Strauss (1995), assuming that theory deals with social processes, described it as involving a systematic linking of concepts, grounded in data, and able to be tested (by comparison with further cases).

Theory allows for both explanation and prediction.[1] It can be thought about at different levels.

Levels or types of theory

Theory development begins with ideas or concepts as analytical tools. Linkages (or relationships) are established between concepts, initially at a *local level*. Often in qualitative research, theory development does not extend beyond local theory, grounded in the particular experience of a particular sample. *Substantive theory* at a mid-range level integrates and further develops discrete local theories around a particular social or behavioural phenomenon. As the scope, range, and conceptual complexity are extended, theory becomes more abstract, less tied to the specific detail of the phenomenon; this is referred to as *formal* or *general theory*. At a higher level of abstraction again, we have *grand theory*. Examples might be:

- local theory – factors influencing neighbourhood involvement in the local school;
- substantive theory – cognitive dissonance theory; health belief model; emotional labour; adoption of innovation;
- formal/general theory – labelling theory; theory of reasoned action;
- grand theory – Parsons' structural functionalism; Mead and Blumer's symbolic interactionism; Giddens' structuration theory; Marx's dialectical materialism.

Strauss (1995: 9) summed up the primary differences in theories as being twofold: whether they were substantive or formal; and whether they were general or local. He preferred to differentiate theories by locating them dimensionally, rather than by level. Thus, theories vary in degrees of:

abstraction (generality of conception)

scope (number of substantive areas studied)

range (extent of relevance – i.e., types of groups, organizations, and societies)

specificity (of detail of grounding; of theoretical sampling expectations)

conceptual complexity (development and linkage of concepts – density; linkage with [an]other theory or theories)

applicability (relevance – i.e., extent and range – to aspects of 'the real world').

(Strauss, 1995: 10)

Strauss suggested that if all six dimensions are positive, then this is close to being a general theory.

Theory building

To move from description to theory requires that you start to ask 'Why?' and 'How?' and that you pay particular attention to clauses beginning with 'because'.

---

[1]There is no clear demarcation in the literature between causal theory and explanation, and so I will follow that trend by using either term as seems fit.

Your developing theory will start with some scrappy ideas, and be couched in terms of possibilities. You will develop those ideas, specifying the concepts you are working with and identifying more or less predictable relations between them, shifting constantly between empirical data and reflection regarding the larger significance of what you are seeing.

> Theory building is a process of going from raw data, thinking about that raw data, delineating concepts to stand for raw data, then making statements of relationship about those concepts linking them all together into a theoretical whole, *and at every step along the way recording that analysis in memos*. (Corbin & Strauss, 2008: 106, emphasis added)

Systematically building evidence through taking propositions developed from your data and assessing them against further data will add more confidence to your conclusions, as will comparison with the conclusions of other studies. At some stage in the process, building toward a substantive theory from your data will require deliberate engagement with existing frameworks and understanding.

> Confirming that what has already been well established also applies to your particular sample is not in and of itself terribly satisfying, but locating your findings within a larger context does create the platform upon which you can justify the particular extensions, elaborations, and enrichments that your study findings contribute. (Thorne, 2008: 205)

A role for qualitative research?

In proposing that qualitative research was not just for exploration, Miles and Huberman argued:

> We consider qualitative analysis to be a very powerful method of assessing causality … Qualitative analysis, with its close-up look, can identify *mechanisms*, going beyond sheer association. It is unrelentingly *local*, and deals well with the *complex* network of events and processes in a situation. It can sort out the *temporal* dimension, showing clearly what preceded what, either through direct observation or *retrospection*. It is well equipped to cycle back and forth between *variables* and *processes* – showing that 'stories' are not capricious, but include underlying variables, and that variables are not disembodied but have connections over time. (1994: 147; emphasis in original)

Established strategies for developing explanatory theory from qualitative data are described below, but first, some necessary foundations for your work.

Foundations for explanatory theory

I begin this section with 'classic' approaches to developing theory that have provided the basis for 'scientific method' as it has been known and taught in most disciplines. These approaches are foundational to the randomised controlled trial (RCT), still promoted as the supposed 'gold standard' approach to establishing causality, particularly in health and education. These approaches have attracted a barrage of criticism from philosophers and educationalists in the US in particular, for example with Shadish, Cook, and Campbell (2002: 9) describing experimentation as generating 'causal description' rather than causal explanation, the latter being best determined through other (typically qualitative) methods. I go on, therefore, to outline a critical realist view of causality, in which the focus is on identifying mechanisms for causation within contexts.

Hume's regularity theory and Mill's canons as a basis for causal analysis

David Hume argued that we cannot prove causation; all we can ever observe is the constant conjunction of events, and this is a sufficient basis for empirical science. Ascribing causation (e.g., that A causes B) is based on three conditions:

- covariation – that when A changes, so does B;
- sequence – that the change in A has to occur before the change in B; and
- elimination of alternative factors which might be responsible for both A and B.

These three conditions establish *a pattern of causation* rather than reasons for it. Because the process of causality is unobservable, explanation (from this viewpoint) has to be derived from the theory informing the causal hypothesis.

Based on Hume's theory, John Stuart Mill laid out canons for systematically matching and comparing cases in order to establish causal relationships. A cause (or contribution to cause) of the phenomenon in question might be identified by:

- a single common factor between otherwise different cases that is always associated with the outcome (method of agreement); or
- a single difference between otherwise identical cases that is routinely associated with presence or absence of the outcome (method of difference).

It is difficult to establish these conditions because they assume, first, that all other external factors are controlled, and second, that a single factor, acting alone, can be sufficient cause. They do, however, allow for the falsification of hypotheses; hence the reliance in social science on setting a null hypothesis as the basis for testing, and the adoption of these canons as the basis of experimental research.

In theory-building comparative analysis, cases sampled from the field of study need to be sufficiently similar that they can be compared with respect to the outcome or issue of interest, but at the same time, they have to have sufficient diversity for comparisons to have any meaning. The 'most similar, different outcome' (MSDO) design is most applicable for exploratory studies involving very small numbers of cases (e.g., three or four), where the goal is to narrow down the range of conditions under which an outcome might occur; while the 'most different, similar outcome' (MDSO) approach is appropriate for theory-testing studies involving a slightly larger (e.g., 15–25) number of cases (Berg-Schlosser & De Meur, 2009).

Deterministic versus probabilistic logic

Causality for human behaviour is not so simple however. Complex intentions operate in a context of others' intentions and actions where they combine to affect each other as well as the outcome. Causes of any event or behaviour are multiple and conjunctural (they act together). The same causes, in a different environment, will have different effects; different combinations of causes can have the same effect.

The multidimensional nature of experiences and processes investigated in social and behavioural research raises a critical issue for those undertaking analyses using single cases or small samples. Not only might there be multiple conditions required for an event, but those conditions might be both interactive and additive in creating the effect. Drawing conclusions on the basis of observing a small number of cases, where you are looking at outcomes in relation to the presence or absence of potential causal factors, rests on deterministic rather than probabilistic logic, and hence, there is a higher risk of reaching wrong conclusions (Lieberson, 1992; see Box 11.1).

- In a deterministic approach to establishing causal propositions, the presence of a given condition will *lead to* a specified outcome.
- From a probabilistic perspective, the presence of a given condition will increase *the likelihood of* a specified outcome. Probabilistic assumptions, however, require a larger sample as a basis for drawing conclusions.

The counter to this problem lies in *not* seeing factors being considered in comparative studies as single dimensional and independent, and in building a rich understanding, through qualitative data, of the multidimensional and interdependent processes that are involved in any aspect of individual or societal behaviour. To reiterate a theme of an earlier chapter for the current context, thorough understanding of the dynamics of each case is an essential prerequisite for any cross-case comparative analysis.

Box 11.1

The application of deterministic logic to a small sample (*n* = 2)

Stanley Lieberson (1992) used the scenario of two alcohol-affected drivers running a red light to illustrate his concern with deterministic logic based on small-*n* samples (based on Mill's arguments about causation). Neither was speeding, but in one case, a car enters from the right and an accident results; in the other, there is no other car and no accident. The fact of the car entering from the right, by this logic, must be the (sole) cause of the accident. There is no consideration

(Continued)

(Continued)

given to the interactive or additive effects of either alcohol or running the red light. If both cars have an accident but each varies in one way from the other, it is impossible to specify the cause. If running the red light was dropped from the analysis (e.g., those data were not collected) then in the case of both cars having an accident despite other differences, inebriation would be seen as the cause. The omission or inclusion of additional factors can radically change conclusions, such that it could be possible to have conditions leading to a conclusion that sobriety was the cause of an accident!

A critical realist perspective on causal processes: understanding mechanisms

Critical realists require a different kind of evidence for causation, distinguishing between a regularity conception of causation (based on Hume) and a generative (or 'intentional') conception of causation. Whereas the former is based on descriptive (observable) variables viewed from an outsider's perspective (variance theory), the latter takes an insider's perspective of relationships among intentional states and actions to identify the mechanism by which something is caused (process theory). One generates causal description, the other, causal explanation. These two aspects are complementary (Maxwell, 2012).

Causation, from a critical realist perspective, does not necessarily involve a physical mechanism. Because mind (including, for example, concepts, beliefs, values) is seen to be part of reality, meaning and intention can explain individual and social phenomena. Validity of a theory is therefore not simply evidenced in that theory's capacity to predict accurately; it requires explanation of *how* the mechanism is bringing about the event or outcome, and how that mechanism is impacted by local conditions at the time (Sayer, 2000). This focus on identifying mechanisms that come between context and consequence, particularly where these might be cognitive or emotional, has particular relevance to methods used in social research, requiring that an interpretive, often qualitative approach be employed (Maxwell, 2012; for an example, see Gutierrez' study of factors involved in workplace-related psychological injury below, Box 11.3). Furthermore, understanding *why* a relationship exists strengthens the internal validity (or trustworthiness) of the conclusions reached (Eisenhardt, 2002).

The context in which a process occurs is critical to that process. Put it in a different environment, and you don't just have different conditions, you potentially also have a different process. Because specific outcomes are contingent on context, the details of which we are not always aware, causal processes will not perform with consistent regularity. We need therefore 'to understand outcome *patterns* rather than seek outcome *regularities*' (Pawson, 2006: 22). Causal connections are established via 'context, mechanism, outcome configurations' (2006: 25) – a pattern that bears much similarity to the 'coding paradigm' of Corbin and Strauss.

Logic and argument: four paths to inference

Most of us have heard of deduction and induction as pathways to conclusions since early in our academic careers. Increasingly, the term abduction, with its pragmatist roots, is being used to describe an alternative form of reasoning, and to a lesser extent we read of retroduction. None of these approaches to drawing inferences is inherently of more value than another; rather, each has relevance in different situations. An inductive approach, historically, has a strong association with qualitative methods, but given an appropriate question, each of the four pathways to inference can be used with qualitative data.

Deduction

Deduction is a formal approach to logic in which a valid conclusion will follow if the premises for that conclusion are true. Thus, if the premise is that A leads to B, then:

If B is present, then A must also have been present; alternatively
If A is present, then B will follow; and
If B is not present, then A was not present.

Deductive logic is sometimes expressed in propositions such as:

All women are mortal.
I am a woman.
Therefore I am mortal.

This kind of logic makes sense in that context where there is 100 per cent certainty. It is less appropriate in the context of complex, multifactorial social and health research: for example, in drawing conclusions about whether an educational intervention A will necessarily lead to improvement B in children's learning.

Deductive logic underpins scientific (hypothetico-deductive) method.[2] On the basis of existing theory, a proposition is developed: that A will lead to B. Because it is easier to disprove something than prove it, for experimental testing this proposition needs to be stated in the form of a null hypothesis: that there is no relationship between A and B. The hypothesis is evaluated in terms of its predictive success when tested in a controlled situation. If indeed the null hypothesis is rejected, then the alternative hypothesis is assumed to be true (albeit subject to modification on the basis of new information). The need to show, in an experimental

---

[2]It is often wrongly assumed that all science is based on 'the scientific method' epitomised by hypothetico-deductive logic and randomised, controlled experimental research.

setting, that if A is not present then neither will B occur, creates a particular problem for qualitative studies, especially evaluation studies based on a single case.

As a qualitative researcher you use deductive logic when you develop formal propositions from existing theory (i.e., accessed through the literature in your subject area) or from your own earlier investigations, and then set out to gather data that will allow you to confirm or disconfirm your proposition. Alternatively, you might use principles of deductive inference making to question and eventually understand the premises behind statements that people make (see below).

Induction

In inductive research, conclusions are 'grounded' in data, as the researcher starts from data and works to develop empirical generalisations that can then be applied to similar situations. Although inductive logic is often associated with theory-emergent approaches in qualitative research, it is equally the basis for a great deal of quantitative and statistical research, especially that generating probability-based statements from data mining or survey techniques. The assumption is that if A is found to be related to B in this set of data, it is likely to be similarly associated in other parallel data settings. Adding understanding of why it might be associated strengthens the conclusions and extends the possibility of applying what has been learned to other settings.

Abduction

Abductive logic, first described by Charles Sanders Peirce and consequently closely connected with pragmatist philosophy, involves an iterative or dialectical interplay between existing theoretical understanding and empirical data, so that the theory is recontextualised, leading to fresh interpretation and potentially to a modified theoretical framework. To assess theoretical plausibility, mechanisms explaining regularities in the data are compared with other areas that are well understood; they are elaborated, and then assessed against further data for their explanatory value (through their predictive capacity).

Abduction does not follow rules of formal logic in the sense that it offers a plausible interpretation rather than a logical conclusion derived from premises. Abductive approaches are commonly applied in qualitative and mixed methods studies where the goal is to generate theory rather than to generalise from a sample to a population.

Retroduction

Retroductive inferences are drawn by answering the question: 'What made this possible?' It is rather like a backwards approach to logic modelling where an attempt is made to work out the components and steps that must have been necessary to lead to a current phenomenon. Where possible, speculative explanations are assessed against historical or archival data.

The development of a Foucaultian genealogy, for example, depends on retroductive logic, at least in its initial stages until supporting data can be amassed. Explanations for behaviour are often retroductive, 'He must have been ...'; indeed, a great deal of assessing causality relies on retroductive logic. We are looking at 'an end point whose existence connotes the occurrence of certain prior events' (Mohr, 1982, quoted by Miles and Huberman, 1994: 147).

Differentiating causal mechanisms from misleading associations

Part of my stated purpose in having you carry out comparative analyses based on demographic attributes followed by relational analyses on specific associations was to have you move from seeing differences associated, say, with gender or age, to asking what it is about being female, or being over 60, that might have contributed to those differences. *Causal analysis must go beyond identifying superficial, demographically based associations to identifying the mechanisms by which such associations have their influence.* A classic example here is analysis of gender and pay levels, where it has been found that simply raising the pay of female employees to an equivalent level with males for equivalent work roles does not bring about gender equality in pay. There are a number of other intervening factors, or mechanisms, that work to ensure that even when they are doing equivalent work, females are likely to be paid less (Reskin, 1998). It is the task of the researcher to identify the 'intervening variable(s)' and the mechanisms associated with them.

Similarly, you will need to beware of seeing causation in spurious or partially spurious associations. If adolescent mothers are more likely to have lower-birthweight babies than older mothers, is that because there is something about being younger that impacts on birthweight? Well, no: rather, adolescent mothers are more likely to smoke, for example, than older mothers, and smoking during pregnancy has been associated with lower birthweight for the baby; adolescent mothers are likely to have poorer nutrition and medical care; and so on. Age of the mother, in itself, has no relationship at all to the birthweight of her child. Being informed by background knowledge, experience, and substantive theory as to potential mechanisms will guide your analyses here.

Logic-based questioning: finding the major premise

When people make statements of 'fact' as if everyone just knows they would be true, Becker (1998) raises a challenge: what is the major premise behind the statement, the assumption(s) on which it rests? For example, let's say you are walking along the street with a friend, and you notice a group of adolescent males gathered on the corner. 'Those boys are going to be trouble', says your friend. What is the premise behind this statement? Questioning your friend about his thoughts as he said that (assuming he doesn't walk off in a huff) will reveal the assumptions he (and presumably others) make about boys who gather on corners (Box 11.2).

| Box 11.2 |

Finding the major premise: what makes a patient 'a crock'?

In a research context, Howard Becker (1998) used logic-based questioning to understand why a medical student referred to a very talkative patient with multiple physical complaints as 'a crock', in a clearly disparaging way. When Becker asked, the student's first attempt at explaining what he meant by crock (doesn't everyone just know?) was to suggest it was someone with a psychosomatic illness. But this didn't stand up when they met the next patient, who had a (presumed) psychosomatic illness with a real physical consequence; so after much further discussion amongst, now, a group of students, they decided a crock was someone with many complaints but no discernible physical pathology. But why was that a problem for them? Surely they would meet crocks in future practice? Yes, but they couldn't learn anything from them in school, because all you ever needed to do for them was talk to them – a lesson learned from the first encounter. They could waste a lot of a student's time, but did not add to their 'clinical experience', which is what they were in school for. A third reason for disliking crocks was finally unearthed: that crocks could never be the subject of a medical miracle, because they weren't 'really sick'.

As Becker continued his research into 'boys in white', he found that traces of these three abstracted ideas – the significance of clinical experience, the value of time, and the meaning of medical responsibility (you can't cure someone unless you can kill them) – permeated throughout the training experience of the medical students, explaining far more than just their distaste for crocks.

Learning what a crock was was thus a matter of carefully unravelling the multiple meanings built into that simple word, and especially of working out the logic of what was being told to us, finding the major premises on which student (and staff, for that matter) activities were based. The trick here is not dazzling and requires plenty of work, consisting as it does of following up the uses and meanings of terms that seem, when we first hear them, strange and even unintelligible. Making people explain what we don't understand, and checking it against what we see and hear, produces the missing premises in the arguments they routinely make to explain and justify what they do. (1998: 157)

Similarly, Becker suggests:

▶ challenge when someone says something isn't something – 'That isn't art', for example – for clues about norms, privilege, and appropriate behaviour or policy toward that object; or

▶ investigate what is being implied when someone states something as a necessity – 'You must ...'

In these cases: 'When you find the unstated premise, ask what in the lives of the people involved makes it necessary or useful for them to make the argument they make, and to keep its major premise to themselves' (1998: 160).

Puzzle solving with 'conjectures and refutations'

The arena for much qualitative research is the community, where experimental designs for research are rarely appropriate. Even quasi-experimental designs, in so far as they require a comparison group of some kind, are difficult to implement from practical and ethical standpoints. Researchers attempting to identify causal relationships in the community setting, therefore, have developed a range of alternative strategies and guidelines for practice, such as those outlined in this and later sections. Several come from evaluation research, where there is an explicit goal of demonstrating a causal relationship between a programmatic input in a given context, and its consequent impact on people within that context, with the hope of being able to generalise from that experience to other parallel situations.

Janice Morse (1994; see earlier in this chapter) suggested that much theorising was about developing 'best guesses', and then checking them out. In the preface to *Conjectures and refutations*, Karl Popper observed: 'The way in which knowledge progresses, and especially our scientific knowledge, is by unjustified (and unjustifiable) anticipations, by guesses, by tentative solutions to our problems, by *conjectures*. These conjectures are controlled by criticism; that is, by attempted *refutations*, which include severely critical tests' ([1963] 2002: xi). On the basis that useful theory *must* also be capable of being refuted, Popper argued that confirmation of a theory should count only if it is the result of a risky prediction; and only if it has been genuinely tested by an attempt to falsify it, or to refute it ([1963] 2002: 46–7).

Several strategies used in qualitative theory building, including those that follow in this section, rely on conjecture as to an explanation, particularly where it is not possible to directly observe or interact with those involved in the process(es) being studied. While you are probably not claiming to be doing 'science' as that term is commonly understood, nevertheless, by applying principles of refutability (e.g., through using theoretical sampling and constant comparison to test predictions) you will sharpen your theory development when you are relying on the strategies below.

Inference to best explanation (IBE)

Inference to best explanation (IBE) draws on inductive or abductive reasoning to find the hypothesis or proposition that provides the 'best' explanation of available evidence, recognising that knowledge is never certain but that 'we can learn from our mistakes' (Popper, [1963] 2002: vii). You are using IBE when you develop an explanation that accounts for all the facts, that explains your data, and that is plausible enough or simple enough to be accepted (Harman, 1965).

IBE draws heavily on your background knowledge and assumptions (Day & Kincaid, 1994). It does not, as some suggest, add credence to a hypothesis; rather it involves your deciding amongst competing hypotheses, based on your best background knowledge. This background knowledge might be 'more or less essential, extensive, detailed, and certain' (1994: 287). You are likely to rely on internal evidence – that which is understood and acceptable within your discipline – but you will also need to be able to answer the external sceptics who will challenge your sources and methods. Generally, IBE as an approach to explanatory argument is likely to be more successful in some settings, especially in those that share background context, than in others. If you are writing as a student, for example, you might assume that your examiners will have a shared background knowledge; but once you begin to present your work to a wider (external) audience, this will not necessarily be the case, and you will need to address, more thoroughly, the concerns of the sceptics by demonstrating the basis for that knowledge and for the quality of your evidence and sources.

Let's say, then, that you develop some propositions based on the simplest, most plausible, most comprehensive explanation you can come up with, given the available evidence. Will it fit all cases? Probably not, but the inference based on your explanation is justified until you have evidence that refutes it, or a better (more plausible) explanation. For example, we assume that a DNA sample is evidence of who did the crime until a sceptic questions the validity of the way in which the sample was collected, transported, or stored. Both negative cases and the sceptic send us back to reconsider our propositions and the evidence for them in a way that must, eventually, lead to our either dismissing our results or modifying them, and/or perhaps to strengthening our argument.

Modus operandi (MO)

In an evaluation setting, Michael Scriven (1976) outlined a model for drawing causal inferences, using a qualitative approach and based on abductive logic, with criteria that bear resemblance to criteria for IBE – an approach he referred to as detecting the *modus operandi* for a programme or process of change:

> Modus operandi (MO) was conceptualised by evaluation theorist Michael Scriven (1976) as a way of inferring causality when experimental designs were impractical or inappropriate. The MO approach, drawing from forensic science, makes the inquirer a detective. Detectives compare clues [patterns of evidence] discovered at a crime scene to known patterns of possible suspects [causes]. Those suspects whose MO (method of operating) does not fit the crime scene pattern are eliminated from further investigation. (Patton, 2002: 471)

Detectives distinguish between a criminal's MO, which is likely to evolve over time, and his signature – a particular twist to the way he conducts his crime, which tends to stay the same over time. The signature is the more vital element in apprehending and convicting the perpetrator of the crime, although the MO provides important clues along the way (Douglas & Douglas, 2006).

We use MO in everyday causal inference, for example, to figure why the toaster doesn't work, or that a particular person's heart attack was their cause of death. The consequence of death is a physical signature of a heart attack (with the culmination of the 'crime' sometimes being prevented by the intervention of another person). In the case of the heart attack victim, we draw a conclusion based on the presence of the signature, and do not resort to experimental evidence (Mohr, 1998). Similarly, the signature of a broken element is sufficient to explain the lack of heat in the toaster; we do not need to experiment with toasters by breaking their elements to demonstrate that. Often, as in this case, we also understand the mechanism. What can the qualitative researcher learn from such situations, to apply in building causal hypotheses when using an approach that does not provide for comparison (as in an experiment) and that involves human behaviour rather than something tangible like a toaster element or a heart attack?

The modus operandi, and its signature, are evident through patterns of behaviours:

▶ Look at the modus operandi in your current inquiry situation; identify patterns in the evidence before you, and 'conjure up' possible causes for that pattern.

▶ Treat each possible cause as a 'suspect', and compare what is known about that suspect with the pattern of evidence you have.

▶ Progressively eliminate those that do not fit, until you are left with the most likely operative reason or causal pathway (the 'best explanation').

Argument by analogy

In a similar vein to identifying the MO of a causal process, one of Brewer and Hunter's (2006) suggested strategies for puzzle solving requires seeing similarities among disparate entities and asking whether what is known to be true about one might be generalised to another. Thus you would work by example, analogy, or metaphor, applying exemplars from one situation to another. Brewer and Hunter suggest that the legitimacy of the use of exemplars or analogies is ultimately based upon the community of practising scientists accepting such models (2006: 56–7).

Defining and testing rival explanations

Thinking about potential rival explanations for an outcome from the start of your study is useful in terms of alerting you to additional data you might need to collect in order to dismiss those explanations. In the absence of that foreknowledge, however, it can still be useful for you to identify and deal with rival explanations at a later stage, as a way of both silencing critics and sharpening analysis. The most direct rival explanation is that the outcome you observed came about for some reason other than your hypothesised cause. Robert Yin (2003) lists several methodological and substantive variations on this rival explanation to consider in the context of conducting evaluative case studies. Can you demonstrate, for example in a programme where you are testing the value of a particular intervention, that the results were not random, or that they did not result from some other form of input or co-occurring change, or that although the intervention was effective, it could not have been better explained by an alternative theory?

Having defined dimensions of interest from the alternative theory or from a consideration of rival explanations, the process is then one of comparing one or more cases across those dimensions, or comparing with a hypothetical case or established benchmarks. It just may be that one of the rival explanations you consider does provide a better explanation of your results than the one you originally proposed. It may not be what you expected, but if your evidence supports it, then you have learned something new, and your project has a result for you to report and to re-evaluate in a further study. If you are able to dismiss all rival explanations, then having done so, you will be able to argue even more convincingly for what you have found.

Yin illustrated the strategy of testing rival explanations by referring to Graham Allison's (1971) study of the 1962 Cuban missile crisis, in which the United States confronted Russia over placing missiles on Cuba that were capable of being aimed at the US. Allison proposed three competing theories to explain what happened in this single (non-repeatable) case: that the US and Russia were rational actors in the situation, that they performed as complex bureaucracies, and/or that they were politically motivated groups of people. He then compared each for its capacity to explain the choices made and the resulting course of events.

Tracing causation through narrative

Statistical models, even those with names that suggest causal modelling (such as path analysis, structural equation modelling) can only ever *suggest* causal paths through demonstrating association between variables; they are not, in the absence of theory, a sufficient basis for *establishing* causality. A narrative captures the importance of context, the meaningfulness of human experience, thought, and speech within time and place; it provides opportunity to understand implicit as well as explicit rationales for action within a holistic framework. While the statistical approach is attempting to build an abstracted, more general causal theory, the narrative approach is seeking comprehensiveness of understanding within the individual case. Working with longitudinal data benefits causal analyses in both approaches, in so far as it provides data about the temporal ordering of factors being considered along with information about other potentially intervening factors in the causal relationship.

Taking a more individualised, narrative approach to establishing causation is likely to assist in overcoming some of the dangers of misleading and spurious associations (as outlined earlier in this chapter). As well as providing information about the sequence of events, in narrative data you have access to the participants' perspectives on their agency and on bringing about changes in their lives or other events. Was it loss of employment that led to ill health, or ill health that led to loss of employment? Nevertheless, with narrative data you can still be subject to the problem of being unwittingly misled by the obvious (rather than operative) reasons for an action, particularly if you are dealing with retrospective action. In the course of narrating some aspect of one's life, events of the past will be restructured in the light of the present (Elliott, 2005). Narratives are modified also to preserve the integrity of identity. They need to be interpreted, therefore, holistically and within their audience context. Pressing for detail in the narrative can help to overcome some of the tendency to present a more socially desirable image.

Jane Elliott (2005) argued cogently for combining statistical and narrative strategies in determining causality. Narrative approaches point to potential influencing factors, and multivariate statistical analyses of survey data or of data from existing (e.g., national) databases help to sort out the relative influences of those factors; alternatively, with data collected concurrently, qualitative comments give meaning to statistical associations. Elliott cites examples by Maume (1999) and Rank (1989). Box 11.3 gives an example of the use of narrative accounts to provide essential detail to understand the mechanism of causation for psychological injury at work.

For causal analysis, you will want to consider, in particular:

- the structure of the narrative, including the sequencing of events (perhaps draw a timeline?);
- what follows from keywords such as 'because';
- open statements of reasons for action, excuses, attributions to other people (the latter may be projections of their own rationale).

⌐ Box 11.3 ⌐

The contribution of narrative accounts to an understanding of the role of interpersonal conflict in psychological injury at work

Rod Gutierrez (2006; cf. Box 2.5) employed a mixed methods approach based on narrative reports to develop an understanding of the causes of psychological injury in the workplace. Following a qualitative review of the entire dataset (156 cases), he identified and extracted binary data from the reports of the claimant, their employer, and an independent psychologist. Multivariate statistical analysis of these data showed that lack of social support combined with interpersonal conflict was the major contributor to an outcome of psychological injury. Interpersonal conflict did not discriminate on its own, and the expression of dissatisfaction with workplace factors was not sufficient to warrant a clinical diagnosis of psychological injury. These analyses

(Continued)

(Continued)

showed, also, that employees and employers had very different views of the nature of events leading to the claim, particularly in relation to interpersonal conflict and the employer's right to undertake 'reasonable actions' in modifying work arrangements.

Gutierrez followed up the statistical analyses with qualitative analyses of a cross-sectional sample of 18 of the narratives to investigate further the role of interpersonal conflict, the role of low support, and the content of rejected communications about distress, and to identify what common (interrelated) factors were present in accepted cases. Interpersonal conflict was reported by almost all claimants: why then, were only some accepted as having an injury? First, from comparative analysis of narratives about conflict, he determined that 'claimants who had been assessed as suffering from a diagnosable disorder described interpersonal conflict in a personal and emotive manner, whereas claimants who were assessed as not suffering from a workplace-related diagnosable disorder spoke of interpersonal conflict relating to workplace factors and situations' (2006: 201). This involved, for example, discriminating between those who might be led to question themselves as workers in relation to some aspect of their job, and those who questioned themselves as people. These more personal attacks, experienced as internalised interpersonal conflict leading to a redefinition of self, were common to all claimants diagnosed as having a psychological injury (i.e., all those whose claim for compensation on that basis was successful).

After investigating also the role of support, Gutierrez concluded that 'work factors in themselves are not sufficient to cause psychopathology, but the way in which claimants make sense of workplace factors has a significant impact on the development of a disorder, especially when workplace factors cause claimants to redefine their perceptions of themselves in a personal manner' (2006: 211). For example:

> I was devastated and I didn't feel it was entirely my fault although I acknowledged there were things I could fix. I felt I'd let everyone down and they didn't have any confidence in me and didn't feel like they could talk to me. I didn't know what else to do. I started to think I was useless and hopeless.

He found also that the assessing psychologist was able to differentiate between a claimant's vocational discontent or dissatisfaction with some aspect of their workplace and clinically relevant distress, based on the narratives provided in each case.

From these (and further) qualitative analyses, Gutierrez was able to map the broad process which most claimants followed in developing a claim for psychological injury following an experience of interpersonal conflict. This process involved five steps: attribution of personal meaning and conclusion of lack of support; adverse emotional experience; clinical symptom development and saturation point; seeking medical attention; and lodging a claim for compensation (2006: 218–19).

Puzzle-solving essentials

You are probably, by now, beginning to detect some common ideas running through these various ways of thinking about and doing causal explanation. Those that are evident to me are:

▶ They all build on your having sufficient background experience and/or knowledge to recognise possible causal factors and to determine the plausibility of competing hypotheses.

▶ Similarly, the theoretical basis for your study will provide a guide to your analysis.

▶ You will need to keep going back to data to test ideas, and potentially to add new, theoretically selected data (of the same or a different kind) to confirm or refute explanatory hypotheses.

▶ At the same time, don't be afraid to develop hunches or make conjectures about what you think might be going on – as long as you are then prepared to evaluate each of those against your data. Ideally you would be drawing on your memos recorded throughout the analysis process as a resource for these conjectures.

And some essentials that I would add:

▶ Listen again for clues in what your participants have said.

▶ Review earlier memos.

▶ Keep challenging (questioning) the hunches and conclusions you develop from your data.

▶ After a period of immersion in your data, take time out to wander and ponder.

▶ Keep writing!

Case-based strategies

In these strategies, the goal is not to look so much at regularities across all cases, as to gain as great an understanding of causal relationships and mechanisms as possible through in-depth analysis of a smaller number of selectively chosen cases. Comparisons are used to strengthen the conclusions drawn.

Analytic induction

Analytic induction is a case comparative method developed from methods employed and described by Florian Znaniecki (1934), with a goal of abstracting and generalising from the particulars of events related to a topic or phenomenon. It was developed by Alfred Lindesmith in the 1940s as a tool to identify the essential factors that make someone or something what it is. Analytic induction has been used classically in studies of deviance, for example, to identify what made someone an addict (Lindesmith, 1947; Becker, 1963; see Box 11.4) or an embezzler (Cressey, 1953). It deals only with cases where the condition is present. Using essentialist logic and Mill's method of agreement, Lindesmith's strategy identifies only necessary conditions, rather than sufficient conditions, to produce universal rather than probabilistic statements. As the world and our understanding of it are subject to change, however, so are our theories.

To use analytic induction:

▶ Work with one case at a time. Develop an explanation about the causes of the phenomenon you are studying from that case.

▶ Introduce a second case. If there are differences, then according to the method of agreement, those differences are ruled out as being causative.

▶ Add further cases, developing a more refined set of criteria. Any retained criterion has to apply in all cases.

▶ If a case exhibits something different that will require a different explanation, then rule that case out as an example of the phenomenon being studied – i.e., tighten the definition of what is being studied (Figure 11.1).

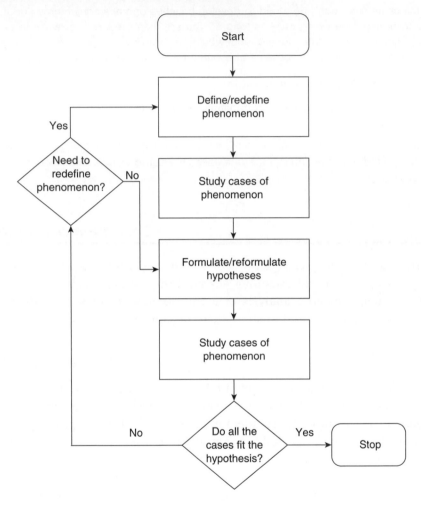

Figure 11.1   The process of analytic induction

Source: Hammersley and Atkinson, 2007: 187

⌐ Box 11.4 ⌐

Classic examples of the use of analytic induction

Alfred Lindesmith (1947) concluded that it took a three-step process to define an opiate addict, using a rigorous form of analytic induction in his dissertation study based on interviews with over 60 morphine or heroin addicts (reported by Becker, 1998):

- A user of opiates takes enough to become physiologically adapted.
- The user experiences an interruption to their use of opiates and develops withdrawal distress.
- They interpret the symptoms as due to their not having the drugs, and understand themselves as addicts, and so they take a shot of the drug. Thereafter they will engage in whatever behaviour is necessary to maintain their supply of drugs.

If someone experienced withdrawal distress but did not take further drugs, they were not an addict in Lindesmith's terms. Controversially at the time, Lindesmith's definition did not suggest that personality factors were involved. While there might be many other correlates of addiction, they could not be part of the definition as determined by this method.

Donald Cressey's (1953) study of embezzlers (those who violate financial trust) is perhaps the most often quoted example of analytic induction. Cressey limited his study to those people who had no intention of committing fraud when they took a position of trust (a difficult sample to locate!). They were people who had, or developed, non-shareable financial problems. Because they were in a position of trust, they felt free of scrutiny and so opportunity was present. They rationalised their theft by believing, for example, they were just borrowing the money and that they would return it, that they deserved it because their skills were not appropriately recognised in monetary terms, that the company didn't need it, and so on. Cressey concluded from his study that there were three essential elements in every fraud – 'the fraud triangle' of motivation, opportunity, and rationalisation.

Theory elaboration

The goal of theory elaboration, as a method, is to develop a theory about a phenomenon that spans different units and levels of analysis by drawing on a maximum variation sample of that phenomenon, so that the contrasts created by the differences in the sample contribute to 'more fully specified constructs' and identification of 'the processes that create, maintain, and change patterned behaviour' (Vaughan, 1992: 181).

Working through one example of a particular phenomenon at a time, Diane Vaughan (1992: 174) alternates between units of analysis of different size, complexity, and function in order to 'elaborate sociological theory'. With each new case she reassesses her current theory, rejecting, confirming, or extending it as needed, until the theory can be more fully specified. Ambiguity and contrasts are welcome. For example, a study of 'taking responsibility' might embrace both parents with a baby in neonatal intensive care, and the chief executive in an oil company. Cases might be selected intra-organisationally or inter-organisationally, and will not necessarily be ordered from micro to macro; ideas developed within the larger organisation might be explored by studying their application in a smaller work unit. With each contrasting level of analysis, the refined theoretical model is tested through comparison with the new case. The selection of 'wildly varying' cases helps to avoid force-fitting the case to theory.

A carefully constructed profile for each case lays a sound foundation for each comparative step in this approach. The process is initially guided by an existing, loosely held theoretical model or concept. Each case is examined with respect to its own uniqueness, with careful attention given to the interactional and contextual elements of the social structure it sits within and to the characteristics of the surrounding environment. As the cases are compared, similarities and differences are identified, and their consequences for the theoretical model evaluated. The process is repeated as many times as is needed to explain all relevant aspects and to dismiss rival explanations. Yin (2003: 122), who refers to this broad approach as a replication strategy (commonly used in small-n case studies), warns that the iterative nature of the method means it is 'fraught with danger' because of a tendency to drift from the original goal. Vaughan (1992), however, remains open to a shift in direction when she finds that the case being examined turns out, instead, to be a case of something else. As with most things, whether or not this is a problem to be guarded against depends on the purpose of your study.

Event structure analysis (ESA)

In event structure analysis (ESA) cases are constructed and compared as whole narratives, with the emphasis on narrative sequence. ESA is used to impute causality in, for example, historical processes, cultural events, motivational processes, and organisational changes. 'Narrative explanation takes the form of an unfolding, open-ended story fraught with conjunctures and contingency, where what happens, an action, in fact happens because of its order and position in the story' (Griffin, 2007: 4).

The strategy was developed by David Heise (1989) who also developed the supporting Java-based Ethno software (available free and with supporting documentation at www.indiana.edu/~socpsy/ESA/). Event(s) being studied are 'unpacked' – broken down into their constituent parts and sorted into chronological order. Chronologically sequenced event elements are listed and then entered one at a time into Ethno with coding for the agent, action, object, instrument, setting, alignment, product, and/or beneficiary of each event. With each entry, the researcher is challenged with a series of yes–no questions to establish whether and how already listed event elements are linked to the current element; questions might be about a prerequisite, an implication, a historical causation, or a counterfactual (a hypothetical alternative event sequence). The researcher therefore has to account for the event, and the analysis depends entirely on the researcher's (necessarily comprehensive) data-driven understanding. ESA's value 'is largely heuristic, centered on how it relentlessly probes the analyst's construction, comprehension and interpretation of the event' (Griffin, 2007: 5). The contribution of the software is to take the components the researcher has entered and, with the researcher's responses to its questions, then show 'how some events are necessary for other events, and how abstract events are represented in concrete happenings' (Heise, 2007). A project using ESA, including a causal diagram drawn by Ethno, is outlined in Box 11.5.

Box 11.5

Using event structure analysis with actor network theory to analyse causality

Marisa Ponti (2012) undertook an evaluative case study of Semantic OPAC (SemOP1), a project designed to evaluate subject access and search functionality in Italian open public access catalogue (OPAC) interfaces. SemOP1 had been set up as a distributed, collaborative project coordinated by four library and information science academics and professionals and drawing on the contribution of 13 student assistants. Ponti drew on both actor network theory and event structure analysis to identify strategies used by the collaborators to work together, to establish goals, and to seek and enrol helpers and resources for the project. Actor network theory provided a framework for examining how relations between human and non-human actors were created, sustained, and adapted over time (Latour, 1987).

From interview data and documentary sources, Ponti mapped the series of transactions and events throughout the project in a long narrative. This was then decomposed into a table listing 33 events that contributed to the collaboration along with the actors involved in each. As she entered the events into Ethno, she responded to 119 (mainly counterfactual) questions, in order to link events. The resulting diagram of the event structure is shown in Figure 11.2 (the program does not *generate* the causal connections, rather, it translates them into diagrammatic form based on the researcher's interpretation of those events). Ponti then interpreted the diagram in causal terms, in associated text. She concluded that ESA helped to harness the explanatory power of narratives, allowed close examination of the interaction between actors, and forced the researcher to differentiate between antecedent and causal actions. It made clear the reasoning processes applied when specifying linkages, contributing to the transparency of the analysis.

(Continued)

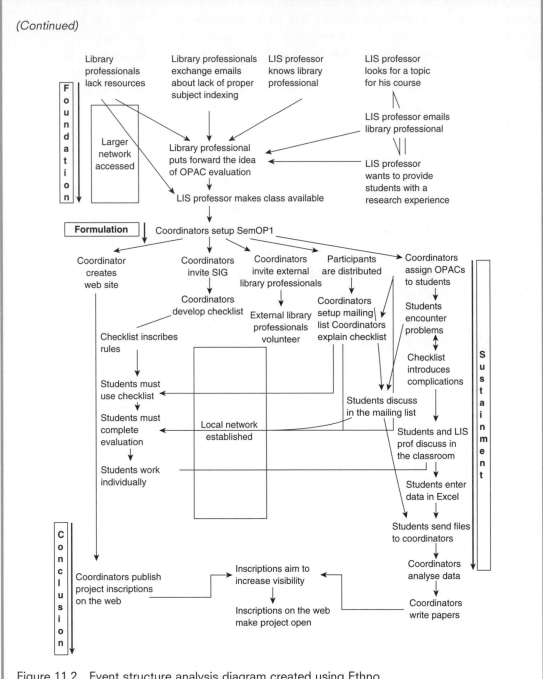

Figure 11.2   Event structure analysis diagram created using Ethno

Source: Ponti, 2012: Illustration 1

Qualitative comparative analysis (QCA)

Configurational comparative methods, still more generally known as qualitative comparative analysis (QCA), comprise particular strategies for cross-case comparative analysis for small- and medium-n studies that are gaining increasing recognition in the social science community since their introduction by Charles Ragin in 1987. Intended to cross the boundary between variable-oriented and case-oriented methodologies, these methods allow you to analyse multiple cases by applying both inductive and deductive methods with key variables while preserving their case configurations. Like all comparative methods involving qualitative data, they build on good case-level knowledge combined with theoretical understanding. Relevant cases and a limited set of quantitatively or qualitatively derived variables across those cases are selected (preferably no more than seven, and fewer for a small number of cases), along with an outcome variable, which may be positive, negative, or contradictory. In the original 'crisp-set' form of analysis, all variables are dichotomised, and a truth table is constructed to include all possible configurations of variables across cases, with individual cases then assigned to the relevant row (e.g., Table 11.1). Adjustments are made, if possible, to remove or reduce contradictory outcomes. Drawing on the logic of set theory, Boolean algebra is then applied to the table to generate potential necessary and/or sufficient conditions for the specified outcome. From this, a minimum set of interrelated 'prime implicants' of general significance for the given outcome is derived (Box 11.6). Unlike incremental additive statistical (regression-based) models, QCA may present multiple constellations of factors that, taken together (i.e., in conjunction), lead to the same result, rather than a single list of variables with their 'contribution' to explaining variance. These provide a complete set of explanatory solutions, expressed in algebraic form, for the factors and outcome being considered. Simplistic models, therefore, are rejected in favour of diversity that is more reflective of the complexity of the situation being studied (Berg-Schlosser, De Meur, Rihoux, & Ragin, 2009).

The basic method for QCA, which relied on dichotomising all variables, has been extended to deal also with multi-value data (mvQCA) and fuzzy-set data (fsQCA).[3] A range of computer programs has been written to assist in these

---

[3]In fuzzy data the boundaries between categories overlap. For example, if income is measured as a continuous variable but is then categorised into very low, low, medium, and high, the cut-off points between categories are rather arbitrary. Does it really make that much difference if your annual income is $50,000 compared to $49,999? Rather than the category a person is in being based on a cut-off, a measure of 'setness' is determined based on how close one is to the cut-off point, possibly in conjunction with other factors. Thus the person at $49,999 would be seen as not very different from the person at $50,000, as each would be split almost equally between two sets.

analyses. These, along with further information, are available (free at the time of writing) from COMPASSS (COMParative methods for the Advancement of Systematic cross-caSe analySis) at www.compasss.org.

| | Box 11.6 | |

Comparative qualitative analysis: an illustrative example

Bakker, Cambré, Korlaar, and Raab (2011) employed crisp-set qualitative comparative analysis to examine the necessity and sufficiency of five conditions (shown in Figure 11.3) hypothesised to favour transfer of project knowledge from a time-bounded project to a parent organisation. The 12 cases for the study came from seven inter-organisational projects that ranged in focus from construction to education and the arts. Data were derived from interviews with members of both project teams and parent organisations. Key variables were dichotomised, enabling the construction of a truth table (Table 11.1). The results placed the responsibility for successful knowledge transfer unambiguously in the hands of the parent organisation – the organisation that set up the project. Transfer was not the result of a single organisational factor, however; it also necessarily involved giving attention to cognitive and/or temporal relational factors between the organisations involved.

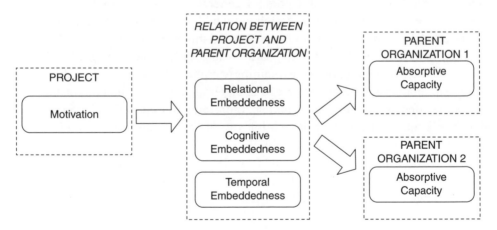

Figure 11.3   Factors potentially impacting knowledge transfer from project to parent organisation

Source: Bakker et al., 2011: 496, Figure 1. Used with permission from Elsevier.

Table 11.1 Truth table of Boolean conditions for successful transfer of knowledge

Case number	R Relational embeddedness	C Cognitive embeddedness	T Temporal embeddedness	A Absorptive capacity	M Motivation	Z Successful knowledge transfer
1, 2	0	0	0	0	0	0
3	0	0	1	1	1	1
4	1	1	1	0	1	0
5	0	0	1	0	1	0
6, 7, 8	1	1	1	1	1	1
9	1	1	0	1	1	1
10	0	1	0	0	1	0
11	1	0	0	1	1	0
12	0	0	0	0	1	0

Source: based on a dichotomous data table for each case provided by Bakker et al., 2011: 498

The Boolean minimisation for those projects where transfer was successful (Z = 1) was:
$$C*R*A*M + T*c*r*A*M \rightarrow Z^{4,\ 5}$$

This can be read as:

successful transfer of knowledge gained in a project occurs where there is:

high cognitive embeddedness (C) AND high relational embeddedness (R) AND high absorptive capacity (A) AND high motivation (M)

OR

high temporal embeddedness (T) AND low cognitive embeddedness (c) AND low relational embeddedness (r) AND high absorptive capacity (A) AND high motivation (M)

Because of the common terms (redundancy), this can be rewritten as:
$$A*M(C*R + T*c*r) \rightarrow Z$$

(Continued)

---

[4]Labels written in lower case represent the 0 condition (i e , absence) for those variables. In set theory, * represents AND (i.e., both together) and + represents OR (i.e., alternatives).

[5]Five alternative configurations predicted unsuccessful transfer.

(Continued)

Thus, absorptive capacity and motivation appear to be necessary but not sufficient for knowledge transfer. This result can be further simplified (by allowing the software to impute from non-observed cases) to:

$$A*T + A*C + A*r \rightarrow Z$$

or, to remove redundancy

$$A(T + C + r) \rightarrow Z$$

This minimal model suggests that absorptive capacity of the parent organisation is the only necessary (but not sufficient) condition for successful knowledge transfer; absorptive capacity has to be combined with a high degree of temporal *or* cognitive embeddedness. Motivation has been eliminated because it can be high in cases that are not successful. (Within-case knowledge suggested that low relational embeddedness (r), which appears as a rather anomalous element, was related to one idiosyncratic case, and so this was dismissed by the authors in further discussion.)

Exploring extreme, deviant, or negative cases

We have come to expect that some cases will not fit the theories we develop. Statistical analysis of survey data, for example, works on probabilistic principles, and statisticians discount extreme or deviant cases as 'outliers' that result from randomness in the sample, from measurement error, or possibly from some unknown additional variable. Qualitative researchers, in contrast, usually seek to explain all cases, and see a deviant or negative case as an indication that they need to consider additional information and/or to restructure their understanding of what is going on. Indeed, the deviant case is valued in so far as it can lead to new and unforeseen patterns of cause and effect, and perhaps to consideration of new variables. As Judith Green observed: 'The key to developing rigorous and valid theory using the constant comparative method is the search for deviant cases ... A full report of qualitative analysis should account for deviant cases and how they have contributed to refining theory' (1998: 1065).

One of the first tasks you will have is to determine whether the 'negative case' really negates the explanation you have developed and the propositions that might come from that, or whether instead it shows that your explanation does not apply in all circumstances. Whatever it turns out to be, it will enrich your analysis (cf. Box 10.11).

When deviant cases are found through survey or experimental research, researchers often turn to qualitative methods to explore further data relating to these cases (Box 11.7). David Byrne described a process wherein he used SPSS (a statistical analysis package) to generate clusters or types within a large existing dataset, then qualitative comparative analysis (QCA) to establish causal pathways for each of those types, and NVivo to explore contradictory cases revealed by the initial runs of QCA – a process he described as something like 'a tool-based version of the hermeneutic circle' (Byrne, 2009b: 261). For the qualitative phase, as well as coding data, he noted the possibility of generating attribute-style measures to attach to cases, through the process of engagement with the data. In qualitative software tools, attributes of cases do not have to be predetermined and fixed, but can be created 'on the fly' as their relevance becomes apparent. These can then be fed back into the QCA as new or refined variables for the causal analyses.

⌐ Box 11.7 ⌐

Using qualitative methods to explore a case not meeting quantitative predictions

In a longitudinal study of processes by which educational leadership impacts school effectiveness, Teddlie and Stringfield (1993) predicted that schools would maintain their effectiveness status over a five-year period between the third and fourth waves of data collection. What the researchers found was that about half of the schools either improved or declined during the five years, and that one school stood out with regard to its improvement on measures of student achievement and teacher behaviour, such as time on task (a classroom management score), despite being from an area of poor socioeconomic status with predicted low performance. The researchers then employed a qualitative case study approach to explain their quantitative results. What they found was that a new principal had been appointed during the interim period, and when they explored his actions, they found that he had recruited new, high-calibre teachers for the school; that he regularly monitored each classroom by making frequent, unscheduled, short visits – a process that gave him good knowledge of the strengths and weaknesses of his teachers; that he then focused personal assistance and professional development to redress any weaknesses; and that he actively managed instructional time by allocating and enforcing the academic schedule. Case analysis had revealed the cause of the anomaly in the statistical prediction.

Theoretical development and integration in grounded theory

Already, the idea of thinking in terms of Strauss' coding paradigm is familiar to you, as a way of relating structure to process for the phenomenon you are studying (cf. Chapters 6, 8, and 10). Processes can be complex and fluid, constantly varying in response to changes in structural conditions, including the differing perspectives of different actors. Something that is a condition in one setting might be a consequence in another; or a consequence becomes a condition for the next phase in the process.[6] For example, misadventure or negligence during surgery will have consequences that vary in severity. These then prompt a range of possible responses in the patient, with the mode of the patient's reaction then becoming the condition for whether they seek legal redress, receive other forms of help, or just get on with their life.

Conditions creating the variation in a process range from the micro (e.g., interactions with significant others) to the macro (e.g., world events). Corbin and Strauss (2008) employed the idea of a conditional matrix as a prompt to consider not just the immediate circumstances surrounding an action, but also the wider setting. In her study of Vietnam veterans, Corbin (in Corbin & Strauss, 2008) considered the growth of American involvement in Vietnam to the point where it became an American war, and the impact on returned soldiers of the changing mood of people at home regarding Vietnam and those who went there. Processes can be studied at any level of the conditional matrix.[7]

Through your constant working back and forth through your data, one or two ideas are likely to assume prominence in your thinking about what is going on in your data – but you may not yet be satisfied that those ideas sufficiently explain or integrate all that you have been seeing in your data. Maybe you never will: not all grounded theorists subscribe to the idea that a single core variable will, or should, be found to 'explain' all of the infinite variety that exists in your data. There are differences among grounded theorists, as well, on the issue of whether the core, integrative category should be a 'basic social process' (expressed as a gerund, i.e., a noun derived from a verb and ending in 'ing'; e.g., Glaser, 2002) or whether it might alternatively be a phenomenon (a main idea) that incorporates a process (or processes). In her study of Vietnam veterans, Corbin wasn't satisfied that 'surviving' adequately described what she was seeing in her veterans' data because they were too oriented to physical survival (Corbin & Strauss, 2008: 266). After reviewing earlier memos and further thought, she found an earlier concept of 'survival: reconciling multiple realities'

---

[6]This is why you are advised *not* to structure your coding on the basis of whether you are seeing something as a condition, process, or consequence, but rather to classify codes according to the type of content they represent, using other tools to show theoretical relationships between them.

[7]Although the conditional matrix has been a feature of all versions of these authors' accounts of developing a grounded theory, it is rarely a feature of studies purporting to be based on their methodology.

that allowed her to 'bring out the physical, psychological, social and moral problems inherent in war and the ways that persons respond to these both during and after returning from war' (Figure 11.4).

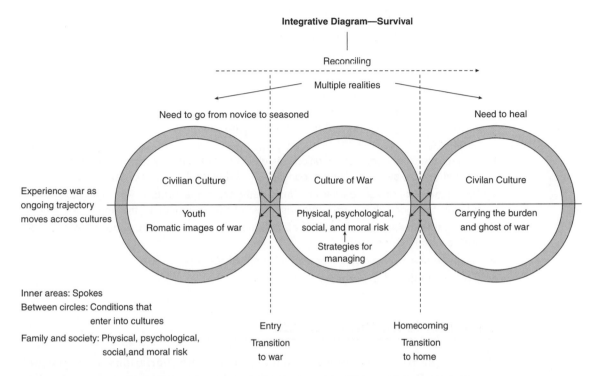

Integrative Diagram—Survival

Reconciling

Multiple realities

Need to go from novice to seasoned   Need to heal

Civilian Culture   Culture of War   Civilan Culture

Experience war as ongoing trajectory moves across cultures

Youth Romatic images of war   Physical, psychological, social, and moral risk   Carrying the burden and ghost of war

Strategies for managing

Inner areas: Spokes
Between circles: Conditions that
            enter into cultures
Family and society: Physical, psychological,
           social,and moral risk

Entry   Homecoming
Transition   Transition
to war   to home

Figure 11.4   Corbin's integrated model of 'Survival: reconciling multiple realities' for Vietnam veterans

Source: Corbin and Strauss, 2008: 271, Figure 12.1

How can you reach this point of recognising (or constructing) an integrative (core) category or process? The following suggestions are adapted from those listed by Corbin and Strauss (Chapters 5 and 12):

▶ Write the storyline – 'what seems to be going on here' – just from what you already 'know' from your data. If necessary, reread quickly through a few interviews or your case summaries, identifying the main issue raised by each.

▶ Your central or core category will be an abstract concept that best 'ties together' all these issues. You can relate all your other important concepts and categories to it in some way.

▶ If this is not a category that you have been directly coding to (which is quite possible), then test its explanatory relevance across each of your cases.

▶ Use diagrams to help focus your ideas about the relationships between categories.

▶ Record what you do at each step in long, thoughtful memos: 'running logs of analytic thinking'. Create links between your thoughts and the data that prompted them.

✓ If you have more than one possible core category, decide on one for the present, and work with that (put the other into the 'next paper' or 'next project' box).

Having identified a core category around which you can integrate your analysis, the next steps involve seeing how other categories link to it:

▶ Specify the dimensions of that category (the elements within it that can vary) and where it sits in relation to each of those (its 'properties').

▶ What are the processes (or subprocesses) embedded within it? These might be the actions, strategies, interactions, and/or emotions that are associated with that category.

▶ Perhaps there are particular conditions attached to it? Or different dimensions of the process will come into play under different conditions? And these will have consequences ...

▶ Telling the story of your data via the main category is one strategy for helping to see how other categories link in, and serves as a test of the adequacy of that main category.

▶ Having told the story and established a framework, check for gaps and inconsistencies, and rework if necessary.

▶ Fill in the descriptive details for each element of the story.

▶ Create a model of the process.

Visual tools for theory building

Visual tools for theory building include, once again, variations on matrix displays, and diagrammatic displays such as flow charts, causal networks, and timelines. As always, the effort of putting data into a visual form both requires and ensures thorough knowledge of the data and understanding of the issues.

Patton's process/outcomes matrix for prompting causal reflection

Patton described creating cross-classification matrices as 'an exercise in logic'. 'The logical process involves creating potential categories by crossing one dimension or typology with another, and then working back and forth between the data and one's logical constructions, filling in the resulting matrix' (2002: 468). This matrix doesn't directly provide you with 'answers'; rather, in the process of filling the cells in the matrix you are prompted to consider causal possibilities, and then to review your data to see if in fact there is any evidence to support each possible cause–effect configuration. Table 11.2 is a partial 'mockup' example of such a matrix, in the context of research activity. (You will need to allow for much more space than I can afford here.)

Table 11.2 Matrix of linkages between processes and outcomes

Processes	Impacts observed in:		
	Engagement in research	Productivity from research	Work with students
Involvement in collaborative/team projects	Stimulus to learning for those who took commitment seriously: *What is absolutely clear about that is that it was done in a team ... they may well have been consciously mentoring but really it was a very cooperative supportive, coming into a team, and it helped me enormously ... So I would say I got started in research by being in with a very supportive team.*	Help through slow periods: *You need someone to bounce ideas off, and to keep you spurred on...* Combining skills: *So I then teamed up quite soon with another 'young turk'. ... we were young and single and just really went for it. We ended up in a space of – after our first year we would have had about 10 papers on the go, after 2–3 years.*	From a student who worked on projects with his supervisor: *Having a mentor with whom to collaborate, one learns much more about the research process than is possible working alone.* From an academic: *There's just nothing nicer than a lab full of eager students you know and you banter and you joke but all the time you're also working towards this research goal.*
Allocation of block time to allow immersion	Experienced researchers group observation notes: spoke extensively about the value of a period of immersion in their research, where they were fully absorbed with data/analysis, and of the consequences of that – especially when they were a full-time research student or had study leave: *Study leave is when you get the muse back – for at least six months.* Market researchers – no time for developing ideas or quality → frustration	Time needed to develop ideas: *It takes time for a project to reach a critical point. All things take time. And any scientist or any person in research needs to give it time and not to be impatient. If you want to do something worthwhile it takes time.* Time needed to write: *... and a lot of people don't realise, when you're writing a book about your research, that you take two or three years before it comes up, they think it is just 'a drop of a hat'.*	...
Training provided for skills development	...	...	
Apply pressure through promotions system	...		etc.

Source: design based or Patton, 2002: 474, Exhibit 8.11

▶ Create a matrix in which you put processes (actions) in the rows, and list types or some other dimension of outcomes across the columns. Processes might include the implementation inputs for an evaluation project, or processes identified through coding. Outcomes could be different types of changes seen (or expected) as a result of those processes, changes observed at different time points, or impacts at different levels (e.g., individual, group, institutional). Deciding how to frame the matrix – how to define the rows and columns – is an important part of the exercise.

▶ Each cell generates a data analysis question, and so the next task is to draw on your data and your memos to fill in the cells using summaries and illustrative quotes which explain or elaborate on each specific linkage, and to interpret the strength of the connections (some cells may remain empty).

Explanatory effects matrices

Miles and Huberman (1994) developed an array of matrices designed to tap into causal processes and outcomes, for their various innovation projects. These are summarised in Table 11.3, and illustrated with excerpts from some of their examples in Figures 11.5–11.7. They can be prepared on paper, in a Word table, in Excel, or by creating a framework matrix in NVivo. Some, like Patton's matrix in Table 11.2, send you hunting through your data to find answers; others have you laying out data in a way that will help you to see patterns. If you are using QDA software, employ the query functions in the software to locate data and explore the relationships between factors, using both intersection (AND) and proximity (NEAR) operators. Additionally, creating a case-by-variable (coded category) matrix using QDA software is a straightforward and effective way of considering outcome and predictor factors together (Figure 11.8). You may be able to summarise cell content from matrices produced in the software as suggested in Chapter 9, or alternatively run a series of simpler queries or case comparison matrices and amalgamate the results in your own tables.[8]

In many ways, these matrices are similar to those you encountered in Chapters 9 and 10, where you set things out in order to discern contrasts and patterns. The main difference here is that you are doing so with an explicitly explanatory purpose – and this will influence both the kinds of things you put into the matrices and the way you lay them out, particularly the ordering of the rows in case-based matrices. The idea is that from these matrices you should be able to move on to build causal models and also make predictions – and then test those by referring back to your data.

---

[8]Ordered case comparison tables containing summaries for key themes are the basis for Framework Analysis, a strategy described in detail by Ritchie and Spencer (1994) that is now supported by a dedicated tool within NVivo.

Table 11.3 Miles and Huberman's explanatory and predictive matrices

Type	Data tabulated	Construction notes	Value for analysis	Limitations
Within-case analyses				
Explanatory effects matrix (Figure 11.5)	Tabulate inputs as seen by users; the user's assessment of the value (importance) of those inputs; the effects of those inputs; with an additional column for the researcher's comments and explanation	Separate row for each response from a participant or participant group	First impressions of causal mechanisms from participant perspective	Doesn't reflect complexity because each participant or group is in a separate row
Case dynamics matrix (Figure 11.6)	Tabulate issues, strains, dilemmas arising in the situation; researcher labelling (abstraction) of the underlying issue, observed response strategies, and eventual resolution or outcomes	Separate row for each issue Add a rating for type or success of outcome	Identify dynamics for each issue; see patterns in issues and types of solutions	Doesn't cover 'non-issues' or positives. Heavily inferential, so keep checking back to notes and data
Cross-case displays (understand the dynamics of each case first!)				
Case-ordered effects matrix	Tabulate cases sorted by degrees of major causal factor; aspects of the causal factor relevant to the case; types of effects or outcomes, e.g., short or long term; who or what was affected; or more specific outcome categories	Order of cases is critical for visual interpretation	Can cope with diversity of effects – provide leads for theory building and testing. Can identify deviant cases	Can be very complex – need to create summary tables from larger display. More descriptive than explanatory
Case-ordered predictor–outcome matrix (Figure 11.7)	Tabulate cases sorted according to an outcome; add data for each case on main antecedent factors that might have contributed to the outcome. Select predictors on logical or theoretical or empirical grounds	Cases in rows. Scale outcomes and predictors (on basis of clear rules applied to indicators)	Using comparison to assess relationships between predictors and outcomes	Lack of variation in some scales; choice of predictors
Predictor–outcome consequences matrix	As above, including relevant predictors for the intermediate outcome, and then adding in consequences of the intermediate outcomes (a three-step matrix)	Previous outcome becomes intermediate predictor	Starting to build a causal chain, understand mechanisms	

Location	User's Assessment	[Ongoing Assistance] Types Provided	Short-run effects ("state" of users)	Longer-run consequences (able/unable to do)	Researcher Explanation
Peer Users	+	Helped w/planning Gave ideas, sugg'ns Gave encouragement	How it could work Filled in gaps Not alone; there's help	Strong users of the off-campus program; they know how to do it	One user was experienced in this approach and brought others up to speed

Figure 11.5   Explanatory effects matrix: ongoing assistance

Source: Miles & Huberman, 1994: 149, Box 6.2 (one row of five)

Strains, difficulties created	Underlying issues (as seen by researcher)	How coped with	How resolved: type of resulting change
Conflicting expectations: should parents or teachers do activities?	Work load. Parent-teacher role conflict.	"Explaining" that teachers could not take primary responsibility for out-of-school activities.	Increased use of "batched" activities, many set up by coordinator. (Procedural change)

Figure 11.6   Case dynamics matrix: innovation as a force for organisational change

Source: Miles & Huberman, 1994: 150, Table 6.1 (one row of six)

Creating a conditional matrix using software

Let's say you have identified a range of conditions under which a core process might become evident, and you have also identified a range of consequences potentially resulting from that process. Assuming you have data simultaneously coded for all three elements – under what condition, what process (action, strategy, interaction) has what consequences – then you could create a conditional matrix with conditions on one axis and consequences on the other, and with the text in the cells restricted to material coded at that core process. The text within each cell, then, would show if that process ever did create a link between a particular condition and a specified consequence, and it would show how that process operated under those circumstances (what its properties were at that time).

Realistically, your coding is likely to not be so thorough as to allow you to do that effectively without suddenly having to do a lot of catch-up coding (i.e., the cells are mostly empty)! Creating the matrix that puts conditions together with consequences, on an unrestricted basis, could then be a worthwhile, more exploratory exercise to try. The overall patterning of 'hits' in the matrix is no longer meaningful in terms of a single core process, but you can learn a great

Ease of early use,[a] by sites	Commitment			Understanding			Resources/ Material	Skills	Training
	Users	Building Principal	Central Office Admin.	Users	Building Principal	Central Office Admin.			
Smooth early use									
Astoria (E)	√√	√√	√√	√√	√√	√√	√√	√√	√
Burton (E)	√	√	√√F	√	0	√√F	√√F	√	√√
Mostly smooth									
Lido (E)	<u>√√</u>F	√√	?	√	√	0	√√F	√	√√
Mixed[b]									
Calston (E)	√√	√√	√√F	√	√	√√	0B	√F	√√
Perry-Parkdale (E)	√√F	0	√√	√√	0	√√	√√	√B	√√
Rough									
–Banestown (E)	√√F	<u>√</u>	√√F	√	0	√	√B	√B	√B
–Masepa (E)	√√	√	√√F	0B	0	√	0B	0B	√
Carson (L)	√√F	√√F	√√	√B	<u>√</u>	√	√	√B	√B
Dun Hollow (L)	√	√	√	√√	√√	√√	√B	√√F	√
–Plummet (L)	√√F	√√F	√√	<u>√</u>	√B	√	√B	√F	0
–Provile (L)	√B	√B	√F	<u>√</u>	√	(√)B	<u>√</u>	√	√
Tindale (L)	0B	√√F	√√F/B	<u>√</u>	√√	√	<u>√√</u>F/B	√	√√

(E) externally developed innovation
(L) locally developed innovation

[a] field researcher judgement from users' responses and/or from observation of practice in use
[b] smooth for some users, rough for others
<u>underline</u> signifies field researcher estimate that factor was decisive in affecting ease of early use

F= factor facilitated early use
B= factor was barrier to successful early use
√√ fully in place
√ partly in place
0 mostly absent, missing
? missing data

Figure 11.7   Case-ordered predictor–outcome matrix: degree of preparedness as related to ease of early implementation

Source: Miles & Huberman, 1994: 214, Table 8.5 (partial)

Note: this matrix surprisingly showed that preparedness did not appear to be a key factor in ease of early implementation of the programme, although some preparedness conditions mattered more than others. Many of the factors were considered unimportant for many of the cases (indicated by lack of underline), suggesting additional or alternative predictors were at work. This took the researchers back to the case reports where they identified five alternative factors to consider, not related to preparedness. What this additional analysis showed was that the 'smooth' sites were making much less substantial changes than the 'rough' sites, and with a high degree of latitude for change; under these conditions (small changes, high latitude), preparation was not as critical as it was for those sites making major changes with variable degrees of latitude.

Matrix Coding Query - Results Prev	challenge	intellectual stimula...	satisfaction
Andrew	0	1	0
Beverly	1	0	0
F3	0	1	0
Jill	0	0	0
Karen	0	0	0
Margaret	0	0	0
Sandy	1	0	0
Simon	1	0	0
Stephen	0	1	0
Elizabeth	1	0	1
Frank	1	1	1
Ange	1	0	1
David	1	1	1
F1	1	1	1
F2	0	0	1
James	1	1	1
Joseph	1	1	1
Paul	1	1	1
Rachel	0	1	1
Jeanette	1	0	1
Kristie	1	1	1
Shane	1	0	1
Stuart	1	1	1
Susan	1	1	1

Figure 11.8   Case-ordered predictor–outcome matrix using NVivo

Note: the numerical pattern in this matrix suggests a strong link between experiencing challenge and/ or stimulation through research and satisfaction, the assumption being that experiencing satisfaction through research will then prompt greater engagement in research. The next step in checking this association would be to look at the text in the cells to confirm whether that linkage is evident in the text, and to investigate what is being said in those cases where one is present without the other.

deal from the text in the cells about which processes are more critical than others in explaining the links between conditions and outcomes (Box 11.8). Perhaps these processes are embedded within a more embracing core category?

Alternatively (or as well), you could run a matrix that tabulated the dimensions of a process with outcomes (consequences), and when reviewing the content of the cells, check the text for relevant conditions (use coding stripes showing conditions to help).

Or ... come up with your own variations using the matrix-building feature of your software. Schatzman (1991), for example, would add 'perspective' to the explanatory equation, pointing out that if you were selecting a job from a moral or ethical perspective rather than an economic survival perspective, you would be more interested in a workplace with a compatible philosophy than in one that offered higher pay.

Box 11.8

Using software to create a conditional matrix

In the matrix in Figure 11.9, text coded with environmental conditions mentioned by researchers has been intersected (in the Boolean sense) with outcomes – showing if and when those conditions were

	A : motivation	B : falling awa...	A : motivation	B : falling awa...
1 : autonomy	2	2	1	0
2 : competing demands	1	2	0	0
3 : competitive	0	1	0	0
4 : encouraging-supportive	10	2	6	0
5 : funding	2	1	1	0
6 : insecurity	0	4	0	3
7 : opportunity	0	3	0	2
8 : role model	2	0	0	0
9 : serendipity	2	0	2	0
10 : time issues	5	6	2	1
11 : working conditions-d...	10	15	3	7

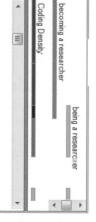

Ange

I think the PhD process is important for that one--the indulgence of--if you're lucky to receive a scholarship, to be paid to *read* for three years and to design the project you want to do, the way you want to.

David

I agree, and it occurs to me it never comes again. I can remember those three years, doing it full time, even though you're living on the smell of an oily rag, it was--it never came again, you know what I mean. It was always then dividing your week up and looking for the day at home so you could read newspapers or whatever, and microfilm in my case. Unless I have the day at home, I'm absorbed utterly in running the great big competition machine the university now is. So yes, it never comes again.

Reference 2 - 0.18% Coverage

So SDL is research as well, it's when you get the muse back--for at least six months.

Figure 11.9   Conditional matrix showing the relationship between environmental factors and engagement in research using NVivo

(Continued)

(Continued)

motivating or discouraging to the researcher. The two columns in the middle show 'hits' across all data; the two columns on the right show only those data which are coded also at *becoming a researcher* (i.e., excluding any coded at *being* a researcher). Examination of the text in the cells revealed:

- the centrality of *being encouraged* by others in the processes of taking up and persisting in researching (evident across multiple conditions, i.e., not just in the row labelled 'encouraging');
- the importance of opportunity (time) to become *totally immersed* in the research project, such as during a full-time PhD period; and
- the *pressured insecurity* that comes about through restricted access to time and funding – primarily for established researchers, but where these created doubts for some beginning researchers, it led to their giving up on the idea of a research career.

Creating causal networks and flow charts

Causal networks show directional relationships between elements (objects; phenomena; variables) in the situation you are studying. When they are combined with text that tells the story of the linkages, you will move toward an explanation of what happened. As always, reducing a series of events to a diagram with directional linkages forces you to evaluate each of the elements of what happened, and how each impacted on each other element. To a considerable extent, building causal networks will draw on what you have learned through puzzle solving and the matrix analyses you have done already.

Guidelines for construction (see Figures 11.10 and 11.11 for examples):[9]

- ▶ Base your causal networks on data, not background theory.
- ▶ Start with a critical event, key concept, or social process, and build around it.
- ▶ Build in fragments of theory already recorded in diagrams or memos.
- ▶ Draw on timelines and earlier time-based analyses to help you get things in order; causal networks assume temporal relationships.
- ▶ As you become increasingly familiar with your data, develop causal hunches: 'If this has happened, it must have been because ....'

---

[9]These guidelines assume 'hand-drawn' construction. Note the similarity in Figure 11.11 to the computer-generated causal map that was produced using Ethno, shown in Figure 11.2.

▶ Ask what had to come before what, or what followed from what, in order to establish a sequence of causal and consequential steps. Make sure there are no missing steps.

▶ Check for alternative pathways and loops (e.g., Figure 11.10): did everyone follow the same route?

▶ Whether you start with a basic model which you modify or build one 'from scratch', progressively modify and refine your causal map throughout the project.

▶ Are there gaps in your model? Return to your data, or seek out additional data.

▶ Do you have data to support each linkage you have drawn? If not, can you get it?

▶ Always add explanatory text to give meaning and added detail to the connections. This will help you ensure that the model is coherent and comprehensive (modify it as needed).

▶ Make predictions from your causal models, and then (if possible) gather (post-project?) data to test those predictions, preferably data of a non-intrusive form. For example, did a change become institutionalised? Was the new researcher who experienced mentoring, skills development, and time to work on a project still engaged in research two years later?

Background factors: School governance
                     Policy environment; economic environment
                     Funding
                     Community and neighbourhood

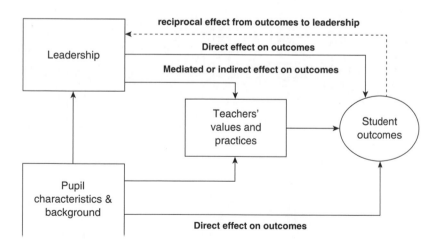

Figure 11.10   A simplified causal model of educational leadership with its direct, indirect, and reciprocal effects on student outcomes

Source: Levačić, 2005: 201, Figure 1

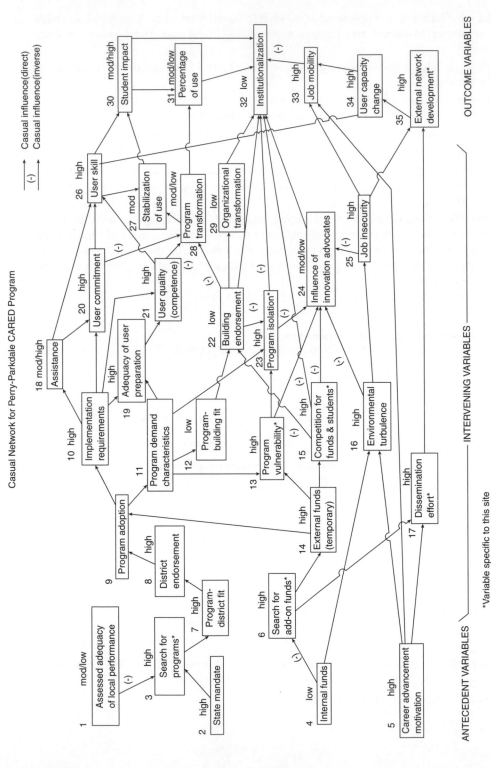

Figure 11.11 Example of a complex, comprehensive causal model

Source: Miles and Huberman, 1994: 154, Figure 6.1

✓ Don't try to draw a complete causal network too early in the project or it will drive your interpretation of new data. Be content with fragments until you have considered variations in the phenomenon and in experience of it.

✓ Have colleagues (and possibly some participants) check your diagram: can they interpret it?

Writing about your developing theory

In the methods chapter

▶ Identify the general approach and the kinds of steps taken in establishing linkages and processes from your data (as for relational analyses).

▶ Explain the logic that underpins your methods of theory development. For example, indicate whether you are creating a deterministic model or one that suggests probable causal pathways, and the extent to which you worked deductively, inductively, abductively, or retroductively (illustrate to clarify if necessary).

▶ Indicate the relative roles played by background theory and your data in deriving your theoretical conclusions.

In the results chapter

▶ Explain the theoretical conclusions you have reached, showing the progressive steps through your data that took you to your conclusions. Illustrate with selected tables and models, ensuring that there is adequate explanation accompanying these.

✓ Depending on your disciplinary background, presentation of theoretical propositions can range from their being explicitly stated, for example as hypotheses, through to their being woven into a narrative.

Further reading

Maxwell (2012: Chapter 3) presents a critical realist understanding of causality and the essential role of context and individual belief, values, motives, and meanings as explanations for events. Alternatively, see Maxwell (2004) or Maxwell and Mittapalli (2010).

Danermark, Ekström, Jakobsen, and Karlsson (2002: Chapter 4, 'Generalization, scientific inference and models for an explanatory social science') explain how critical realism impacts on methodology in the social sciences. They include a detailed outline of the four paths to drawing inferences.

C. Wright Mills (1959), in *The sociological imagination*, critiques grand theory and 'abstracted empiricism'.

Reichertz (2010) establishes a view of grounded theory based on abductive logic, linking back to Charles Sanders Pierce.

Miles and Huberman (1994: Chapters 6 and 8) cover within-case and across-case displays for predicting and explaining causal patterns.

Bergene (2007) reviews case-based comparative methods from a critical realist perspective, arguing for iterative case studies that combine detailed within-case analysis with comparative analysis.

Griffin (1993) uses Ethno in a social-historical causal analysis of events surrounding the lynching of an African-American following an argument in which he killed a white tenant farmer in Mississippi in 1930.

Rihoux and Ragin (2009) provide a comprehensive guide to all forms of qualitative comparative analysis (QCA).

Lee (2011) explains how fuzzy sets work and reviews three studies on welfare reform that were conducted using fsQCA.

12

Developing coherent understanding

You are nearing the end of a long road. As you draw near to your destination your pace quickens a little, and yet at times the end still seems so far away. Critical insights and critical decisions are needed to sharpen the focus of your work, and to bring it to a coherent conclusion where data, methods, and product all 'dance to the same tune'; with arguments and evidence drawn together to support the critical 'take home message' or thesis you wish to present.

In this chapter you will find:

- guidelines to help you clarify your focus;
- guidelines for making use of rich, interpretive description;
- strategies to integrate your theoretical understanding;
- a range of models that integrate and convey a key understanding;
- tips and tricks for bringing it together.

Even while you are putting it all together, you are still refining your analysis.

Coherent understanding?

Coherence: clear, comprehensible, articulate, lucid, rational, sound, logical, consistent, reasoned; logically or aesthetically consistent and fitting together as a harmonious or credible whole (Encarta Dictionary, 2010). That sounds like an appropriate goal for your writing about your work!

You planned for coherence in design when you began your project (cf. Chapter 2). Now it's time to consider how you might create the kind of coherent conclusions and presentation that will do justice to your research, your topic, your participants – and convince others of the value of your work. This coherence will, in the first instance, be found in the goals you set for your work.

▶ This is the time to revisit your vision of what you were hoping to achieve, your original purpose statement, and the questions that flowed from that.

▶ If you have moved on, then map out carefully how things have changed, and why. The chances are that your project has taken you into paths never considered at the outset.

▶ Work from that to develop a renewed vision of what your project might achieve, and what questions you can answer. (It is likely that your specific questions will have changed more than your overall purpose.)

▶ From that, think through to the form your findings might take to answer those questions and meet your purpose, and use that to guide you in bringing everything together.

There are times when you think it will never come together

You're drowning in data, codes, stories, maps, and matrices, with memos everywhere – will you ever have a coherent story to tell?

> In many ways, this is like having a large set of building blocks, and experimenting with the different ways their form and structure enable and constrain what you are capable of constructing. (Thorne, 2008: 167)

Persistence and immersion are the keys to the process here:

▶ Review your memos for consistent ideas, themes, and concepts flowing through them.

▶ Tell someone about your project, perhaps making a recording as you do. Gradually you will be able to tell it in three or five minutes rather than an hour (quite a few theses have 'come together' over my kitchen bench, as dinner was being prepared).

▶ Explore existing substantive and general theory for unifying ideas.

▶ If you have developed an explanatory theory or core concept, focus other concepts and elements of what you have found around that; if they don't fit, work on resolving the contradictions; if they don't belong, edit them out and save them for another day.

There is more than one type of what 'together' is

This book has had an academic orientation with a consequent bias toward theory building, but not all projects will conclude with a neat theoretical statement that encapsulates the core of everything you have found. This is particularly so for non-thesis projects, for projects that have a more practice oriented or professional focus, or for projects that are simply exploratory, designed to 'suss out' the field in preparation for a further phase of work. Perhaps, from your data-driven research, you have written a novel or created a performance that will convey an important message or provide an insightful interpretation of some aspect of the human condition? A report for a sponsoring body or for public consumption will be constructed differently from an academic paper or dissertation based on the same project. Even where you do end up with a central process or concept to frame your work around, there will likely be 'ifs and buts' – divergences, differences, and variations that you need to explain.

> When you emphasise description, you want your reader to see what you saw. When you emphasize analysis, you want your reader to know what you know. When you emphasize interpretation, you want your reader to understand what you yourself have understood. In different ratios, for different purposes, we try to accomplish all three. (Wolcott, 1994: 412)

I would argue, however, that even if your primary goal is largely achieved with description it is useful to go beyond that.[1] Lyn Richards (2009: 135) likened raw description to describing the scene of a crime without trying to solve the crime. For example, if you have been funded to identify how people have responded to a new development in housing styles, think about how those people understand housing, or 'home', and its relationship to family and security. Then you could identify some principles that would guide future innovative housing developments, and so on. Don't just summarise your data, or think that it is sufficient to 'allow your participants to speak'.

There is likely to be more than one 'together' from any project

What is the main message you want to come out of your research? Is it the same for all purposes and all stakeholders? A paper generally should be written around a single 'take-home message'; a dissertation will necessarily be more complex, although it is typically putting forward a central thesis that brings together the work you have done. There have been quite a few occasions when I have sat down with a late-candidacy doctoral student to help sort out which thesis he or she wants to write out of three or four equally plausible possibilities. The questions you face now, therefore, are:

- What is most important for now, and what can be put off for the next report, paper, or project?
- What can you realistically achieve with the time and resources at your disposal?

Setting aside some of what you have found does not mean you have wasted effort (as if learning through experience can ever be wasted effort); you will be able to make opportunities to present each of those other ideas in other forums, or you will develop them through further research, or perhaps you will have students who can take up one or other of the issues you have raised. When Lynn Kemp (cf. Box 10.10;) interviewed her participants with a spinal injury, they didn't just talk about community services (the focus of her project), they also discussed at length issues around personal relationships, employment, further education, and leisure and recreation. These 'chunks' of data became an ideal base for student projects in an environment where she was no longer able to dedicate the necessary time to develop them herself.

---

[1]Going the 'extra mile' has two important consequences: (1) you will be offered further contracts or opportunities to conduct research; (2) if you are in the 'game' of applying for (university-based) research grants, you will need to have produced theoretically oriented papers from your commercial contract projects to convince the assessors of those applications that you are capable of doing so, and that what you want to achieve in the new project cannot be met through contract research (Bazeley, 1998).

What will be sufficient?

Lyn Richards has observed that a satisfactory outcome offers more than your participants could have reported. In *Handling qualitative data* (2009: 146), she suggests five signs of sufficiency for an analysis:

- simplicity – a 'small polished gem of a theory, not a mere pebble of truism' that reflects what you have learned from your data;
- elegance and balance – well-crafted, grounded in data, and coherent;
- completeness – it explains all: 'nothing is left sticking out, unconsidered or unexplained';
- robustness – it doesn't fall over with new data; and
- it makes sense to relevant audiences (even if they disagree).

I have a Welsh Springer Spaniel dog. When he was younger, it was fascinating to watch him cross a field. He would course back and forth in what appeared to be a very indirect route until he picked up a scent: his brain made the connection with rabbit, and so then he would move rapidly and directly in line with that scent. Coherence and sufficiency require that, having moved along a tortuous and uncertain path until you have found the scent, you make the connections and you are then able to progress directly to the goal.

Coherence through description

Description has been written about earlier as a tool for analysis. The focus now shifts to ways to generate description, based on analysis, that will be useful in your study and ultimately for your audience. Description continues to have benefits for deeper analysis, in so far as the exercise of recording the detail of events and experiences always prompts further reflective thought and interpretation. It is also, for many, a good place to start because it is 'doable'.

To a greater or lesser extent, descriptive writing will always have a place in the record of a study and may indeed be the primary component of the final product – if that is what best suits the purpose of the study (Sandelowski, 2000; Stake, 1995). As noted by Wolcott:

> Description provides the foundation upon which qualitative inquiry rests. Unless you prove to be gifted at conceptualizing or theorizing, the descriptive account will usually constitute the major contribution you have to make. The more solid the descriptive basis, the more likely it will survive changing fads and fashions in reporting or changing emphases in how we derive meaning from our studies. Give your account a firm footing in description. (2009: 27)

There are wide differences of opinion expressed in the literature, however, regarding the issue of whether descriptive reporting from data constitutes 'research'. Atkinson is one who

> want[s] to insist that data should be analysed, and not just reproduced and celebrated (as sometimes happens with life-histories, and some visual materials) … Consequently, there

is too much social research that collects, reproduces and celebrates individual 'stories', without grounding them in a sustained analysis of their forms and functions. (2005: 11)

What role then should description play in a research report? When and how can it be useful? There would be few who would argue with Wolcott's directive to 'start with a straightforward description of the setting and events' (2009: 27) – as outlined below. It is the use of a descriptive style of reporting as a major vehicle of communication that is more contentious. Descriptive reporting has been justified as a legitimate outcome of research:

- when it provides straightforward answers to practical questions for practitioners and policy makers (Sandelowski, 2000; Thorne, 2008); or
- when it presents sufficiently detailed information to allow listeners and readers to understand an experience 'as it really is' and to draw their own meanings and significance (Colaizzi, 1978; Patton, 2002; Stake, 1995).[2]

As ethnographers, Emerson et al. seek 'to use and balance this tension between analytic propositions and local meanings' (1995: 170) by producing a narrative that incorporates analytic themes or concepts but presents them through data-centred 'tales' that will interest an outside audience.[3] The 'persuasive force' of ethnographic writing derives from an 'interplay of concrete exemplification and discursive commentary' (Atkinson, 1990: 103). Even if your task is a practical evaluation or synthesis, Pawson (2006) argues it should comprise a theoretical component, and Smith et al. (2009) suggest that writing an *interpretive* phenomenological analysis involves interweaving analytic commentary with the raw extracts that are included as evidence.

Situating the study

Description of the context, sample, and cases for the study is an important *preliminary* step to complete for analysis, so that both analyst and reader can make sense of and position the results of the study.

Begin your account by outlining the physical, social, organisational, political, historical, religious, and/or cultural context in which the study occurred, so that the reader can 'locate' the study. Within that broader context, note how unique or representative were the particular people, objects, or places studied. Then focus on the events and actions you will be writing about, any aspects that are relevant to your

---

[2]This raises the issue of whether 'drawing meaning and significance' is the job of the researcher or the reader. There is a danger that this approach can degenerate into the presentation of 'undigested' data as a form of final report.

[3]See Barbara Tedlock (2000) for a very comprehensive listing of ethnographic studies presented in a variety of non-traditional formats. Many of these have become classics in the field. Again, there is a danger that the inexperienced writer will focus on the tale and neglect the deeper analytic and theoretical content.

analyses. For example, these might include physical, socioeconomic, and service provision characteristics of the location where data were gathered in an evaluation of a community intervention; the design of the building, the structure of staff roles, and the characteristics of the target client group in a welfare service; or the philosophy of service and discursive practices surrounding welfare in that service. Much of this information will have been recorded during the processes of data gathering and early analysis (cf. Chapters 3 and 4), but other details will have been omitted; assumed knowledge and tacit understandings need to be made explicit.

You will, of course, also need to situate your study substantively (within the literature on your topic) and theoretically, if your data and analyses are to contribute to a broader understanding of the knowledge and issues covered by them.

Rich description

The expression 'thick description' is frequently quoted in writing about qualitative analysis. The term originated with Gilbert Ryle (1971), who had used it in presenting his theory of mind to demonstrate that mental processes (mind) were evidenced in behaviour, rather than being a separate entity. Ryle's example, taken up and extended by the anthropologist Clifford Geertz (1973), was to consider the meaning of briefly closing one eye. This could simply be the result of a tic, or it could be a wink that is communicating a secret understanding, or perhaps it is an observer who is parodying someone else's wink. Because the description of an action needs contextual information and an explanation of the cultural significance (signified intentions and meanings) of the action for it to convey meaning, Geertz argued that thick description was an essential element of ethnographic research.

Denzin added a constructivist perspective to the term, part of the trend to see thick description as having an inherent interpretive purpose:

> A thick description does more than record what a person is doing. It goes beyond mere fact and surface appearances. It presents detail, context, emotion, and the webs of social relationships that join persons to one another. The description evokes emotionality and self-feelings. It inserts history into experience. It establishes the significance of an experience or the sequence of events, for the person or persons in question. In thick description the voices, feelings, actions, and meanings of interacting individuals are heard ... *It contains the necessary ingredients for thick interpretation.* (1989: 83, emphasis added)

Current popularised use of the term has extended it to broadly cover any kind of description that is reasonably detailed. 'How much description is enough to earn the accolade of "thick description"?' asks Harry Wolcott (2009: 94). 'How much context is enough to make a study "contextual"? To avoid being shallow, how deeply must we delve to present a case "in depth"?' Some classical anthropological works and ethnographies comprise very detailed and full descriptions. Becker describes Agee and Evans' (1941) publication, *Let us now praise famous men*, about three tenant families during the depression, for example, as a masterpiece of 'minute, detailed description, the kind of description that lets you see how much summary, how much generalization, is contained in the most exhaustive social science descriptions' (1998: 80). Agee and Evans devoted 54 pages, supported by photographs, to describing a sharecropping family's four-roomed shack. Becker noted that while the incredible detail of that account allowed the reader the opportunity to do their own interpreting, in that instance, of the misery of lives lived in these surroundings, the danger is that 'full' description *can* become very trivial and boring. As an anthropologist friend of mine commented when we were discussing this issue, it is important to differentiate between thick description and flowery description. My choice to use the term 'rich' rather than 'thick' is threefold: to imply that description should incorporate a wealth of data-derived 'goodies' within it; to avoid perpetuating the misappropriation of the term that was used by Geertz to convey much more than common descriptive writing; and to avoid any connotation of its simply involving use of a lot of words.

Your ability to produce rich description will depend on your having recorded 'rich data' through long-term involvement, intensive interviews, and careful observation recorded in detailed field notes (Maxwell, 2013: 126). Box 12.2 shows how Leoni Degenhardt (cf. Box 2.10) drew on her journals, notes, transcripts, and literature to construct a richly detailed account of the process of implementing a new approach to learning within the school of which she was principal. Records made throughout the course of the study were essential to that construction.

Box 12.1

Drawing on field journals and other data to create rich description

Radical new pedagogy

In 1999 an external education consultant had made a significant impact on teachers (II08), helping them to see that students had different ways of learning. However, as discussed earlier, the 2000 student surveys identified that the school still catered more for dependent learners than for independent or collaborative learners. The 2001 strategy set the goal of developing Student Growth Plans [SGPs] for every student and, by 2002, the term 'radical new pedagogy' was in use. This was a contentious term, as the following comments illustrate:

> I think it's really interesting how in the first few weeks of my being here, I noticed … the word 'radical' came on … Are we radical? And there was a complete fluff … 'No, we mustn't use the word radical, we're not radical.' And it actually confronted something about the image of the place, you know we're [educating] the nice girls to marry nice boys, it wasn't that we wanted to be radical (laughter). (IF08)

(Continued)

(Continued)

There was ongoing and often heated discussion of the term 'radical' (J200303; IF08). Some HoDs[4] disliked the term, believing it contained an implied criticism of current teaching and learning, and so did the Implementation Team, who wanted to replace it with 'exciting' or 'innovative' in order not to scare staff. The Implementation Team considered that SGPs needed to be 'marketed' to staff, some of whom were experiencing anxiety and unrest about their jobs (J200303). Despite this, the leadership team determined that the term 'radical' would remain, and would be included in their advertisements for the inaugural Year 7 2004 team members, as the following quote from a member of the leadership team explains:

> It is honest to keep it in, as the change IS radical … If we remove the word, and yet speak about radical, it is a disconnect. (J200303)

By the following month, the angst about 'radical' seemed to have subsided, as this entry in the researcher journal indicates:

> We worked through the Year 7 Team member advertisement and conditions. The Implementation Team is now 'over' the radical issue … they see it as honest to describe the new ways with this word. It helped when they saw the article about the Australian Science and Mathematics School [an innovative school visited by the principal and some other staff] in Adelaide. (J200304)

'Radical new pedagogy' was more than incremental improvement but a profound change in what was taught, how it was taught and assessed, and in the relationships between teacher, learner, and parent. It implied several things:

1　a move away from teacher-directed to student-directed learning …
2　authentic learning …
3　a different approach to curriculum design …
4　incorporation of holistic elements.

[Each of these points was discussed in relation to changes at the school and supported by reference to data, theory, and literature.]

Source: Degenhardt, 2006: 163–4

Interpretive description

In so far as choices are made about what to include in a description, what to leave out, how to value different sources, and how to present material, all description is interpretive. Forms of expression chosen also convey a level of interpretation: for example, 'hurrying home' implies a motive not present in 'walking rapidly'; 'heated discussion' (Box 12.1) suggests a level of emotional involvement not present in 'debate'. Interpretation is particularly evident in reports of what was felt, and in meanings attributed to events or actions.

---

[4]Heads of departments.

Essentially, according to Wolcott (1994: 287), description becomes interpretive through 'mulling'. Build on intensive reading, interpretive memoing, coding, and summarising, and exploration of variations and cases that don't fit. Then cluster these ideas and understandings, sequence and weave them together into an overall account or story that goes beyond thematic reporting. Interpretive description includes the circumstances, meanings, intentions, strategies, and motivations of those who are the subject of the description (Schwandt, 2007: 296). Even with phenomenology, that most descriptive of methodologies, van Manen suggests that 'themes are only fasteners, foci, or threads around which the phenomenological description is facilitated' (1990: 91).

> Interpretive description requires an analytic form that extends beyond taking things apart and putting them back together again. It requires that we learn to see beyond the obvious, rigorously testing out that which we think we see, and taking some ownership over the potential meaning and impact of the visions that we eventually present as our findings. (Thorne, 2008: 142)

Thorne goes on to describe 'a good thematic description' as being distinct from a topical summary in so far as it reflects an overall organising structure, so that the description is a part of a new conceptualisation of the issues being researched. It is *'ordered and organized to reveal aspects that would have been obscured through any other presentation framework'* (2008: 173, emphasis added).

Guidelines when writing descriptively

▶ Start with full descriptive narrative even if you're not sure about the course your analysis will take – and then cut it as the direction becomes clearer. Keep backups of pre-cut versions as they can be useful to check on later interpretation.

▶ The process of writing a narrative, in itself, will prompt further analytic thinking. In particular, look for cases that don't fit, and actions, experiences, or emotions that are incongruous. These will help to jolt you out of your stalled or routine thinking, conventional categories, and things you take for granted.

▶ Don't neglect to observe and report the commonplace. Things that seem like 'givens' to you will not necessarily be so for others. People have a tendency to neglect the expected aspects of an environment, and focus on the unusual.

▶ If your purpose is to describe, then resist the temptation to intrude on that with researcher interpretive asides. Highlight your interpretive comments until you can decide whether to leave them there, footnote them, or collect them under a new heading to mark the shift in focus.

▶ Draw on literary conventions and techniques for presentation to assist in communicating what you have learned, but balance an enthusiasm for unusual forms of presentation with your need to communicate meaningful results in a form that is useful for your audience.

▶ Provide case-oriented connecting and contextual detail, to facilitate interpretation. Case analyses and vignettes are often used to illustrate the outcomes (or some other aspect) of a study.

▶ Displays communicate powerfully with most audiences, and can help to clarify description for both author and audience (Box 12.2).

▶ Use quotations from verbatim transcripts to support or illustrate points being made, but do not rely on them to make the point. One of the best pieces of advice I ever heard regarding use of quotes was from Lyn Richards: write a complete draft of your results with *no quotes* included, before introducing some for illustrative purposes. This helps to ensure your reliance on the set of data as a whole for evidence to support what you are saying, rather than a single quote. One quote is *not* evidence, and should not be tendered as such, although a carefully selected quote can assist in illustrating the point you are making.

▶ Where quotes are included, they should be brief, reduced to convey the essential point only.

▶ If multiple quotes are being used throughout a set of results, provide an abbreviated form of identification (e.g., a pseudonym that is used consistently through the report) so that the reader can assess whether all are being drawn from the same participant, or widely across the sample.

▶ Whether or not you incorporate academic literature into your descriptive writing is very much a question of purpose and style. Emerson et al. (1995) suggest, for ethnographic writing, including literature that highlights your analysis (as in the example in Box 12.1), but in many situations it can be a distraction.

Box 12.2

Using a diagram to help clarify your description[5]

In the process of drafting an article on what makes a good care worker, a doctoral student described the skills used by care workers to build and maintain good relationships with their clients:

> Particular skills that were singled out were communication skills, skills in negotiating and managing difficult situations, being able to take initiative and be flexible, to exercise judgement, to be sensitive to and recognise people's needs and to deal with problems as they arose. In order to build a working relationship with people, the participants stated they needed to be able to listen carefully and respond appropriately to the client. They spoke of needing highly developed 'people skills' that would enable care workers to see things from the client's point of view. They spoke of the importance of being able to empathise and connect with people, to be able to talk and to listen when it was appropriate.

Puzzling about how the categories listed in this passage might be more clearly presented led to seeing that the various skills mentioned could be seen as two kinds of communication, with a focus on the centrality of relationship. This suggested the following approach to presenting the skills listed:

> Communication skills of care workers were demonstrated in two primary ways:

- through their ability to negotiate and manage difficult situations; and
- through their capacity to listen and respond to the client.

---

[5]Example adapted from Bazeley (2009: 11–12).

Together, these skills reflect the practical and emotive dimensions of an ability to *take account of the client* – a critical feature of what makes for good care work (Figure 12.1).

The student's article could then continue by elaborating on how the different skills involved in each of these two types of communication contributed to what could be seen now as a core process of taking account of the client.

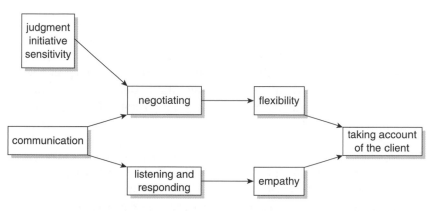

Figure 12.1   The role of communication skills in 'taking account of the client'

Numbers in descriptive reporting

The debates and disputes which arose with the push to carve out a distinct inter-pretivist and constructivist niche for qualitative research in the 1980s had much to do with stimulating rejection of anything numerical by researchers adopting qualitative methods. Nearly 30 years later, the debates have moved on, yet some still approach incorporating numbers in a qualitative report with great anxiety. Counting things reflects the 'numbered nature of phenomena', however, and is part of the descriptive process (Sandelowski, 2001: 231). Counting recognises that all data inherently combine quantitative and qualitative features. Numbers, as much as words, are the result of an interpretive process that depends, for exam-ple, on how questions are framed, how participants respond to those questions, and how the researcher interprets those responses and the patterning of responses.

- Use of counts communicates more effectively and reliably than does use of vague terms such as 'most' or 'some' to indicate more or less frequent occurrence of some feature in the text.
- Counts can be viewed as reflecting the importance of various emergent themes, although it can be argued that frequency and importance are not necessarily synonymous (e.g., Seale's 2001 study, described in Box 6.12, made use of counts for this purpose).
- Counting summarises patterns in data, such as from comparative and relational matrix analyses, and can allow possible interrelationships to be more easily identified for further exploration (cf. Chapters 9 and 10).

- Counting, as a counter to biased impressions, helps to maintain analytical integrity (Boxes 12.3 and 12.4).
- Counts prompt further analysis: why are so few in this group recorded as saying X (Box 12.4)?
- Numbers help to present evidence and can be used in arguing for the strength of a conclusion. They are particularly valuable when you want to persuade policy makers to take action.

Whether one should use counts of the number of participants who mention something or the overall frequency with which something is mentioned depends on the context in which counts are being obtained and used and the possible meanings of a zero (0) count in that context. Using codes that do not have a high degree of specificity, relying on numbers to tell the whole story, and not providing sufficient context to allow the reader to properly interpret the numbers are also cause for concern if you are using counts derived from qualitative coding (Bazeley, 2010a; Sandelowski, Voils, & Knafl, 2009). If you are drawing conclusions based on numbers, beware:

🛑 Numbers should *not* be reported in a way that suggests a representative sample where this did not exist (i.e., you cannot make *statistical* generalisations to a population from the kinds of samples used in the majority of qualitative studies).

🛑 If you are drawing conclusions specifically from numerical comparisons, you should have a basic understanding of probability theory (specifically, the central limit theorem) in relation to sample error and hypothesis testing; and

🛑 Avoid reporting in a form that gives a false sense of precision or rigour.[6]

🛑 Beware reducing evidence to the amount of evidence. Evidence must be placed in the context of an account that reflects what has been learned from interpreting the text, sound, images, movement – perhaps even statistical reports – that comprised the data for your qualitative study.

| Box 12.3 |

Using counts to challenge researcher impressions

The text search tools provided by software can often be usefully employed to check impressions. A workshop participant studying the growing acceptance of community-owned banks was sure that people trusted these smaller cooperatives more than the 'Big Four' corporate banks. She used text search to locate all the times 'trust' was mentioned, and found it eight times in her 20 interviews – but each time was as part of an interviewer's question. To resolve this, my workshop participant needed to check each interview for the context of her question: was she leading the interviewee, or was she responding to and clarifying something the interviewee had already been saying? As Lyn Richards has observed: 'Every researcher has a war

---

[6]In quantitative work, for example, the convention in reporting numbers is to not give more decimal places than were used in gathering the data; a difference (e.g., of 0.2°C in body temperature) might make for a statistically significant difference between (moderately large) groups, but not have any meaning or significance for the individuals in those groups.

story of a dominant theme that grabbed their attention, a word that seemed to occur every-where, but which in the hard light of day was being contributed seldom and then mainly by the members of the research team!' (2009: 164–5).

¬ **Box 12.4** ⌐

Using counts to maintain analytical integrity

Heidi declared that she had identified a number of universal characteristics of people who adopt a pattern of lifelong learning. She was struggling, however, to see where to go in her write-up beyond saying that, and listing the characteristics. As my conversation with her continued, she began to talk about some characteristics being more important than others. How did she know that, I asked? She then revealed a list of the characteristics, ordered by the number of sources coded for each. Ah! Each source represented a single case – and not all characteristics were coded for all 12 cases. How then could she say that *all* these characteristics were universal? Importantly, this observation sent her off into an exploration of why some were coded for only some cases, who wasn't coded for particular characteristics, and so on – thus enriching and potentially changing the whole direction of her analysis.

The ethics of descriptive reporting

Descriptive reporting always carries the likelihood that the identity of your informants or participants will be evident to others, particularly in a report based on a study undertaken within a particular community or organisational setting.

- In some studies, participants explicitly give their permission for their identity to be revealed, and indeed, may request that their real names be used. This is the exception, rather than the rule. In these cases, ethical researchers will assess whether their participants are correctly weighing the risks associated with disclosure. They will point out any possible consequences to them of such revelation, such as reactions from within their community, and will clear the text (or photographs) with them before publication (Guenther, 2009).
- Where confidentiality and anonymity have been promised, unless a participant is simply one among many and not able to be distinguished from 'the mass', identifying details associated with description of individuals or particular groups or quotes from individuals will need to remain undisclosed, or be altered to inhibit recognition by the likely (and any possible) audiences for the report. This can require more than simply providing pseudonyms or adjusting ages; even if identities are 'disguised' or simply not reported, someone within a particular community can be recognisable, for example, from the form of expression contained within an illustrative quote.[7]

---

[7]In a recent report of a management study within a smallish organisation, I ensured that any quotes contained in the report were representative of multiple comments – and made this clear in the report and to the manager. She, nevertheless, still tried to attribute particular comments to particular people – often wrongly.

The inclusion of photographs or other visual material within a report adds a further complication, primarily with regard to the issue of anonymity – something that is not dealt with just by pixelating faces or covering eyes within a photograph. Claudia Mitchell (2011) provides an example of how something as innocuous as a pair of slippers, photographed by a young girl as part of a 'feeling safe' or 'feeling not so safe' project, could potentially cause a problem if displayed and seen in that context by her stepfather, who routinely used them to hit her. In their discussion paper based on a series of focus groups and interviews, Rose Wiles and colleagues point to the 'ongoing tension between, on the one hand, research participants' rights and researchers' desire for participants to be seen and heard and, on the other hand, researchers' real and perceived responsibility to protect participants' (Wiles, Coffey, Robison, & Heath, 2010: 2). These are situated decisions that call for individual judgements, making it difficult to set guidelines (e.g., for institutional ethics review boards). Wiles et al. 'make the case that (i) respondents' status and "vulnerability" in combination with (ii) the nature of the research and (iii) the ways that visual (and other) data are used and presented should be key issues in making informed decisions about anonymity' (2010: 17), with identifiable images linked to interpretive ('psychologising') text or text relating to sensitive issues being the most problematic and most likely to require anonymisation.

 You might consider seeking additional permission *after* an interview regarding which of various ways interviewees are willing to have you use their story. This could be, for example, as one of three options: (a) using it only as part of an aggregated dataset for writing articles, (b) for use also as an anonymised example in a written report or text, or (c) using it as a specific example in a written report or text with the person and/or other data about them identified. In that case (and perhaps also for option b), the text of the example needs to be cleared with the person from whom it was obtained before publication. As well as gaining specific permission for use, this step also ensures the accuracy of the report.

Theoretical coherence

Description was a good place to start. Now you need to move on. If you've been following the general pathway proposed in this book, you will have progressed from empirical observation to conceptual ideas, to exploring relationships between those ideas, and perhaps to identifying explanations for how the things you observed happen or work. The task now is to bring those ideas together to build and present an integrated model, a theoretical statement (a thesis), or a coordinated picture of what you have found that will answer your questions and achieve your purpose.

The magic of theory 'emerging from the data'

In 1994, Janice Morse lamented the inability of researchers to describe *how* they analysed data, and their tendency to summarise the process of theory development as 'emerging from the data'. Nearly 20 years later, this is still a common lament. Theory 'emerges' for those who have thoroughly worked the data, *who are steeped in it*, and who, at a particular time (often when waking up, in the shower, cooking dinner, out walking, or talking to a colleague), have that flash of insight, an 'Aha!' moment, where they see how things might come together. Not only does this require thorough preparation, it also requires follow-up work where the flashy, insightful idea is pursued back through the data, to check that it really does have some meaning and significance (it often doesn't). The idea or theory, then, emerges through your working to achieve comprehensive knowledge and deep understanding of the data; it does not emerge 'out of the blue'. To a significant extent, increasing sensitivity to the data comes through the use of intensive analytic memos, through which you refine and test ideas. Using those memos to dialogue with yourself will contribute strongly to your capacity to record what you have found, as well. So – no magical emergence, just hard work occasionally brightened by fresh understanding or awareness of a new connection that 'makes sense'.

'Making sense' theoretically

What does it mean to develop theoretical coherence or integration? Is coherent theory necessarily explanatory? Richards (2009: 177) argues that most theory is just about what goes with what. It seems to me, though, that there always has to be something holding those things together; things are associated because one is influencing the other, or because something else is influencing them both – and so process and explanation of some sort come into play.

A theory that transcends description by integrating what has been learned from data to present the 'gestalt' will have:

- abstracted from the particular to the general, with concepts that apply across cases and potentially to related areas beyond those cases and the immediate topic;
- a fabric that links those concepts into a coordinated structure with implications for the phenomenon being studied;
- detail that reflects the complexity of the situation studied, the multiplicity of factors that create, sustain, and change events, processes, outcomes; but also
- a simplicity that allows an observer to see and understand the core of the theory;
- it will 'fit' with data, 'work' as an explanation of those data, without loose ends;
- it will 'ring true' – making sense to the participants and other stakeholders; and
- it will have relevance beyond the specific data that gave rise to it.

Shapes of theoretical coherence: what might yours look like?

There are multiple ways you might pull your fragments of theoretical analysis with their supporting data together into an integrated whole, to say something worthwhile, and so a coherent presentation of what you have found might take any one of a variety of forms. These include (but are not restricted to):

- integrative concepts that have explanatory power;
- classifications and typologies that reveal and clarify;

- identification of patterns and pathways;
- presentation of a thesis – a propositional relationship;
- drawing on existing theory for coherent explanation;
- an extension to or refinement of existing theory;
- a model demonstrating essential relationships and processes for your theory.

You might add to this list from your own reading of the literature in your discipline area.

Integrative concepts that have explanatory power

▶ Present a detailed analysis of the dimensions and structure of an important concept, showing how these retain their essential character as they become focused or extended under different circumstances (cf. Chapter 8). Show indicators for those dimensions to guide operationalisation of the concept so it can be used in further research.

▶ You have developed a *new* concept to integrate your observations. For example, Morse (1999) reported how she and her colleagues developed 'compathy' to describe the way nurses interacted with and calmed patients in the trauma room. Your concept will need now to be described and defined, and its explanatory value explained.

▶ You have been engaged in developing a grounded theory: integrate the main concepts and processes you have identified around a core category and/or process (cf. Chapter 11 and Box 12.5).

▶ Show how a narrator 'performs' his story, for example, to preserve his sense (self-concept) of masculinity in the face of debilitating disability (Riessman, 2008).

▌ Box 12.5 ▐

Practice justification as an integrating concept for risk factor management in primary health services

Rachel Laws, at the University of New South Wales, studied the implementation of brief lifestyle intervention for risk factor management[8] in primary care practice for one metropolitan and two rural community nursing and allied health teams (Laws, Kemp, Harris, Powell Davies, Williams, & Eames-Brown, 2009). She used a mixed methods approach, with a major component based on grounded theory methodology. Her overall model (shown in Figure 12.2) 'suggests that clinician perceptions shape their risk factor management practices through the process of *practice justification*' (2009: 5) – a process supported through *commitment* and beliefs about *capacity*. She then addressed the issue of how various patient, provider, and contextual factors impacted on practitioners' likelihood to engage in risk factor management.

---

[8]Known as SNAP – intervention to improve risk factors related to Smoking, Nutrition, Alcohol and Physical exercise.

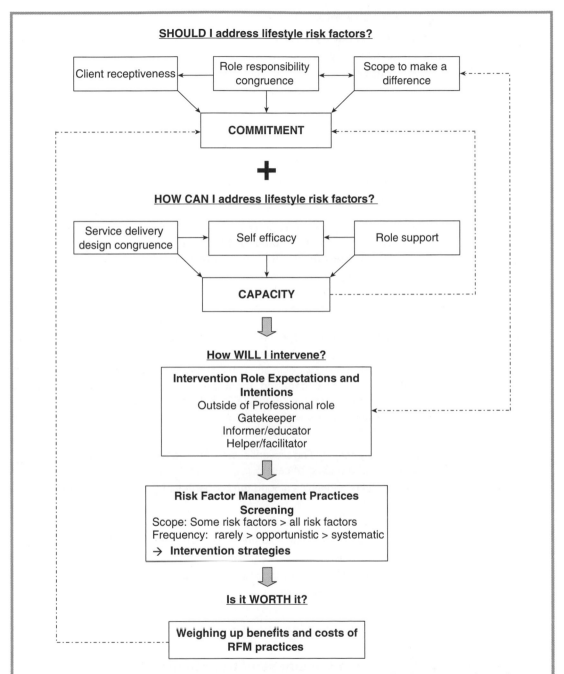

Figure 12.2 The 'practice justification' process: a model of how clinician perceptions shape their risk factor management practices

Source: Laws et al., 2009: 7, Figure 1

Classifications and typologies that reveal and clarify

Classification systems and typologies fall partway between description and theory. While some are very enthusiastic about them, seeing them as a way of clarifying the territory of a subject or phenomenon, others see them as little more than description that doesn't offer anything new. If you are presenting a classification system or typology as the *product* of your study, then each component in it must be based in data rather than speculation, and you will need to take extra care to show how it contributes to knowledge and understanding.

Your classification system or typology might come directly out of the (re)structuring of your coding system; through the cross-classification of two key dimensions; or as a result of clustering concepts derived from your data. Alternative approaches follow:

▶ Identify a way of grouping concepts or categories that reflects your participants' ways of describing things (described by Spradley, 1979, as domain analysis) and from which you can theorise about their perspective on the world (or some small part of it at least).

▶ Your method of clustering concepts has resulted in a taxonomy that brings order to a mass of concepts such that it will have practical benefits for further work: think of the benefit that has come from Linnaeus' classification of plants, for example. When clustering and ordering of a taxonomy are based on principles that have been derived from the data, this allows the system to deal with new categories, or new information about existing categories.

▶ A typology is often built by cross-tabulating two critical dimensions identified in your data. You would then show how doing so, with the resulting 'types' populating each cell, adds to what is known and understood about the processes operating in that setting (Box 12.6). Drawing on the work of Kluge (2000), Sellerberg and Leppänen (2012: 25–30) identified four (potentially overlapping) steps in an analysis, following indexing and annotating data, to develop a typology:

　○ compare data fragments to find similarities and differences, leading to identification of dimensions and grouping of cases;

　○ locate meaningful relationships among the properties of those narratives grouped together;

　○ identify and compare these as types; consider how they differ;

　○ theorise the typology by relating it to previously formulated knowledge.

▶ Test your typology by asking:

　○ Are all cases covered by the typology (without forcing)?

　○ Does the pattern hold at all times?

┐ Box 12.6 ┌

A typology of bankrupt small-business entrepreneurs

Ann-Mari Sellerberg and Vesa Leppänen (2012) used narrative analysis with positioning theory to develop a typology of bankrupt small-business entrepreneurs in Sweden. Bankrupt entrepreneurs experience a sharp disruption to their economic and social lives, impacting on their ability to make choices about their business, their reputation, and their professional and personal relationships. In telling their stories, as they reflected on and reconstructed their experience, the 22 entrepreneurs described themselves in relation to their economic activity relative to their economic network, and in their relationships with other economic actors, thus creating the dimensions for construction of a typology (Table 12.1).

Constructing this typology led the authors to then ask (of their data) why the entrepreneurs described themselves so differently, and what the consequences of doing so might be. They found three variables relevant to the 'Why?' question that helped to explain the relative positioning and response of each group of entrepreneurs: the location of the business (large or small community); the integration of the entrepreneur in the community (high or low); and the meaning of doing business (personal or general interest). As the interviews were conducted quite soon after the event, their data regarding consequences were more speculative, but they were able to suggest that the Swedish creditor-friendly model of managing bankruptcy 'may result in a drain of particular types of knowledge and drive from the market' (2012: 75), because it is those who are better integrated into smaller communities who are most likely to withdraw from the market.

Table 12.1 A typology of the economic relationships of bankrupt small-business entrepreneurs

Relationships with economic actors	Position in their economic network	
	Participation	*Marginalisation*
Equal: able to take initiative and negotiate	The undeterred (*n* = 6)	The analytical (*n* = 1)
Unequal: subordinate, without power to act	The withdrawn (*n* = 4)	The rejected (*n* = 11)

Source: adapted from Sellerberg and Leppänen, 2012: 31, Table 1

Pattern identification

▸ Identify and explain a pattern or pathway such that you can build predictions on the basis of it; then you are moving beyond description to theory building. For example, exploration of the career development of early career researchers allowed Laudel and Glaser (2008) to identify critical factors in the process of moving from dependent to independent researcher (cf. Box 9.8).

▸ Identify patterns in discursive (or other types of) practices, then 'unpack' them to show how each patterned form of interaction is used, and for what purposes (Antaki et al., 2003).

▸ Interpret observed patterns of behaviour for their cultural meaning and relevance. Then bring these together to show their fit within a whole cultural system, and the principles by which that system operates (e.g., Van Maanen, 1979).

▸ Place narrative patterns based on elements such as genre and structure within a context that provides the rationale for their development, explains the purpose they serve within that context, and/or provides insights into the life and experience of the narrator (e.g., Frank's 1995 illness narratives; cf. Box 7.5).

▸ You have traced the patterned archaeology of events that has allowed your subject to become what it/he/she is. Now it is possible to conceptualise an 'other' – to see a different way of being (Tamboukou, in Andrews et al., 2004).

Argue a thesis – a propositional relationship

This is the classic form in which an integrated theory is presented for a dissertation. In inductively or abductively driven research (cf. Chapter 11) this will typically be presented and argued at or near the end of the work as a conclusion to the research you have conducted. In contrast, if you started from a theoretical proposition, your conclusion will show whether your data supported, modified, or refuted that proposition.

▶ Your thesis is introduced, presented, and then explained and supported by use of evidence from the research you have conducted. For example, in my dissertation I argued that: 'Community development is an effective strategy for the promotion of mental health in a disadvantaged community' (Bazeley, 1977). This proposition was elaborated through a series of models (cf. Figures 12.6 and 12.7) and then supported and elaborated from data and literature.

▶ Alternatively, put forward a central proposition supported (or refined by) several related propositions for which you have evidence (Box 12.7).

▶ Show how the elements you have identified as essential to defining or generating a process or concept (e.g., through a process of analytic induction or theory elaboration) achieve that purpose.

⌐ Box 12.7 ⌐

A thesis with related propositions

John Eastwood's (2011) dissertation was designed to challenge prevailing approaches to epidemiological research by examining the particular issue of maternal depression from an ecological and critical realist perspective (cf. Box 1.2). His thesis was:

> In the neighbourhood spatial context, in keeping with critical realist ontology, global-economic, social and cultural level generative powers trigger and condition maternal psychological and biological level stress mechanisms resulting in the phenomenon of maternal depression and alteration of the infants' developmental trajectory. (2011: 409)

He then drew on his empirical findings and an accompanying theoretical framework to put forward 11 (falsifiable) propositions, each elaborated in accompanying models to show context, mechanism, and outcome. These included, for example:

> *Proposition 4:* Maternal psychological stress triggered by 'mismatched' expectation tends to cause (increase) depressive symptoms in the context of loneliness, isolation, lack of emotional support, lack of practical help, limited social network, limited support services, financial stress and poor health. (2011: 419)

> *Proposition 10:* Expectations of mothers (and wives and daughters) is a cultural level mechanism that tends to increase maternal psychological stress in the context of strong bonding social networks, weak bridging networks, language barriers, poor access to services and information, and cultural practices. (2011: 423)

Draw on existing theory for coherent explanation

▶ Draw on an existing theory to provide a coherent explanation for a pattern you are seeing in your data.

Miles and Huberman (1994: 261) found that in some of their schools, teachers worked extremely hard on implementation of new programmes, and asserted strongly that there had been improvements as a result – improvements for which they found little substantiating evidence. In other sites where there was less personal investment, there were fewer or more accurate claims. To understand the meaning of this pattern beyond those immediate schools, they explored established theories. They dismissed the idea that it was just group conformity to mistaken judgements (Asch's conformity theory), but decided it did fit with Festinger's idea of *effort justification* which states that people justify high levels of effort expended by seeing more results than are really there – a component of his cognitive dissonance theory. This lent plausibility to their finding and gave a theoretical explanation for the patterns they observed in these and other situations (an example of abductive inference drawing).

Similarly Turner (1981), in a grounded theory study, generalised from observing an argument over queuing for cement to conflict over marginal territory to problems of resource allocation, which led him to the relevance of economic demand theory for what he was seeing. He noted that this was very different from starting with economic demand theory and then fitting data to it.

Extend or refine existing theory

▶ Use your study to elaborate or refine an existing theory. Most refinements will be 'incremental' rather than revolutionary; the latter usually is possible only after a sustained programme of work and reflection, perhaps over a lifetime!

In her study of primary care clinicians' adoption of risk factor management practices (cf. Box 12.5), Rachel Laws found similar associations between patient and contextual factors and lifestyle intervention as had been reported in previous studies, but she then showed how her findings contributed an understanding of *process* to explain those associations. Additionally, she extended theoretical considerations of role adequacy in clinical practice by going beyond commonly used notions of self-efficacy to include the issue of congruence of new practices with current ways of working. Dominant psychological theories of motivation and action, with their primary focus on the role of individual cognitive factors in shaping behaviour, were extended also by her identifying the way in which the service delivery environment also shaped beliefs and practices (Laws et al., 2009).

Demonstrate essential processes and relationships via a model

Models vary in their degree of complexity. They help you to discover, or see anew, what goes with what, as you are 'forced' to find a place for each object and to check each relationship.

▶ Rework and refine your original conceptual model or logic model to incorporate what you have learned from your study.

▶ Develop a visual model that sums up the key elements of the process you have identified.

▶ Show how your theorising about a pattern or pathway works out in practice in one or more settings through a model or series of models.

Examples of models that have been presented in papers, articles, and/or dissertations follow in the next section (see also Figure 12.2).

Coherence through display

Throughout this book I have demonstrated the value of using various forms of display through all stages of a study, from developing a conceptual framework through analysis to developing theory. Let's look now at some ways displays have been used to provide a coherent presentation of the results of an analysis. Treat these as examples, rather than as exact models for you to follow; use them as a point of departure for thinking about your own work.

Even at this stage, the preparation of a visual model, chart, or other form of display will continue to stretch your analytic thinking. It forces you to condense all that you have learned into a restricted space, and consequently to identify what's most important in what you have found for your thesis, report, or article. By using visual strategies well, you can convey a big idea and/or a large amount of information in a small space, but beware the danger of distorting your observations for the sake of simplicity or elegance.

Capturing the essence

I am reminded of the famous quote by Blaise Pascal: 'The present letter is a very long one, simply because I had no leisure to make it shorter.' Lynn Kemp's model (Box 12.8) was built on the basis of much more complex maps of interrelated categories but, in its essential form, it holds within it a wealth of meaning that perfectly summed up both the desires and the experiences of her participants with a spinal cord injury.

▐ Box 12.8 ▐

A simple but effective model

In her mixed methods study of people living in the community with varying degrees and levels of spinal cord injury, Lynn Kemp (1999) had evaluated a series of common models for determining need for services and had found that all fell short of achieving their purpose. From her qualitative interviews with 40 participants, supplemented by lengthy additional comments from 30 survey respondents, she reached an understanding of need for services as being that which would allow the person with a spinal cord injury to fulfil their plan to be 'ordinary' (cf. Box 10.10). Just occasionally, services supported the plan of the person with an injury to engage in ordinary relationships and to make independent choices about daily activities, but more often, in order to receive services, the recipient had to accept difference and fit with predetermined stereotypes: they had to have sufficient (obvious) need to be worthy of services; they had to be dependent but not too dependent; they had no control over how and when those services were provided; and they had to be grateful for receiving them. Her model of this central conclusion came out of careful consideration of categories derived from her participants' narratives and the relationships between those categories, strongly supported by the theoretical and research literature.[9]

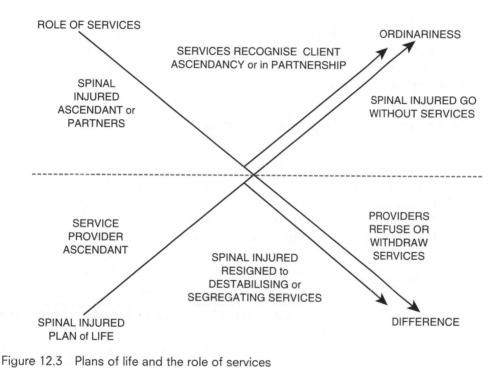

Figure 12.3   Plans of life and the role of services
Source: Kemp, 1999: 177, Figure 27

Tabling a pattern

Not all visual models will be diagrammatic. Carl Auerbach and colleagues (Auerbach, Salick, & Fine, 2006) sought to develop a systematic way of helping clinicians to make decisions about treatment in cases of multicontextual

---

[9]It was first drawn, however, in a moment of tranquillity in a coffee shop on a serviette with a borrowed pen!

trauma where the sufferer is at risk of post-traumatic stress. Working from a resilience- rather than a damage-based perspective, they used an elaborative grounded theory approach to investigate and theorise the natural process of recovery from trauma, starting from a base in trauma literature. They then explored the relevance of the theoretical constructs suggested by the literature in a series of studies of survivors of five specific, different traumas, modifying the constructs with each successive group (and revisiting earlier data) until no further modifications were needed. From this, they developed a 'stages and issues model of trauma and recovery' (Figure 12.4) that reflected the four stages all of their participants went through (in columns), along with three core issues that arise during recovery (rows). When the model is applied to people experiencing a specific type of trauma, the specific themes populating the cells will vary slightly, but the pattern is the same. This then provides the clinician with a structured procedure for developing an intervention strategy with any particular case.

Modelling a core category and associated processes

Models for core categories with associated conditions and processes typically result from grounded theory studies. Two examples have been seen already: Juliet Corbin's model of 'survival: reconciling multiple realities' in Figure 11.4, and Rachel Laws' model of 'practice justification' in Figure 12.2.

Grounded theory based in symbolic interactionism was used by Landier et al. (2011) to develop and validate a model explaining the process of adherence to

STAGES/ ISSUES	TRAUMATISATION/ SHATTERING DIAGNOSIS AND DESPAIR	SAFETY CHOOSING TO GO ON	REPROCESSING BUILDING A WAY TO LIVE	INTEGRATION REENTERING LIFE
STRENGTH	The body fails	Finding an inner strength	Reclaiming the physical body	Moving forward
CONNECTION	Withdrawal from social world	Reaching out	Getting involved	New empathy and giving something back
MEANING	Loss of old life and inability to register	Formulating a plan	Cultivating hope	Finding personal meaning

Figure 12.4   The stages and issues model for PTSD following acquired physical disability

Source: Auerbach et al., 2006: 370, Figure 1

treatment for children and adolescents with acute lymphoblastic leukaemia (ALL). Treatment involves essential daily self or caregiver administration of oral chemotherapy, for a period of around two years. The process therefore depended on a parent or caregiver taking responsibility for ensuring treatment was maintained (*doing our part*), with the outcome being mediated by the caregiver and/ or patient making the connection between treatment and the disease (older adolescents were most likely to be those who did not maintain strict adherence). From their analysis of interviews with 17 patients and 21 caregivers who had completed treatment, they identified three stages in the process of adherence: *recognizing the threat*; *taking control*; and *managing for the duration*, described through their quite detailed theoretical model (Figure 12.5), with supporting evidence in the text.

Network drawings and flow charts

As suggested by the previous chapter, network drawings and flow charts are a popular and useful way to show the complexity of causal relationships such as are found, for example, in community settings.

I can illustrate the use of a flow chart by reference to my own doctoral work in which I set out to understand the mental health needs of and resources available to people (primarily single or separated women with children) living in a medium-rise section of a public housing estate (Bazeley, 1977). Figure 12.6 provided an overview of the key concepts and overall linkage established between community development and mental health. It was followed by three component charts, each showing in detail the mechanisms (theorised and observed) that played a part in linking specific aspects of community development to components of mental health. The second of these is shown in Figure 12.7.

What was important here, for construction of these diagrams, was that on the journey through my research I progressively clarified key concepts for my research: a three-step definition of mental health relevant to a community context; the implications of disadvantage with respect to mental health based on the literature and then supported by a multi-pronged community study; and a conceptual understanding of community development (which had been an unanticipated component of the project) based on experience in the community that was then supported by literature. These clarifications greatly facilitated my being able to visualise, theorise, and substantiate the links between community development and mental health as I came to the conclusion of my project; indeed, building the final model was possible only because I had undertaken these clarifications (especially as I faced the typical tight deadline by that stage!). The way I often talk about this now with students is to ask them to write, at the end of each section

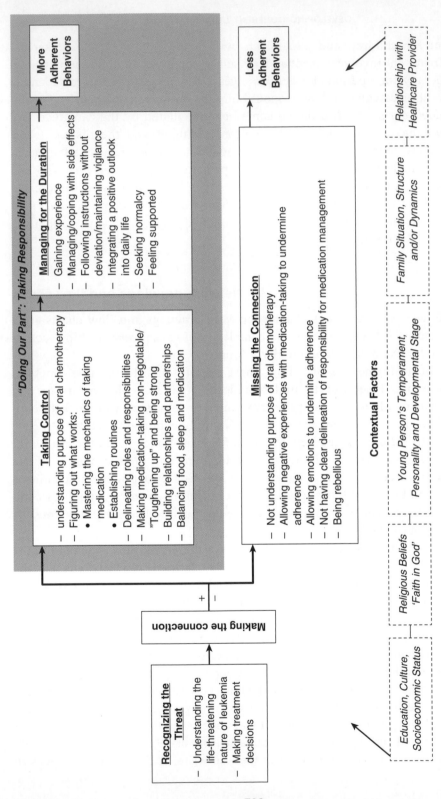

Figure 12.5 'Doing our part': a theoretical model of the process of adherence to oral chemotherapy for children with acute lymphoblastic leukaemia

Source: Landier et al., 2011: 208, Figure 1

of their work, what they are taking forward from that section. This ensures each component of their writing becomes focused and each can then contribute to building a conclusion – as well as providing a valuable 'road map' for the reader on their way through.

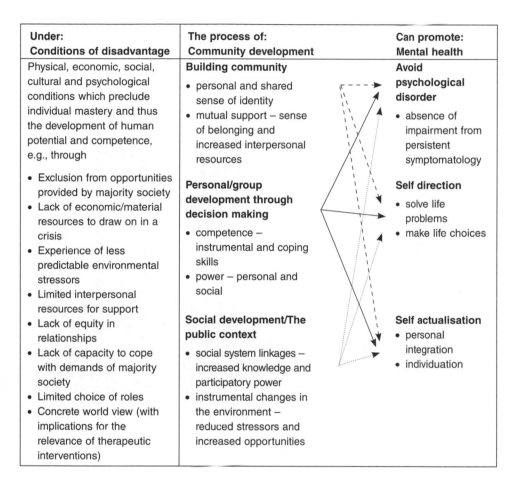

Figure 12.6   Community development as a strategy to promote mental health in a disadvantaged population

Source: Bazeley, 1977· 424, Figure 11.1[1]

---

[1]Adapted from the original for clarity in the absence of the accompanying text: column 1 has been added, detail in columns 2 and 3 has been reduced.

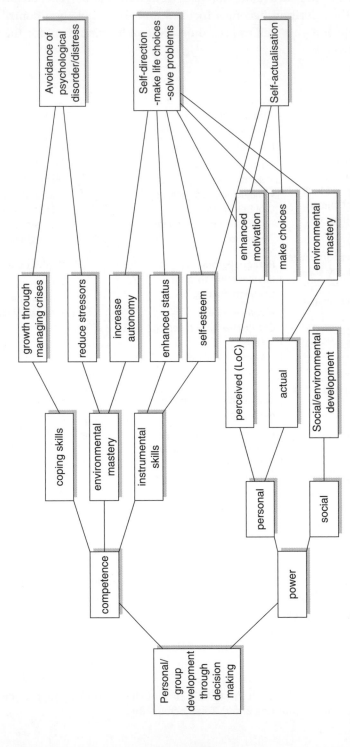

Figure 12.7 Details of specific linkages between development through group decision making and mental health outcomes

Source: Bazeley, 1977: 425, Figure 11.1

A collection of tips and tricks for bringing it together

Enter your skiff of musement [allowing the mind to wander; a mental game without rules], push off into the lake of thought, and leave the breath of heaven to swell your sail. With your eyes open, awake to what is about or within you, and open conversation with yourself: for such is all meditation! … It is, however, not a conversation in words alone, but is illustrated, like a lecture, with diagrams and with experiments. (Peirce, 1931–35, Vol. 6: 315, quoted in Reichertz, 2010: 20).

▶ Develop a 'hunch' and see if it works.

▶ Talk it. As you tell your peers and colleagues about your work, their questions will help you to clarify where it is all going. When Justin was telling me he was going to write a paper comparing workers in two similar organisations, I asked: why do the comparison? What will it tell you, other than that this group differs from that in these ways? He then realised the point of his article would be about *how* the comparative structures and funding arrangements for the two types of organisations might impact differently on the working life and satisfaction of employees. This provided a framework for writing, leading to a conclusion.

▶ Tell it. Practise presenting your research in three minutes: check out the three-minute thesis competition at 3mt.grad.ubc.ca/about/2012-finalists/ or www.postgraduate.uwa. edu.au/news/3mt/.

▶ Draw it. Create a conference poster without regular text that captures the essence of your work.

▶ Write it. Try writing the abstract for your article or thesis. If that is a problem, go back and write an abstract for each chapter or section.

▶ Read for stimulation and ideas (not just academic literature; cf. Gersick, 1988, in Box 10.3).

▶ Stop reading and just start writing. Then keep writing, constantly referring back to your data for information and ideas. (You might end up 'ditching' a lot of it; make a 'cuts' file for those bits you might use later or that you can't bear to throw away.) As you keep working at it, and become immersed in it, order will come.

▶ Check out some likely theories (maybe review those that you included as part of your conceptual framework).

▶ Join a writing circle where you can share and discuss work (yours and others') as it proceeds.

▶ Think about how you used to write the undergraduate essay. You did your library research, made notes, sorted them, and figured out what you would say from that. Then you wrote an introduction explaining how you were going to approach the topic; you developed your points or arguments through a series of paragraphs that drew on what you'd learned from the reading you did (one point per paragraph, with a topic sentence to start each paragraph); and you wrapped it up in a conclusion. Pulling a thesis or report together in your concluding chapter is similar: figure what you want to say out of all the work you've done, introduce it, clarify definitions and assumptions, support it with evidence from your research (which has been well described in previous chapters), and write the conclusion. The difference is that in a concluding chapter for a dissertation, you're most likely going to put the concluding statement (the thesis) up front in the chapter; it's not designed to lead your readers on a treasure hunt!

▶ For each issue covered as you progress through writing up your results, create a keypoint summary about what you are doing and finding.

▶ Sit on it. This section of this chapter came about after I thought I'd finished writing it.

Writing about developing coherence

In the methods chapter

▶ Briefly outline any strategies used to assist in bringing your work to a coherent conclusion.

In the results chapter

▶ Think about what the organising principle will be for writing your findings. In general, it is best that this *not* be according to what method you used, or whose voice (which participant group) the findings were derived from. Rather, use a thematic, topic, or issue basis for arranging your results, and draw together all the data and theory you have developed for each component of your topic. As part of that, you might show what you learned from different methods or different participant groups – from how they were similar or what you learned from their differences.

▶ Have a full draft ready well before it is due to be submitted or sent. I find I rework almost every sentence and paragraph that I write, often multiple times over, before I am satisfied with how each reads. It is helpful, too (if not essential), to have other people review it before it is finalised.

Further reading

Mills (1959: Appendix) lays out necessary preparation and then a series of steps to aid the release of 'the sociological imagination', to bring your study together for presentation in written form.

Miles and Huberman (1994: Chapter 10) list and briefly elaborate 13 'tactics for generating meaning' (many of these have been covered in this and earlier chapters). In Chapter 11, they review ethical issues related to analysing and reporting qualitative research.

Richards (2009: Part III, Chapters 7–9) provides ideas and strategies for making sense of your data.

Corbin and Strauss (2008: Chapter 5) is on achieving theoretical integration for those using grounded theory methods.

Seale (1999: Chapter 9) expands on the issue of using numbers in qualitative research.

Wolcott (2009) provides helpful guidelines on writing up your qualitative study.

13

Defending and extending: issues of quality and significance

Matthew Miles (1979: 591) once famously asked: 'How can we be sure that an "earthy", "undeniable", "serendipitous" finding is not, in fact, wrong?' When you conduct research, you want to create a piece of work that will stand up to challenge and be of value to others as well as yourself. The quality and significance of your research will be evident in an approach and execution that exhibits the work of a creative, reflective, and competent craftsperson, and a product that informs, inspires, and empowers others. When these are present, you are able to *defend* your work, and you or others can then *extend* it through application to similar settings, through further research, or into guidelines for practice. The generally endorsed principles I outline in this chapter for quality of data, processes, product, and outcomes speak to that practical task,[1] and reaffirm or add to those I have outlined throughout this book, and to those given specifically for your consideration as you designed your project in Chapter 2.

In this chapter you will consider:

- those qualities that will encourage others to see your methods and conclusions as credible, trustworthy, dependable, valid;
- strategies that help to ensure quality and credibility in your research;
- strategies needed if your research is to be able to contribute to others beyond the immediate situation from which they were derived;
- ways to extend the theoretical significance of your work;
- issues involved in reporting from your research, in so far as they represent and impact on those about whom you are reporting.

---

[1]My intention in this chapter is to focus on the 'doing' of quality and validity, rather than to engage in the extensive debates about the concepts of validity and reliability.

The issue of quality

Philosophers and theorists will argue about what is real, what is truth, and the extent to which we construct individual and shared realities, as discussed in Chapter 1. Because we have different viewpoints on what constitutes truth and whether truth can be known, there are no absolute, agreed standards for the quality and significance of research. That does not mean, however, that 'anything goes'. An absolute claim to accuracy of representation may not be necessary for your research to be useful, but, as Maxwell (1992) noted, your research does have to be credible.

Traditionally, researchers talked about demonstrating validity and reliability in reaching research conclusions, with particular processes and criteria attached to these terms. Yvonna Lincoln and Egon Guba (1985), in marking out a special territory for qualitative inquiry, rejected that traditional terminology and proposed alternative criteria for quality in qualitative research: trustworthiness, credibility, dependability, confirmability, and transferability. Lyn Richards (2009) suggested thinking about validating as a verb, with its emphasis on an active process of ensuring strong conclusions, rather than validity as a descriptive noun. While qualitative researchers might have rejected traditional terminology and the kinds of procedures for ensuring validity that were derived from experimental research, they have not rejected the concept of needing to demonstrate that there is a sound basis for the researcher's inferences about the phenomenon being investigated. In broad terms, the practical question to answer is: what do you need to do to avoid having your audience dismiss the work that you have done, and the inferences you have derived from that?

As you work through this chapter:

▶ Reflect on the propositions or conclusions you have developed through your research, running an inner dialogue that anticipates the kind of dialogue you might have with an external audience as they challenge:

  ○ the appropriateness and adequacy of the methods you used for your particular study;
  ○ whether your conclusions are supported by evidence; and
  ○ the significance, or 'so what?', of your work.[2]

▶ Make use of the audit trail you have created through memo writing as you worked through your project. This and your database of evidence are your most valuable resources for this stage of your work.
▶ Look to provide specific comments and give examples, based on your data, as you work through the considerations and questions below, rather than just suppose.

---

[2]The word 'significance' is used in this chapter (and indeed, throughout the book) in a non-statistical sense to imply a sense of importance, meaningfulness, worth.

Questions to consider

These questions to consider are the kinds of questions that are likely to be asked by an academic audience, thesis or journal reviewers, recipients of reports, sceptical journalists, or a curious (and informed) public. Be prepared to pre-empt them (e.g., aided by the strategies that follow), but also to have responses to hand for when the questions come (Box 13.1). Note that it is not the data or the processes themselves which generate quality, but rather *the appropriate use* of data and methods, and the inferences you draw from them.[3] In addressing questions of quality, I will focus on epistemic (rather than political) considerations and principles (Hammersley, 2008).[4]

Quality of data

- How did you arrive at your final sample? (Was it as intended?) How did that impact your conclusions?
- How has your presence as an observer or your questioning of participants impacted on the situation being investigated?
- Have you obtained sufficient contextual information to allow you to interpret your data? Will it be sufficient for others to explore the comparative relevance of your conclusions for their situation?
- Did your methods provide you with necessary data to answer your questions (e.g., was there a long enough period of exposure to site or participants)? If not, where did the data fall short and how has this limited or changed your analysis and conclusions?

Quality of process

- Were procedures implemented as designed? If not, how and why were they changed?
- Was your choice of methods determined by the question, or by convenience or fashion? Did you consider alternatives to the methods you eventually chose? (Interviews dominate qualitative methods, especially in human services professions, often leading to journalistic commentaries rather than analytic outcomes.)
- How did you get from data to conclusions?

  o Did your coding scheme develop beyond free-listed descriptive or common-sense categories, e.g., to develop schematically organised abstract or theoretical concepts? Did you establish connections between your concepts, e.g., based on observed patterns of association?
  o Were your categories 'saturated' (substantively grounded, theoretically conceptualised, fully elaborated)?[5]
  o Did you take time to reflect on and write memos about your developing understanding and the puzzles associated with those reflections, memos, and understandings?

---

[3]Maxwell (2013), among others, noted that validity is a property only of inferences, not of the methods used to obtain them.

[4]In developing these questions, I have drawn primarily on the following references to supplement my ingrained understanding: Flick (2007b), Hammersley (2008), Maxwell (1992), and Seale (1999; 2004).

[5]The issue of reliability (confirmability) in coding was addressed in Chapter 5.

Quality of product

- How useful are your findings and conclusions for your intended purpose?
- Do they increase and deepen understanding of the phenomenon you studied?
- Are there clear links between your data, evidence, and argument, such that there is consistency across these areas and your conclusions are supported by evidence?
- Did you do more than summarise and report categories?
- Have you relied on quotes for evidence? Are they adequately contextualised so that the reader can confirm their meaning? Can your findings be understood and 'stand up' if all quotes are removed? Can you demonstrate that the conclusions you have reached are based on the data as a whole, for example by showing the frequency of codes, themes, or patterns across all the data? Quotes from original data should be used only to illustrate results, not as evidence for them; proof texts have never been an adequate substitute for hermeneutic scholarship.
- Is there evidence of critical thinking in the conduct of your research and analysis of your data?
- Have you drawn conclusions for your readers? *You* are the one with the knowledge and experience that are needed to do that.
- Are your findings clearly structured and expressed? Impressive, complex language that unnecessarily coins new words and obscures meaning offers little to most readers.

Quality of outcome

- Does your research contribute to knowledge or theory within its field?
  - Does it offer new information to yourself or others working in that field or discipline?
  - Does it confirm or extend existing information in that field?
- Does your research contribute to practice and policy?
  - Does it offer new information for those contexts?
  - Is it acceptable to and accepted by relevant communities of practice?[6]
  - Does it contribute to social change, foster social justice, facilitate empowerment?[7]

Box 13.1

Demonstrating quality criteria

Having presented her model on practice justification for risk factor management in primary care services (cf. Box 12.5), Rachel Laws set about showing how her study findings compared with previous research and existing theories before outlining implications for practice at individual, service, and system levels. She concluded her dissertation with a section covering study strengths and limitations, using a series of tables (e.g., Table 13.1) to address quality criteria for the research process and product.

---

[6]A negative in this instance does not necessarily imply research that is lacking in trustworthiness or credibility.

[7]Although I consider that many of the practices promoted by a transformative approach to research (cf. Chapter 1), such as actively hearing the voices of participants in research, potentially contribute to the quality of the knowledge produced by research, I also consider that criteria of, say, whether social research brings about a more just society or empowers the weak, speak more to the *value* of research than to its *quality*.

Table 13.1 Demonstrating the quality of the research product: theoretical model

Quality criteria	Evidence from the current study
Credibility Logical links between the data and the analysis and argument presented	• Prolonged engagement in the setting by the researcher • Synergistic use of both quantitative and qualitative data • Multiple sources of qualitative data: interview and journal notes • Mixed methods and case study analysis demonstrate the usefulness of the model in understanding variations in clinicians' lifestyle risk factor management practices
Resonance Representation of the 'emic' perspective of participants and fullness of the studied experience	• Presentation of the results includes discussion of the language used by participants as well as implicit or taken for granted meanings • The use of theoretical and purposeful sampling ensures that fullness of the studied experience was represented in the analysis
Originality The analysis provides a new conceptual rendering of the data, extending or providing new insights	• Comparisons with existing literature and theory demonstrate the new insights provided
Usefulness Contribution of the research to knowledge, practical application and further research	• Insights provided by the model make a unique contribution to understanding the lifestyle risk factor management practices of PHC clinicians and have been used to make practical recommendations to improve such practices • The results have stimulated ideas for further research

Source: Laws, 2010: 338, Table 70

Strategies to increase the trustworthiness and credibility of your conclusions

All too often, reports or articles from qualitative projects contain unsupported assertions, undigested data, and/or impressionistic journalism. Throughout this book you have been introduced to strategies designed to strengthen your analysis and ensure that you build well-supported conclusions from your data. To the extent that you have already conducted comparative analyses, considered alternative explanations, investigated negative cases, and gathered together all relevant evidence in preparing your claims, you have already done almost all you can in terms of practical strategies to help ensure the quality and credibility of your results. Now it's time for some final checks, and, if possible, a period where you can 'sit on it' and then go through your work with fresh eyes once more, reviewing the inferences you have drawn from your work, before it is disseminated at last.

Just as your analysis methods varied depending on the nature of the phenomenon you were studying and the kinds of questions you were asking about it, so your strategies for ensuring trustworthiness, or validity, will depend on the nature and purpose of your project (Maxwell, 2013). Some of the strategies I outline below will add to your stockpile of strategies to use for asserting the validity of your inferences; others will serve more as brief reminders of things that (I would hope) you will have already done. It is not anticipated that you will employ all of these strategies; if you have been thorough on the way through, then you may not need to do much more than refer to your audit trail of memos and models to explain how you arrived at the best explanations or interpretations possible, in answer to your research questions.

Compare and triangulate results

▶ Check against other data (where appropriate), and/or look for complementary data.

▶ Alternatively, compare cohorts (different sample groups) or analyse part of your data, then the remainder, and compare results.

▶ Seek out alternative explanations, conclusions, or interpretations and test these against your data.

▶ Compare your findings with those reported in the literature or predicted by alternative theories.

Triangulation, as a strategy for validation, usually involves independently obtaining one or more alternative sources of (qualitative *or* quantitative) data and checking to see if the inferences you draw from that data are comparable with those obtained in the first instance. This process is not as straightforward as it sounds, however. For example, using different methods will double the time and resources required for the study, and each is likely to address different aspects of the question.[8] Sandra Mathison identified three possible outcomes from triangulation – convergence, inconsistency, and contradiction – and concluded that: 'In practice, triangulation as a strategy provides a rich and complex picture of some social phenomenon being studied, but rarely does it provide a clear path to a singular view of what is the case' (1988: 15).

Theoretical triangulation, checking out alternative theories and rival explanations related to the phenomenon using the evidence you have, is an alternative to a purely data- and methods-based strategy. This also might send you off to gather more data as you realise that your evidence is lacking in some way.

---

[8]There is an extensive literature on triangulation as a strategy for validation. It is covered in detail in many texts on mixed methods, as well as many qualitative methods texts. Alternatively, a search on the term will generate many finds. It is of interest that Denzin, who did much to popularise the term and the concept (e.g., Denzin, 1978), later repudiated it as a strategy for validation.

Generate predictions and account for negative cases

▶ Develop predictions based on your results, and test them against further data. Add further cases, to see if your theory can be applied.

▶ As you endeavour to account for all cases, treat as suspicious conclusions like: 'Most (or some) people said. ...' This immediately prompts the question: what about the rest? Alternative viewpoints warrant exploration and demand explanation. It is quite probable that not everybody experiences something in the same way, but we need to know this, and to know what and why this is.

Transparency of process and product

Transparency involves clear explanation of process that allows the reader to understand how you, as researcher, progressed from initial purposes, assumptions, and questions through data analysis to the results, interpretation, and conclusions of your study. These procedures need to be articulated clearly enough that others can assess their appropriateness and so they could potentially replicate them.

As there are multiple versions practised of any given methodology, it is never sufficient to simply say, with regard to your methodological process, 'grounded theory was used for this study' or 'a phenomenological approach was taken in interpreting the interviews'. (Even worse is to say, 'The data were analysed with NVivo' – or any other of a range of programs.) It is imperative that you describe just what it was that you did to select your sample and to gather and analyse your data, with the kind of detail I have been suggesting in the 'Writing about ...' sections of this book. If you have to compress your description of method for a journal article, it is still necessary to indicate (in summary) the kinds of processes you engaged in, rather than passing it off by naming a methodology. This is because one of the reader's best chances of assessing the quality of your article or thesis is to be able to trace the steps you took to arrive at your results and conclusions.

Transparency requires critical self-reflection (reflexivity). Achieving transparency will depend, as with so many other aspects of qualitative method, on your having kept an adequate record of your management of the research process and your approach to data analysis. Transparency designed to increase trustworthiness intersects with ethics, for example, in relation to fairness in reporting, or where it might conflict with confidentiality (Box 13.2).

Box 13.2

Transparency and the 'dark matter' of qualitative research

Naomi Weiner-Levy and Ariela Popper-Giveon (2011) describe what is left out of qualitative research reports as the 'dark matter' of qualitative research. They describe two main types of omissions other than those raised by space limitations: (a) personal experiences and biases of the researcher that

(Continued)

(Continued)

threaten privacy, are embarrassing, or threaten confidentiality; and (b) categories or themes that are left out because they are uncomfortable or inconvenient for the researcher or the participants. They suggest that the not-so-random elimination of uncomfortable categories from a report can affect interpretation of the results by the reader, and provide two examples from their own research.

- By omitting reference to payments made to Palestinian traditional healers by their clients, the 'spirituality' of the process was emphasised and the respect for such healers, who help marginalised women resume family roles, was preserved. This was, however, at the cost of cloaking the financially exploitative aspects of the relationships between the healers and their clients.
- Discussion of 'homicide for family honour', although mentioned frequently by them, was omitted from accounts of 'trailblazing' Druze women seeking higher education. Not mentioning their 'deviant' views left unexplained why these women were so careful to adhere to other specific behavioural norms. It also deprived the reader of a full understanding of the power of education for women in this community.

Weiner-Levy and Popper-Giveon concluded by recommending that aspects of a study which cannot be covered because of lack of space (if not also for other reasons) should at least be listed, to provide balance and transparency to the report. Sometimes this is necessary, just to ensure they are brought to the researcher's attention as they consider how they will present their data and conclusions.

Member checking or respondent validation

Member checking or respondent validation, that is, seeking agreement from participants and/or other stakeholders regarding the conclusions you have reached, is often promoted as a useful strategy for ensuring the quality of your results and the faithfulness of your interpretation of them. Issues related to respondent validation of data collected (e.g., through interviews) were discussed in Chapter 2; the focus here will be on checking your findings and conclusions. This can be a beneficial strategy in a number of situations:

- Where you are wanting to check the accuracy of descriptive information.
- If there are remaining uncertainties in your study, checking back with the source participants or community can help to clarify these. Similarly, they can comment on, and perhaps provide additional information about, what they regard as errors of judgement on your part (it is then up to you to decide how much of that opinion you take 'on board').
- Riessman (2008: 191) described situations where participants' stories might be fractured and lacking in coherence, such as for those who have survived trauma. Returning to the 'community of experience' could help make sense analytically of the thematic convergence and divergence across the stories.
- To obtain feedback on your interpretive analysis: this may generate further data.
- Clearing your use of respondent quotations or other data with the persons concerned by showing how you plan to use them, where surprise exposure and/or inadequate context could cause embarrassment, is important – although primarily from an ethical rather than a validation point of view.
- And finally, confirmation can be encouraging!

At the same time, member checking of the final results, conclusions, and interpretations *for the purpose of validation* raises issues that you need to keep in mind as you consider the appropriateness of this strategy:

- Not all participants will be the same and will have the same response to your report: so with whom are you checking?
- Are participants likely to be any more reliable as member checkers than they were when interviewed?
- What are you asking them to check: their part in a report (e.g., that there is a category in a typology that represents them), or the whole report?
- Research is often reported in multiple forms and contexts: are you going to ask them to check each one?
- The length of time between data collection and final analysis and publication could mean that participants have moved on. Perhaps life is different and they are no longer interested?
- If your interpretation is different from theirs, does that necessarily render it invalid? Any situation can be interpreted in multiple ways, even by the people experiencing it.
- What would be an appropriate response if your audience rejects your conclusions? Does your whole project become useless? (You could record that a dissenting viewpoint was expressed.)
- Is member checking redundant because your employment of theoretical sampling ensured that divergent views were always checked out against further data from either the original or additional participants?
- Your interpretation of people's contributions may go beyond their interest and comprehension, for example where a core process is abstracted from a range of subjective viewpoints, where you employ abstract concepts, develop broader theory, or delve into social or psychological unconsciousness. Your findings, therefore, may need 'translation' to be understood by a lay audience.

The issues in how participants are represented in your research and how you might meet obligations to report back to participants are different from member checking or respondent validation for checking validity or quality of results. Additionally, in projects designed in cooperation with a community (such as for participant action research), participants will clearly expect to have a level of control over the conduct and results of the research phases of the project. Issues of reporting back and representation are discussed later in this chapter.

Peer debriefing and consensual validation

- ▶ Test your conclusions with peers to clarify interpretations, and to check for gaps and for bias.
- ▶ Present your findings at a conference, to generate questions and discussion by peers, before finalising them for publication.
- ▶ If the findings of your research are accepted by a community of scholars as part of collective knowledge, and are useful as a 'point of departure for others' work', this suggests quality and value, although it can take some time to establish this (Riessman, 2008: 191).

Generalisation and transferability

As with validity, there has been discussion in the qualitative literature about the appropriateness of terms and concepts used to express the idea of what was traditionally known, for experimental or survey research, as external validity or generalisation. In that context, the idea was that precise sampling procedures made it possible to make statements about a larger population based on what was learned from a sample drawn from that population. As qualitative studies rarely achieve the required degree of precision in representative sampling, and don't aspire to, clearly the concept of generalisation in that sense is inappropriate. Rather, qualitative researchers have focused on theoretical or analytic generalisation, with the goal of developing theory with application beyond the immediate context. The term *transferability* was introduced by Lincoln and Guba (1985) as an alternative to generalisation, specifically to refer to case-to-case transfer of knowledge – the only form of generalisation they see as legitimate.

The important issues for researchers analysing qualitative data therefore are what is able to be generalised (applied more broadly) or transferred (from case to case), and under what conditions that can occur. The assumption underlying these questions is that there can be value in a qualitative project, even in a single case study, that will have relevance in a wider or alternative setting or time – that your work has significance (meaning or application) beyond the immediate here and now.

From single cases: the importance of context

Observation of single events or single cases generates contextualised, local knowledge from which can be derived unique understanding of causal processes and mechanisms that respects their situated complexity (Miles & Huberman, 1994). Sufficient information to assess applicability to a new situation is needed to facilitate case-to-case transfer of a programme or idea.

> As we begin to reflect on the state of general knowledge and social science, it is clear that much of what we know derives from classic case studies. Goffman (1961) tells us what goes on in mental institutions, Sykes (1958) explains the operation of prisons, Whyte (1943) and Liebow (1967) reveal the attractions of street-corner gangs, and Thompson (1971) makes food riots sensible. Examples could be multiplied to show that it is not only the skill and notoriety that these writers bring to their cases that establish them as standard interpretations. Lesser-known works have had the same effect on all of us. Rather, these kinds of case studies become classic because they provide models capable of instructive transferability to other settings. (Walton, 1992: 125–6)

The capacity for transferability from a single case rests in the level of detail provided and whether that records the full complexity of it, so as to contextualise the lessons learned from it (Firestone, 1993). It also assumes that the user of the information has differentiated critical from superficial characteristics in deter-mining its usefulness in the new situation (Flick, 2007b).

The idea that we can learn from a single case and use that information more broadly relates to the concept of a case presented in Chapter 1: that each singular person or event embraces a degree of universality, reflecting dimensions of the social structures and order of their time. What is learned from individual cases or case studies reflects this: it is not that we can describe the characteristics of a larger population, survey style, but rather that we gain understanding of the way some aspect of society works – an understanding of processes and principles, theory rather than facts. Such theory might then be applied, with appropriate modifications to take account of variations in context, to a new setting within that society, or perhaps even more widely. The single case allows also for qualita-tive exploration of process and causality that is foundational to causal generalisa-tion (Maxwell, in press).

From multiple cases: the importance of comparison

With multiple-case analyses, each case effectively acts as a replication of the study in a different person or setting. This gives some assurance that the results obtained are not completely idiosyncratic – that they will be more broadly appli-cable. The analytic benefit of having comparison cases is that it improves under-standing of processes and consequent explanations by allowing exploration of the way in which those processes are impacted by local conditions. As with single case studies, retaining full comprehension (and description) of the context of each case remains critical both to understanding and to applying results from cross-case analyses. When results are applied, if predictions are supported in other sites, this strengthens the analytic outcomes. Having multiple cases, then, allows you to:

- identify what is common across cases;
- test and confirm your findings on fresh cases;
- determine the ways in which variations in context shape the consequences of a common process;
- strengthen understanding by considering 'outlier' cases.

Theoretical extension

As suggested above, the primary benefit to be derived from qualitative analyses, beyond applicability to a local situation, is in their contribution to theoretical understanding about personal and interpersonal experiences and social pro-cesses. I will address two strategies in particular in this context, but I would remind you also of the importance of linking your work back to the theoretical literature and placing it in that context, so that your readers can see how you have challenged or added to knowledge in your substantive, theoretical, or methodological field.

Elaborating from local to substantive or general theory

In Chapter 11, theory elaboration was described as a strategy for developing theory by sampling from very diverse cases during its development. The strategy of elaborating theory to be described here is based on a similar concept and process, with the intention of taking what might be described as a local theory, developed through researching a small number of cases, to a higher level of generality, to move from a specific finding to 'middle-range' generalisation.

'The trick in developing theory,' Janice Morse observed, 'is to move from the particular to the general in small steps' (1994: 31), case by case – and the clue in doing so is to explore contrasts. If you stay with one area of study, such as one level of organisation, you will build in biases deriving from that particular context (Vaughan, 1992). Constant comparison, applied to an ever-widening and diverse range of possibilities, remains a key process throughout. Begin with replications and comparisons within the same general topic area to move from local to substantive theory, then cross borders into other topics and discipline areas to move from substantive to more general theory. Strauss noted, for example, that 'the theory of awareness context developed in *Awareness of Dying* (Glaser & Strauss, 1965) can be elaborated by looking at materials on con men, spies, government officials, court testimonies, and so on' (1995: 13). As each varied source is considered, it adds potentially useful concepts, contextual relationships, and conceptual complexity; the theory is extended in scope and so promises greater applicability to the world of practical action.

Strauss (1995) suggested two further strategies for elaborating theory:

▶ Take a proposed or developed theory and speculate about the effect of altering each component of it, asking questions stimulated by the alterations. Strauss applied this approach to elaborate Davis' (1961) grounded theory on deviancy disavowal, a theory 'about how persons with visible disabilities go about controlling this potentially damaging information to themselves when in a brief initial encounter with a nondisabled stranger' (1995: 15). What if, rather than being inexperienced with disability, the stranger has a spouse who was disabled, or is a physical therapist? What if the disability is invisible to the stranger; what difference does it make if it is more or less negative? How would each of these conditions affect the interaction between the two? And so 'one can continue with this comparative analytic game' – and reach a point where you can link this theory with other theories, for example, on stigma, awareness contexts, or intimacy.

▶ Read widely, including literature such as novels, biographies, and plays, for sensitising concepts and theoretical insights from the events and anecdotes contained therein. Many researchers point to the parallels between sociological themes and those portrayed in more popular literature – which is not surprising in so far as each reflects (or constructs) some facet of social life.

As theory becomes more general, it 'necessarily gathers up and helps to integrate what previously have been discrete theories, and elements of theories, that bear on the phenomena you are focused upon' (1995: 17). Such theory will always be subject to further theoretical sampling, testing, and refining.

Extending theory through synthesis: meta-ethnography and related approaches

Qualitative metasynthesis shares many characteristics with primary qualitative analysis, but uses completed studies as data rather than interviews or other original (unanalysed) sources. Qualitative synthesis (as meta-ethnography) was first detailed by Noblit and Hare (1988) with the goal of developing general or formal theory by combining the evidence of multiple qualitative studies. Others have since extended or refined their methodology, with as many as 11 different variations in approaches to qualitative synthesis being identified and reviewed by Dixon-Woods et al. (2005), Barnett-Page and Thomas (2009), and Major and Savin-Baden (2011). These approaches share many features, and can be categorised as falling into two major types: aggregative syntheses and interpretive syntheses. Table 13.2 summarises the key differences in these, in relation to the major steps in undertaking a qualitative synthesis.

A synthesis is different from a literature review, being designed to generate *new* results through a methodologically rigorous approach, rather than just report or review literature. Authors often have a practice or policy orientation, with the majority of qualitative syntheses having been conducted in health (especially nursing), and to a lesser extent, in education, with relatively few in other fields.

The first tasks that both aggregative and interpretive syntheses share are:

▶ Determine the purpose of and question to be informed by the synthesis.
▶ Identify and locate relevant studies for the synthesis. These are likely to include 'grey literature' as well as articles in journals, theses, and books. Use library databases, websites, recommendations of experts in the area, chain articles through following up references and citations.
▶ Set out inclusion and exclusion criteria for the material to be considered.
▶ Determine a policy regarding quality issues in the studies to be considered.
▶ Scan the studies that have been found, to ascertain coverage and key issues related to the topic.

Already you will be facing some major issues and decisions about your choice of literature to include in your qualitative synthesis:

• Setting a boundary on 'qualitative' can be difficult. For example, interpreted results from statistical analyses of survey or experimental data are also likely to be of value – but you may have to 'borrow' some skills to assess the quality of inferences from those.
• Initial assessment of what literature to include is typically done on the basis of keyword searches and scanning of abstracts – leading to spurious inclusions and sometimes notable absences.

- There needs to be sufficient detail of how the original analysis was done and the results from that to enable reanalysis, but these details are often missing in reports of studies.
- An article of otherwise poor quality might contain, nevertheless, some useful ideas; some distinguish between 'fatally flawed' and 'superficially flawed', eliminating only the former.

The next steps you take will largely depend on the purpose of your synthesis and the method chosen for completing it, as suggested in Table 13.2. An interpretive approach to synthesis is illustrated in Box 13.3.

Table 13.2   Two broad approaches to qualitative synthesis

Stages	Type of qualitative synthesis	
	Aggregative	**Interpretive**
Purpose	Synthesis	Analysis
Question(s)	Carefully specified *a priori*	Refined throughout analysis
Choosing relevant studies • inclusion criteria • quality criteria	May limit range or type of studies to be considered, attempt to find all available within specifications; Strict quality criteria for inclusion	Relevance more important than strict quality criteria, theoretical sampling based on issues raised as analysis proceeds
Reading and recording	Summarise and record details against pre-set criteria or categories, e.g., in a table, spreadsheet, or database format; privileges similarity	Coding, categories and themes developed iteratively with analysis, e.g., using QDA software; use each study to build on or refute others
Data analysis and synthesis	Aggregation of results. Summaries and conclusions based on overall patterns	Interpretive analysis and theorising; construction of new meanings. Contextual data important

---

Box 13.3

Using qualitative synthesis to study access to healthcare by vulnerable groups

In a system where everyone is entitled to free healthcare, such as in the UK, there nevertheless remains a vulnerable population who do not equally access those health services. Much has been researched and written on this issue, and so this was the literature that Mary Dixon-Woods and colleagues (2006) set out to systematically review and synthesise, starting with an 'anchor' question rather than a precise question with *a priori* definitions and categories. From an initial 100,000 articles and other items related to access, they identified 1200 potentially relevant records. They took a purposive then theoretical sampling approach to these, eventually reviewing 119 articles related to access by relevant groups in the UK. Quality was judged during the process of the review. Relevant information was summarised and then coded using QDA software, using a critical ('dynamic, recursive, and reflexive') approach to identify themes, categories, and patterns. The authors noted, in their discussion, that

> Subjecting a question to continual review and refinement, as we did, may make it more difficult for those conducting critical interpretive reviews to demonstrate, as required by conventional systematic review methodology, the 'transparency', comprehensiveness, and reproducibility of search strategies. This dilemma between the 'answerable' question and the 'meaningful' question has received little attention, but it underpins key tensions between the two ends of the academic/pragmatic systematic review spectrum. (2006: 11)

To explain what was happening with access and equity for vulnerable groups, they developed the 'synthetic' construct of *candidacy* to describe 'the ways in which people's eligibility for medical attention and intervention is jointly negotiated between individuals and health services' (2006: 7). Having described the conditions under which candidacy operated, the authors were then able to bring their work together in a final, one-paragraph, synthesising argument. What they had achieved was to move from the morass of multiple and diverse studies to an integrated, concise statement of the key processes and equity issues in accessing a universal healthcare system by vulnerable groups.

Ray Pawson (2006), with his focus on programme evaluation and its significance for policy development, wrote about synthesis in that context, from a critical realist perspective. He also took an interpretive approach to synthesis, with a central claim that: *'Research synthesis operates through processes of policy abstraction and theory-building rather than data extraction and number crunching'* (2006: 78, emphasis added). In making the point that synthesis is about contributing to theory, not delivering a verdict on a programme or policy, he emphasised the importance when dealing with interventions of evaluating the theories and logic models that provide the foundation for the interventions, and the personal, interpersonal, and systemic contexts in which they were conducted. That some cases may emphasise outcomes, others context, and others process is managed in an analytic process where each study is worked through one at a time, to see how it 'supports, weakens, modifies, supplements, reinterprets or refocuses the preliminary theory' (2006: 96) and so data from one study are used to make sense of a pattern in another. The 'lines of enquiry' driving the analysis are: *'What ... works, for whom, in what circumstances, in what respects and why?'* (2006: 94, emphasis in original). Pawson illustrated his approach with analyses of three programmes: sex offender registration, youth mentoring, and public disclosure through league tables.

Audiences and representation

Having received data from participants, communities, or archives, you have an obligation not only to analyse and interpret what you have found, but also to create an account of that to share with others, including those from whom you received it. Outcomes from your research in the form of print or other media will be shaped according to your intended audience, by your epistemological approach, and by ethical issues (Box 13.4). Your audiences will range from academic peers (and future generations of academics) to funding or commissioning bodies, policy makers and practitioners, and those whose data they were. For each of these audiences, the content and form of presentation will require your judgement about what is most relevant for that audience, and how it is best communicated to them.

Three questions that arise in this context are:

- whether, in what form, and at what time you have a responsibility to report back to participants or participant communities;
- whether it is possible to effectively represent another's voice to a wider audience – a question referred to in the literature as 'the crisis of representation';
- how to ensure that your research makes a difference.

| Box 13.4 |

Representation and reporting: two perspectives

Stories of people trying to sort out who they are figure prominently on the landscape of postmodern times. Those who have been objects of others' reports are now telling their own stories. As they do so, they define the ethic of our times: an ethic of voice, affording each a right to speak her own truth, in her own words. (Frank, 1995: xiii)

But giving voice or empowering the powerless through extensive quotation, however desirable it might be in its own right, is not the same as analysing what is said. (Antaki et al., 2003: 16)

Reporting back

Reporting back to your participants via member checking is often problematic when employed *as a strategy for validation* of your results. Providing feedback to those who contributed to your research *as a moral obligation* is an entirely different question. Reporting back is often a requirement of the commissioning of the research (e.g., in an evaluation study), or it may be that you are working jointly with participants to publish the outcomes of a collaborative project. If neither of these is the case, there might well remain an obligation, where possible, to make information about what has been learned from participants' contributions available individually to those participants or to a participating community – particularly as in a qualitative project, the contribution is likely to have been quite intensive or extensive. To do so is to validate the value of their engagement in the research, and to satisfy their aroused curiosity about the project.[9] Nevertheless, as for member checking, there may be times or situations where reporting back is problematic, irresponsible, or unethical.[10]

The primary difference from member checking is the form in which information is provided, and to whom. In this instance, you are not specifically seeking participants' confirmation of your findings; your interpretation is your responsibility. For those who are interested, what is likely to be most appropriate is a summary of the main points of what you have found from the participant group as a whole without focusing on or identifying individual members. Focus on those points most likely to be of interest to them, and allow discussion; they do not want a theoretical treatise. For reasons covered under member checking, this information should be made available to participants, rather than imposed on them, and sensitivity to the dynamics of the local situation is called for (Box 13.5).

⌐ Box 13.5 ⌐

Sensitivity in sharing results of research

In a roundtable forum, Carolyn Ellis (Ellis et al., 2008) recounted the considerable embarrassment and loss of faith that resulted when a university colleague had shared some of Ellis' observations from her first fieldwork project about people in an isolated fishing community with members of that community.

> The fisher folk had known I was doing research. But I had been there for 9 years, and they forgot. At this point, to them I was pretty much just Carolyn coming to the community to visit. They were extremely hurt by what they heard. I had described them as smelling like fish and other things equally devastating. These people had become really good friends of mine. I loved them and cared for them, and what I said was very painful for them and also for me. I went back to the community and talked with them. Some people forgave me. Some people never did forgive me. (2008: 272)

Some years after this incident, she reflected on the ethical issues of research that are not usually considered by an institutional research board in an article about returning to the field (Ellis, 1995).

In my study of mental health needs and resources in a public housing estate, following an exploratory phase involving participant observation, key informant interviews, a household interview-based survey with over 80 per cent of resident

---

[9]Ensuring the results of an evaluation or a commissioned study reach all those who contributed, including those in less powerful positions, can be difficult, especially if negativity was expressed about the gatekeepers occupying the more powerful positions.

[10]For example, when a participant in a study expects to recover from what is actually a terminal degenerative condition, such as motor neurone disease.

households, and documentation of social indicator data, I personally delivered an invitation to each of the 256 households to a meeting in the local school to hear about what I had found; 27 took up the invitation. The information was presented orally and in a printed version that made extensive use of diagrams to summarise what I had found out about the community. As a consequence of presenting that information, considerable discussion ensued and a new neighbourhood group was formed to work on solutions to some of the problems and issues revealed by the research.

Reporting back to constituent organisations or communities is often an empowering action for those communities – one that you need to be ready for as it may involve you in further follow-up responsibilities. Influencing policy makers and powerbrokers is more difficult, often frustratingly so. After spending several years in an ethnographic study where he was involved with 'gang girls and the boys they know', Mark Fleisher (2000) declared that his problem wasn't learning about youth crime or identifying its causes and effects. His greatest challenge was learning how best to bring his research to the attention of lawmakers, in a form that was useful to them: 'While we publish and save ourselves from perishing, our informants perish in the ghettos we leave behind' (2000: 248).

The crisis of representation

Recognition of the incapacity of a researcher to effectively represent the culture, life experiences, and voices of participants, labelled as 'the crisis of representation', was considered to be the fourth major 'moment' in the history of qualitative methods by Denzin and Lincoln (2000: 16). Sandelowski observed:

> Qualitative researchers have generally found comfort in the belief that qualitative methods permit more intimate, empathetic, and, therefore, more accurate portrayals of the lives of the participants in their studies than quantitative methods. But the crisis of representation has shown this belief to be naive, at best, and hubris, at worst. (2006: 10)

The concept of a crisis of representation stems from French postmodern thinking of the 1960s. In a 1972 conversation with Foucault about political power and the role of intellectuals in representing the conditions of 'the masses', Deleuze observed: 'you were the first – in your books and in the practical sphere – to teach us something absolutely fundamental: the indignity of speaking for others ... that only those directly concerned can speak in a practical way on their own behalf' (Foucault & Deleuze, 1977: 209). In speaking for others, we disempower those who might speak for themselves – even if we are part of the group being represented:[11]

> In both the practice of speaking for as well as the practice of speaking about others, I am engaging in the act of representing the other's needs, goals, situation, and in fact, *who they*

---

[11]This, in itself, raises issues of what group membership might mean (Alcoff, 1991–2).

are. I am representing them *as* such and such, or in post-structuralist terms, I am participating in the construction of their subject-positions … such representations are in every case mediated and the product of interpretation (Alcoff, 1991–2: 9, emphasis in original)

At the same time, Alcoff suggests:

The declaration that I 'speak only for myself' has the sole effect of allowing me to avoid responsibility and accountability for my effects on others; it cannot literally erase those effects. (1991–2: 20)

The solution, as Alcoff points out, is *not* to say nothing at all, particularly where the goal is to speak out against oppression or injustice, but to look for ways of lessening the dangers of speaking for others:

the practice of speaking for others remains the best possibility in some existing situations. An absolute retreat weakens political effectivity, is based on a metaphysical illusion, and often effects only an obscuring of the intellectual's power. (1991–2: 24)

Indeed, to recommend or even suggest that we never speak for others, or attempt to represent their position, would silence us as social scientists, and would deny us an opportunity to act as transformative agents in the social and political worlds. The ideal situation might be to sufficiently engage those designed to be participants in research as co-researchers that they are empowered to both steer the ongoing direction of the research and speak for themselves. Where this is either not possible or not appropriate, consider and apply the following strategies so as to reduce the dangers involved in representing participants to the wider world:[12]

▶ Analyse why you feel you need to speak for others.
▶ Engage in a process of critical self-reflection through keeping a journal.
▶ Balance your own perspectives with a broader literature.
▶ Reflexively interrogate your own position in relation to both research participants and audience, the context of the research and speaking about it, and your personal interests – and how these impact on what you are saying.
▶ Take responsibility for your perspective, actions, and words.
▶ Attempt to assess the effects of your work, and presentations from it; then learn from that for future studies.
▶ Offer opportunities for others to represent you, in order to better understand the phenomenon of being represented.

A final reflection

As you contemplate where your analytical endeavours have taken you, apply reflexive thought to the ways in which any limitations of method (which you will

---

[12]These are drawn from Alcoff (1991–2), Patton (2002), Schwandt (2007), and Seale (2004).

have outlined at the end of your methodology section) might have impacted on the results you obtained and what you have been able to say with them as a consequence. The goal here is not to put an unjustified 'gloss' on things, or to condemn your own work, but to openly and transparently evaluate those impacts. 'The researcher should not waste time trying to eliminate "investigator effects"; instead, she should concentrate on *understanding* those effects' (Delamont, 2002: 8). Having done so, you are in a position to point out the value of your contribution as well as its limitations.

Writing about quality and significance

In the methodology chapter

▶ Record the strategies used to ensure that your work has met criteria of quality.
▶ Anticipate criticisms and discuss them.
▶ Record steps taken to facilitate the possibility of generalisation or transfer of your work to other locations or projects.
▶ Indicate how you deal with the ethical issues raised by your representation of others' lifeworlds.

In the results chapters and conclusion

▶ Provide enough detail to convince readers you understand what the issues are for your topic, and that you have a firm basis, through having done detailed analysis, for what you have learned about those issues.
▶ Think about what it was that led you from your questions and data to your conclusions, and convinced you of them. Now use that evidence and understanding to convince your readers.
▶ Provide sufficient context for your findings that others can transfer what you have learned to parallel situations.
▶ Indicate how limitations in your methods might have affected your conclusions.

Exercises

Exercise 1: Quality of research

▶ Review a research study and ask the following questions of it:
   o What rival explanations might there be for the findings from the study?
   o How are their claims made plausible by the researchers?
   o Do the authors comment on any threats to the validity of their results? Are there any such, or any other threats that you can see?
   o Are the claims supported by sufficient evidence to be credible?

Exercise 2: Representations

▶ Carol Bacchi (1999: 12–13) offers the following questions to guide analysis of policy-oriented problems. Try them on a sample policy-oriented article.

o How is the problem represented in either a specific policy debate or a specific policy proposal?

o What presuppositions or assumptions underlie this representation?

o What effects are produced by this representation? How are subjects constituted within it? What is likely to change? What is likely to stay the same? Who is likely to benefit from this representation?

o What is left unproblematic in this representation?

o How would responses differ if the problem were thought about or represented differently?

Further reading

Seale (1999; 2004) describes and provides examples of criteria for quality and generalisation in qualitative research.

Lincoln and Guba (1990) outline *resonance, rhetoric, empowerment,* and *applicability* as criteria for judging the quality of case study reports.

Maxwell (2012: Chapter 8; 2013: Chapter 6) addresses issues of what validity means from a critical realist perspective, and suggests strategies to increase the validity of inferences from your research.

Pawson (2006) provides extensive coverage of the logic, theory, and practice of interpretive synthesis in the context of evaluation studies. A shorter version is available in Pawson (2008).

Firestone (1993) discusses three forms of generalisation from qualitative data: sample-to-population extrapolation, analytic generalisation, and case-to-case transfer. He details the usefulness and hazards of each and details strategies to improve capacity to generalise from qualitative data.

Strauss (1995) is a very readable record of a lecture he gave in which he describes and illustrates (in some detail) the process of elaborating theory.

Whyte, in an appendix for the fourth edition of *Street corner society* ([1943] 1993), responds to criticism of his representation, or 'exploitation', of the young men of Cornerville.

Mitchell (2011) discusses, and illustrates through nine case examples, a range of ethical and political issues that can arise in community-based visual research projects on sensitive subjects with regard to privacy issues as well as ownership and use of photographs in various reporting contexts. She provides guidelines and examples of consent forms for such projects.

After-Words

As I draw to the end of a long, arduous, but enjoyable journey of writing, I am all too conscious of what I have and have not been able to include in this book. My goal, throughout, has been to provide a range of ideas and strategies for analysis for those who choose to take a qualitative approach in their research, as well as those who find themselves dealing unexpectedly with qualitative data. It has also been my goal to make these strategies accessible, at the risk of being accused of oversimplifying or trivialising important issues held dear by ardent methodologists. My hope in doing so is that these ideas, strategies, and guidelines will assist students, academics, and practitioners who engage in qualitative analysis to develop their skills in critical, reflexive thinking, with consequent benefits for the depth of their interpretive understanding and the quality of their reporting.

Two themes have permeated my approach to qualitative analysis:

1 Maintain a habit of writing reflective notes throughout your study, from initial planning through to completion.
2 Constantly challenge your data, asking questions of each item, each statement, each interim conclusion, leading you to see them in new ways or to seek more information.

To these, I would add a third 'prescription': enjoy the process!

C. Wright Mills (1959) described research – and analysis in particular – as an intellectual craft. He was more interested in learning from experience and history than from theoretical formulations about procedures, suggesting that research is inseparable from life experience. Keeping a journal of personal experience, professional activities, studies under way, and studies you might think of doing – capturing fleeting thoughts and ideas, interesting observations, and even dreams – was, for Mills, a most essential task for a researcher to undertake. 'Imagination is often successfully invited by putting together hitherto isolated items, by finding unsuspected connections' (1959: 201). The imagination that finally brings things together 'in considerable part consists of the capacity to shift from one perspective to another', combining ideas no one expected could be combined, doing so with a 'playfulness of mind ... as well as a truly fierce drive to make sense of the world' (1959: 211).

Mills captured the playfulness and inquisitiveness that I also believe drive the researcher's imagination and work. Perhaps this book will have contributed to both, for you. Writing it has done so, for me.

References

Abbott, A. (1992). What do cases do? Some notes on activity in sociological analysis. In C. Ragin & H. Becker (Eds.), *What is a case? Exploring the foundations of social inquiry* (pp. 53–82). New York: Cambridge University Press.

Agee, J., & Evans, W. (1941). *Let us now praise famous men.* Boston: Houghton Mifflin.

Åkerlind, G. S. (2005). Variation and commonality in phenomenographic research methods. *Higher Education Research & Development, 24*(4), 321–334.

Åkerlind, G. S. (2008). An academic perspective on research and being a researcher: an integration of the literature. *Studies in Higher Education, 33*(1), 17–31.

Alcoff, L. M. (1991–2). The problem of speaking for others. *Cultural Critique. 20*(Winter), 5–32.

Alexander, B. K. (2005). Performance ethnography: the reenacting and inciting of culture. In N. K. Denzin & Y. S. Lincoln (Eds.), *Handbook of qualitative research* (3rd ed., pp. 411–442). Thousand Oaks, CA: Sage.

Allison, G. T. (1971). *Essence of decision: explaining the Cuban missile crisis.* Boston: Little, Brown.

Andrews, M., Day Sclater, S., Squire, C., & Tamboukou, M. (2004). Narrative research. In C. Seale, G. Gobo, J. F. Gubrium, & D. Silverman (Eds.), *Qualitative research practice* (pp. 109–124). London: Sage.

Antaki, C., Billig, M., Edwards, D., & Potter, J. (2003). Discourse analysis means doing analysis: a critique of six analytic shortcomings. *Discourse Analysis Online, 1,* Available from www.shu.ac.uk/daol/articles/v1/n1/a1/antaki2002002-paper.html.

Atkinson, P. (1990). *The ethnographic imagination: textual constructions of reality.* London: Routledge.

Atkinson, P. (2005). Qualitative research: unity and diversity. *Forum: Qualitative Social Research, 6*(3), Article 26, 25 paragraphs.

Attride-Stirling, J. (2001). Thematic networks: an analytic tool for qualitative research. *Qualitative Research, 1*(3), 385–405.

Auerbach, C. F., Salick, E., & Fine, J. (2006). Using grounded theory to develop treatment strategies for multicontextual trauma. *Professional Psychology Research and Practice, 37*(4), 367–373.

AusAID (2005). *AusGuideline 3.3 The logical framework approach.* Canberra: Commonwealth of Australia. Available from www.ausaid.gov.au/ausguide/pdf/ausguideline3.3.pdf.

Australian Securities and Investments Commission (2002). *Hook, line & sinker: who takes the bait in cold calling scams?* Sydney: ASIC.

Ayres, L. (2000a). Narratives of family caregiving: four story types. *Research in Nursing and Health, 23* (September), 359–371.

Ayres, L. (2000b). Narratives of family caregiving: the process of making meaning. *Research in Nursing and Health, 23* (October), 424–434.

Ayres, L., Kavanaugh, K., & Knafl, K. A. (2003). Within-case and across-case approaches to qualitative data analysis. *Qualitative Health Research, 13*(1), 1–13.

Bacchi, C. L. (1999). *Women, policy and politics: the construction of policy problems.* London: Sage.

Bacon, F. (1620). *Novum Organum II.* Reprinted as: Preface to *The New Organon: or True directions concerning the interpretation of nature.* Available from University of Adelaide, ebooks.adelaide.edu.au/b/bacon/francis/organon/.

Baker, S. E., & Edwards, R. (2012). How many qualitative interviews is enough? *NCRM Methods Review Papers.* Retrieved from eprints.ncrm.ac.uk/2273/.

Bakker, R. M., Cambré, B., Korlaar, L., & Raab, J. (2011). Managing the project learning paradox: a set-theoretic approach toward project knowledge transfer. *International Journal of Project Management, 29*(5), 494–503.

Barnett-Page, E., & Thomas, J. (2009). Methods for the synthesis of qualitative research: a critical review. *NCRM Working Paper Series 01/09*, 1–25. Retrieved from eprints.ncrm.ac.uk/690/.

Bazeley, P. (1977). *Community development for mental health.* PhD, Macquarie University, Sydney.

Bazeley, P. (1998). Peer review and panel decisions in the assessment of Australian Research Council project grant applications: what counts in a highly competitive context? *Higher Education, 35,* 435–452.

Bazeley, P. (2006a). The contribution of computer software to integrating qualitative and quantitative data and analyses. *Research in the Schools, 13*(1), 63–73.

Bazeley, P. (2006b). Research dissemination in creative arts, humanities and the social sciences. *Higher Education Research and Development, 25*(3), 215–229.

Bazeley, P. (2007). *Qualitative data analysis with NVivo.* London: Sage.

Bazeley, P. (2009). Analysing qualitative data: more than 'identifying themes'. *Malaysian Journal of Qualitative Research, 2*(2), 6–22.

Bazeley, P. (2010a). Computer assisted integration of mixed methods data sources and analyses. In A. Tashakkori & C. Teddlie (Eds.), *Handbook of mixed methods research for the social and behavioral sciences* (2nd ed., pp. 431–467). Thousand Oaks, CA: Sage.

Bazeley, P. (2010b). Conceptualising research performance. *Studies in Higher Education, 35*(8), 889–904.

Bazeley, P., & Jackson, K. (in press). *Qualitative data analysis with NVivo* (2nd ed.). London: Sage.

Bazeley, P., & Kemp, L. (1995). The 'p's and 'q's of immunisation clinics: a review of public immunisation services. *Environmental Health Review Australia. 24*(2), 27–34.

Bazeley, P., Kemp, L., Stevens, K., Asmar, C., Grbich, C., Marsh, H., & Bhathal, R. (1996). *Waiting in the wings: a study of early career academic researchers in Australia.* National Board of Employment Education and Training Commissioned Report no. 50. Canberra: Australian Government Publishing Service.

Becker, H. ([1953] 2006). How to become a marihuana user. In J. O'Brien (Ed.), *The production of reality* (4th ed., pp. 140-148). Thousand Oaks, CA: Pine Forge.

Becker, H. (1963). *Outsiders: studies in the sociology of deviance.* New York: Free Press.

Becker, H. S. (1998). *Tricks of the trade: how to think about your research while you're doing it.* Chicago: University of Chicago Press.

Bergene, A. C. (2007). Toward a critical realist comparative methodology: context sensitive theoretical comparison. *Journal of Critical Realism. 6*(1), 5-27.

Berg-Schlosser, D., & De Meur, G. (2009). Comparative research design: case and variable selection. In B. Rihoux & C. Ragin (Eds.), *Configurational comparative methods* (pp. 19-32). Thousand Oaks, CA: Sage.

Berg-Schlosser, D., De Meur, G., Rihoux, B., & Ragin, C. (2009). Qualitative comparative analysis (QCA) as an approach. In B. Rihoux & C. Ragin (Eds.), *Configurational comparative methods* (pp. 1-18). Thousand Oaks, CA: Sage.

Bernard, H. R., & Ryan, G. W. (2010). *Analyzing qualitative data: systematic approaches.* Thousand Oaks, CA: Sage.

Biesta, G. (2010). Pragmatism and the philosophical foundations of mixed methods research. In A. Tashakkori & C. Teddlie (Eds.), *Handbook of mixed methods research in the social and behavioral sciences* (2nd ed., pp. 95-117). Thousand Oaks, CA: Sage.

Birks, M., & Mills, J. (2011). *Grounded theory: a practical guide.* London: Sage.

Bletzer, K., & Koss, M. P. (2006). After-rape among three populations in the Southwest. *Violence Against Women, 12*, 5-29.

Bogdan, R., & Biklen, S. K. (1992). *Qualitative research for education: an introduction to theory and methods* (2nd ed.). Boston: Allyn & Bacon.

Boote, D. N., & Beile, P. (2005). Scholars before researchers: on the centrality of the dissertation literature review in research preparation. *Educational Researcher, 34*(6), 3-15.

Bowers, B. J. (1989). Grounded theory. In B. Sarter (Ed.), *Paths to knowledge: innovative research methods for nursing* (pp. 33-59). New York: National League for Nursing.

Boyatzis, R. E. (1998). *Transforming qualitative information: thematic analysis and code development.* Thousand Oaks, CA: Sage.

Braun, V., & Clarke, V. (2006). Using thematic analysis in psychology. *Qualitative Research in Psychology, 3*, 77-101.

Brew, A. (2001). Conceptions of research: a phenomenographic study. *Studies in Higher Education, 26*, 271-285.

Brewer, J., & Hunter, A. (2006). *Foundations of multimethod research: synthesizing styles* (2nd ed.). Thousand Oaks, CA: Sage.

Brinkmann, S. (2012). *Qualitative inquiry in everyday life.* London: Sage.

Brinton, C. (1938). *Anatomy of a revolution.* Englewood Cliffs, NJ: Prentice Hall.

Bruce, C. D. (2007). Questions arising about emergence, data collection, and its interaction with analysis in a grounded theory study. *International Journal of Qualitative Methods, 6*(1), Art. 4, 1-12. Retrieved from www.ualberta.ca/~iiqm/backissues/6_1/bruce.pdf.

Bryman, A. (2006). Integrating quantitative and qualitative research: how is it done? *Qualitative Research, 6*(1), 97-113.

Butow, P. N., & Lobb, E. A. (2004). Analyzing the process and content of genetic counseling in familial breast cancer consultations. *Journal of Genetic Counseling*, *13*(5), 403–424.

Byrne, D. (2009a). Case-based methods: why we need them; what they are; how to do them. In D. Byrne & C. Ragin (Eds.), *Handbook of case-based methods* (pp. 1–10). London: Sage.

Byrne, D. (2009b). Using cluster analysis, qualitative comparative analysis and NVivo in relation to the establishment of causal configurations with pre-existing large-*N* datasets: machining hermeneutics. In D. Byrne & C. Ragin (Eds.), *Handbook of case-based methods* (pp. 260–268). London: Sage.

Carey, M. A., & Asbury, J. (2012). *Essentials of focus groups*. Walnut Creek, CA: Left Coast Press, Inc.

Carley, K. (1993). Coding choices for textual analysis: a comparison of content analysis and map analysis. *Sociological Methodology*, *23*, 75–126.

Caron, C. D., & Bowers, B. J. (2000). Methods and application of dimensional analysis: a contribution to concept and knowledge development in nursing. In B. L. Rodgers & K. A. Knafl (Eds.), *Concept development in nursing: foundations, techniques and applications* (pp. 285–319). Philadelphia: Saunders.

Charmaz, K. (2006). *Constructing grounded theory*. Thousand Oaks, CA: Sage.

Cisneros-Puebla, C. A. (2004). 'To learn to think conceptually': Juliet Corbin in conversation with Cesar A. Cisneros-Puebla. *Forum: Qualitative Social Research*, *5*(3), Art. 32, 53 paragraphs.

Clark, A. (2007). Understanding community: a review of networks, ties and contacts. *NCRM Working Paper Series 9/07*, 1–39. Retrieved from eprints.ncrm.ac.uk/469/.

Clarke, A. E. (2005). *Situational analysis: grounded theory mapping after the postmodern turn*. Thousand Oaks, CA: Sage.

Clarke, A. E. (2009). From grounded theory to situational analysis. In J. M. Morse (Ed.), *Developing grounded theory: the second generation* (pp. 194–233). Walnut Creek, CA: Left Coast Press, Inc.

Coffey, A., & Atkinson, P. (1996). *Making sense of qualitative data*. Thousand Oaks, CA: Sage.

Colaizzi, P. F. (1978). Psychological research as the phenomenologist sees it. In R. S. Valle & M. King (Eds.), *Existential phenomenological alternatives for psychology* (pp. 48–71). New York: Oxford University Press.

Coll, A. M. (n.d.). *Experience of pain after day surgery*. School of Care Sciences, University of Glamorgan. Pontypridd, Wales.

Collins, C. C., & Dressler, W. W. (2008). Cultural consensus and cultural diversity: a mixed methods investigation of human service providers' models of domestic violence. *Journal of Mixed Methods Research*, *2*(4), 362–387.

Conroy, D. L. (1987). *A phenomenological study of police officers as victims*. PhD, The Union Institute, Cincinnati, OH.

Cooper, G. (2008). Conceptualising social life. In N. Gilbert (Ed.), *Researching social life* (3rd ed., pp. 5–20). London: Sage.

Corbin, J. (2009). Taking an analytic journey. In J. M. Morse (Ed.), *Developing grounded theory* (pp. 35–53). Walnut Creek, CA: Left Coast Press, Inc.

Corbin, J., & Strauss, A. L. (2008). *Basics of qualitative research* (3rd ed.). Thousand Oaks, CA: Sage.

Cressey, D. R. (1953). *Other people's money: a study in the social psychology of embezzlement*. New York: Free Press.

Creswell, J. W. (2003). *Research design: qualitative, quantitative and mixed methods approaches* (2nd ed.). Thousand Oaks, CA: Sage.

Crossley, N. (2008). Pretty connected: the social network of the early UK punk movement. *Theory, Culture and Society, 25*(6), 89–116.

Crossley, N. (2011). Using social network analysis: researching relational structure. In J. Mason & A. Dale (Eds.), *Understanding social research: thinking creatively about method* (pp. 75–89). London: Sage.

Crotty, M. (1998). *The foundations of social research*. Sydney: Allen & Unwin.

Cumming, J. (2007). *Representing the complexity, diversity and particularity of the doctoral enterprise in Australia*. PhD, The Australian National University, Canberra.

Danermark, B., Ekström, M., Jakobsen, L., & Karlsson, J. C. (2002). *Explaining society: critical realism in the social sciences*. London: Routledge.

Davidson, J., & di Gregorio, S. (2011). Qualitative research and technology. In N. K. Denzin & Y. S. Lincoln (Eds.), *Handbook of qualitative research* (4th ed., pp. 627–639). Thousand Oaks, CA: Sage.

Davis, F. (1961). Deviance disavowal. *Social Problems, 9*, 120–132.

Day, T., & Kincaid, H. (1994). Putting inference to the best explanation in its place. *Synthese, 98*(2), 271–295.

Degenhardt, L. M. (2006). *Reinventing a school for the 21st century: a case study of change in a Mary Ward school*. PhD, Australian Catholic University, Sydney.

Degenhardt, L. M., & Duignan, P. (2010). *Dancing on a shifting carpet: reinventing traditional schooling for the 21st century*. Melbourne: Australian Council for Educational Research.

De Gioia, K. (2003). *Beyond cultural diversity: exploring micro and macro culture in the early childhood setting*. PhD, University of Western Sydney, Sydney.

Delamont, S. (2002). *Fieldwork in educational settings* (2nd ed.). New York: Routledge.

Denning, S. (2001). *The springboard: how storytelling ignites action in knowledge-era organizations*. Portsmouth, NH: Butterworth-Heinemann.

Denzin, N. K. (1978). *The research act: a theoretical introduction to sociological methods* (2nd ed.). New York: McGraw-Hill.

Denzin, N. K. (1989). *Interpretive interactionism*. Newbury Park, CA: Sage.

Denzin, N. K. (2001). *Interpretive interactionism* (2nd ed.). Thousand Oaks, CA: Sage.

Denzin, N. K. (2003). *Performance ethnography: critical pedagogy and the politics of culture*. Thousand Oaks, CA: Sage.

Denzin, N. K., & Lincoln, Y. S. (2000). Introduction: the discipline and practice of qualitative research. In N. K. Denzin & Y. S. Lincoln (Eds.), *Handbook of qualitative research* (2nd ed., pp. 1–29). Thousand Oaks, CA: Sage.

Denzin, N. K., & Lincoln, Y. S. (Eds.) (1994; 2000; 2005; 2011). *Handbook of qualitative research*. Thousand Oaks, CA: Sage.

Dey, I. (1993). *Qualitative data analysis: a user-friendly guide for social scientists*. London: Routledge & Kegan Paul.

Dey, I. (2004). Grounded theory. In C. Seale, G. Gobo, J. F. Gubrium, & D. Silverman (Eds.), *Qualitative research practice* (pp. 80–93). London: Sage.

Dickson, A., Allan, D., & O'Carroll, R. (2008). Biographical disruption and the experience of loss following a spinal cord injury: an interpretative phenomenological analysis. *Psychology and Health, 23*(4), 407–425.

Dixon-Woods, M., Agarwal, S., Jones, D., Young, B., & Sutton, A. (2005). Synthesising qualitative and quantitative evidence: a review of possible methods. *Journal of Health Services Research and Policy, 10*(1), 45–53.

Dixon-Woods, M., Cavers, D., Agarwal, S., Annandale, E., Arthur, A., Harvey, J., et al. (2006). Conducting a critical interpretive synthesis of the literature on access to healthcare by vulnerable groups. *BMC Medical Research Methodology, 6*(35), 1–15.

Douglas, J. E., & Douglas, L. K. (2006). Modus operandi and signature aspects of violent crime. In J. E. Douglas, A. W. Burgess, A. G. Burgess, & R. K. Ressler (Eds.), *Crime classification manual: a standard system for investigating and classifying violent crimes* (pp. 19–30). San Francisco: Wiley.

Drew, P. (2003). Conversation analysis. In J. A. Smith (Ed.), *Qualitative psychology* (pp. 132–158). London: Sage.

Eastwood, J. (2011). *Realist theory building for social epidemiology: building a theoretical model of neighbourhood context and the developmental origins of health and disease using postnatal depression as a case study*. PhD, University of New South Wales, Sydney.

Eisenhardt, K. M. (2002). Building theories from case study research. In A. M. Huberman & M. B. Miles (Eds.), *The qualitative researcher's companion* (pp. 5–35). Thousand Oaks, CA: Sage.

Elliott, J. (2005). *Using narrative in social research: qualitative and quantitative approaches*. London: Sage.

Ellis, C. (1995). Emotional and ethical quagmires in returning to the field. *Journal of Contemporary Ethnography, 24*, 711–713.

Ellis, C. (2004). *The ethnographic I: a methodological novel about autoethnography*. Walnut Creek, CA: AltaMira.

Ellis, C., Bochner, A., Denzin, N., Lincoln, Y., Morse, J., Pelias, R., & Richardson, L. (2008). Talking and thinking about qualitative research. *Qualitative Inquiry, 14*, 254–284.

Emerson, R. M., Fretz, R. I., & Shaw, L. L. (1995). *Writing ethnographic fieldnotes*. Chicago: University of Chicago Press.

Encarta UK Dictionary (2010) Seattle: Microsoft Corporation

Esposito, N. (2001). From meaning to meaning: the influence of translation techniques on non-English focus group research. *Qualitative Health Research, 11*(4), 568–579.

Ezzy, D. (2002). *Qualitative analysis: practice and innovation*. London: Routledge.

Fairclough, N. (2003). *Analyzing discourse: textual analysis for social research*. New York: Routledge.

Farnsworth, J., & Boon, B. (2010). Analysing group dynamics within the focus group. *Qualitative Research, 10*(5), 605–624.

Fielding, J. (2008). Coding and managing data. In N. Gilbert (Ed.), *Researching social life* (3rd ed., pp. 323–352). London: Sage.

Firestone, W. A. (1993). Alternative arguments for generalising from data as applied to qualitative research. *Educational Researcher, 22*(4), 16–23.

Fleisher, M. (2000). *Dead end kids: gang girls and the boys they know.* Madison, WI: University of Wisconsin Press.

Flick, U. (2007a). *Designing qualitative research.* London: Sage.

Flick, U. (2007b). *Managing quality in qualitative research.* London: Sage.

Flick, U. (2009). *An introduction to qualitative research* (4th ed.). London: Sage.

Flyvbjerg, B. (2004). Five misunderstandings about case-study research. In C. Seale, G. Gobo, J. F. Gubrium, & D. Silverman (Eds.), *Qualitative research practice* (pp. 420–434). London: Sage.

Foucault, M., & Deleuze, G. (1977). Intellectuals and power: a conversation between Michel Foucault and Gilles Deleuze (D. F. Bouchard & S. Simon, Trans.). In D. F. Bouchard (Ed.), *Language, counter-memory, practice: selected essays and interviews* (pp. 205–217). Ithaca, NY: Cornell University Press.

Frank, A. W. (1995). *The wounded storyteller: body, illness, and ethics.* Chicago: University of Chicago Press.

Fransella, F., Bell, R., & Bannister, D. (2003). *A manual for repertory grid technique* (2nd ed.). Chichester: Wiley.

Friese, S. (2012). *Qualitative data analysis with Atlas.ti.* London: Sage.

Frost, P. J., & Stablein, R. E. (1992). *Doing exemplary research.* Newbury Park, CA: Sage.

Fry, G., Chantavanich, S., & Chantavanich, A. (1981). Merging quantitative and qualitative research techniques: toward a new research paradigm. *Anthropology and Education Quarterly, 12*(2), 145–158.

Gee, J. P. (1986). Units in the production of narrative discourse. *Discourse Processes. 9,* 391–422.

Gee, J. P. (1991). A linguistic approach to narrative. *Journal of Narrative and Life History, 1*(1), 15–39.

Gee, J. P. (2011). *How to do discourse analysis: a toolkit.* New York: Routledge.

Geertz, C. (1973). Thick description: towards an interpretive theory of culture. In C. Geertz (Ed.), *The interpretation of cultures: selected essays* (pp. 3–30). New York: Basic.

Gergen, K. J., & Gergen, M. M. (1988). Narrative and the self as relationship. In L. Berkowitz (Ed.), *Advances in experimental social psychology* (pp. 17–56). San Diego, CA: Academic.

Gersick, C. J. G. (1988). Time and transition in work teams: toward a new model of group development. *Academy of Management Journal, 31*(1), 9–41.

Gherardi, S., & Turner, B. (2002). Real men don't collect soft data. In A. M. Huberman & M. B. Miles (Eds.), *The qualitative researcher's companion* (pp. 81–100). Thousand Oaks, CA: Sage.

Gibbs, G. (2007). *Analyzing qualitative data.* London: Sage.

Gibson, W. J., & Brown, A. (2009). *Working with qualitative data.* London: Sage.

Giddings, L. S., & Grant, B. M. (2009). From rigour to trustworthiness: validating mixed methods. In S. Andrew & E. Halcomb (Eds.), *Mixed methods research for nursing and the health sciences* (pp. 119–134). Chichester: Wiley-Blackwell.

Gilbert, L. S. (2002). Going the distance: 'closeness' in qualitative data analysis software. *International Journal of Social Research Methodology, 5*(3), 215–228.

Gilligan, C., Spencer, R., Weinberg, M. C., & Bertsch, T. (2003). On the listening guide: a voice-centred relational method. In P. M. Camic, J. E. Rhodes, & L. Yardley (Eds.), *Qualitative research in psychology: expanding perspectives in methodology and design* (pp. 157–172). Washington, DC: American Psychological Association.

Giorgi, A., & Giorgi, B. (2003). Phenomenology. In J. A. Smith (Ed.), *Qualitative psychology* (pp. 25–50). London: Sage.

Glaser, B. G. (1978). *Theoretical sensitivity*. Mill Valley, CA: Sociology Press.

Glaser, B. G. (1992). *Basics of grounded theory analysis: emergence vs. forcing*. Mill Valley, CA: Sociology Press.

Glaser, B. G. (2002). Constructivist grounded theory? *Forum: Qualitative Social Research, 3*(3), 47 paragraphs.

Glaser, B. G., & Strauss, A. (1965). *Awareness of dying*. Chicago: Aldine.

Glaser, B. G., & Strauss, A. (1967). *The discovery of grounded theory: strategies for qualitative research*. Chicago: Aldine.

Goertz, G. (2006). *Social science concepts: a user's guide*. Princeton, NJ: Princeton University Press.

Goffman, E. (1961). *Asylums: Essays on the social situation of mental patients and other inmates*. Garden City, NY: Anchor Books.

Goffman, E. (1989). On fieldwork. *Journal of Contemporary Ethnography, 18*(2), 122–132.

Grbich, C. (2007). *Qualitative data analysis: an introduction*. London: Sage.

Green, J. (1998). Commentary: grounded theory and the constant comparative method. *British Medical Journal, 316*(7137), 1064–1065.

Green, N. (2008). Formulating and refining a research question. In N. Gilbert (Ed.), *Researching social life* (3rd ed., pp. 43–62). London: Sage.

Greene, J. C. (2007). *Mixed methods in social inquiry*. San Francisco: Jossey-Bass (Wiley).

Griffin, L. J. (1993). Narrative, event-structure analysis, and causal interpretation in historical sociology. *American Journal of Sociology, 98*(5), 1094–1133.

Griffin, L. J. (2007). Historical sociology, narrative and event-structure analysis: fifteen years later. *Sociologica*, (3), 1–17.

Guba, E. G. (1978). *Toward a methodology of naturalistic inquiry in educational evaluation*. Los Angeles: Center for the Study of Evaluation, University of California.

Guenther, K. M. (2009). The politics of names: rethinking the methodological and ethical significance of naming people, organizations, and places. *Qualitative Research. 9*(4), 411-421.

Guest, G., Bunce, A., & Johnson, L. (2006). How many interviews are enough? An experiment with data saturation and variability. *Field Methods, 18*(1), 59–82.

Gutierrez, R. (2006). *Workplace psychological injury: a mixed methods investigation into workers' compensation claims*. PhD, University of Sydney, Sydney.

Halai, N. (2007). Making use of bilingual interview data: some experiences from the field. *The Qualitative Report, 12*(3), 344–355. Retrieved from nova,edu/ssss/QR/QR12-3/halai.pdf.

Hammersley, M. (2008). *Questioning qualitative inquiry*. London: Sage.

Hammersley, M., & Atkinson, P. (2007). *Ethnography: principles in practice* (3rd ed.). Abingdon: Routledge.

Harden, A., & Thomas, J. (2005). Methodological issues in combining diverse study types in systematic reviews. *International Journal of Social Research Methodology, 8*(3), 257–271.

Harman, G. H. (1965). The inference to best explanation. *Philosophical Review, 74*(1), 88–95.

Harper, D. (1992). Small *N*'s and community case studies. In C. Ragin & H. Becker (Eds.), *What is a case? Exploring the foundations of social inquiry* (pp. 139–158). New York: Cambridge University Press.

Heise, D. (1989). Modelling event structures. *Journal of Mathematical Sociology, 14*, 139–169.

Heise, D. (2007). Event structure analysis. Retrieved 7 April 2012 from www.indiana.edu/~socpsy/ESA/.

Hepburn, A., & Potter, J. (2004). Discourse analytic practice. In C. Seale, G. Gobo, J. F. Gubrium, & D. Silverman (Eds.), *Qualitative research practice* (pp. 180–196). London: Sage.

Hodgkinson, P. (2008). Grounded theory and inductive research. In N. Gilbert (Ed.), *Researching social life* (3rd ed., pp. 80–100). London: Sage.

Holsti, O. R. (1969). *Content analysis for the social sciences and humanities*. Reading, MA: Addison-Wesley.

House, E. R. (1991). Realism in research. *Educational Researcher, 20*(6), 2–9.

Huberman, A. M., & Miles, M. B. (Eds.) (2002). *The qualitative researcher's companion*. Thousand Oaks, CA: Sage.

Hunter, J. D., & Cooksey, R. W. (2004). The decision to outsource: a case study of the complex interplay between strategic wisdom and behavioural reality. *Journal of the Australian and New Zealand Academy of Management, 10*(2), 26–40.

Hycner, R. H. (1999). Some guidelines for the phenomenological analysis of interview data. In A. Bryman & R. G. Burgess (Eds.), *Qualitative Research* (Vol. 3, pp. 143–164). London: Sage.

Iyer, R. (2009). Entrepreneurial identities and the problematic of subjectivity in media-mediated discourses. *Discourse and Society, 20*(2), 241–263.

Janesick, V. J. (2000). The choreography of qualitative research design: minuets, improvisations and crystallization. In N. K. Denzin & Y. S. Lincoln (Eds.), *Handbook of qualitative research* (2nd ed., pp. 379–399). Thousand Oaks, CA: Sage.

Johnston, L. H. (2006). Software and method: reflections on teaching and using QSR NVivo in doctoral research. *International Journal of Social Research Methodology, 9*(5), 379–391.

Kelle, U. (2004). Computer-assisted qualitative data analysis. In C. Seale, G. Gobo, J. F. Gubrium, & D. Silverman (Eds.), *Qualitative research practice* (pp. 473–489). London: Sage.

Kelly, G. (1955). *The psychology of personal constructs*. New York: Norton.

Kemp, L. (1999). *Charting a parallel course: meeting the community service needs of persons with spinal injuries*. PhD, University of Western Sydney, Sydney.

Kendall, G., & Wickham, G. (2004). The Foucaultian framework. In C. Seale, G. Gobo, J. F. Gubrium, & D. Silverman (Eds.), *Qualitative research practice* (pp. 141–150). London: Sage.

Kluge, S. (2000). Empirically grounded construction of types and typologies in qualitative social research. *Forum: Qualitative Social Research*, *1*(1), Art. 14, 14 paragraphs.

Knafl, K. A., & Ayres, L. (1996). Managing large qualitative data sets in family research. *Journal of Family Nursing*, *2*(4), 350–364.

Knigge, L., & Cope, M. (2006). Grounded visualization: integrating the analysis of qualitative and quantitative data through grounded theory and visualization. *Environment and Planning A*, *38*, 2021–2037.

Knowlton, L. W., & Phillips, C. C. (2009). *The logic model guidebook*. Thousand Oaks, CA: Sage.

Koller, A. (1983). *An unknown woman: a journey to self-discovery*. Toronto: Bantam.

Krog, A. (2010). In the name of human rights: I say (how) you (should) speak (before I listen). In N. K. Denzin & M. D. Giardina (Eds.), *Qualitative Inquiry and Human Rights* (pp. 125–135). Walnut Creek, CA: Left Coast Press, Inc.

Kvale, S. (1996). *InterViews: an introduction to qualitative interviewing*. Thousand Oaks, CA: Sage.

Kvale, S. (2007). *Doing interviews*. London: Sage.

Labov, W. (1997). Some further steps in narrative analysis. *Journal of Narrative and Life History*, *7*, 395–415.

Labov, W., & Waletzky, J. (1967). Narrative analysis. In D. Tannen (Ed.), *Essays on the verbal and visual arts* (pp. 12–44). Seattle: University of Washington Press.

Lakoff, G., & Johnson, M. (1980). *Metaphors we live by*. Chicago: University of Chicago Press.

Landier, W., Hughes, C. B., Calvillo, E. R., Anderson, N. L. R., Briseño-Toomey, D., Dominguez, L., et al. (2011). A grounded theory of the process of adherence to oral chemotherapy in Hispanic and Caucasian children and adolescents with acute lymphoblastic leukemia. *Journal of Pediatric Oncology Nursing*, *28*(4), 203–223.

Langellier, K. M. (2001). 'You're marked': breast cancer, tattoo and the narrative performance of identity. In J. Brockmeier & D. Carbaugh (Eds.), *Narrative identity: studies in autobiography, self, and culture* (pp. 145–184). Amsterdam: Benjamins.

Latour, B. (1987). *Science in action*. Cambridge, MA: Harvard University Press.

Laub, D. (1991). Bearing witness, or the vicissitudes of listening. In S. Felman & D. Laub (Eds.), *Testimony: crises of witnessing in literature, psychoanalysis, and history*. New York: Routledge, Chapman & Hall.

Laudel, G., & Gläser, J. (2008). From apprentice to colleague: the metamorphosis of early career researchers. *Higher Education*, *55*(3), 387–406.

Laws, R. A. (2010). *Putting prevention into practice: developing a theoretical model to help understand the lifestyle risk factor management practices of primary health care clinicians*. PhD, University of New South Wales, Sydney.

Laws, R. A., Kemp, L., Harris, M. F., Powell Davies, G., Williams, A. M., & Eames-Brown, R. (2009). An exploration of how clinician attitudes and beliefs influence the implementation of lifestyle risk factor management in primary healthcare: a grounded theory study. *BMC: Implementation Science, 4*(66), 1–15.

Lee, S. S. (2011). Fuzzy-set method in comparative social policy: a critical introduction and review of the applications of the fuzzy-set method. *Quality & Quantity*, 1–18. DOI: 10.1007/s11135-011-9633-8.

Levačić, R. (2005). Educational leadership as a causal factor: methodological issues in research on leadership 'effects'. *Educational Management Administration & Leadership, 33*(2), 197–210.

Lewins, A., & Silver, C. (in press). *Using qualitative software: a step by step guide* (2nd ed.). London: Sage.

Lieberson, S. (1992). Small *N*'s and big conclusions: an examination of the reasoning in comparative studies based on a small number of cases. In C. Ragin & H. Becker (Eds.), *What is a case? Exploring the foundations of social inquiry* (pp. 105–118). London: Cambridge University Press.

Liebow, E. (1967). *Tally's corner: a study of Negro streetcorner men.* Boston: Little, Brown.

Lincoln, Y. S., & Guba, E. G. (1985). *Naturalistic enquiry.* Beverly Hills, CA: Sage.

Lincoln, Y. S., & Guba, E. G. (1990). Judging the quality of case study reports. *International Journal of Qualitative Studies in Education, 3*(1), 53–59.

Lindesmith, A. (1947). *Opiate addiction.* Bloomington, IN: Principia.

Lofland, J. (1971). *Analyzing social settings: a guide to qualitative observation and analysis.* Belmont, CA: Wadsworth.

Louis, K. S., & Miles, M. B. (1990). *Improving the urban high school: what works and why.* New York: Teachers College Press.

MacQueen, K. M., McLellan, E., Kay, K., & Milstein, B. (1998). Codebook development for team-based qualitative analysis. *Cultural Anthropology Methods, 10*(2), 31–36.

Major, C. H., & Savin-Badin, M. (2011). Integration of qualitative evidence: towards construction of academic knowledge in social science and professional fields. *Qualitative Research, 11*(6), 645–663.

Marshall, C., & Rossman, G. B. (2006). *Designing qualitative research* (4th ed.). Thousand Oaks, CA: Sage.

Marshall, C., & Rossman, G. B. (2010). *Designing qualitative research* (5th ed.). Thousand Oaks, CA: Sage.

Marshall, H. (2002). What do we do when we code data? *Qualitative Research Journal, 2*(1), 56–70.

Marton, F. (1981). Phenomenography: describing conceptions of the world around us. *Instructional Science, 10*, 177–200.

Mathioon, S. (1988). Why triangulate? *Educational Researcher, 17*(2), 13–17.

Matthews, H. F. (1992). The directive force of morality tales in a Mexican community. In R. G. D'Andrade & C. Strauss (Eds.), *Human motives and cultural models* (pp. 127–162). New York: Cambridge University Press.

Maume, D. (1999). Glass ceilings and glass escalators. *Work and occupations. 26*, 483–509.

Maxwell, J. A. (1992). Understanding and validity in qualitative research. *Harvard Educational Review, 62*(3), 279–300.

Maxwell, J. A. (2004). Causal explanation, qualitative research, and scientific inquiry in education. *Educational Researcher. 33*(2), 3–11.

Maxwell, J. A. (2006). Literature reviews of, and for, educational research: a commentary on Boote and Beile's 'Scholars before researchers'. *Educational Researcher, 35*(9), 28–31.

Maxwell, J. A. (2012). *A realist approach for qualitative research*. Thousand Oaks, CA: Sage.

Maxwell, J. A. (2013). *Qualitative research design* (3rd ed.). Thousand Oaks, CA: Sage.

Maxwell, J. A. (in press). The importance of qualitative research for causal explanation in Education. *Qualitative Inquiry*.

Maxwell, J. A., & Loomis, D. (2003). Mixed method design: an alternative approach. In A. Tashakkori & C. Teddlie (Eds.), *Handbook of mixed methods in social and behavioral research* (pp. 241–271). Thousand Oaks, CA: Sage.

Maxwell, J. A., & Miller, B. A. (2008). Categorizing and connecting strategies in qualitative data analysis. In P. Leavy & S. N. Hesse-Biber (Eds.), *Handbook of emergent methods* (pp. 461–477). New York: Guilford.

Maxwell, J. A., & Mittapalli, K. (2010). Realism as a stance for mixed methods research. In A. Tashakkori & C. Teddlie (Eds.), *Handbook of mixed methods research for the social and behavioral sciences* (2nd ed., pp. 145–167). Thousand Oaks, CA: Sage.

McCance, T. V., McKenna, H. P., & Boore, J. R. P. (2001). Exploring caring using narrative methodology: an analysis of the approach. *Journal of Advanced Nursing, 33*(3), 350–356.

Mead, G. H. (1934). *Mind, self and society*. Chicago: University of Chicago Press.

Mertens, D. M. (1996). Breaking the silence about sexual abuse of deaf youth. *American Annals of the Deaf, 141*(5), 352–358.

Mertens, D. M. (2007). Transformative paradigm: mixed methods and social justice. *Journal of Mixed Methods Research, 1*(3), 212–225.

Mertens, D. M. (2009). *Transformative research and evaluation*. New York: Guilford.

Mertens, D. M. (2010). *Research and evaluation in education and psychology* (3rd ed.). Thousand Oaks, CA: Sage.

Miles, M. B. (1979). Qualitative data as an attractive nuisance: the problem of analysis. *Administrative Science Quarterly, 24*, 590–601.

Miles, M. B., & Huberman, A. M. (1994). *Qualitative data analysis: an expanded sourcebook*. Thousand Oaks, CA: Sage.

Mills, C. W. (1959). *The sociological imagination*. New York: Oxford University Press.

Mishler, E. G. (1979). Meaning in context: is there any other kind? *Harvard Educational Review, 49*(1), 1–19.

Mishler, E. G. (1986). *Research interviewing: context and narrative*. Cambridge, MA: Harvard University Press.

Mishler, E. G. (1991). Representing discourse: the rhetoric of transcription. *Journal of Narrative and Life History. 1*(4), 255-280.

Mitchell, C. (2011). *Doing visual research*. London: Sage.

Mohr, L. (1982). *Explaining organisational behavior*. San Francisco: Jossey-Bass.

Mohr, L. (1998). *The causes of human behavior: implications for theory and method in the social sciences*. Ann Arbor, MI: University of Michigan Press.

Morgan, D. L. (2007). Paradigms lost and pragmatism regained: methodological implications of combining qualitative and quantitative methods. *Journal of Mixed Methods Research, 1*(1), 48–76.

Morrow, S. L., & Smith, M. L. (1995). Constructions of survival and coping by women who have survived childhood sexual abuse. *Journal of Counseling Psychology, 42*(1), 24–33.

Morse, J. M. (1994). 'Emerging from the data': the cognitive process of analysis in qualitative inquiry. In J. M. Morse (Ed.), *Critical issues in qualitative research methods* (pp. 23–43). Thousand Oaks, CA: Sage.

Morse, J. M. (1997). 'Perfectly healthy, but dead': the myth of inter-rater reliability. *Qualitative Health Research, 7*(4), 445–447.

Morse, J. M. (1999). Qualitative methods: the state of the art. *Qualitative Health Research, 9*(3), 393–406.

Morse, J. M. (2000). Determining sample size. *Qualitative Health Research, 10*(1), 3–5.

Morse, J. M., & Mitcham, C. (1998). The experience of agonizing pain and signals of disembodiment. *Journal of Psychosomatic Research, 44*(6), 667–680.

Morse, J. M., & Richards, L. (2002). *Readme first for a user's guide to qualitative methods*. Thousand Oaks, CA: Sage.

Morse, J. M., Stern, P. N., Corbin, J., Bowers, B., Charmaz, K., & Clarke, A. E. (Eds.) (2009). *Developing grounded theory: the second generation*. Walnut Creek, CA: Left Coast Press, Inc.

New, C. (1998). Realism, deconstruction and the feminist standpoint. *Journal for the Theory of Social Behaviour, 28*(4), 349–372.

Noblit, G. W., & Hare, R. D. (1988). *Meta-ethnography: synthesizing qualitative studies*. Newbury Park, CA: Sage.

Northcutt, N., & McCoy, D. (2004). *Interactive qualitative analysis: a systems method for qualitative research*. Thousand Oaks, CA: Sage.

Nussbaum, M. C. (1992). Human functioning and social justice: in defence of Aristotelian essentialism. *Political Theory. 20*(2), 202–246.

O'Brien, J. (Ed.) (2006). *The production of reality* (4th ed.). Thousand Oaks, CA: Pine Forge.

Orona, C. J. (1990). Temporality and identity loss due to Alzheimer's disease. *Social Science and Medicine, 30*(11), 1247–1256.

Patton, M. Q. (2002). *Qualitative evaluation and research methods* (3rd ed.). Thousand Oaks, CA: Sage.

Pawson, R. (2006). *Evidence-based policy*. London: Sage.

Pawson, R. (2008). Method mix, technical hex, theory fix. In M. M. Bergman (Ed.), *Advances in mixed methods research* (pp. 120–137). London: Sage.

Peirce, C. S. (1931–35). *The collected papers of Charles S. Peirce*. Cambridge, MA: Harvard University Press.

Pelz, D. C., & Andrews, F. M. (1976). *Scientists in organisations*. Ann Arbor, MI: Institute for Social Research, University of Michigan.

Peräkylä, A. (2004). Conversation analysis. In C. Seale, G. Gobo, J. F. Gubrium, & D. Silverman (Eds.), *Qualitative research practice* (pp. 165–179). London: Sage.

Poirier, S., & Ayres, L. (1997). Endings, secrets, and silences: overreading in narrative inquiry. *Research in Nursing & Health*, *20*, 551–557.

Poirier, S., & Ayres, L. (2002). *Stories of family caregiving*. Indianapolis: Center Nursing.

Polkinghorne, D. E. (1988). *Narrative knowing and the human sciences*. Albany, NY: University of New York Press.

Ponti, M. (2012). Uncovering causality in narratives of collaboration: actor-network theory and event structure analysis. *Forum: Qualitative Social Research*, *13*(1), Art. 11, 42 paragraphs.

Popper, K. ([1963] 2002). *Conjectures and refutations: the growth of scientific knowledge* (2nd ed.). London: Routledge.

Potter, J., & Edwards, D. (1992). *Discursive psychology*. London: Sage.

Prell, C. (2012). *Social network analysis*. London: Sage.

Punch, K. (1998). *Introduction to social research: quantitative and qualitative approaches*. London: Sage.

Putnam, R. D. (2000). *Bowling alone: the collapse and revival of American community*. New York: Simon and Schuster.

Rae, N. (2003). *The ch'i of the brush*. New York: Watson-Guptill.

Ragin, C. (1987). *The comparative method: moving beyond qualitative and quantitative strategies*. Berkeley, CA: University of California Press.

Ragin, C. (1992). Cases of 'What is a case?' In C. Ragin & H. Becker (Eds.), *What is a case? Exploring the foundations of social inquiry* (pp. 1–18). New York: Cambridge University Press.

Ragin, C., & Becker, H. (Eds.) (1992). *What is a case? Exploring the foundations of social inquiry*. New York: Cambridge University Press.

Rank, M. R. (1989). Fertility among women on welfare: incidence and determinants. *American Sociological Review*. *54*, 296–304.

Reichertz, J. (2010). Abduction: the logic of discovery of grounded theory. *Forum: Qualitative Social Research*, *11*(1), Art. 13, 39 paragraphs.

Reskin, B. (1998). Bringing the men back in: sex differentiation and the devaluation of women's work. *Gender and Society*, *2*, 58–81.

Richards, L. (2009). *Handling qualitative data* (2nd ed.). London: Sage.

Richardson, L. (2000). Writing: a method of inquiry. In N. K. Denzin & Y. S. Lincoln (Eds.), *Handbook of qualitative research* (2nd ed., pp. 923–948). Thousand Oaks, CA: Sage.

Ricoeur, P. (1970). *Freud and philosophy: an essay on interpretation*. New Haven, CT: Yale University Press.

Riessman, C. K. (2008). *Narrative methods for the human sciences*. Thousand Oaks, CA: Sage.

Riessman, C. K., & Quinney, L. (2005). Narrative in social work: a critical review. *Qualitative Social Work*, *4*(4), 391–412.

Rihoux, B., & Ragin, C. (Eds.) (2009). *Configurational comparative methods*. Thousand Oaks, CA: Sage.

Rist, R. C. (1980). Blitzkrieg ethnography: on the transformation of a method into a movement. *Educational Researcher*, *9*(2), 8–10.

Ritchie, J., & Spencer, L. (1994). Qualitative data analysis for applied policy research. In A. Bryman & R. G. Burgess (Eds.), *Analyzing qualitative data* (pp. 173–194). London: Routledge.

Ryle, G. (1971). The thinking of thoughts. What is *'le Penseur'* doing? *Collected Papers* (Vol. 2, pp. 480–496). London: Hutchinson.

Saldaña, J. (2009). *The coding manual for qualitative researchers*. London: Sage.

Sandelowski, M. (2000). Whatever happened to qualitative description? *Research in Nursing & Health, 23*(4), 334–340.

Sandelowski, M. (2001). Real qualitative researchers do not count: the use of numbers in qualitative research. *Research in Nursing & Health, 24*(3), 230–240.

Sandelowski, M. (2006). 'Meta-jeopardy': the crisis of representation in qualitative metasynthesis. *Nursing Outlook, 54*(1), 10–16.

Sandelowski, M. (2008). Foreword. In S. Thorne (Ed.), *Interpretive description*. Walnut Creek, CA: Left Coast Press, Inc.

Sandelowski, M., Voils, C. I., & Knafl, G. (2009). On quantitizing. *Journal of Mixed Methods Research, 3*(3), 208–222.

Sanford, N. (1970). Whatever happened to action research? *Journal of Social Issues, 26*(4), 3–23.

Sartre, J.-P. (1981). *The family idiot: Gustave Flaubert, 1821–1857* (Vol. 1). Chicago: University of Chicago Press.

Savage, J. (2000). One voice, different tunes: issues raised by dual analysis of a segment of qualitative data. *Journal of Advanced Nursing, 31*(6), 1493–1500.

Sayer, A. (2000). *Realism and social science*. London: Sage.

Schatzman, L. (1991). Dimensional analysis: notes on an alternative approach to the grounding of theory in qualitative research. In D. R. Maines (Ed.), *Social organizations and social process: essays in honor of Anselm Strauss*. New York: Aldine De Gruyter.

Schmittmann, V. D., Cramer, A. O. J., Waldorp, L. J., Epskamp, S., Kievit, R. A., & Borsboom, D. (2011). Deconstructing the construct: a network perspective on psychological phenomena. *New Ideas in Psychology*, 1–11. DOI: 10.1016/j.newideapsych.2011.02.007.

Schwandt, T. A. (2000). Three epistemological stances for qualitative inquiry: interpretivism, hermeneutics, and social constructionism. In N. Denzin & Y. Lincoln (Eds.), *Handbook of qualitative research* (2nd ed., pp. 189–214). Thousand Oaks, CA: Sage.

Schwandt, T. A. (2007). *Dictionary of qualitative inquiry* (3rd ed.). Thousand Oaks, CA: Sage.

Scott, J. (2012). *Social network analysis* (3rd ed.). London: Sage.

Scott, S. B., Bergeman, C. S., Verney, A., Longenbaker, S., Markey, M. A., & Bisconti, T. L. (2007). Social support in widowhood: a mixed methods study. *Journal of Mixed Methods Research, 1*(3), 242–266.

Scriven, M. (1976). Maximising the power of causal investigation: the modus operandi method. In G. V. Glass (Ed.), *Evaluation studies annual review* (Vol. 1, pp. 120–139). Beverly Hills, CA: Sage.

Seale, C. (1999). *The quality of qualitative research*. London: Sage.

Seale, C. (2001). Sporting cancer: struggle language in news reports of people with cancer. *Sociology of Health and Illness, 23*(3), 308–329.

Seale, C. (2004). Quality in qualitative research. In C. Seale, G. Gobo, J. F. Gubrium, & D. Silverman (Eds.), *Qualitative research practice* (pp. 409–419). London: Sage.

Sellerberg, A.-M., & Leppänen, V. (2012). A typology of narratives of social inclusion and exclusion: the case of bankrupt entrepreneurs. *Forum: Qualitative Social Research*, *13*(1), Art. 26, 75 paragraphs.

Shadish, W. R., Cook, T. D., & Campbell, D. T. (2002). *Experimental and quasi-experimental designs for generalized causal inference*. Boston: Houghton Mifflin.

Sheridan, J., Chamberlain, K., & Dupuis, A. (2011). Timelining: visualizing experience. *Qualitative Research*, *11*(5), 552–569.

Shin, K. R., Kim, M. Y., & Chung, S. E. (2009). Methods and strategies utilized in published qualitative research. *Qualitative Health Research*, *19*(6), 850–858.

Silverman, D. (2000). *Doing qualitative research: a practical handbook*. London: Sage.

Silverman, D. (2010). *Doing qualitative research* (3rd ed.). London: Sage.

Sin, S. (2010). Considerations of quality in phenomenographic research. *International Journal of Qualitative Methods*, *9*(4), 305–319.

Singh, S. (1997). *Marriage money: the social shaping of money in marriage and banking*. Sydney: Allen & Unwin.

Slaney, K. L., & Racine, T. P. (2011). What's in a name? Psychology's ever evasive construct. *New Ideas in Psychology*, 1–9. DOI: 10.1016/j.newideapsych.2011.02.003.

Smith, E. E., & Medin, D. L. (1981). *Categories and concepts*. Cambridge, MA: Harvard University Press.

Smith, J. A., Flowers, P., & Larkin, M. (2009). *Interpretative phenomenological analysis*. London: Sage.

Smith, J. A., & Osborn, M. (2003). Interpretative phenomenological analysis. In J. A. Smith (Ed.), *Qualitative psychology* (pp. 51–80). London: Sage.

Spradley, J. P. (1970). *You owe yourself a drunk: an ethnography of urban nomads*. Boston: Little, Brown.

Spradley, J. P. (1979). *The ethnographic interview*. New York: Holt, Rinehart & Winston.

Stake, R. E. (1995). *The art of case study research*. Thousand Oaks, CA: Sage.

Stake, R. E. (2000). Case studies. In N. K. Denzin & Y. S. Lincoln (Eds.), *Handbook of qualitative research* (2nd ed., pp. 435–454). Thousand Oaks, CA: Sage.

Stake, R. E. (2010). *Qualitative researching: studying how things work*. New York: Guilford.

Stevens, P. E. (1996). Focus groups: collecting aggregate-level data to understand community health phenomena. *Public Health Nursing*, *13*(3), 170–176.

Strauss, A. L. (1987). *Qualitative analysis for social scientists*. Cambridge: Cambridge University Press.

Strauss, A. L. (1995). Notes on the nature and development of general theories. *Qualitative Inquiry*, *1*(1), 7–18.

Sykes, G. M. (1958). *The society of captives: a study of a maximum security prison*. Princeton, NJ: Princeton University Press.

Sykes, I., Friedman, V., Rosenfeld, J. M., & Weiss, T. (2006). Learning from success: leveraging tacit knowledge and introducing collective learning into organizations. Unpublished paper. Myers-JDC-Brookdale Institute.

Tan, F. B., & Hunter, M. G. (2002). The repertory grid technique: a method for the study of cognition in information systems. *MIS Quarterly*, *26*(1), 39–57.

Teddlie, C., & Stringfield, S. (1993). *Schools make a difference: lessons learned from a 10-year study of school effects*. New York: Teachers College Press.

Tedlock, B. (2000). Ethnography and ethnographic representation. In N. K. Denzin & Y. S. Lincoln (Eds.), *Handbook of qualitative research* (2nd ed., pp. 455–486). Thousand Oaks, CA: Sage.

Thompson, E. P. (1971). The moral economy of the English crowd in the eighteenth century. *Past and Present. 50*, 76–136.

Thorne, S. (2008). *Interpretive description*. Walnut Creek, CA: Left Coast Press, Inc.

Turner, B. (1981). Some practical aspects of qualitative data analysis: one way of organising the cognitive processes associated with the generation of grounded theory. *Quality and Quantity, 15*(3), 225–247.

Van Maanen, J. (1979). The fact of fiction in organizational ethnography. *Administrative Science Quarterly, 24*(4), 539–550.

van Manen, M. (1990). *Researching lived experience: human science for an action sensitive pedagogy*. New York: State University of New York Press.

Vaughan, D. (1992). Theory elaboration: the heuristics of case analysis. In C. Ragin & H. Becker (Eds.), *What is a case? Exploring the foundations of social inquiry* (pp. 173–202). New York: Cambridge University Press.

Walton, J. (1992). Making the theoretical case. In C. Ragin & H. Becker (Eds.), *What is a case? Exploring the foundations of social inquiry* (pp. 121–137). New York: Cambridge University Press.

Warr, D. J. (2005). "It was fun...but we don't usually talk about these things": analyzing sociable interaction in focus groups. *Qualitative Inquiry. 11*(2), 200-225

Webber, R. (1997). The media's representation of young people who kill. *Interlogue, 8*(1), 13–21.

Weiner-Levy, N., & Popper-Giveon, A. (2011). The absent, the hidden and the obscured: reflections on 'dark matter' in qualitative research. *Quality & Quantity*, 1–14. DOI: 10.1007/s11135-011-9650-7.

Whyte, W. F. ([1943] 1993). *Street corner society: the social structure of an Italian slum* (4th ed.). Chicago: University of Chicago Press.

Wiles, R., Coffey, A., Robison, J., & Heath, S. (2010). Anonymisation and visual images: issues of respect, 'voice' and protection. *NCRM Working Paper Series 07/10*, 1–25. Retrieved from eprints.ncrm.ac.uk/1804/.

Willig, C. (2003). Discourse analysis. In J. A. Smith (Ed.), *Qualitative psychology* (pp. 159–183). London: Sage.

Willis, K., Green, J., Daly, J., Williamson, L., & Bandyopadhyay, M. (2009). Perils and possibilities: achieving best evidence from focus groups in public health research. *Australian & New Zealand Journal of Public Health, 33*(2), 131–136.

Wodak, R. (2004). Critical discourse analysis. In C. Seale, G. Gobo, J. F. Gubrium, & D. Silverman (Eds.), *Qualitative research practice* (pp. 197–213). London: Sage.

Wojnar, D. M., & Swanson, K. M. (2007). Phenomenology: an exploration. *Journal of Holistic Nursing, 25*(3), 172–180.

Wolcott, H. F. (1992). Posturing in qualitative inquiry. In M. D. Le Compte, W. L. Millroy, & J. Preissle (Eds.), *The handbook of qualitative research in education* (pp. 3–52). New York: Academic.

Wolcott, H. F. (1994). *Transforming qualitative data: description, analysis and interpretation*. Thousand Oaks, CA: Sage.

Wolcott, H. F. (2009). *Writing up qualitative research* (3rd ed.). Thousand Oaks, CA: Sage.

Yin, R. K. (2003). *Case study research: design and methods* (3rd ed.). Thousand Oaks, CA: Sage.

Yorgason, J. B., Roper, S. O., Wheeler, B., Crane, K., Byron, R., Carpenter, L., et al. (2010). Older couples' management of multiple-chronic illnesses: individual and shared perceptions and coping in type 2 diabetes and osteoarthritis. *Families, Systems, & Health, 28*(1), 30–47.

Zaltman, G. (1996). Metaphorically speaking. *Marketing Research, 8*(2), 13–20.

Znaniecki, F. (1934). Analytic induction. In F. Znaniecki (Ed.), *The method of sociology* (pp. 249–331). New York: Farrar & Rinehart.

Index